FOR BREAD JUSTICE AND FREEDOM

a political biography of George Weekes

FOR BREAD JUSTICE AND FREEDOM
a political biography of George Weekes

by

Khafra Kambon

NEW BEACON BOOKS
London: Port of Spain

First published in 1988 by New Beacon Books Ltd., 76 Stroud Green Road, London N4 3EN, England.

ISBN 0901241 89 X (hardback)
     0901241 90 3 (paperback)

Typeset in Great Britain by William Clowes Limited, Beccles and London

DEDICATION

To all those who have
struggled and sacrificed
towards the goal of
building a Caribbean nation.

CONTENTS

vii

ACKNOWLEDGEMENTS

The author wishes to thank the Executive and members of the Oilfields Workers Trade Union who made it possible for this book to be written.

I particularly want to thank George Weekes for the patience he showed through many long interviews, conversations and discussions of his reactions to many episodes in his life.

I also wish to thank Winston Leonard who transcribed several hours of taped interviews, who conducted interviews on my behalf with Walter Annamunthodo, John La Rose and C.L.R. James, and who further assisted in slugging through newspaper sources and extracting relevant information.

A number of other people contributed in different ways to the preparation of this book.

Valuable information was provided through interviews with Theresa Weekes (wife of George Weekes), Barbara and Sybil Weekes (sisters of George Weekes), Cyril Weekes (George's son), Thelma Williams, Doodnath Maharaj, Lennox Pierre and Jack Kelshall. Many other individuals provided information in informal conversations and discussions.

Prudence Guppy typed the handwritten transcripts of the taped interviews.

I also received willing assistance from the OWTU's librarian, Donna Coombs-Montrose, who made all sources in that library available to me and provided a wide range of choice in the selection of photographs for the book. Dereck Scotland photocopied many of the documents needed for research.

Assistance also came from librarians at the University of the West Indies, St Augustine, who allowed me to use the West Indian Reference Room at the library over the period.

I am extremely grateful for the helpful comments made on the draft manuscript by Olabisi Kuboni, Dr Roy Thomas of the

University of the West Indies, St Augustine and Dr Tony Martin of Wellesley College in Boston.

Thanks to John La Rose who meticulously went through the text with an editor's eye, and to his wife, Sarah White, who took the copy through the final stages of publication.

Writing this book was demanding on my family as well as myself. Fortunately my wife, Asha, has always shared my commitments. My children, Shabaka, Khafra and Mariamma, were very understanding for their young ages, though their enthusiasm for the project was at times outweighed by their preference for a little more attention from their father. I sure appreciate their contribution in this regard.

Finally I wish to thank all those who shared with me the profound personal political experiences that determined my approach to writing this book.

In the sense of all these contributions it was a collective enterprise. But for all the views expressed and the manner of their expression, I take full responsibility.

ACRONYMS

ACDC	Action Committee of Democratic Citizens
AFL-CIO	American Federation of Labour – Congress of Industrial Organisations
AIFLD	American Institute of Free Labour Development
ATSE&FWTU	All Trinidad Sugar Estates & Factory Workers Trade Union
AWU	Amalgamated Workers Union
BEWCHRP	British Empire Workers & Citizens Home Rule Party
BEWPRU	British Empire Workers Peasants & Rate Payers Union
BWIA	British West Indian Airways
CADORIT	Caribbean Area Division of the Regional Labour Organisation
CARIG	Committee Against Repression in Guyana
CATTU	Communications and Transport Workers Trade Union
CIA	Central Intelligence Agency
CLS	Committee for Labour Solidarity
COLA	Cost of Living Allowances
COSSABO	Conference of Shop Stewards and Branch Officers
CPTU	Council of Progressive Trade Unions
CSA	Civil Service Association
CWU	Communication Workers Union
DAC	Democratic Action Congress
DLP	Democratic Labour Party
ECA	Employers Consultative Association
ESIU	Electricity Supply & Industrial Workers Union
FWTU	Federated Workers Trade Union
ICFTU	International Confederation of Free Trade Unions
ICFTU	Islandwide Cane Farmers Trade Union
ILO	International Labour Organisation
IRA	Industrial Relations Act
IRO	Inter-Religious Organisation
ISA	Industrial Stabilisation Act
ISCOTT	Iron and Steel Company of Trinidad & Tobago
KTO	Kern Trinidad Oilfields
MMM	Mass Membership Meeting
NAR	National Alliance for Reconstruction
NFL	National Federation of Labour
NJAC	National Joint Action Committee
NIS	National Insurance Scheme

NOC	National Oil Company
NTUC	National Trade Union Congress
NUFF	National Union of Freedom Fighters
NUGFW	National Union of Government & Federated Workers Trade Union
NUGE	National Union of Government Employees
NWA	Negro Welfare Association
NWCSA	Negro Welfare Cultural & Social Association
ONR	Organisation for National Reconstruction
OPEC	Organisation of Petroleum Exporting Countries
OWTU	Oilfields Workers Trade Union
PDP	Peoples Democratic Party
PNM	Peoples National Movement
POPPG	Party of Political Progress Group
PPP	Peoples Progressive Party (Guyana)
PSA	Public Services Association
SWWTU	Seamen & Waterfront Workers Trade Union
TCL	Trinidad Citizens League
TICFA	Trinidad Islandwide Cane Farmers Association
TIWU	Transport & Industrial Workers Union
TLL	Trinidad Leaseholds Limited
TLP	Trinidad Labour Party
TPD	Trinidad Petroleum Development Company
T&TEC	Trinidad & Tobago Electricity Commission
T&TTU	Trinidad & Tobago Teachers Union
TTUTA	Trinidad & Tobago Unified Teachers Association
TUC	Trades Union Congress
TWA	Trinidad Workingmen's Association
UCIW	Union of Commercial & Industrial Workers
UF	United Front
ULF	United Labour Front
UMROBI	Universal Movement for the Reconstruction of Black Identity
UNIA	Universal Negro Improvement Association
UNIP	United National Independence Party
URO	Union of Revolutionary Organisations
UWI	University of the West Indies
WASA	Water & Sewerage Authority
WEA	Workers Educational Association
WFM	Workers Freedom Movement
WFP	Workers and Farmers Party
WFTU	World Federation of Trade Unions
WIIP	West Indian Independence Party
WINP	West Indian National Party
WPA	Working Peoples Alliance

CHAPTER 1

A PEEPHOLE ON THE SOCIAL FERMENT

Sixty years later, the picture remained stamped in the memory of George Weekes, an image of trees drawing apart, giving way in front of the lone bus out of the village in the early morning. The bumpy road from Toco, in the North Eastern extremity of the island of Trinidad, to Sangre Grande, the last outpost of relative modernity in the 1920's, was one adults travelled only out of necessity. Many people still preferred to travel in and out of Toco by boat.

But in the mind of a child, seated next to his father in the privately owned bus, all thoughts were on the beauty of the thick forest, with its tall trees standing close guard against the narrow, winding road, not the bumps from ruts and stones that tortured the vehicle shocks on the upgraded track that served as a road.

The eyes of the young George would peer at the road ahead, looking for the red glows in the mist of morning that would signal the charcoal carts emerging from the still dark forest onto the roadway ahead. This was the sight George loved the best. The casual moving donkey carts, lit by flambeaux or lanterns to warn of their presence from a distance. At this time the charcoal burners would be heading for the towns to sell their 'coal' to the housewives.

The stern Pa Weekes knew what a joy a rare trip like this was for his second son, George, his "eyeball" as the old people would say, an energetic boy born to Edgar and Rebecca Weekes on March 9th* 1921 in the remote village of Toco. Sitting with all the upright seriousness typical of a schoolmaster in those days, Pa Weekes was very much aware of the tremendous excitement in the short, wide eyed boy, who was anxiously waiting to see that

---

* Because of problems in registration at the time, George's birth certificate carries the date — April 27th.

1

strange other world that awaited them when the last green leafed sentinels would draw back and reveal the town of Sangre Grande.

The journey from Sangre Grande to Port of Spain, the capital of the country, would be a much easier one. On these trips George could hardly contain his excitement, especially when he disembarked from the bus at the southern end of Frederick Street in Port of Spain and felt the hustle and bustle of the city, on this its busiest street. He would look forward eagerly to the tram car ride or the horse and buggy ride to visit his relatives. It was a joy to be reunited, even briefly, with his mother, who was separated from his father while he was still quite young. It was a joy to see his younger sisters, Barbara and Vinola, who lived with her on Sackville Street in Port of Spain, and to see his older brother Kenny, who stayed with Aunt Ollie (Mendez) in Boissiere, a village on the outskirts of the capital.

What George loved best was when he made the journey to Port of Spain, not just for a short visit, but to spend longer periods during school vacations. His most enjoyable childhood days were at Aunt Ollie. There he really felt at home. The Mendez family was a large one with many children, and very warm. To add to the happiness, being there meant being away from his ever strict father who just did not know how to show the kind of love George received in Boissiere and from his mother.

Despite his own excitement, George was not unaware of the seriousness of his father's mission on many of his trips. There would be grim faces and earnest voices when his father met with other teachers discussing concerns of the adult world. George's glimpses of such meetings would remind him of similar discussions he often witnessed at home in Toco. Sometimes he overheard what was being said at their own home. It was all about the 'advantage'* taken on teachers in the colony.

Edgar Weekes did not discuss his problems with George, but often enough George heard the expressions of bitterness in the meetings and knew how his father chafed at some of the restrictions imposed on him. Already underpaid, like everybody else, Edgar Weekes was like a prisoner on remand, with the Anglican priest as parole officer. He couldn't simply board the

---

* 'To take advantage of' is a common colloquial expression meaning to exploit or abuse from an advantageous position. The term 'advantage' is consistently used in this chapter with similar meaning.

village bus, with its quaint name — 'Within The Time' it was called — and head for Sangre Grande or Arima or Port of Spain. The imported priest, who represented the religion of the British rulers, had the authority to decide when the headmaster of his school, the Toco E.C School, could leave the village.

When the priest was on vacation or out of the village for any reason, George's father could not leave at all. In addition to being headmaster, he functioned as a lay preacher, often substituting for the priest, especially in outlying areas. With the priest absent Edgar Weekes had to stay and conduct services not only in Toco, but in the surrounding villages like Sans Souci and Matelot.

This activity helped him to keep in touch with other teachers. They sought ways to deal collectively with their problems. But the struggle that would lead to the legal recognition of trade unions by employers was yet to succeed.

George's childhood perception of his father's anguish and passionate involvement in organising to do something about the problems, was just one tiny window opened on the social landscape of growing anti-colonial conflict. But it was too small a peephole for a child to see the gathering storm.

All he felt was sadness and anger as a witness to a headmaster's grim meetings in Toco and Port of Spain, especially as that headmaster was 'Pa'. It was 'Pa' who was being wronged by somebody. George knew his 'Pa' did not deserve that kind of treatment. How could anyone do that to 'Pa' who never left Port of Spain without getting something special for George, without some surprise to take home for Nellie and Sybil, George's older sisters, who would be waiting anxiously at home. Why would anyone make life so hard for 'Pa' and those other teachers? True they all beat the daylights out of you. But they weren't bad. They were trying to make something of you, making sure you could read and write and count, and that you were polite. That was important in those days, you had to be polite, you had to have respect, and manners! Whoever was hurting 'Pa' and all these people was doing something really terrible.

But such adult matters were not the most important concerns of an energetic boy in the countryside. On the journey back home, by the time the bus left Sangre Grande, the darkness was already gathering. The lights of the bus cut through the darkness ahead but the night hung a heavy black curtain on the trees behind. As the time machine moved from the world of electric lights and flush toilets to the world of lamps and lanterns and candles and cesspits far in the backyard, the angry voices of teachers in Port of Spain would be only one of many memories.

Through his restricted window on the world, George, though not conscious of it, was seeing an extension of a historic ferment occasioned by the growth pangs of those forces which he himself would later become an integral part of. Indeed he would assume a leadership role in their development.

George's birth coincided quite closely with the rebirth/revival of the working class movement, which was intimately linked to the movement for self-government in Trinidad and Tobago. In 1919, as stirrings of unrest developed, strongly influenced by soldiers returning from World War I, by the ideas of Marcus Garvey and by the reverberations of the Russian Revolution, seven British battleships had called at Port of Spain during the course of the year, to let workers know very unambiguously the price of struggling for human dignity in a British colony. Anti-colonial riots that year had reached the far village of Toco, just two years before George was born. Two workers, one of East Indian descent on the sugar plantations of Trinidad, and one of African descent in Tobago, paid the ultimate price and became the first martyrs of the workers' movement in the 20th century*. Death here symbolically spanned the great divides all movements for emancipation in the twentieth century have had to deal with in this land — the most critical being the racial division of African and Indian, and the other, the sensitive and exploited division between the people born on the island of Trinidad and those born in Tobago.

In the aftermath of the colony-wide struggles of that time mandatory prison sentences were imposed on officers and members of the Trinidad Workingmen's Association identified as leaders of the revolt, James Brathwaite (Secretary), James Phillips (Asst. Secretary), Bruce McConney and Fenton.[1] Another Assistant Secretary of the TWA, a Garveyite by the name of Edward Selier Salmon, was deported to Jamaica.[2] Fourteen workers arrested in Tobago were sentenced to prison terms ranging from one and a half to three years.[3]

---

* Beharrysingh on Woodford Lodge estate and Nathaniel Williams in Scarborough, Tobago.

A PEEPHOLE ON THE SOCIAL FERMENT

The repression failed to stop the resurgence of this organisation, which had originally been formed in 1898 and had fizzled out after the mass disturbances (the Water Riots) of 1903. Alfred Richards, a druggist, revived the TWA in 1906 and by 1919, under the leadership of James Brathwaite, it proved itself a strong force again. With the election of Captain Arthur Andrew Cipriani as president of the Association in 1922, the marked growth in the organisation's membership, which was evident from 1920, was further accelerated. The organisation made significant inroads among East Indian workers in this phase of growth.

The level of Indian participation in the TWA under Cipriani's leadership marked a new milestone in the political development of Trinidad and Tobago. It was an advance on what had taken place in 1919 when Indian involvement in the uprisings created panic among whites. Writing about that period Brinsley Samaroo points out that "increasing restlessness caused panic among the country's white population. A group of them, led by George F. Huggins, petitioned the colonial office for the immediate arming of the colony's white men and the permanent stationing of a white garrison in the colony. In previous years, they wrote, the indentured Indian under white control could be looked upon as a 'substantial guard against troubles with the negroes and vice versa'. With the abolition of Indentureship such a counterpoise had ceased to exist."[4] However, although workers from both numerically dominant groups participated in the mass uprising, the TWA did not have an organisational base or a commanding influence among Indian workers in 1919. The advance of 1922 is the success achieved in bringing the struggles of Africans and Indians, on issues of workers' interests, under the umbrella of a single mass organisation.

On wider national issues, such as the demand for constitutional reform and the movement for self-government, the consensus across racial barriers was severely hampered by the work of certain East Indian organisations. The East Indian National Association and sections of the East Indian National Congress, both middle-class-based organisations, cultivated fears among the East Indian population that African domination, which they portrayed as more fearful than British Crown Colony rule, would be the corollary of decolonisation.

5

Cipriani's role was a seemingly incongruous one — a member of the white planter class leading a Black working class organisation. But his credentials for leadership came first of all from his championship of the cause of Black Caribbean soldiers in Egypt against the vicious racial discrimination of the British during the First World War. On his return to Trinidad and Tobago, Cipriani founded a soldiers' union, seeking the re-settlement of soldiers. He travelled throughout the country lecturing on the war and praising the competence of the West Indian soldiers. He further enhanced his image by outspokenness on issues relevant to workers and national development. He made the best of the distinct advantage his colour and class background gave him in dealing with the colonial authorities.

There is also a feeling that Cipriani's colour was an advantage in terms of those whom he led. Sahadeo Basdeo advances the opinion that the TWA's selection of a racially 'neutral' figure as leader, facilitated the entry of Indians into the movement.[5] While this factor cannot be discounted at the specific time, it is also important to appreciate the new constellation of emerging social forces which had been signalled, prior to Cipriani's leadership, by mass Indian participation in the growing unrest of 1919. The later experiences of non-'neutral' leaders (in the racial sense), like Tubal Uriah Buzz Butler, the leader of mass revolt in the 1930's, and later, George Weekes, also indicate other possibilities. However, the effect of a 'white', not a 'neutral' champion, on the psychology of colonial workers, African and Indian, is not to be underestimated in the meteoric rise of Cipriani as the spokesman for "the barefooted man"*, those he often referred to, with perhaps unconscious contempt, as his "followers", "the unwashed and the unsoaped". This is not to deny the zeal with which Cipriani went about his chosen cause, the abilities he brought to the task and, for a decade, the relative effectiveness of his actions, judged within the context of his times.

The activities of Edgar Weekes with teachers was one spark of the movement of the 20's. But Toco, with its fertile ground for provisions** and vegetables, for cocoa and bananas, was not such fertile ground for the radicalism of the times. The basis of

---

* Cipriani's term
** 'provisions', more usually 'ground provisions', refers to root crops such as dasheen, tannia, cassava and others.

discontent was there in the poverty and depression of the area, the lack of opportunity. Even a family that was considered relatively well off, like the Weekes family, could not always afford tea from the shop. George quite enjoyed the 'bush' tea which was substituted. George's sister, Sybil, knew the common experience of going to the shop and asking for the favour of a 'pinch' of salt and a 'dust' of flour. With his father being a headmaster, George would in fact have been considered middle class. But the line of class division, in a practical sense, was little more than the ability to afford shoes to wear to school.

So if the Toco of the 1920's did not reverberate as strongly as many other parts of the country with the social and political vibrations of the times, it was not because of any semblance, not even the slightest semblance of relative material well being. But important factors were missing.

This was not an era when electronic communication could fill gaps created by physical remoteness. Radios were not common anywhere in Trinidad and Tobago and there was no local radio station. In Toco the battery radio owned by the priest and the police wireless system were the sum total of electronic communications. Electronic communication was so far removed from his world that the young George hardly even heard music outside of the church, where his father struggled against arthritic pains to pedal the organ he was compelled to play. George used to be delighted to hear the blacksmith sing as he worked. On the rare occasion that the police band would come on a ship, it would be a real treat to hear military music. Beyond that he would hear music bands that accompanied excursions to the village. Sometimes he got a taste of Indian music this way and he was particularly attracted to the organ. These experiences were more treasured because of the absence of the sound of radios. Generally, communication by way of the written word was not very effective either. Only a few newspapers reached the village and they reached one day late.

The low level of formal communication was a disadvantage but by no means decisive. The people had developed their own 'word of mouth' system of communication. Such informal systems of communication have played important roles in organised resistance throughout the country's history. But there were other disadvantages. The work environment made it harder for the movement of the 20's and 30's to grip Toco than it was for it to seize the oil belt, the sugar belt and the urban areas of the North. In Toco, many of the people were small independent peasants and fishermen. There were a few large estates, but nothing really approaching a mass labour force.

In the absence of mass concentrations of labour, which would have facilitated ready organisation, the movement of the 1920's would have needed a well grounded cadre to organise the potential in this remote village. Such elements of organisation as there were in Toco after 1919 did not reach the level to achieve mass mobilisation. At most pockets of identification developed, which were not generally influential enough to transform the mood of the village, to turn awareness and empathy with the wider movement into open revolt as in the earlier period.

George himself did reap some benefits, though, from the activities of those individuals who had the consciousness to keep abreast of national and, as far as it was possible, international developments. One such person was a tailor, Mr Arthur. He would eventually be the first to introduce a young George to the speeches of Butler in *The People*, a radical newspaper. There were never more than a few such individuals. They encouraged discussion of issues, but did not rise to fill the role of mass organisers. So in the absence of effective organisation or even agitation, life in the village continued virtually undisturbed by the mass movement in the wider society.

In this environment, George enjoyed his youth to the fullest. While Cipriani led workers to achieve the eight hour day, while he led the mass movement to capitalize, in the limited ways possible, on the first dent in the Crown Colony system (from 1925, a narrow franchise and seven elected representatives in the twenty five (25) man Legislative Council), George led the field of primary school boys in running races or he led his unofficial team in stick fights.

But it was not always plain sailing for the young George, just as it was not always plain sailing for the young self-government movement. Pa Weekes wanted his son to be different from the other boys in the village. After all he was a headmaster's son. He couldn't just roam the village getting into the kind of mischief that young boys generally got into. George did not share the view of his disciplinarian father. He only had two sisters at home for company. That was no good, when after all there were important things to do, like catching crabs and flying kite. George would unfailingly run away to do what was important. Deep inside he was really rebelling against his father. The reports of his activities would come back. George's father would 'bench' him, as he benched the pupils at school. Once he beat George in so much anger, the rage pushing all question of 'favourite' aside, that Nellie and Sybil had to intervene for mercy.

These two sisters would be in charge of George when Edgar Weekes was not at home. That would be a headache for poor Nellie especially. George was not a rude or disrespectful child. So she did not have that problem. But the moment she was not looking, George would be gone. At one point the only strategy she could think of to keep him within bounds was to tie a rope around his waist, while he flew his kite from the yard and she prepared a meal in the kitchen. Every now and again she would give the rope a slight tug to make sure there was tension at the end of it . . .

In the 1930's the feeling would increasingly grow in the society that Cipriani was tied at the end of a rope, pulled by the British Labour Party and the British Trades Union Congress and that he held the masses in check with his leadership. The tension at the end of that rope was the striving of the people to adopt new and more effective forms of leadership than Cipriani provided at the time.

Change was coming. The young George and the young nationalist movement were entering new phases of development at about the same time.

Just over the age of 10, George moved out of Toco. He went to live with his mother on Sackville Street in Port of Spain and continued his schooling, begun at the Anglican school in Toco, at the Richmond Street Boys School. He quickly built up a reputation for fighting and acquired the nickname, "Tiger" . . .

After a little more than 10 years under Cipriani, the vanguard movement of the workers, which had been transformed from the Trinidad Workingmen's Association to the Trinidad Labour Party in 1932, started experiencing an exodus, both of the mass membership and of important leaders.

Before the exodus there were rifts at the top over strategy. There were signs of trouble over a number of issues. For example, on the question of when to observe May Day. Cipriani, associated as he was with Lord Passfield and the Fabian socialists in Britain, opted as they did for an observance on the nearest Sunday. Quintin O'Connor, on the other hand, and other influential TWA members, such as Jim Barrette, insisted on the observance of Labour Day on May 1st.

More serious differences at the leadership level arose over the new emphasis signalled by the organisation's change of name. The change from TWA to TLP was a reaction to the Trade Union Ordinance of 1932. The main deficiency of this act, which Cipriani had agitated for locally and in London, was that it did not provide the protection necessary for trade unions to operate effectively. Employers could sue trade unions to recover losses and damages suffered as a result of a strike. Given the glaring limitations of the act, Cipriani decided, on the advice of the British Trades Union Congress, not to register the TWA as a trade union. He himself had long achieved political prominence as a representative of labour; he had been elected to the Legislative Council since the 1925 election and he was several times Mayor of Port of Spain. Now he decided that the full weight of the TWA should be directed at seeking first the political kingdom.

Quintin O'Connor, later to be General Secretary of the Federated Workers Trade Union, was one of those who disagreed with Cipriani's strategy. He felt the formation and registration of trade unions could take place side by side with the political struggle, despite the restrictions of the ordinance. Nevertheless, O'Connor remained in the TLP. Tubal Uriah Buzz Butler, who was to emerge as a national hero, disagreed with Cipriani too, but he also held on. Because the leaders who were against the subordination of trade union activity remained in the Trinidad Labour Party, the Cipriani-led movement did not break up immediately. But with the loss of cohesion at the top and mushrooming, unattended problems below, the breakup was not far off.

Cipriani's waning influence with the masses was first most apparent in the sugar belt around 1934. The constitutionalist politics of the 1920's had run its course. Certainly it held out no further hope for East Indian workers in the sugar belt, who were fighting to cope with increasing impoverishment which was part of the general depression affecting the society. The Trinidad economy was feeling the effects of an international economic depression engulfing the capitalist countries.[6] Sugar workers turned their backs on the compromising TLP leadership and soon resorted to direct mass action. In that same year, 1934, strikes in the sugar belt progressed into violent conflict.[7]

That was only the beginning. In 1935 Adrian Cola Rienzi, a lawyer, who was one of the most influential leaders of the TLP, broke with Cipriani and the TLP and he formed the Trinidad Citizens League. Butler, a former oil worker, who was by now exerting greater mass influence than Cipriani, left the TLP as well, and in 1936 he launched the British Empire Workers and Citizens Home Rule Party. The basis was laid for a different kind of politics.

While this political evolution was taking place George Weekes had progressed from elementary school to Tranquility Inter-mediate School. But after one year of post-primary education, he was taken out of school because of family problems and he had to return to the countryside. At the time, still in the early 30's, some more awareness had touched him. Among other things he would hear his brother Kenny, who attended Queens Royal College, talking with his friends about world affairs. The discussions were interesting, but nothing to disturb the energies and preoccupa-tions of youth.

Some social images from his urban experiences however remained embedded in his mind. Shuttling between his mother's home in down town Port of Spain and Boissiere, on the outskirts of the city, where his brother lived, George could not help but notice the type of housing in St Clair. The huge mansions stood out in stark contrast to housing he saw in other areas even around the town, and naturally the contrast was far greater in relation to what he knew in Toco. He also could not help but notice that the only people who seemed to live in those mansions in St Clair were white.

George's mind would wander past the mansions and their occupants to some repeated observations in Toco, that always troubled something, somewhere at the back of his mind. Those occasions when there would be a sudden burst of feverish activity in the village, a frenzied preparation. Every action of that adult world would say that something important was about to happen. The old buildings had to be made to look especially good. On the day people would dress for a big occasion. The anti-climax would come in the form of a white official — some school inspector or government representative, making a rare appearance to perform a special function in the village.

George felt instinctively that there was something wrong about the level of excitement, concern and even fear that heralded the visits of these white officials, just as there was something wrong in the visual message of St Clair. His pre-teen mind could not define the wrong. His uneasy thoughts were not consciously shaped by exposure to any particular set of ideas. His reaction was an embryonic rebellion of instincts, that part of the psyche of colonised peoples that says no, that in the wider society was beginning to say no more vociferously, as it became more self-conscious and ideologically motivated under the influence of Garvey and Garveyism.

Trinidad in fact had a strong branch of the Garvey organisation, despite the fact that the paper, *The Negro World*, was banned. In the 1920's Trinidad was ranked second to Cuba in terms of the movement's organisation in the Caribbean.[8] But the name 'Garvey', even if it was heard by the young George, did not dwell in his imagination — not at that time. His thoughts were not burdened by any concept of colonialism, which symbolically reasserted itself in the village with each representation of authority in the form of a white man. The only resident symbol in the village of the total British domination of the colony, was the priest. Out there you would hardly ever see the few white estate owners. Now and then you spotted a white overseer on a motorcycle. It was not like the town, where the governor's mansion, and at times the governor could be seen around the savannah, or where you could see white officialdom converging on the rebuilt Red House*, where the Legislative Council met, or be conscious of the economic dominance of white merchants. It was not like the sugar belt where the white overseers exacted back breaking labour for starvation wages, or the oilbelt where the blatant racism of the British managers was supplemented by that of their South African kith and kin.

The full psychological impact of this oppressive corner of the British empire was not felt in the Toco of George's upbringing in the 1920's and early 1930's. The vocabulary of anti-colonialism, anti-racism, anti-white domination; the ideas of self-

---

* The Red House had been burnt to the ground during the disturbances of 1903.

government, democracy, the right to vote, the right to organise trade unions, even more radical ideas of a workers' state, fuelled by the Russian Revolution of 1917 and incorporated into a group like the Negro Welfare Cultural and Social Association*, led by Elma Francois; all these were part of the milieu of the times. But the forest stood between this ferment and the village of Toco with only a narrow roadway of communication. When George did cross this roadway, the dominant image would be that of his loving mother, kind, friendly, the type of person who gave freely of advice and assistance, who therefore maintained very good relationships with neighbours. She was not into the politics of the day, neither were Barbara and Vinola, George's younger sisters who lived with her. The personal environment therefore did not provide the inputs for George to link St Clair with the whole social order, which was created by colonialism.

It was a social order founded on concepts of the racial supremacy of whites. British colonial rule, with its inherent racism, elevated whites generally, not just Britishers, above the Black inhabitants of the islands, whether slave or free. This was so from the time the British captured the island of Trinidad from the Spaniards in 1797 and established political control over a colony where most of the whites were French. The group, which up to today is regarded as the French Creole elite, were able to thrive under British rule because they were white. The association of power, economic control, wealth and social status, with whiteness, was reinforced. This social environment was typical of the British Caribbean colonies. Arthur Lewis very aptly described this aspect of the region in the 1930's:

> The white population is relatively small, averaging about 3% of the total, this being exceeded only in the exclusively sugar plantation islands of Barbados (7%), St Kitts (6%) and Antigua (4%). But this tiny white element dominates every aspect of West Indian life. Economically and politically the white man is supreme; he owns the biggest plantations, stores and banks, controlling directly or indirectly the entire economic life of the community. It is he whom the Governor most often nominates to his councils, and

---

* This organisation is often simply referred to as the 'Negro Welfare Association' (NWA)

13

for his sons that the best government jobs are reserved.
Socially, the whites in general constitute the
aristocracy.[9]

The challenge to this social order, the challenge to alien
political rule, to overbearing economic exploitation reached a
highpoint in 1937. On the 10th of June, Butler exhorted the
workers of the country:

The hour has come to show your might and power to
get things for yourselves. Our brutal Taskmasters
have proudly and cruelly turned down our Prayers,
our petitions for more pay and British conditions of
Life and Labour in the oil Industry of the Colony.

These men and bosses have challenged us to prove
our right to life and happiness . . .

Sons of freedom as we are, we bravely accept the
challenge.[10]

He alerted the workers to be on standby for the call to what he
elsewhere described as "a fight to the finish". The fight soon
came.

The revolutionary upheaval that year, in Butler's words, the
"struggle for the Liberation of the land from the Spoiler, the
Oppressor and the Exploiter", touched the teenaged George
Weekes more profoundly than he thought at the time.

His mind had become more alert to political events after
receiving its most conscious political jolt shortly before the
eruption. The jolt had come from outside. The invasion of
Ethiopia by Mussolini in 1935. George was in Port of Spain at
the time with his mother. He could not help but be caught up in
the emotional shockwaves that brought with them an awareness
of a wider world out there, to which he was connected.
Somewhere in the psyche there was an umbilical connection
with the invaded country. It was not individual. It made a
community react.[11]

Organisations reacted, such as the NWCSA which mounted a
massive campaign of protest. Weekes saw and felt the collective
reaction. Objectively he saw it and instinctively he felt it. It was
within him too. People wanted to volunteer to fight. They felt
'advantage' was being taken. Some went to Cipriani seeking to
volunteer. Some went to Butler.

One country taking 'advantage' of another. But that was far
away. His mind had not yet drawn the parallel with his

homeland. But a name the people called, 'Butler', became a part of a nascent awareness. That name was about to emerge from the mist of George's political unconsciousness.

On June 19th 1937, George was back in Toco. In the village, peaceful and slow moving like the gardener on his donkey. In the village with the pure air that George loved to breathe, the smell of the sea. The women, like on any other day, could be seen carrying buckets of water on their heads, their erect black bodies swaying with a stately rhythm. They would stand up and talk comfortably, in tune with the casual pace of the village. Not a drop of water would spill from the perfectly balanced buckets. Under the charm there was a life of poverty and hard work, but borne as though it was the natural order of things. But far, far away from the tranquil village, on June 19th 1937 the order was being upset.

The news came into the village. The older people knew the name Butler, just as they had known the name Cipriani. They gathered in excited groups. Their hero had escaped. The police had gone to arrest him, arrest the mighty Butler, because they were afraid of him. He made the whites tremble. He was making Black people see the light, making the workers understand the power that lay in their hands, telling them they should "hold the reins". They were poor, working hard and kept poor to make English men from overseas rich. Prices were rising higher, so the poor people were getting poorer. Not a penny more for their labour. Massa in the oil companies, Massa in the sugar companies, Massa in South, Massa in North, they were deaf to the cries of the poor workers, living in overcrowded barracks and shacks. They were deaf to the cries of the hungry who could find no jobs. Butler was making them hear. So they sent the police to arrest him. Corporal Charlie King was foolish enough to try. In front of the people, while Butler was talking to them. In Fyzabad, where tempers were hot. They burnt Charlie King to death.

The flames from the corpse of Charlie King lit the ready torches of revolt. By the time the uprising was suppressed by British troops and the local militia and police, 14 people were dead, including two policemen, 59 had been seriously injured, and hundreds had been arrested.

George could sense the importance of the events, but he could not define that importance. He was isolated from the drama and the trauma. The strikes, stretching from the oil fields, to the cane fields to the docks, and the gunshots, like the mass meetings and the demonstrations that preceded them, were far away, reaching his world on the printed page but mainly by the spoken word, spoken more around him than to him. However, what filtered in was enough to widen that world. More unaccustomed thoughts were falling into place. He already knew about one country, a white country, invading another country, a black country and taking 'advantage'. Now troops from another country, a white country, had invaded his country and he was learning about 'advantage' closer at hand. He knew more about that word 'advantage' in 1937. It had become larger than the personal, larger than the image of his struggling father and the other teachers. There were other workers out there crying 'advantage'. Blood was spilled because of 'advantage'. The estate workers, who did hard tasks on the estates in Toco, whose lot was poverty no matter how hard they worked, they seemed to understand what it was all about, they were talking about 'advantage' too. Not only out there beyond the forest. At home in the village. In peaceful Toco.

All through the English speaking Caribbean the message and the action spread. On the heels of the troops, the British government sent the Commissions to find out causes, to suggest measures to placate. Forster Commission to Trinidad, Moyne Commission through the islands, including Trinidad and Tobago. New constitutional forms were wrested through the struggle, including universal adult suffrage, which was implemented in Jamaica in 1944 and in Trinidad and Tobago in 1946. The trade union movement entered a more definitive stage. The Oilfields Workers Trade Union was one of the unions born out of that travail. Born with a mission — to stop 'advantage'. George Weekes' destiny was taking shape. But he was blissfully unaware of it.

CHAPTER 2

LOVE, WAR, AND THE BIRTH OF IDEOLOGY

The teenaged Theresa Brown observed the young man who lived in the apartment next door on Kitchener Street in Woodbrook* coming home in his uniform for the first time. She did not even know he had joined the Volunteer Regiment. He kept so much to himself. She knew his name was George. She was very close to his sister, Vinola Weekes. They confided in each other, went out together with the same group of friends. But George was never a part of that group. She thought to herself that he did look quite handsome in his military uniform.

At one point he was gone for a long time. The day he came back, she and Vinola were standing in the yard. Mother and sisters, everybody came out excited. There he was so cool and Theresa thought he looked more handsome. He greeted the family and he looked at her. Yes, it was so strange. And she felt strange. The way he looked at her. Something happened. He spoke, to her!

"But how you change like that?"

It was a compliment. But what did he mean by that? How did she change? She was trying hard to put a matter-of-fact look on her face, to get her hands to find their natural place (where did she keep them all the time?). Her mind was doing a racing inventory of herself. She thought she was skinny. Why was he looking at her?

Anytime he returned from the barracks after that he would visit her. He moved from the Volunteers to the regular army. She saw his determination to fight the war. He was so serious, always reading something. He didn't seem to have many friends or care for too much company. She often found him hardly

---

* George's mother had moved from Sackville Street to an apartment on Kitchener St in Woodbrook.

communicative. Why did he do all that reading? Whatever the source of his preoccupation with books, it was something he did not share with her, even though a relationship was developing between them. In fact by the time he left for the war in 1943, they were quite close. With the sea between them, he took to the pen. Surprisingly for someone so serious, she found out that he was pretty good at writing sweet nothings.

Theresa thought a lot about the intense young man who was courting her, who had volunteered to go overseas to fight a war from which he might never return. She did not understand what was driving George. As close as they had become before he left on a troop ship, in some ways he was as much a stranger as when she observed him in the few years before they became friends. He locked even those closest to him outside of his deepest thoughts and motivations. If only she could have understood the inner stirrings behind his silences and absorption in books, she would have understood the depth of the call to battle.

To George the call was irresistible. When the Second World War broke out in 1939, he was eighteen. He was not politically involved and understood very little about the constitutional issues that were fought over in Trinidad and Tobago. But there were many things moving George. He had developed a fierce racial pride. He was offended by the portrayal of Blacks in so many of the films he went to see when he lived in the town. He went to the public library and read avidly, seeking out black newspapers that were received from the United States. Reading about the achievements of African-Americans in various fields gave him something to hold on to. He was strongly incensed when Hitler refused to acknowledge the victories of the outstanding black sprinter, Jesse Owens at the 1936 Munich Olympics.

His motivation came from his strong sense of justice too. Reading about the Nazi campaign of extermination against the Jews collided with all his human instincts. The preliminary events leading up to the war drew his attention, made him pay more attention to international affairs. Hitler was taking over neighbouring countries. Austria, Czechoslovakia ... he was going after Poland. There was talk that he would take over Britain too, talk about what he would do to the Blacks.

With all these things pressing on his mind, George abandoned his 24 cents a week motor mechanic apprenticeship on Nelson Street and volunteered for the army when war did break out.

LOVE, WAR, AND THE BIRTH OF IDEOLOGY

> I went to war as a Black man fighting for his Black
> pride and a human being fighting for the humanity of
> our planet.[1]

Joining the army for him was a relief from the exploitation he suffered as an apprentice and to which he saw other workers subjected. It was the same everywhere you went. There was no difference when earlier on he was an apprentice carpenter. Employers were squeezing you dry for next to nothing. In the army he felt independent, he felt he earned his "first real money".

He felt a sense of adventure about the whole thing. The army was posted at various points in the country "to ensure that no Nazi ship or troops come in or infiltrate the country". George felt good to be part of a cause.

> I was attracted to the possibility of action against the
> enemy . . . I did not see anything else in my own mind
> but that cause against fascism.[2]

There was something about the military in its own right that attracted George. He had functioned in the Cubs and the Boy Scouts in Toco. Despite the ups and downs with changes in leadership, he enjoyed the military feel of it, the camp fires, camping out in the night, going out in the bush.

The sense of excitement and adventure of the boy scout was transferred into the soldier, taking pride in the uniform, the tramping of the feet in the heavy boots, the rigorous training he received at the St James barracks, the discipline of army life. In 1940-41 he was in the bush 'for real', serving at the different strategic locations in the country ready to defend, wanting to be called upon to defend.

It was not surprising that when they called for volunteers for the Caribbean Regiment to go abroad to fight, George volunteered immediately. Young love was blossoming at home. Theresa was so pretty. He would miss her. But nothing could supersede the attraction of going to fight against evil. The first love was the love of a cause. He was going to defend race, country and mankind, to fight for justice as he saw it. He did not fear death when it came to that. The pattern of his life was set . . .

Shortly after the war, Vinola Weekes, George's sister, was leaving for Canada. Friends and relatives came around to the Kitchener Street apartment to bid farewell. To say George surprised them would be to put it mildly. As Sybil said:

19

George stand up between the bedroom and the living
room and he make one speech . . . I couldn't believe
. . . He talk so fluently. I was shock.[3]

George Weekes long winter of reclusive silence was over. The
hibernating 'Tiger' abandoned the lair of the shy boy and was
baring sharp verbal claws.

The war had broken the ice.

It was the war. The direct experience of segregation in
Virginia, the first training stop for the Caribbean Regiment. Sit
at the back of the bus. Blacks and dogs not allowed.

It was the war. The physical battles engaged in during the
war. They were not the expected battles against the fascists. The
only time the threat from Hitler was really felt by the Caribbean
Regiment was when they were travelling on the troop ships. The
Atlantic was a hunting ground for German U-boats. Once the
convoy taking the Caribbean troops to Italy came to a dead stop,
all engines were cut, trying to cover their presence by silence
when it was suspected that U-boats were around.

On the sea the threat of the torpedo kept the nerves on edge.
On the land the threat was the fellow soldier. Black versus White,
they battled in the clubs and on the streets of Cairo. The racial
tension was always there, between the British and the Caribbean
soldiers, not only on the off-nights in the Egyptian capital, but in
the military camps in the Suez. In the camps, much of the conflict
stemmed from the British ill-treatment of the Sudanese and other
African regiments. They were treated as the Caribbean soldiers
were treated in Virginia. In the Suez the Caribbean soldiers had
the rights of British soldiers. They could go into the canteens.
The African soldiers were kept out. There were those like
Weekes who would not accept the "British identity" or the
discriminatory exclusion of their kith and kin. They went into
the camps of their brothers and brought them into the forbidden
territory.

It was the war. The new knowledge to re-enforce identity
acquired during the war. The soldiers had the privilege of a few
trips to museums and historical sites in Egypt. George debunked
the propaganda which sought to deny Africans this rich part of
their heritage. His eyes could see and his intelligence could
discern, he was looking at African artifacts, produced in Africa,
by Africans. The Sphinx and the Pyramids were his pride, the
creation and the pride of his people.

LOVE, WAR, AND THE BIRTH OF IDEOLOGY

It was the war. The effect of the female touch during the war. "Tiger", the fighter, forced into fighting again by racism, was only Tiger among his male companions. He was too shy to even dance with the women. One of those beautiful black Sudanese women, who were regarded as the best women in Cairo, took him into a room and taught him how.

It was the war. The jolt to the intellect, which was the most decisive war experience. George's mind expanded on the press debate about the merits and demerits of different social, economic and political SYSTEMS — Fascism, Capitalism, Socialism. The carnage on the battlefields gave urgency to the pens and speeches of the men of thought. George was especially impressed by the speeches and writings of the British socialists. He digested the thoughts of leaders of the British Labour Party like Clement Attlee and Aneurin Bevan. Conceptually he began to understand exploitation and its roots in the organisation of society. He had long been familiar with the effects. He learnt about the nature of colonialism and imperialism. He began to see society differentiated into classes, with the minority capitalist class dominating and preying on the working class. He developed an identification with the working class, its frustrations and its struggles. He was converted to a belief in the justice and the historical necessity of the working class assuming the control of society. On the whole a new profundity of analysis, wider appreciation of international affairs and the ideology of socialism was now added to gut feelings and experiential perceptions.

The George Weekes who came home from the war in 1945 was not the same George Weekes who left Trinidad and Tobago on a troop ship in 1943. The journey through Virginia USA, Italy, Egypt and into a seductive New World of Ideas changed the boy into a man.

Theresa perceived his maturity. She also saw him become more absorbed in reading than before the war. She found that he was even more lonesome in some ways too, though she observed a new pace of activity coming into his life. He was responding to the call of politics.

The man, George Weekes, still had a boyish hunger for knowledge and action. The thrust of his reading now became more political.

When I came back to Trinidad, whenever I could get any type of literature that dealt with Marxism and socialism, I lapped it up. I began buying books as well. When I met Lennox Pierre, he suggested certain books. Whatever he had to lend me I would read. Others I would purchase wherever I could find them.

I would read about the Soviet Union and its development; also I would read the 'Comintern*', a Marxist paper telling you of what was happening all over the world. I would listen to the radio and take interest. I just fell in love with that. I wasn't the classical type of person who would know the Marxist jargon. I saw things from a Just point of view. I had this feeling for Justice ... I thought of what Capitalism represented and had caused. I said that is not for me. I wanted something new, something different, something that was more Just. After reading about Socialism, I said that was for me.[4]

But politics was not the only thing on his mind. Weekes was heading for a milestone in his life, one quite different from political involvement. He had taken Theresa in his dreams to the faraway places he saw during the war. In 1947, he was taking her down the aisle.

The courtship that led to marriage vows at St Patrick's Church in Newtown on June 28th 1947 gave a clear indication of the passion with which Weekes was driven by politics. Not even his starry eyes could tie his movements to the traditional activities associated with wooing. His ideological vision was drawing his steps to political meetings, stealing time from the softer plays of the heart. In the run up to the 1946 election Weekes was attracted to the messages of many of the speakers of the United Front. This was an electoral coalition of the socialist oriented West Indian National Party, the Butler Party, a combination of trade unions and 'socialist' individuals. Butler dropped out of it before the election. So too did the trade unions. Weekes ardently followed their meetings. Jack Kelshall and David Pitt were talking his kind of language when they spoke of nationalisation

---

* The Comintern had by then been transformed into the Cominform and its journal, which Weekes would have been exposed to at the time, was called *For a Lasting Peace, For a People's Democracy*.

of the oil industry. Patrick Solomon impressed him with his stand on issues of constitutional change . . .

With these fires burning in his soul and ideas of change sparking in the colonial environment in which he lived, there was no way marriage could settle George Weekes into a routine of work and home. His involvement was destined to develop beyond listening. There was a powerful magnet out there. In radical movements generally, but embodied with the greatest power in a particular leader whose name was linked to a boyhood consciousness, a hero whispered about in the Toco of 1937 growing to legendary and supernatural proportions as he eluded the British authorities during the uprising that year . . . "they can't catch up with Butler. Butler would be in a car and when they set up the road block and look in the car they can't see him at all" . . .

It was not the mystery, but the militancy that was attracting Weekes ten years later. He had not yet met this giant, Butler. But he could feel a bond in ideology and spirit. Eventually he would take his first step into political activism by registering his name in the Butler union, the British Empire Workers, Peasants and Ratepayers Union. Formally he did not become a member of the Butler party. In practice it made little difference. Butler would have a more profound influence on Weekes than any other single individual. Weekes formed other political associations, he went on to rise to great heights as a trade unionist, to gain national prominence and international recognition. But through it all he never ceased to be a Butlerite or to revere the memory of Butler.

While Butler's influence remained predominant, it is through the influence of some other associates, with whom he came into contact after establishing himself in the Butler movement, that Weekes first formally joined a political party. That party was the West Indian Independence Party (WIIP). The influential figures were Lennox Pierre, a solicitor, and John La Rose, an executive member of the Federated Workers Trade Union.

Before the formation of the WIIP, La Rose belonged to a marxist study group in Port of Spain which, in 1948, teamed up with the formerly powerful Negro Welfare Cultural and Social Association to form the Workers Freedom Movement. At the time the NWCSA was little more than a name carried by Jim Barrette, Christina King and Lucius Mondezie. The Workers Freedom Movement was closely associated with and later incorporated another marxist study group from Point Fortin, led by Lennox de Paiva. At this time, Lennox Pierre was chairman of the progressive-leaning Youth Council. Pierre encouraged the Workers Freedom Movement to become affiliated to the Youth Council and he himself became a member of the WFM.

Pierre's cultural and political activities drew Weekes towards him. The young solicitor was prominently associated with the steelband movement, at a time when the instrument and its players were fighting against ostracism. He took progressive stands on national political issues. For example, the Youth Council, under Lennox Pierre's leadership, supported Patrick Solomon's minority report on constitutional reform in 1948. Solomon's submission was harshly critical of the reactionary official report submitted by the O'Reilly Commission. Eric Williams described Solomon's report, which emphasised the responsibility of the people for their own affairs, as "a decisive document in the political and constitutional history of Trinidad and Tobago".[5]

Weekes' association with La Rose developed at the beginning of the 1950's. In that period, La Rose, representing the Workers Freedom Movement, held meetings throughout the oil belt presenting the oil workers with a wealth of information on the oil industry which the WFM cadre were able to get through their contacts with the Labour Research Department in Britain. Weekes was then a pipefitter with Trinidad Leaseholds Ltd, one of the major oil companies at the time. In 1952 Pierre, La Rose, Jim Barrette of the Negro Welfare Association, John Poon and others founded the West Indian Independence Party in combination with John Rojas, President General of the OWTU and Quintin O'Connor, leader of the Federated Workers Trade Union. The close association of Weekes, Pierre and La Rose would remain unbroken through Weekes' 35 years as an active trade unionist, 25 of which he would spend as President General of the OWTU.

Apart from directly political activity, Weekes was very impassioned about any movement dealing with the positive projection of African identity.

> Anything that dealt with Black people's struggle for
> identity that I knew about and could assist in any way
> I would be involved in it.[6]

24

LOVE, WAR, AND THE BIRTH OF IDEOLOGY

He joined the African Nationalist Movement, formed in 1947, which changed its name to the Pan African League in 1948. This movement, which had its headquarters in Montrose, Chaguanas, was led by Harrison Johnson and David Modeste. Members of this association laid the foundations for the establishment of the Ethiopian Orthodox Church in Trinidad and Tobago in December 1952. Weekes was also an active member of the Port of Spain-based Universal African Nationalist Movement, a direct offshoot of Garvey's UNIA. He sometimes took Theresa to meetings. Through these organisations he was exposed to another line of thought that complemented the early stirrings deep down in his soul. He learnt about Marcus Garvey and his Pan-African school of thought. He could identify with the message which had lost none of its power years after Garvey's death in 1940:

> Be as proud of your race today as your fathers were in the days of yore. We have a beautiful history, and we shall create another in the future that will astonish the world.[7]

He learnt about the expansive organisation which Garvey had built and his persecution by the United States authorities. He learnt about the debate between Du Bois and Garvey about how and where the African-American would find his rightful place in the sun. He was now able to put instinctive feelings about a people and their roots into a philosophical perspective.

All this exposure would have implications for the political and economic destiny of Trinidad and Tobago. But first the effects of the knowledge and the experience gained by George Weekes would be felt within the Oilfields Workers Trade Union.

CHAPTER 3

TURNING POINT FOR THE OWTU

June 29th 1960.

A.M. There is tension in the air at Beaumont Hill, scene of increasingly bitter negotiations over the past few months between Texaco Trinidad Inc., the US oil giant, and the Oilfields Workers Trade Union, Trinidad and Tobago's most powerful unit of organised labour.

Today would not be just another round of negotiations. At 2.15 p.m. a 48 hour ultimatum to the company would expire. The company must either budge and budge significantly from the 4% wage increase they were offering, or face the consequences of strike action. The union is demanding 30%, having reduced their original claim for a 40% general increase in pay.

Across the nation there was an air of expectancy. Texaco was by far the largest company operating in Trinidad and Tobago. There was also the danger of the strike, if it was called, escalating to engulf the entire oil industry. Motorists were rushing to stock gasoline. Housewives, especially in the towns, were worrying how they would cook as kerosene, on which most kitchens were dependent, would inevitably cease to flow from the pumps. Mothers wondered how they would get their children to school, in cases where they had to travel. Workers were calculating the distances they would have to walk, or ride if possible, to get to their jobs.

The teams faced each other around the table in the company building that overlooks the sea at Pointe-a-Pierre. The deceptive calm of the sea gave no hint of the potential national crisis, which could erupt at any moment affecting the industry which provided at the time 30% of government revenues and earned 89% of the country's foreign exchange.

TURNING POINT FOR THE OWTU

John Rojas, the President General of OWTU leading the union team, looked nervous. Every instinct in him was urging him to plead with the company as he had done earlier in the negotiations to yield at least enough for him to be able to pacify the workers. All Texaco had to do was make a more reasonable offer and he would do all in his power to call off the threatened strike. One of Rojas' Vice Presidents, Fitzroy McCollins, was glaring angrily at George Weekes, who was on the negotiating team as president of the powerful Pointe-a-Pierre branch of the union. They had come close to blows as the pressure to call the strike mounted in the union. McCollins argued vociferously that no workers were going on strike. They had too many financial commitments — hire purchase, rent, mortgages, loans . . .

Weekes and other 'Rebels' on the team, as well as those who supported their line, were in an angry, fighting mood. For Weekes, this battle was ideological and national, as well as industrial. The multi-national corporations were not only plundering the resources of the country, but they were treating the workers and the union with contempt, and, for the years gone by, Rojas and his Executive had been letting them get away with it.

Even as the hours ticked away before the ultimatum expired, Weekes could see the arrogance in the white faces on the other side. He had never forgotten Butler's references to the expressions of contempt which oil workers had to deal with from the very early days. A slur that always remained fixed in his mind was the comment of one manager who said, "Black dogs can only bark, they cannot bite". Butler had taught them differently, but only for a while. Unfortunately, Butler was in hiding when the OWTU was formed under his inspiration in July 1937. When he did emerge from hiding to testify before the Forster Commission of Enquiry into the disturbances, he was arrested. In December 1937 he was convicted on charges of sedition and he spent the following 18 months in prison. Butler therefore missed the opportunity to chart the course of the union in its critical formative period. Even on his release from prison he was denied the chance to shape the destiny of the OWTU. He was sidelined, or so the existing Executive of the union thought, into a specially created post of General Organiser. It was supposed to be title without responsibility. Butler did not take it that way. Whatever the title, he was rapidly organising the

27

union for the kind of struggle which gave birth to it in the first place. He was quickly thrown out because Rienzi, Rojas and the other OWTU leaders were determined that Butler would not gain control of the union. They were prepared to pull out all stops to ensure that the militancy of Butler would not tarnish the image of 'responsible' trade unionism which they had been compromising so strenuously to cultivate.

When Butler was expelled from OWTU and he formed his own union, the British Empire Workers Peasants and Rate Payers Union, the oil companies collaborated with Rienzi and Rojas by denying him representation of oil workers. There was an even more vicious accommodation between Rojas and the oil companies in the late 40's, aimed at finally destroying Butler's influence among oil workers.*

Weekes was very much aware that these historical events were some of the important, unacknowledged factors in the current negotiations. Though Texaco did not become a major oil company in Trinidad until their purchase of the assets of Trinidad Leaseholds Limited in 1956, they understood the deals of the 40's, and the effect of such backroom collusion on the effectiveness of Rojas leadership. Their arrogance was therefore supported by the feeling that they were up against a man whom they had on a string. His inclination to beg when he should have been demanding during the negotiations confirmed their opinions, and they were taking a sadistic pleasure in seeing a man who had opposed their entry into the country squirming before their 'might'.

They were also calculating on the divisions within the union paralysing its ability to act decisively. They knew about the growth of the 'Rebels' in Pointe-a-Pierre, a group George Weekes now led though he was not a founding member. They knew about the 'Rebels' vibrant opposition to Rojas which had led to near-violent clashes within the union. This explains the impertinence with which Texaco representatives had previously dismissed any strong talk by the union during the negotiations, openly accusing the team of bringing their internal confusion to the table to create problems for the company.

This time the company had miscalculated. The OWTU team retired to an adjoining office and Rojas signed the strike notice

_____
* Further details are presented later in this chapter

with trembling hands. Delivery of the notice wiped the smug look from the faces on the management side. They followed the union team out of the office and stood amazed as they drove away. What could have entered the heads of the 'dogs' for them to start biting again!

June 29th 1960. 2.15 p.m.

The company's miscalculation is confirmed. Straight from Beaumont Hill, Weekes and the other Pointe-a-Pierre officers had gone to the Texaco refinery. The call was given for the appointed time: 2.15 p.m., a call echoed by other branch officers and organisers who were on standby throughout the union's branches. As the hour reached, the workers in Pointe-a-Pierre downed tools en masse. The same was happening in all fields. From Pointe-a-Pierre, a 5000 strong blue shirted army burst through the refinery gates heading for San Fernando. Workers, by the hundreds, were pouring out from other areas of the company's operations. Weekes had done what he had to do according to his concept of 'responsible' trade unionism. He saw to it that there were meetings with workers and company officials before the exodus to ensure that all precautions were taken to avoid any potential disaster such as a major fire, while the workers were on strike.

Just outside of the Paramount Hotel (which was later to be the headquarters of the OWTU), Rojas joined the massive demonstration. He had received the news that the call was overwhelmingly successful and the strike was on. He went into the vehicle with the microphone to lead the workers to King's Wharf, where more thousands of workers from other areas and people generally would converge to hear the union leaders speak at the impromptu meeting. Out in front the demonstration and on the platform at King's Wharf, Big John*, in his broad-rimmed Texas hat would really look big. There would be no signs of the lack of confidence which made him hurry anxiously to the union's Lower Hillside Street headquarters, instead of to the fields, when the negotiating team left Beaumont Hill. Freed from the tension of waiting to hear how the workers would respond, he could raise his chest and his voice and defy imperialism in a way he might have wanted to do since 1937.

The success of the strike, drawing immediately 7000 Texaco workers, shocked the company. At the end of an emergency

---

* "Big John" was a popular nickname for Rojas, among oilworkers.

meeting of the management, they hastily despatched a new offer to the union, raising their offer to 12 1/2%. The revised offer reached Rojas on the platform. But, in his moment of glory, the beginning of the first official strike in the 23 years of the union's history, Big John was not compromising. Not at that time.

As Rojas poured public scorn on the company's offer, Texaco officialdom were left to wonder where they had gone wrong. Rojas too had to weigh the force that had developed in the union. Because he knew that the tail was now wagging the dog. When Texaco officials were counting on the divisions in the union, they were assuming a balance of forces that would neutralize the militants. What the strike was clearly signalling was that George Weekes and the Rebels had come into their own. This was the turning point for the union.

A new attention now had to be paid to the president of the Pointe-a-Pierre branch. He could no longer be dismissed either by oil barons or union executives as just another firebrand agitator. The strike had revealed that it was not just a matter of division in the union anymore. A dramatic transformation had taken place and George Weekes was now indisputably at the helm of the moving forces of change.

Weekes was the type of person who did not remain unknown for long when he came into the oilfields to work at Trinidad Leaseholds Limited in 1949. He was a man with a mission, intense, proselytizing, debating, combative, generating ideological and political controversy that profoundly stirred the minds of workers. He replanted seeds of a liberating vision in a harsh environment of oil and grease, of steel and wells and compressors, and employers as hard as the machines. He nourished the vision to grow beyond concerns over wages and working conditions, critical as such concerns were and are, to wider considerations of self-hood, of world view, of economics and government.

The young, exuberant George Weekes felt an urgency about converting every worker to beliefs that to him were incontrovertible. Their blackness must be a symbol of pride and a call to arms against oppression, not a stigma of inferiority or a rationalization for accepting second class status. Often he felt a deep hurt when he would "hear a Black man crying down his own people, his own blackness. For when you as a Black man condemn Black, you condemn yourself".[1] He also preached to them that they must stand up consciously as part of a working class movement which would defeat imperialism and lead the country to socialism.

The expression of these views set raging ideological fires in the oil belt:

> Debates were very heated between myself and others who disagreed with me . . . Sometimes during lunch time or tea-break in the Canteen area I used to be in strong dialogue . . . These arguments were a constant affair. Sometimes you would be engaged in serious work on the job and they would come and pick you out. You could be between heated furnaces making up some line or doing some other hard work that demands all your attention but the fellas would be so interested in what they want to discuss that they will come and interrupt you.[2]

The arguments came from all sides, sometimes with those who "had been schooled in the white man's thought so strongly that when you spoke about Black people, they didn't want to hear that". Sometimes the arguments were against those who "were supportive of blackness" but didn't have the "socialist outlook. They were conservative and although we agreed on the question of Black, when it was necessary to take a progressive line, it conflicted with their line of thought".[3] And of course there were the arguments against those who would have nothing to do either with blackness or socialism.

From these bases, arguments and discussions went on to "politics in general — what was happening in the country, the position this leader or that leader took . . ."[4]

Weekes' image among oil workers grew in the heat of the controversy he stimulated. He was reaching the majority of workers with what he had to say and even where there was opposition, there was respect:

> We had disagreement on certain points. But in spite of this disagreement there was always respect and regard from even those who disagreed with me on different projections.[5]

Workers respected and were inclined to believe Weekes because of the conviction and honesty with which he spoke, because they sensed that he was talking "from a strong feeling deep down inside".[6] He was also appealing to some of the innermost suppressed feelings of a people oppressed and dehumanized in a racist system.

He dealt directly with the internal wrangles in the union too. He was an articulate and bitter opponent of Rojas and the OWTU leadership. His first basis of opposition was an unswerving loyalty to Butler. He could not forget Rojas' treatment of Butler. For him, like for most oil workers, Butler was their true leader and the rightful leader of the union, a union "built upon the name of Butler, kept together by the name of Butler"[7] as the Chief Servant had once reminded Rienzi in a letter.

When Rienzi assumed leadership of OWTU as its first president, it was widely understood that he was acting for Butler. His credibility with the oil workers was enhanced by his association with Butler. Rienzi was Butler's defence lawyer in 1937 and acted as an intermediary between Butler, on behalf of the workers, and the colonial government.[8] On his record Rienzi deserved this consideration. The way he boldly played his part in the months of crisis, during the 1937 rebellion, further endeared him to the workers. Their response to him was an early demonstration that African workers (oil workers were predominantly African) were prepared to accept an Indian leader once they were convinced he represented their views and interests. It was also testimony to the revolutionary influence of Butler. He had been able to surmount the racial cleavage engineered by colonialism to keep the two major dominated peoples in the society apart. He gave both Africans and Indians at the mass level a more wholesome vision based on a revolutionary nationalism, racial pride and common class interests.

Rienzi, however, was to fall into the mould, which seduced so many other Black professionals who championed the cause of labour during the early and mid-twentieth century in Trinidad and Tobago. The theory of struggle proved far more appealing than the realities of confrontation with the colonial authorities, which resulted in death and serious injury, imprisonment and loss of jobs. It also meant harsh financial sacrifices, especially for the early trade union leaders and champions of labour. No doubt in the environment of 1937, with its bloody background of 14 shot dead and 59 seriously wounded, the British-defined role for trade unions in the West Indian colonies must have had some undue attraction. In the Forster Commission report on the 1937 rebellion, we find a very succinct statement of the perspective on trade unions which was to hold sway with the colonial authorities:

> Such a movement, given sympathetic guidance by Government and a tolerant encouragement on the part of employers during the transitional stage of its development, is the surest means of securing industrial stability and the removal of extremist tendencies.[9]

The British government fought hard to persuade the industrialists and planters on the validity of this point of view.

The colonial authorities in Britain and Trinidad and Tobago also had to persuade the employers about the individuals who were gaining control of the unions, in particular Adrian Cola Rienzi, who had crossed swords with Cipriani on many occasions. As president of the San Fernando branch of the TWA, he sent a cable on the anniversary of the Russian Revolution in 1927 congratulating the Russian leaders for ten years of "successful government". In the cable he also pledged the support of the Trinidad workers in "the struggle for world socialism". This cable was intercepted and put in the hands of the governor.[10] So the Rienzi, who was first president of both the Oilfields Workers Trade Union and the All Trinidad Sugar Estates and Factory Workers Trade Union, was a man under close surveillance by the colonial government for a long time. But the British government did not easily panic at the prospect of such men assuming potentially powerful positions. They had a great deal of confidence in their instruments of control. They saw the colonial intellectual as manipulable. They saw the trade union itself as an instrument of control. They sent down 'guides' from the Colonial Office and the TUC in Britain to help the early movement along the approved path which was apolitical and non-confrontational. The first emissary in this role was A.G.V. Lindon, designated an industrial advisor, who had a tremendous influence in setting the pattern of operation for trade unions.

The confident attitude of the British government could be seen in the position the colonial office adopted when Trinidad Leaseholds Limited tried to prevail on the governor to refuse to recognise the newly-formed union led by Rienzi. The oil company managers rested their argument on the grounds that

(i) they did not believe the workers (meaning "ignorant Blacks") capable of trade union organisation and (ii) they saw Rienzi as a "bad hat" (dangerous communist). The Colonial Office answered the concerns of TLL on July 31st 1937 by pointing out:

(a) . . . it is the government's policy, which on general grounds the Secretary of State must strongly support, to encourage the formation of trade unions, (b) the only people who are capable of doing this are the very people who have been known as "red" in the past, and you have got to put up with them and hope they'll get paler.[11]

Early trade unionism in Trinidad and Tobago and Rienzi lived up to the British government expectations so perfectly that there was no room for Butler, the "fanatical negro" as he was called by the Forster Commission, or the "curious phenomenon" as he was termed by F.W. Dalley. Dalley, who was sent to Trinidad by the British government to investigate the causes of the 1946-47 labour unrest, quite accurately perceived the divergences in the trade union movement, which made Butler an outcast from the OWTU. Divergences which were to surface again in 1960 in the same union, with George Weekes as the central figure. Only this time the "threat" could not be ostracized. Dalley said in 1947:

Responsible trade unions and 'Butlerism' cannot exist side by side: they are incompatibles.[12]

He also expressed the view that "the workers of Trinidad should be helped to realise this by all the responsible elements of the colony".[13]

By the time Dalley was writing this, Rienzi had become so pale that you could not even find a trace of pink, far more "red" in the actions of the former president of OWTU, turned Crown Counsel for the colonial government.

Butler, with his forceful re-emergence on the labour scene, was the reason for Dalley's investigation. The Chief Servant had been removed from the labour scene with the outbreak of World War II in 1939. Conveniently, the British government had detained him before he could get too far in organising his own trade union base, following his rejection by the OWTU leadership. But once freed from his imprisonment and forced exile on Nelson Island, which lasted for the duration of the war, Butler issued a strong challenge to the colonial authorities with massive strikes and demonstrations in 1946 and 1947. The colonial government co-operated zealously with the oil and sugar companies, which were most affected by Butler's actions, in ruthlessly suppressing this new upsurge of the workers. In this they were fully supported by Rojas, who, in 1943, had taken over from Rienzi in the OWTU, and other 'responsible' trade unionists.

Thousands of workers who had responded to Butler's call were thrown out of their jobs. Hundreds of them settled on Crown Lands to form a new village called Strikers Village. The blows were so devastating that this period represented, as Annamunthodo said, "the beginning of the end of Butler as a Labour leader".[14] The great hope of the establishment and its trade union allies was that Butlerism as well as Butler had been crushed. The oil companies were well pleased with the role of Rojas and the OWTU Executive, who had sent a letter to the Dalley Commission of Enquiry condemning Butler and singing their praises[15]; so pleased that they rewarded him by instituting a check off system and the closed shop in the oil industry in 1948. It was a resounding triumph for 'responsible' trade unionism.

Up to 1960, Texaco could feel that they were riding the crest of this victory. They never felt that the counter trends experienced in the oil industry, the unofficial or 'wild cat' strikes which erupted from time to time, were indicative of any spirit which could find dominance in industrial relations again. They had seen Butler triumph in national elections in 1950. The Governor, Hubert Rance, and the colonial authorities conspired with Albert Gomes and others to deny Butler and his party representatives ministerial office then, but the fact was, Butler's party had won the largest number of seats among parties contesting. The oil executives had seen Butler win his own seat again in 1956. But, despite the political victories, the Chief Servant did not appear to present any threat on the labour scene. Even politically, it was clear that his time was past. Though he won his seat in 1956 and his party had one other successful candidate, there could be no doubt that he was now eclipsed by Dr Eric Williams as the leader of the masses.

The Texaco brigade were not only outsiders in nationality, they were even more hopelessly outsiders to the spirit of resilience of the people, blinded victims of their own racial contempt. Walter Annamunthodo expresses the effect Butler had on people even when he was defeated. Speaking about 1947 he said:

> I am among those who responded to his call for positive action. That single step has filled my life with unending pride.[16]

These sentiments were expressed 30 years later and could be taken as a gauge of the spirit of those who 'responded to the call'. George Weekes was one of the young men deeply affected by the call and its consequences. The dramatic events took place before he had joined the Butler union. At the time he was working in Port of Spain as a conductor on the trolley buses of the City Corporation. He was not able to attend the long march from San Fernando to Port of Spain in January 1947. But he strongly identified with its purpose. He identified with the rage which caused stones to be thrown outside the Red House when the striking and unemployed workers from the South linked up with public workers in Port of Spain and reacted to police harassment and the shooting of Cyril Larodé. He was angered when two days later, the notorious Commissioner of Police, Colonel Muller, known as "Two gun Muller", led a raiding party that ransacked Butler's headquarters at 29 Old St Joseph Road in Port of Spain, wilfully damaging the printing press in the process. At that time Weekes only knew of the headquarters by its reputation. But it was ground that would soon be well known and sacred to him. The efforts of the establishment to crush Butler were actually drawing Weekes closer to the movement. Apart from being moved by the ideas and militancy of Butler himself, he was impressed by the courage and determination of the Butlerites, and he was feeling his manhood challenged by the repression of the colonial government.

These were critical factors in Weekes' decision to get involved. From the sidelines he was seeing a number of people expressing the right ideas. But it is Butler and the Butlerites whom he saw really taking up the fight against injustice, the fight for workers' power. As much as Weekes was attracted by radical ideas, he was even more attracted when the ideas were combined with action. Once he made the decision to become involved, there was no turning back. He became a regular visitor to the headquarters of the Butler party. This is where he would go on afternoons after work and during breaks to meet with stalwarts like James Lynch and assist in the work of the party. He enrolled in the Butler union and his political activity picked up a new pace. In later years he had the opportunity to sit in the headquarters and talk extensively with the Chief Servant himself on many occasions.

So when Texaco thought that 'responsible' trade unionism was still the order of the day, they had failed to recognise that Butler was reborn again in the labour movement, in the OWTU, in the person of Butler's "son", George Weekes. In 1960, they were getting the first inkling, though they may not have recognised it at the time, why Butler referred to Weekes as his "son"*.

The oratory which quickly made George Weekes an influential figure among the oil workers was developed on the platforms of the Butler party. Weekes' first public speech was made to sugar workers in the Curepe area in a meeting chaired by James Lynch. From there he went on to become a regular speaker on Butlerite platforms. Up to that time in the late 40's, he had not yet seen or met Butler. The first time he saw Butler in person was in 1950 when Butler returned from England after spending almost two years there.

As Weekes established himself as a man with an assurance of what he was saying, a passion for the goals of the movement, and the ability to communicate effectively with an audience, his moments of glory came when he would speak on the same platform with Butler. He first had this experience at Harris Promenade in San Fernando. After Butler had been elected to parliament in 1950, the Chief Servant (as Butler designated himself) introduced a revolutionary practice of reporting to the people after every session of Parliament. He would hold a mass meeting at Woodford Square in Port of Spain on a Friday afternoon, after the meeting of the House was over, and discuss the current issues with the people. This would be followed by a similar session in San Fernando on the Monday. Weekes soon became one of the regular speakers who appeared on these platforms and who spread the word at other meetings throughout the country, along with other activists who would become his long standing associates, such as Stephen Maharaj and John Abraham, who would later become Vice President of OWTU. His dynamism on the platforms of Butler throughout

---

* In later years, when George Weekes was President General of the OWTU, Butler referred to him as his "son".

the South, where he was exposed to the mass of oil workers, combined with his education and agitation of the workers on the company grounds, spread and deepened his influence in the industry.

The ideas which Weekes was putting forward, also bore the stamp of Butler. Weekes was coming from a background of wide reading and his intellect was being fed by his involvement in a number of organisations, which gave him a consistent view of revolutionary change that was uncluttered by the sentiments of British Empire loyalty that were a point of contradiction in Butler's radicalism. Butler, nevertheless, represented in Weekes' imagination the most dynamic crystallization of some fundamental ideas which were the ground of his own motivation. Butler's consistent cry to "Let those who labour hold the reins" appealed to the socialist in Weekes. Butler's vehement anti-imperialism was what Weekes felt instinctively as much as he held on to it ideologically.

Butler referred to himself as "Butler the Black" in his confrontation with the white establishment, indicating a racial pride which he generally exuded, and which touched deep chords of response in the mind and soul of his young protege, equally proud of his identity. Butler's racial pride was not a racist ideology, which excluded his acceptance and appreciation of others, or blinded him to the common bonds of suffering of oppressed people. Butler fought for the ideal of African-Indian unity, and championed the cause of Indian workers with the same love, sacrificial zeal and boldness, that he battled the cause of African workers. For him there was no separation in that fight against the colonial/imperialist domination. He was the leader of the workers, the oppressed, the exploited, who in this society were all Black — African and Indian — against the oppressors, predominantly white and foreign. It was the same with Weekes, which would give him an appeal, similar to Butler's, with Indian as well as African workers.

Butler's cry for "Home-Rule" was transformed into a demand for total Independence in Weekes' own unambiguous vision. Like Butler, Weekes saw nationalisation of major industries such as oil as the ideal way to go, a means of establishing an independent economic base. For Weekes this was a necessary foundation of national independence.

Above all the old veteran and hero and the young "warrior worker"* shared a common spirit and idea on the approach of the trade union within the context of an imperialist dominated society. Workers were not organised into trade unions to beg favours from the multinationals but to demand their rights, a concept that was being revived in the 1960 strike.

These ideas communicated readily in the oil industry of the 1950's. They were part of the heritage of the workers. They were latent in the wake of the 1947 repression and under the confusion caused by the dualism of the union leadership that mouthed a radical ideology but practised an undignified collusion with industry magnates. Weekes made the Butlerite ideas assume a new reality in the 50's. Fighting from within the union he was less hampered by obstacles that acted against Butler at the time. Butler was still reaching the consciousness of the oil workers, up until he went to England again in 1953. But Butler was on the outside of their day to day struggle. Weekes, as an extension of Butler within the union, was able to struggle concretely for these ideas. This he did at a wider political level, like Butler, and, very important for the workers, he struggled in direct confrontation with the oppressive employers and compromised union leaders. In this way he spearheaded the resurgence of radical ideas as a practical, moving force in the workers' lives, especially in the late 50's.

In Weekes, the workers were not just seeing ideas. More importantly they were perceiving a sense of struggle, a genuine commitment, that same defiant personality that had made Butler their true leader. Weekes's involvement in the Butler movement had steeled him in many ways for leadership. As he rapped and mobilised from day to day, with relentless energy and dedication, with a captivating single-mindedness of purpose, the workers were experiencing the re-emergence of the spirit of Butler in the oilfields.

Texaco would only feel the change when their 7000 employees left the refinery and the fields and converged on Harris Promenade on June 29th 1960, singing to the tune of a Sparrow calypso**, "4% is murder"[17]. Apex, another foreign oil

---

* Butler referred to his followers as "warrior workers"
** Calypso is one of the major indigenous art forms of Trinidad and Tobago, a form of song often used for social and political commentary. 'Sparrow' is one of the most famous exponents of this art form.

39

company, would still not understand, and rushed rudely into laying off 600 workers, on the excuse that the Texaco strike took away the market for their products. But they never thought it necessary to discuss the matter with the union before taking action. On July 1st all their workers walked off on strike. Shell, with whom negotiations were also underway, thought they could undercut the effectiveness of the strike by importing and distributing the products which the Texaco strike was taking off the market. Their 3000 workers gave them the message that there was a new dispensation in oil when they closed Shell down on the 7th of July.

The *Trinidad Guardian* editorial of June 30th reflected what a shock the strike was for the establishment from the very beginning. They were caught unawares "because of the fact that this particular union (OWTU) has in the past shown on the whole a most commendable restraint and sense of responsibility". They held on to the hope that because the union had never before called a strike it "certainly would not wish its first essay to be a means of disrupting the industry". Looking at the union's "excellent record of sober and skillful bargaining" they could only suspect some "element of politics" in the situation. They could not understand what was taking place.

It was too early to recognise the phenomenon of a renascent Butlerism, or even to identify the precise nature of the "element of politics" or how it fit into the picture. The *Guardian* would become really disturbed, when over the first weekend of the strike, which started on a Wednesday, Eric Williams, the premier of the country would say:

> Government is not concerned. I understand the strike
> is quite a peaceful strike. I do not propose to express
> any opinion on it. At this stage it does not concern the
> Premier of the country.[18]

The *Guardian* paraphrased Williams as saying that the strike action was "what industrial democracy meant — bargaining between employers and workers. Too much people behaved as though it was a question for the government".[19]

The *Guardian*, true to form, took up the cry of the company for the appointment of a Board of Enquiry to settle the dispute, and as the strike wore on they editorialised repeatedly against the government for its "retreat from responsibility".[20] The only significant intervention from the government, however, came on the 7th of July, when Williams called a meeting of OWTU and Texaco representatives to seek an agreement on the maintenance of essential services. As a representative on the union team, Weekes would sit around a table from Williams for the first time. The spotlight, however, would not be on Weekes. He had not yet become a national figure. Fiery, radical rhetoric was not enough to capture great attention from the media. That was a standard feature of trade union practice, which since 1947 had caused little more than localized ripples on the tranquil industrial scene. Weekes himself used to be impressed with the fiery speeches of agitators like Urilton Pierre and Fabien Lesaldo, who were both to oppose him for the OWTU presidency in later years.

The newsmaker on the union side was the President General, 'Big John' Rojas. As the strike developed, he carried the public image of the union, as the main speaker on platforms and speaking to the press. But the backbone of the strike was George Weekes and the Rebels. This is when Weekes would first develop a relationship with Jack Kelshall, who was legal adviser to the union. Kelshall and Telford Georges (later to be a judge), who was another legal adviser at the time, were giving considerable service to the union. In addition to handling legal matters, they were producing almost daily bulletins, keeping workers up to date on progress in negotiations and other matters relevant to the strike.[21]

There was basic agreement with the measures proposed by Williams at the meeting — mainly to keep emergency vehicles in service and to allow people like doctors to get gasoline. In the days to come the union would get the better of the argument with the company in terms of who was entitled to receive gas and the procedures for distribution, which eventually fell very much into the hands of OWTU workers.

The agreement itself was not the most significant thing about the meeting with Williams though. It was a certain apparent harmony between union and government which characterised the strike. This is what prevailed against the *Guardian*'s efforts to get the PNM regime to draw the sword against the workers. It is what scuttled an intended opposition motion in the Parliament to declare a state of emergency, as the pressures started to mount on the population. It is what led to the boldness of many of the other trade unions in supporting the strike — funds raised by stevedores, funds donated by the Seamen and Waterfront

Workers Trade Union (SWWTU), funds and threats of sympathy strikes by Sutton's Amalgamated Workers Union and more. There was even a one hour work stoppage, intended to be national, on July 12th. Though it was not as widespread as the National Trade Union Congress had hoped when they called the strike, since some major unions did not respond, it was wide enough to make an impact.

These developments must certainly have confirmed in the editorial board of the *Guardian,* what they and their financial backers saw initially as the politics in the strike. They would have remembered Rojas complaining in 1959 of the PNM creating confusion in the union and attempting to take it over. The fact is, the PNM influence was at work. But it was only one of the influences in the process of transformation of the union. And what was most fundamental about it was not Rojas' and the *Guardian*'s simple notions of direct manipulation and efforts at a takeover. Of deeper significance was the way in which the mass movement of 1956, which the PNM led, had become a tributary converging with the renascence of the spirit of 1937, a feature which would become very ironical as subsequent history unfolded.

A letter writer in the *Trinidad Chronicle* of May 5th 1959, responding to Rojas charges, was very much on the mark when he said:

> No one can honestly say that the Government has directly interfered with the OWTU. I say 'directly' because I believe that with the advent of the PNM Government, there was interference. But such interference was with the minds and aspirations of OWTU members and has now begun to reflect upon the administration of the OWTU ...
>
> They have been caught up in the whirl of progressive thoughts and reforms and all like Rojas must give way or go down ignominiously.

The writer went on to look at some concrete effects of the "progressive thoughts" in the workers' attitudes to leaders and negotiations:

> They (the workers) need a leader who can appreciate their hardships and not one who takes what he gets at the expense of what they deserve, simply to be regarded in 'high official circles' as 'responsible'.

They need a friend of the workers not a friend of the employers.

Williams, with his anti-colonial rhetoric, had captured the hearts and the imagination of the mass of Africans in the society. In the divided political culture, the mass of Indians remained aloof from the movement he led. It must be said though that Williams' failure to mobilize the Indian masses in the nationalist movement of 1956 had to do with the limitations in his own perspective, as well as the divisiveness of the political culture. These divisions were real and important, but not decisive. Cipriani and later Butler had been able to mobilise the Indian masses at a time when there were East Indian organisations like the East Indian National Congress and the East Indian National Association trying hard to counter the movement for self-government with a narrow ethnic nationalism. Weekes, at the trade union level, in an atmosphere where PNMism and DLPism* were pulling the society apart in 1965, succeeded in the mobilization of Indian workers. The National Joint Action Committee was able to repeat the mass mobilization of Africans and Indians at a more direct political level in 1970.**

Williams' failure with the Indian masses, however, was no obstacle to his overwhelming impact in the predominantly African oil belt. Here his ideological impact was to act as a catalyst in re-stimulating demands which would eventually go beyond where he was prepared to go. Politically he was seeking to destroy the man Butler, but concretely by his own projection as a Black liberator, a nationalist, a fighter who dared the imperialists at the Caribbean Commission, who could speak the language of the masses, he was in fact invoking the spirit of Butler. The mood he created, as fate would have it, helped the rise of the man who would become one of his most tenacious opponents, George Weekes. Weekes is the one who would truly

---

* The Democratic Labour Party (DLP), a combination of Bhadase Maraj's PDP and Albert Gomes' POPPG, was the major opposition party and popularly perceived to be representing Indian ethnic interests, just as the PNM was regarded as representing African interests.

** It is important to note, however, that racial antagonism assumes far more significance in conventional politics, which is where Williams expended all his effort, than in industrial struggles or revolutionary political struggles.

carry the ideas and the spirit, though confined to a more limited arena than Williams who held the reins of government.

However, in 1960 the divergences did not surface. Indeed in a speech after the strike, Williams, in a fighting mood, communicated an approach by the government to industrial relations, which would have made every trade unionist feel a new strength in the battle against the big corporations (mainly in oil and sugar at the time), who were exploiting local labour unconscionably, comfortable in their accommodation with 'responsible' trade unionism.

> You will notice, Ladies and Gentlemen, that I have refrained from discussing the inconvenience to the public, the temporary price increases, the shortage of foodstuffs in various areas ... Strikes inevitably involve public inconvenience.[22]

The 1960 strike did. Over the three weeks that it lasted, anxieties and rumors gripped the country, urban housewives rediscovered the coal pot, the country's streets appeared deserted by motor vehicles, men in 'high positions' rode to work, formally suited in jacket and tie, on horseback or on bicycles, numerous hardships were experienced by the public, one taxi driver was even sent to jail for stealing 72 cents worth of gas from the truck of a contractor ...

But, as Williams continued, on the subject of the strike:

> **It is the effective and in fact often the only way of bringing the workers case to the attention of the public and winning public support and sympathy.** I have been through so many strikes abroad many leading directly or indirectly to a transport crisis, that I for one was determined, once basic essential services were maintained and until a total shutdown was really threatened, that I **would sanction no step whatsoever which savoured of strike-breaking.**[23]

Weekes himself, despite his misgivings about Williams, was seduced by the tenor of the remarks. He had always been supportive of Williams' nationalism. Williams' attitude to the multinationals in this strike was consistent with a progressive nationalism. In his speech he scorned their attempts to force the government's hand, mentioning:

44

A company representative threatened one Minister that his company would not invest another penny in Trinidad. Another company representative accused the Government, through another Minister, of doublecrossing the company and blamed the strike on PNM elements.[24]

Williams was not phased by any of this. He was not phased by the various *Guardian* articles suggesting that the strike would "have an ill-effect on Trinidad's industrial and investment climate" and quoting conveniently unnamed "top economists" to back up their point. Without mentioning the *Guardian,* Williams countered:

> And let no one deceive you. **Outside investors are not scared away by a militant union or by a grim strike.** Quite the contrary, American and British investors know all that needs to be known about tough strikes, and they know that a well-organised and disciplined union is one of the major incentives to investment.
>
> In the midst of the strike another oil company arrived in Trinidad to negotiate concessions from the Government, and while the strike was on I was opening in Port of Spain the Bank of London and Montreal which is already planning branches in San Fernando and Scarborough.[25]

These were impressive projections for how the PNM saw the role of the trade unions, especially in relation to the foreign multinationals, and Williams emphasised the determination of his government to let unions bargain for their members free from government intervention, to "promote union democracy". The party to which Weekes belonged, the West Indian Independence Party, had supported Williams and the PNM in the 1956 elections, except in the Arima constituency, where one of the WIIP members, John La Rose, contested. The WIIP hierarchy had supported Williams as a superior alternative to either the PDP or the POPPG. Whereas Gomes had repressed the unions, Williams attitude to the unions in 1960 seemed justification enough for the support he had received from the radical left.

Weekes' area of reserve remained on the question of socialism. Passing remarks of Williams on this occasion, about "elements" who "sought to lay the groundwork for the establishment of a

socialist party to fight the forthcoming General Elections",
reinforced his view. Williams' writings, in particular *Capitalism
and Slavery*, had convinced some people that Williams was a
socialist. Weekes too was influenced by Williams' writings and
the sheer power of his projection on the political platform. But he
could not discern any policy of socialism in Williams' political
speeches. And neither he nor the leaders of the WIIP accepted
the argument that Williams' avoidance of socialist projections
and occasional expressions of disdain for socialism, during his bid
for political office, were tactical on his part. Weekes and the
WIIP knew, therefore, that under Williams rule, the people
would not experience the ultimate realisation of a state where
exploitative capitalism would be ended and social control
established over the resources of the country. This was enough to
keep Weekes out of the PNM. He however held on to the hope
that at least Williams would represent a progressive stage of
nationalism.

The way in which Williams characterized those whom he
claimed wanted to establish a socialist party, gave a clue to some
contradictions that would affect later relationships between
radical trade unionism, a movement in which George Weekes
would be the leading figure, and the PNM regime.

> Irresponsible elements on the workers' side injected
> race into the strike, talked about emulating Castro,
> advocated nationalisation of the oil industry . . .[26]

Such remarks were obviously slanted against organisers like
George Weekes and others, whose ideas and expressions during
the strike would have formed the basis of Williams invective.
Already Williams was distancing himself from ideas which he
himself had helped to generate.

'Race' does not have to be 'injected' into the colonial situation.
It is implicit in the organisation of production, in the structure of
the society, in the psychological environment. When Williams
himself, coming into politics on the heels of the independence of
Ghana, and using historical analysis as a weapon of emancipation, revived the fighting spirit of the people, the establishment
which opposed him also accused him of injecting race into the
politics.

The race factor goes beyond the national. There is an
international dimension to the racial consciousness of the society
which links the factors of race and rebellion in the psyche of the

46

oppressed. The global pattern of white domination, which evolved over the last 500 years of European expansionism, conquest and colonization, has meant that struggles for freedom and independence in the colonial world became movements of racial as well as national assertion. They were articulated and perceived as struggles of Africans, Asians and others against Europeans, of Black peoples against Whites.

The victory of India over British colonialism in 1947 was a tremendous motivating force, culturally and politically, for Indians living in Trinidad & Tobago. The independence of Ghana in 1957 stirred a greater racial awareness and pride in the local African population. Such racial pride and awareness are powerful political factors in environments with similar patterns of domination, and intensified industrial unrest is a common expression of the new consciousness. When self-definitions change, concepts about what is acceptable, or even tolerable, whether in terms of material conditions and returns for labour or in terms of basic human dignity, also undergo transformation.

A more bitter edge is added to racial feelings where events create a focus on the more extreme practices of white racism, especially the scourge of apartheid in South Africa. In 1960 the peaceful resistance of Blacks in that country was meeting ever more violent resistance. There was local focus stimulated by the trade unions which had taken up the call of the International Confederation of Free Trade Unions (ICFTU) to wage a campaign for the boycott of South African consumer goods. In the midst of the campaign would come the horrifying Sharpeville massacre in March of 1960. All these events were factors in the consciousness which led to the strike of 1960. They are issues which have always been an important spring of motivation for Weekes and they added more urgency and impact to his words as he mobilised on the industrial front.

It is not difficult to see how the Cuban revolution fits naturally into the picture as well. Castro was seen as an extension of the process of anti-imperialism which Williams himself was supposed to represent. The triumph of the revolution in Cuba in 1959 was another ideological spark in the process which culminated in the 1960 strike. During the strike itself, developments in that revolution added more fuel to the workers' struggle. On July 2nd 1960, the Castro government nationalized the refineries of Texaco, Shell and Esso because they refused to handle Russian oil. That kind of action was bound to have tremendous appeal to workers fighting against one of the same companies. The courage of the Cuban example gave more weight to the voices of George Weekes and other militants who had long been advocating that similar steps should be taken in Trinidad and Tobago.

The Premier's brief but pointed denunciations, therefore, indicated ideological inconsistencies which Weekes did not miss. Whatever doubts remained at the fundamental ideological level, however, Williams was giving a sterling performance in the role of a progressive nationalist in the area that mattered most to Weekes, the field of industrial relations.

Nothing Williams said at that point, therefore, robbed George Weekes of the sense of victory which he felt at the outcome of the strike. It had to do with more than the financial gains secured by the workers. The way Weekes saw it:

> The 1960 strike marks the achievement of maturity
> and the realisation that the workers are now powerful
> enough not only to seek, but to fight successfully for
> their rights.[27]

In other words, it was the end of 'responsible' trade unionism which had reigned for 23 years. At most it would limp for two more. Butlerism would rise again, at least for the next 25 years.

The significance of the strike went even beyond this. It lay in the interplay of forces which were battling to give direction to the society, in the combinations and contests of personalities which would long influence the political environment, in the reformulations of ideas about industrial relations, about democracy, about the economy, ideas which would continuously interact and clash in succeeding years. Coming events were casting their shadows, but the shapes were not clearly discerned in the deceptive light of 1960.

Weekes himself was not deeply troubled. At the time he underrated the forces that would undermine the nationalist, pro-labour posture of Williams, a posture which could not be maintained outside of a context of revolutionary change. But that reality was one George Weekes would not confront until 1963.

CHAPTER 4

OWTU GETS A NEW LEADER

In the first half of 1962, if anything seemed to be brewing between Eric Williams and George Weekes, it was an embryonic co-operation between PNM nationalism and radical unionism, as both men moved almost in step to new pinnacles.

They were in fact moving to the beat of different drums, but in the criss-cross of rhythms this was not apparent to the casual observer. In fact at the time most observers would have been caught up with only one of the men, the country's Premier, Dr Eric Williams. The national excitement was about Independence from Britain, the lowering of the Union Jack and the hoisting of national colours, scheduled for August 31st. By legal definition a new nation, the nation of Trinidad and Tobago was about to be born, stepfathered by Eric Williams.

Overshadowed by the euphoria of the times, another birth was taking place. Out of decades of the pain of labour, another offspring of Butler, Militant Trade Unionism, a foetus that seemed doomed to stillbirth in 1937, an infant that gave a brief cry in the late 1940's but was slapped too hard, finally drew its full breath of air, signalling the completion of its birth, step-fathered by George Weekes.

The date was June 25th 1962.

On April 2nd, John Rojas had been forced to submit his resignation as President General of the country's most powerful union, the OWTU. On June 25th George Weekes and his entire Rebel team were elected to office in the union, with Weekes holding the post of President General. As OWTU was a major union, and with all the bitterness and accusations surrounding the change of leadership, the events gained media coverage. They gained some notice from a preoccupied public, but, except for the 12,000 oil workers and other special interest groups, who kept a hawk eye on affairs which had the potential to disturb the inherited social and economic order, it was just another internal union affair. Even Rojas' charges that Weekes was a "communist", or his accusations in his letter of resignation that "disaffection" was "engineered by foreign elements", failed to create any excitement. They had no weight or importance in the pre-Independence atmosphere. In fact many people were relieved to see Rojas go because of his consistent, vocal opposition to Eric Williams in the early years. He did make a turn around in 1961, when he encouraged the National Trades Union Congress (NTUC) to demonstrate in favour of the PNM before a national election. But it was not enough to absolve him with the masses.

Weekes gathered the forces of the union into the mood of the times. Independence is what Butler had fought so long for. Independence was one of Weekes' dreams. National independence was coming as an inferior substitute for the independence of a federated West Indies (another dream), but once the collapse of the Federation had to be taken as a reality, with the withdrawal of Jamaica, there was every reason to hold on to this gain. National independence was coming without the revolutionary leadership and perspective that Weekes would have liked to see, but it was coming. It would still be a giant step forward, and its imminence made him enjoy his triumph in the union even more. He could now fully mobilise the weight of the union to add to the thrust, no longer for formal independence (which was by then fait accompli), but for the substance of independence. Under an independent nationalist government, he pictured the trade union having more scope to deal with the multinationals. There was some WIIP scepticism about whether Williams would turn out to be the "right arm of labour" or the "false arm of labour".[1] But it was easy to believe that the PNM would be committed to giving the unions adequate scope, based on earlier statements by the Premier, Eric Williams, and Robert Wallace, the Minister of Labour.

In this period, the oil workers were mobilised behind Weekes, their trade union leader, and Eric Williams, their maximum political leader, without any sense of the conflicting loyalties which would come later. For six years they had been led by Williams to climb to this mountain top, to freedom it was assumed. For ten years they had struggled with Weekes to bring regeneration to the union.

Now the people were seeing Militant Trade Unionism and 'Independence' delivered close together like twins. Differences in features between these offspring of Butler would only become apparent with growth. In 1962 few could envisage the conflicting paths that would emerge due to different foster guidance and the different circumstances of birth.

'Independence', in the final moment, had come without a sense of struggle. The travail was a distant echo. The pain and the blood was only a memory in the heads of older people. The deceptively easy transition dampened the psychological and spiritual impact of the earlier struggles.

In 1919 men and women, led by the TWA, bounced their heads against the iron bars of Empire. In the 1920's Cipriani marched round and round inside the prison compound, that was the colonial territory of Trinidad and Tobago, shouting, but he would not try the formidable gates. In 1937, Butler assaulted the bars of imperial subjection again. He shook the locks and bent some bars, but the steel of bayonets prevailed. Ten years later men like Mahatma Gandhi and Nehru would break the locks in India, and at the end of another decade, Nkrumah would rip another iron door in Africa. By the 1960's the 'Great' Britain that haughtily sent battleships and troops to decide on questions of rulership in earlier years was a declining shadow, sending diplomats to concur and to guide. Territorial possessions that were the source of fortune in ages gone by were now economic millstones to a weakening colonial power. Britain no longer had any interest in mending broken locks on the prison doors of Empire. Once suitable candidates could be found to take over now burdensome administrations, they were being invited to push the doors open and enter into the new world of neo-colonialism, proudly dressed in national symbols.

In the internal struggle in the union, there were no open doors to push, there was no equivalent of 'smile and handshake' constitutional conferences at Marlborough House*. There was heat and anger and hatred. Workers demonstrated. And their demonstrations were not polite gestures but hostile acts. Factions developed, physical fights occasionally broke out.

---

* The government and the official opposition party of Trinidad and Tobago met with the British rulers at Marlborough House in London, to decide on the draft of an Independence constitution for Trinidad and Tobago.

Divisions did not begin with George Weekes. There were sharp divisions in the union when Weekes joined in 1952, even though the differences that would escalate into serious strife were in a relatively subdued phase at the beginning of the decade of the 50's. Fortunately the division was basically between a clique surrounding the Rojas-led Executive and the majority of the membership. The Executive was one so odious to Weekes as a Butlerite that he had deliberately refrained from joining the union for years after he went to work at Trinidad Leaseholds Limited (TLL) in 1949. When he was persuaded by Lennox Pierre and John La Rose that the best course of action was to fight from inside, rather than just continue to agitate against the Rojas clique from the outside, he found himself walking into a situation that was about to gather renewed momentum and had all the potential for explosion.

After 1948, the many faithful Butlerites throughout the oil fields, were coming to the conclusion that, with deteriorating conditions, they needed whatever measure of protection could be afforded by the trade union. The oil companies, now totally convinced that 'responsible' trade unionism, as represented by Rojas, was a major stabilizing force for the industry, were exerting pressure on the workers to join the union, putting at risk the jobs of those who did not respond. It was clear that at the trade union level, there was no coming back for Butler after the terror of 1947. In fact, while the workers were trekking dejectedly back into the OWTU, he was in London, where he stayed for a rather extended period from 1948 to 1950, agitating for Home Rule.

The influx of new members into the OWTU between 1948 and 1950[2] changed the tone of the union. Rojas was able for a time to make some adjustment to the new, more militant demands. He had no difficulty on the ideological level. He had always preached a radical, socialist ideology. He became one of the founders and first Vice-Chairman of the WIIP (West Indian Independence Party) in 1952, the party that Weekes joined almost immediately after its formation, despite Rojas' prominence. Weekes joined because of his admiration for Pierre and La Rose. The image of the party was such that many years later when Weekes would learn that he was banned from entering the United States, the reason given was that he once belonged to the WIIP, which the Americans described as the "communist party" of Trinidad and Tobago.

When Weekes did join the union he found Rojas in an unenviably contradictory position. Big John was trying to live up to his leftist political image, under mounting pressure from the increasing Butlerite tendencies within the union. At the same time he was trying to assure the imperialist oil companies that he was not departing from the approved methods of 'responsible' trade unionism.

In the early 50's, though Rojas would not call a strike, he led and encouraged several demonstrations of workers and their families. An outstanding feature of this period was the involvement of women in the union's struggles. Female workers and wives were mobilised by the very active Women's Auxiliary, which itself organised and led marches. Rojas featured in all these developments. Under the influence of the WIIP, he paid particular attention to May Day. In 1953 it was a particularly grand occasion, representing the high point of the West Indian Independence Party. The morale of this radical group was extremely high at the time, boosted by the electoral victory of Cheddi Jagan's Peoples Progressive Party in British Guiana. The PPP, a party with which the WIIP had been closely associated, had won 18 of the 24 seats in the April election. The members of the celebrating Trinidad group wore red shirts and chanted the slogan, "British Guiana Today; Trinidad and Tobago Tomorrow".

The new militancy in the oilfields was centered mainly in the more southerly parts of the TLL operations, where the Butler heritage was stronger. Weekes was based at Pointe-a-Pierre, which remained relatively quiet, though it was the biggest branch of the union. By the time he actually joined the union, he was already known by his fellow workers as a militant Butlerite, a zealous young man who always condemned Rojas and the union executive for the betrayal of Butler, who preached incessantly about workers striving to achieve justice through socialism, about the evils of capitalism, imperialism and apartheid, about Black pride. Once he became a member of the union, many workers started to encourage him to run for office so that he could exert more influence on the direction of the union. In a relatively short period this demand would gather an irresistible momentum.

Weekes had to make some psychological adjustment if he was to take up the responsibility being thrust upon him. He had joined organisations before, he had been outspoken within those organisations, he had even become a public spokesman, as was the case in the Butler party. But he had functioned as a floor member, and at the beginning of his challenge to Rojas, he was seeing himself as a floor member agitating for change, not as a leader spearheading that change. Now he was being called upon to take a step in that direction and he could not honourably refuse.

The demands for change in the union were mounting. By 1954 it was clear that Rojas' militancy had only been a passing cloud. The introduction of British troops into Guyana (then British Guiana) in October 1953, when the new government had only spent 133 days in office, and the suspension of that colony's constitution had sent a powerful message to the Left in Trinidad and Tobago. The British had moved so swiftly and decisively against Jagan, the new premier, and Burnham, when they opted for a socialist path of development, that leftwing organisations in Trinidad and Tobago felt the backlash[3]. Rojas, who had ignored all previous efforts of the colonial government to get him to do so, was one of those who pulled out of the WIIP. Both he and O'Connor had their union executives call for their resignations from the party.

There was another area in which Rojas capitulated to the British authorities at this time. He ended his defiance of the colonial authorities and their local cohorts on the question of the membership of his union and the Trades Union Council, of which he was also president, in the World Federation of Trade Unions (WFTU).

The Trades Union Council of Trinidad and Tobago had joined the newly formed WFTU in 1946 on the advice of the British TUC and the Trinidad government. When the British and the Americans decided to break away from that body and form a rival international body, the International Confederation of Free Trade Unions, they wanted the Trinidad group to join them in condemning the WFTU as "communist" and giving up their membership there in favour of the new Western dominated body. Rojas and O'Connor said openly then that "they were not at the beck and call of British unions or the colonial government".[4]

Rojas had also ignored entreaties from Solomon Hochoy to pull out of the WFTU. Solomon Hochoy, who was then in the office of Commissioner of Labour, was later to become the first Governor General of Trinidad and Tobago. In the early 50's he was engaged in furtive behind-the-scenes intrigues and manipulation to pull all other trade union leaders away from the intransigent Rojas and O'Connor when he could not get them to go along with Britain and America.

But in the wake of Guyana and on the eve of the second coming of Dalley, Rojas renounced membership in the WFTU. The word had been out that Dalley was coming to root out communists from the trade union movement in Trinidad and Tobago.

Weekes stood his political ground at a time when only the firmest believers remained with Lennox Pierre and John La Rose to carry on the West Indian Independence Party. He knew that Dalley on his earlier visit in 1947 had overseen the crushing of Butler and he understood the psychology of this visit against the background of battleships in Guyana. True he was not yet a prime target because he held no position of influence comparable to Rojas, but his act of faith in himself, in his beliefs and in the organisation to which he belonged was indicative of the mettle of the man. The workers could have sensed this difference between Weekes and Rojas and they were drawn to Weekes' aura of strength. It was now a matter of putting that strength at the service of the workers in union affairs.

Union office was not long in coming. Weekes scored his first election victory in 'Saltfish Hall' to become a branch committee member for Pointe-a-Pierre in 1955. From then onwards, except for one brief defeat, he would hold office continuously in the union until his decision to resign at the end of 25 years as President General. On his way to becoming President General, he held the office of committee member of the Pointe-a-Pierre branch for two years, Vice President of the Pointe-a-Pierre branch, President of the branch, 1st Vice President of the union and acting President General, in the months between Rojas' resignation and new elections in the union.

The road to power revealed many things about the man, George Weekes. Ideological conviction, commitment to principle, integrity. Perhaps the fact that he was not a man obsessed with power allowed him to keep his integrity intact and not descend to the opportunism so characteristic of leaders and would-be leaders in Caribbean society. It is these strengths in Weekes' character that led him to his first and only defeat in an election in the OWTU. And, ironically enough, Texaco was responsible, without taking any hand in it, possibly without even more than a passing awareness of the election, which was just a simple branch committee election.

In fact it was not really Texaco itself, but the issues surrounding the purchase of the assets of Trinidad Leaseholds Limited by Texaco that brought Weekes down. The controversy brought him into conflict with a newly-formed group of activists at Pointe-a-Pierre, a group that would later become a bastion of strength for George Weekes. Even at this time they had very much in common. Both Weekes and the group were 'rebels' against the sell out ('responsible') trade unionism of Rojas, 'rebels' against what they saw as squandermania in the union and lack of accountability, 'rebels' against the constitutional suppression of the popular will in the union. An alliance between the group of 'rebels', who would in time officially accept the press label 'Rebels', and George Weekes would have seemed a very natural one. Apart from fighting some of the same grouses about the affairs of the union, there was an underlying common source of hostility to Rojas. Some of the key members of the Rebels felt the same loyalty to Butler and hurt at his betrayal by Rojas and others as Weekes did.

But there was a difference that was critical in 1956. Rojas was strongly and vociferously opposed to the American multinational, Texaco, taking over the largest oilfield in the country. He was calling on the British Government to block the sale and themselves purchase the assets of TLL, or at least a 51% share, to hold in trust for the people of Trinidad and Tobago. He argued that the country would soon be self-governing and destined to be part of an independent Federation of the West Indies. Control of basic assets, therefore, should not be sold out to the Americans. He also argued that the Americans would bring their racist attitudes with them.

Despite his strong feelings against Rojas, in his opposition Weekes dealt at the level of policy. He would not oppose what he thought to be right simply because it came from Rojas. He openly supported the position of Rojas, the union executive, and other radical opinion on the Texaco question. He perceived the opposition of the Rebels to Rojas on this issue as more of an anti-Rojas stand than a principled position. And to a large extent he was right, though there was another factor which confirmed the Rebels in their stand, and it was an important factor in the context of mid-1956 (the British government gave the go-ahead for the sale in June). Walter Annamunthodo, one of the early organisers and leading spokesmen of the Rebels, stated his position this way in an interview in 1986:

> Rojas was not in support of the (Texaco) take-over and I was thinking of going along with that, but the bitterness had already gone very far between us and I couldn't. Added to this my will was strengthened by what Williams* told me. He had convinced me when he said that whatever our socialist aspirations were we had to bear in mind that the British company, TLL, did not have the money then to develop the oil industry in Trinidad whereas Texaco had the money and were prepared to spend it. So we should allow the take-over, let Texaco spend the money to expand and develop the industry, after which we can make all sorts of demands, from a labour point of view and also on behalf of the country. Honestly, Williams convinced me along these lines.[5]

Weekes put ideological persuasion and principle before any personal or tactical considerations. He could not compromise his beliefs in order to secure the Rebel base of support, which would clearly have been a considerable advantage in any bid for union office. This was an early indication that Weekes was not obsessed with office and power. He was actually going against the grain of the times because of his convictions. Not only was he alienating the valuable Rebel base of support, but he was actually getting identified with Rojas in the union in a way that was very much to his disadvantage. There was no pretence at rapprochement, there were no joint platform appearances. But in the emotionally charged atmosphere of the debate, it was easy for those who opposed him to caricature him as a supporter of Rojas. Weekes' credibility in the union was too great for the workers to really accept that he was in any sense a Rojas man. But many of them

---

* The late Prime Minister, Eric Williams (at the time he was an aspirant to office).

could not come to terms with support for Rojas on any issue. There were very hardline attitudes against Rojas and the Rebels were the embodiment of these attitudes.

Even these factors might not have been critical in undermining the considerable support Weekes had built up in the union though, without the supplementary influence of the national political factor. At the national political level, Weekes' stand was putting him in the company of the Caribbean National Labour Party, formed by Rojas and O'Connor, following their failure to work out a deal with Williams[6]. Weekes' anti-Texaco stand was putting him in the company of the West Indian Independence Party, a party branded as communist. (Weekes was in fact a member of this party.) Most significantly it was putting him in opposition to Eric Williams.

Dr Eric Williams, the rising star on the political scene, about to crush the Albert Gomes regime, did not confine his support for the Texaco take-over to private meetings. He staunchly advocated it at the massive, pre-election meetings the PNM was holding. In an article in *PNM Weekly*, the party newspaper, Williams quoted a statement by the president of the American Bankers Association 58 years before, where he boasted that America held "three of the winning cards in the game for commercial greatness, to wit - iron, steel and coal". On this basis Williams proclaimed:

> ... the Trinidad oil deal merely signifies for Trinidad and Tobago the fulfillment of America's 'Manifest Destiny', the eclipse of Britain, and the addition of oil to the three trumps (of the US), iron, steel and coal.[7]

The implications of Williams' statements were a slap against any concept of self-determination. But with his charismatic appeal, his words were definitive. In the wake of the Texaco controversy, Weekes found himself out of branch committee membership in the next union election.

This in no way affected Weekes' enthusiasm to fight for what he saw to be just. It did not cause him to shift either from supporting what he thought was right in favour of what was popular. So he crossed the Rebels again, on the issue of South Africa. Apartheid in South Africa was another one of those fundamental issues on which Weekes would not let hostility to Rojas get in the way of what he believed in. The Rebels accused

Rojas of bothering too much about South Africa and not enough about the union membership. They were using the fact that apartheid was one of those issues on which Rojas took a strong and consistent stand, an outrage against which he waged constant propaganda campaigns in the oil belt, to further undermine his leadership. This was one more issue that put Weekes in the contradictory position of defending Rojas, who was his arch-enemy, against the attacks of the Rebels with whom he shared so much.

Despite the conflicts, the Rebels were drawn to George Weekes. There was a magnetism in his honesty and conviction. He was a man who seemed to live for his beliefs. He took full part in the union activities, always a live wire at branch meetings, whether on or off the committee, outspoken and unafraid to cross swords with anybody, consistent in his advocacy of cleansing changes for the union and the rebirth of a militant approach to industrial relations. Despite the post-Texaco setback, there could have been no doubt that the workers at Pointe-a-Pierre were seeing Weekes as a leader. The Rebels knew that. They too were seeing the leadership qualities of this vocal and articulate unionist who did not fail to confront them when he disagreed with them.

Within a short time the inevitable happened. In 1958, George Weekes accepted an invitation to run for Vice President of the Pointe-a-Pierre branch of the union on a 'Rebel' ticket. He won. Another Rebel, Israel Yearwood, won the presidency. The Rebels gained control of the branch. Yearwood turned out to be a disappointment to the Rebels, backpedalling on issues they regarded as crucial and not carrying the fight at the General Council level the way they wanted. In the next election he was replaced by Weekes as President of the branch. The most powerful branch of the OWTU now had a new leader and the stage was set for the battle that would determine the destiny of the union.

In the Rebels, Weekes had solid backing to defeat the old order. This group of activists, which was to play a remarkable role in the transformation of the union, had first reached the stage of definite meeting and collective protest in the mid 1950's in response to the decision of the union Executive to purchase the Palms Club for what they considered to be the exorbitant sum of $85,000.00. They became more consolidated as they continued to meet in secret in a hall at the back of St Paul's Anglican Church on Harris Promenade, meeting under the guise of a football club on Friday afternoons to prepare for the meeting of the branch the following Monday.[8]

With their rise within the Pointe-a-Pierre branch, which paralleled the rise of Weekes, uncomfortable questions began to be raised at the Annual Conference. Questions about financial accountability and the reform of the union rules and constitution. The Rebels were able to question effectively the financial reports of the union because they had accounting assistance from one of their core members, John Gomes, who was a weekly paid worker in the accounting department of Texaco. There was initially too much Rojas support at the level of the General Council and the Annual Conference of Delegates for them to make much headway. But demonstrations against the Rojas Executive started to develop. There were stormy meetings between Rojas and the Pointe-a-Pierre branch. At one such meeting Rojas drew his revolver and rested it on the table. Eventually it was the police who ended that meeting. The vicious fight back from the Executive included the expulsion from the union of three of the Rebel founders, Walter Annamunthodo, Cecil Mitchell and Hugh Norton in 1957[9]. Texaco co-operated by shortly thereafter dismissing Annamunthodo from his job in the oil fields.

But all attempts at repression were in vain. By 1959, when the Rebels were consolidated and in control at Pointe-a-Pierre, under the leadership of George Weekes, there was only one more hurdle to cross to open the way for the removal of the discredited union Executive. The workers needed the vote. They were still at this time confined to voting only at the branch level for branch officers. The nine members of the Central Executive were elected by delegates to the Annual Conference.

In addition there were unnecessary restrictions on who could hold office at any level in the union and the restrictions became more cumbersome for executive office. Voting was manipulated at the branch level, which is where the climb to the top had to begin (you had to be a branch officer to be eligible for election at the executive level). Election dates were not publicized so the clique in office at the branch level simply brought their friends along to re-elect them. Therefore, even to begin to make a breakthrough, Weekes and the Rebels had to print leaflets announcing election dates and mobilising members to come out to the union meeting place, 'Saltfish Hall'. The Hall itself was far too small for the prevailing system of elections by show of hands. The Rebels got the Registrar of Trade Unions to supervise branch elections in order to make a breakthrough possible against the rigged machinery.

At another level they had to tackle the format of the Annual Conference. The Annual Conference was a farce — one day which the Executive packed with speeches, reports and a long lunch break with plenty of alcohol flowing. In this way serious resolutions always got crowded out of the day's proceedings and were left for the loyal General Council (loyal to Rojas) or the Executive to deliberate and decide on at a later date.

The struggle for internal democracy in the OWTU was one occasion on which some form of colonial tutelage did not come into play in a significant development in the trade union movement. A well ingrained characteristic of the movement up to those times was to seek external guidance, from the British Trade Union Congress especially, on every move for trade unions.

However this time around the international associates of the trade union movement were not in the driver's or adviser's seat. Some tried to hold back the forward movement. For example, in April 1959, Robert Goss of the International Federation of Petroleum and Chemical Workers, in Trinidad for an education seminar held by the OWTU, publicly praised the organisation as "one of the finest democratic unions we have seen".[10] But the movement in the OWTU was a grassroots movement, determined to define its own standards, not one concerned about what standards outsiders thought were good enough for them.

It is not only on the question of democracy that the popular movement in the OWTU found itself alienated from the traditional 'friends' of the Trinidad and Tobago and Caribbean trade union movement. Elements in the British Trade Union Congress were openly hostile to the developments taking place in oil and sugar; there was also a strong rebel movement in sugar. This hostility extended to a very rude interference by a TUC representative, Martin Pounder, who spent nine months in the country, supposedly assisting trade unions, especially the sugar workers' union, in their development. He was highly praised for all the "gains" he secured for sugar workers, just as he was high in praise of the Sugar Manufacturers Association who were drawing blood out of stone in the industry. In a speech at a farewell function held for him at the Palms Club in June of 1958, he ranted against the "rebels" in oil and sugar:

> Sugar and oil are winded about rebels — a bunch of fellows seeking only to destroy the unity for which thousands have died all over the world . . . what those rebels are doing is a lot of damned nonsense. It is a tragedy. While others try to build a good relationship between the workers and the employers, the rebels who possess only nuisance value try to destroy it . . . But how long are **we** to tolerate this damned nonsense.[11]

A classical, if contemptuous and intemperate, restatement of the 'responsible' trade union philosophy which was driving people like Weekes and the Rebels to be rebels in the first place. The focus was on "a good relationship between the workers and the employers" not the question of justice for the workers. 'Responsibility' was not the responsibility to seek the needs of the workers and secure the best for them, it was responsibility to "build a good relationship" with the employers, whom Weekes could see walking on the national dignity of workers in the oil belt. To cite a blatant example, they were still hiring South African managers. They had not mended their ways, despite the fact that this was one of the vexatious complaints of workers in 1937, just as it had been in 1919.

That kind of national humiliation was the price workers had to pay for the dominance of the British TUC line, the line of the colonial government (including the Gomes sub-section) and the Rojas line. Workers paid a further price in the material exploitation they suffered. This was clearly reflected in the wages of oil workers up to the strike in 1960, even though in those days oil workers' wages were the highest in the country. A release from CADORIT (the Caribbean Area Division of the Regional Labour Organisation) during the strike pointed out that the rates of pay at Texaco were among the lowest by big companies operating in the Caribbean. Examples showed that hourly rates for welders in the aluminum industry in Jamaica were $1.88; for welders in the Demerara Bauxite company — $1.27; for Texaco welders 88.5 cents. A comparison with labourers in the same industries showed those in Jamaica receiving $1.08 per hour;

those in Guyana receiving 82-90 cents per hour; those at Texaco receiving 59 cents per hour.[12]

These realities, articulated by Weekes and the Rebels, spoke louder than Goss or British TUC representatives. One month after Goss praised the OWTU democracy, the Pointe-a-Pierre branch passed a vote of no-confidence in the union Executive. Dissatisfaction with Rojas' answers to questions on the auditor's report on the union accounts was the immediate issue on which the vote was passed. Rojas spurned the resolution. He painted it all in the press as the work of "agents of the PNM who have been carrying out subversive activities throughout the oil belt".[13] This time Weekes and the others were not to succeed. They were on the way. Remarkable changes were taking place at the branch level in the union. The example of Pointe-a-Pierre was beginning to spread. But the final triumph for democracy in the union, the achievement of 'one man, one vote' was still to come.

The thrust continued. Storm clouds enveloped the union and the winds were battering company and union Executive alike. The atmosphere was hostile, but because of the educational work of the rebel leadership, the hostility had a direction. It was no broad, haphazard division of worker against worker, as the oil companies would have liked to believe, it was no self-consuming anger. The division was between those who represented the old moribund order and the mass of workers with a rekindled Butlerite spirit. Within the mass the bonds of togetherness were growing. A wholesome Caribbean vision was growing, the spirit of Federation.

A dramatic example of the togetherness and the well-channelled anger came in August 1959 when a senior staff engineer, a Jamaican national, was suspended by the Apex oilfields management, because of a dispute with a white Englishman. The engineer was non-Trinidadian and he was not an ordinary worker, he was a member of staff. But there was more than immediate empathy, there was an immediate strike by the workers at Apex. The *Trinidad Chronicle* newspaper on the 9th of August reported:

> The strikers claimed the issue was **national**. A qualified **West Indian** was being denied an opportunity to live.

In all areas of the oil industry the militant spirit was taking over. Strikes were widespread and the union Executive was feeling more threatened than the oil companies. They issued a leaflet denouncing unofficial strikes. They reiterated a warning to the workers in the report of the General Council to the Annual Conference of Delegates in November 1959:

The Council wishes to warn all Councils and Branch committees again that it will not sanction any Wild Cat strikes in the oil industry, these strikes are not doing the union any good . . .

They admitted:

We have had more of these strikes in the year under review than at any other time . . .

And they went on to threaten:

. . . if the workers fail to adhere to the advice of the General Council and the Executive, and continue to take outside advice to run the union, then they would suffer as a consequence.

It is now history that it is the Executive and the General Council who had to take, not the advice, but the instructions of the workers a few months later and call an official strike in the oil industry. Rojas' first strike was his last major act as President General of the OWTU. In the year after the strike, his second Vice President, Fitzroy McCollins, the one who had come close to a physical fight with George Weekes over the very question of the 1960 strike, resigned. As if by poetic justice, he was succeeded in office by none other than George Weekes. The writing was on the wall. It only remained to put it in the constitution. At the 21st Annual Conference of Delegates in November 1961, a resolution from the Pointe-a-Pierre branch calling for the critical amendment of the constitution was passed. The resolution called for 'one man, one vote' in the elections for the Executive of the union.

This was the de facto end of Rojas as the President General of the OWTU. His days were numbered until the next election date. Or so one would have thought. In fact, as it turned out, even such numbers were optimistic. Over the previous few years, the influence of Weekes and the Rebels he led had spread throughout the industry. To the extent that the final move would come from outside the Pointe-a-Pierre branch. It came from the Palo Seco branch, in the form of a vote of no-confidence in the President and General Secretary (J.C. Holder) of the OWTU.

The motion was passed by the General Council on March 27th 1962 and it was all over for Rojas. He was forced to resign. George Weekes took over as Acting President General and he was overwhelmingly confirmed as President General by the first popular democratic vote for the Executive of the union on June 25th 1962. Weekes fought that election on a 'Reformist' ticket. The Reformists were an alliance of the Rebels and other anti-Rojas fighters in the union. The victory was total as the entire Reformist team was voted into office. The team that scored that historic victory consisted of Urilton Pierre, 1st Vice President; Donald Roberts, 2nd Vice President; Cyril Gonzales, General Secretary; Jeremiah Antoine, Asst. General Secretary; William D. Steele, Treasurer; and Trustees, Lionel Bannister, Irving Noel and Charles James. Later elections were fought under the name, 'Rebels'.

There was something truly remarkable about the triumph of George Weekes in the OWTU. He had achieved success without a conscious manipulation of the forces of the time. He never needed to package his ideas and his presentation to suit what was current and popular. His ideological perspective, about which he was very open, and his genuine feel for the very issues which were deeply rooted in the subjective world of the people, ensured his success. Without playing politics, he was buoyed by the political momentum, because what he projected and radiated corresponded at the sub-conscious level with the impact of the new forces in the political arena.

In his own perception he was peripheral to the new national movement, led and dominated by Eric Williams. He was supportive of it, but within a critical, defined context. Any rudimentary analysis at the time could have indicated the differences between the nationalism of Weekes, which included a marxian influenced socialism, and Williams' 'substanceless' nationalism. But the drive and emotional power of mass movements do not communicate so much in terms of specifics and clinical definitions as they communicate at a psychic and subliminal level. So Weekes did not contrive any party affiliation to the PNM in order to enhance his stake in the union. He did not seek any party card. He voiced his areas of doubt and disagreement with the Williams' regime. He was even able to stand against some of the pronouncements of the new Messiah, for example on Texaco, and escape only slightly scathed. The weight of the consciousness which was alive in OWTU still remained with him. His credibility held because, in an important dimension of perception, George Weekes and Eric Williams were manifestations of the same force; they communicated as complementary agents of the same vision, Williams on a grander messianic scale, the National Redeemer; Weekes in a more modest but undeniably forceful way as the Hope of Labour.

However the spirit of independence had to give way to the practice of nation building. There were real and tangible bases of power in the society, the most formidable and backward-looking being the one organised around the exploitation of the country's economic resources. There were conflicts of interests, conflicts of personalities, conflicts of goals and vision, tensions of class and race, all entrenched in the body politic. The ideas and aspirations of those who assumed control of bases of power in the name of the masses, now had to be systematically applied to the reality, either to transform it or to become absorbed in it. The harmony of 1962 is that from the political level and from the trade union level there seemed such a convergence of objective - to transform what was an intolerable colonial legacy. But this process meant confrontation with other established bases of power and ingrained modes of perception which were intrinsically opposed to the goals and spirit of the mass movement. It called for systematic struggle, ideological direction and political will, which had to come primarily from those in political office. As it turned out, abstract promise did not become concrete policy at this level. But at the level of the OWTU, Weekes was on an uncompromising drive to make the promise the reality. The forces that appeared to complement each other were now headed for collision.

CHAPTER 5

CONFRONTATION BEGINS

It did not take long for the inevitable confrontation to come. And when it came it was as unexpected as a thief in the night. The issue was one on which, logically, unanimity of government and union could have been expected. It was the very issue that had forced the resignation of Rojas from the OWTU leadership. The issue was retrenchment in the oil industry, specifically retrenchment by British Petroleum, which had only a few years earlier taken over the assets of three other oil companies - TPD*, Apex and KTO**. In 1962 Rojas had gone against the will of the General Council in the face of BP's decision to lay off 38 workers. The General Council decision was to strike if the company insisted. Rojas came to a compromise where the company found re-employment for some of the men with contractors. The union unreservedly rejected this, since there was no certainty how long such employment would last. Given the strength of Weekes and the Rebels at this time, Rojas was forced to pay dearly for his defiance of the popular mandate.

Within months of Weekes taking office as President General, BP was to test him on the same issue, on a bolder and more provocative scale. The British multinational informed the union of its intention to retrench 200 workers in February 1963. For the new President General that was a declaration of war. On February 16th the OWTU gave BP 24 hours to withdraw the retrenchment notices, and on February 17th, the 2600 BP workers went on strike. Unsuspectingly, Weekes had waved a red flag in front of the PNM bull. Before the strike was over, he was to feel a terrible sense of betrayal by Williams. He was taken by surprise at the time. The first shocker for Weekes was Williams' portrayal of the strike:

---

* TPD = Trinidad Petroleum Development Company
** KTO = Kern Trinidad Oilfields

> Dr Williams met a delegation of my Executives and complained to us that our Union had started the strike to embarrass the Government. He accused my Union of acting like a second Government . . . [1]

The greater shocker, which emphasised that opposition had developed between the two men, was the follow up action Williams decided upon:

> (He) announced that he would set up a Commission to investigate subversion in the Trade Union movement.[2]

Battle lines were drawn.

Despite the government's negative response, the workers triumphed in the long and bitter strike. Weekes and the OWTU had decided "Not a Man must go"*. And not a man went.

As a direct result of the strike and the grit of the workers, who held out for 57 days, job security came to an industry which had shed some 2500 jobs over the preceding five years[3]. To Weekes the result was a validation of his faith in decisive and militant action. But Williams' animosity and threat introduced a new dimension into the trade union struggle, which Weekes would have to be very conscious of in the future.

It was an awakening and a very disturbing one. Weekes was acutely aware of ideological differenes between himself and the government, though he did hold on to some hope that Williams could have had deeper ideological convictions than he stated and these would be reflected in his post-independence programmes. But even if Williams' political philosophy went no further than the concepts he had so far been expressing, it was not easy to understand the hostility of the Premier's reaction to a fight to save the jobs of nationals.

Employment was a national priority. In his presentation of the 1961 Budget, the Minister of Finance (and Prime Minister), Eric Williams, had spoken with alarm of a jobless rate that had grown to 14%[4]. It was just over 6% when the PNM came to power in 1956. Williams had also mentioned that displacement of labour in the oil and sugar industries had a huge impact on this unemployment figure[5]. Weekes was fighting to put an end to this pattern, in the oil industry at least. The immediate threat was a threat to hundreds of jobs. During the course of the strike

---

* The popular slogan of a later strike.

the number of retrenchment notices handed out totalled 350, an even more dread prospect than the 200 initially announced. BP claimed that the extra 150 men had to go in order for the company to meet the new wages they would have to pay. In December of 1962 negotiations with Texaco had concluded and BP knew they would have to pay the same rates agreed to in those negotiations. In the end, on the verge of a strike in the entire oil industry (Weekes had given a ten day ultimatum from March 30th), the company bowed. But instead of emerging as a champion of the national interests in the eyes of the government, George Weekes emerged as an enemy of the state to be investigated for subversion.

It was the beginning of disillusionment for Weekes, not only because of the issue involved, but also because official actions contradicted his image of Williams and the kind of support he expected in the light of that image. Weekes was seeing the Black man who stood up against the Caribbean Commission

> who had to leave the Caribbean Commission because of his blackness. I had hoped . . . that as a man now in power who had suffered at the hands of Metropolitan powers like Britain, France and the United States, Williams would have taken a stronger line in defence of Black people. I saw myself as President General as being complementary to the struggle I expected to be waged by Dr Williams against the oppression of Black people to carry them forward.

> I was therefore disappointed in the 60's when after Independence Dr Williams did not recognise what we were doing . . .[6]

The disappointment was understandable. The confrontation that developed, so suddenly it seemed, was not the type of confrontation that the struggle over Chaguaramas in 1960 would have led the country to expect. Williams' strident demand on the Americans then was "Give us back Chaguaramas!". Chaguaramas, an area on the Western peninsula of Trinidad, had been leased to the Americans by the British for a period of 99 years for the setting up of a naval base. Williams called for the return of the land so that the capital of the West Indies Federation could be sited there. Such a demand, forcefully made by mass meetings and a march in the rain, pointed in the direction of an earnest struggle against imperialism, whether represented in military or other forms, a point well made by Lloyd Best in an article entitled 'From Chaguaramas To Slavery'[7]. But in 1963, the struggle of the popular nationalist forces against imperialist advantage, represented by the OWTU fight for jobs at BP, was overshadowed by the confrontation of the nationalist political leader (the same Williams) against a nationalist trade union leader (George Weekes).

The moment of truth had arrived. Nationalism was no longer allowed the luxury of being ethereal, undefined, all things to all people. Under the pressures of striving for economic development, nationalism split into antagonistic definitions. In this preliminary phase, for the PNM regime, nationalism was now subservience to the multinational corporations, in the national interest as they saw it. For Weekes and the OWTU, it was war against the multinational corporations, in the national interest as they saw it.

Williams' own personality quirks might explain why this betrayal of promise came at the time it did and in the way it did, but it was inevitable. It was in the logic of the path of development chosen, and, along that road, the betrayal would necessarily go much further.

When Williams and the PNM succeeded the Gomes regime in political office, the sense of a new dispensation they communicated to the population was based on some real improvements, but in fundamental ways their perspective was just as flawed as that of the rejected regime. There was improvement in terms of political direction and nationalist attitudes. The PNM advanced the thrust for self-government with the initial intention of independence within a Federation of British Caribbean territories. In this thrust, they secured from the British authorities the right to appoint a Chief Minister and other ministers of government according to the conventions of a party system, they introduced the cabinet system into the country; a bicameral legislature and eventually got agreement on full internal self government in June of 1960. This came into full effect after the December 1961 General Election. These positive measures and emotive public lectures by Williams to explain and justify them raised national consciousness, Black pride and self confidence. In this respect the Williams regime represented a tremendous advance on what went before.

In terms of organisation (the PNM was a real party with a structure) and administrative skills, the new regime was far ahead of the hodge podge Gomes regime. But, in other vitally important ways, the practice of government soon revealed the PNM as a POPPG* with more polish and intellectual veneer. In ideology and concept of development, only superficial impressions distinguished the 'new' from the old. This came out clearly in matters of economic direction. As part of the process leading to self-government, the Eric Williams regime quickly gained more control over the instruments of economic policy. They got down to more professional budgeting, they emphasised respect for the trade unions. But that is as far as it went. There was nothing more, no vision or strategy of economic development and transformation to raise them above the level of Gomes and the governor.

They inherited an economy based mainly on oil and sugar, under the control of foreigners. The new, growing sector, regarded as the key to economic development, was manufacturing, based on a policy of "industrialization by invitation" under the Aid to Pioneer Industries Ordinance of 1950. They completely accepted this structure of economy, and worse, the philosophy of development on which it was based. This philosophy equated industrialisation with economic development. A tragically misguided belief of its proponents was that industrialisation could be achieved rapidly by relying on foreign capital, foreign technology and foreign entrepreneurship. All the government needed to do was to seduce North American and European capitalists with generous incentives, especially tax holidays, and to provide adequate infrastructure for their industries. (A submissive labour force was the one item on the agenda, the PNM seemed not to buy at first.)

One of the first steps of the government was to invite W. Arthur Lewis and Teodoro Moscoso to advise on economic policy. Arthur Lewis was famous for theorising about and applauding the system of development adopted in Puerto Rico, which was highly regarded as the model for this pattern of development. Moscoso was one of the architects of that system in Puerto Rico. By 1959 the PNM regime had established an Industrial Development Corporation to facilitate the entry of these companies into the country, supposedly to industrialise it.

---

* Party of Political Progress Groups, the party led by Albert Gomes.

That was in keeping with the thinking Williams expressed in his very first budget speech. He said:

The possibility is by no means to be excluded that the incentives which we offer to investors are not sufficiently attractive.[8]

In taking this course, Williams was in fact trying to go faster along a road chosen by a colonial commission. The recommendation for Trinidad and Tobago to follow the pattern of economic development, which in a further refinement would be commonly referred to as the "Puerto Rican model", came initially from a commission appointed in 1947 by a colonial governor, John Shaw.[9] The commission reported in 1949 and its suggested approach — to attract investment from abroad by incentives, especially tax incentives — was faithfully pursued by Gomes and company.

Essentially it turned out to be a road of tears. It looked good for a short season and made the PNM's economic policies look good. The economy was soaring in the first few years and the regime was taking praise for it. A look back however would indicate that things started to pick up in 1954 and boomed in 1955,[10] before Williams came to power. The PNM government had come in on the crest of a wave which had nothing to do with their policies. In fact it had nothing to do with the policies of the colonial or Gomes' regime either. Booms, then as now, simply reflected the international fortunes of oil. By 1963, the oil goose was no longer laying golden eggs* and the bankruptcy of PNM's borrowed economic policy was being felt by the mass of the population. Scapegoats had to be found. Who else but "communists", "subversives" and "irresponsible trade unionists".

When Weekes called the strike in 1963 he was dealing with a different reality from say 1960 when government statements weighed so heavily on the side of workers. In 1960 the mass movement was riding a crest. Williams moved with the moral force which came from the mobilised masses, he moved with the authority inherent in a situation where he could have led the movement in any direction (there was the Cuban example at the time). He moved with a decided aim — to emphasise his strength to the enemy, colonialism. And he moved, it would seem, with a real conviction of the role of the trade union movement as a

---

* In 1961 and 1962, the price of oil fell on average by 6 per cent per annum.

dynamic force, which was to be allowed the maximum freedom to struggle for the benefit of workers. C.L.R. James, who was intimately connected with Williams in the early years, says, in relation to the overall radical projections of Williams, which extended to Chaguaramas, West Indian Independence and a strong Federation:

I have incontrovertible evidence to prove that for a great part of the time (Williams) meant what he said.[11]

Whether Williams meant what he said about labour or he was being opportunistic, at that phase of the anti-colonial struggle, the militancy of organised labour suited the purpose of the regime. Williams would not have been overly daunted by thoughts of where the militancy could lead. He would have been convinced that he could use moral suasion or the personal manipulation of leaders to control the trade union movement at any point he thought it necessary.

All this had changed by the time Weekes acted in 1963. The mass movement which was the basis of Williams strength had burnt itself out in disillusionment. The government now felt intimidated more than anything else by any manifestations of it, such as major strikes. The government also felt more dependent on the multinationals. This was the psychological concomitant of a dependence that was real and growing.

Critical economic indicators told the story. Oil retained its pre-eminence in the economy under the control of fewer, bigger and more powerful companies than in the Gomes era. Three of the notorious "Seven Sisters" were in charge — Texaco, Shell and British Petroleum. Oil still accounted for some 85% of exports and approximately 30% of Gross Domestic Product. The country was more dependent on foreign investment. Whereas 37% of investment came from abroad in 1956, 53% came from abroad by 1962.[12] In the pioneer industries, the sector that was supposed to be the vanguard sector of the economic thrust, capital invested was 83% foreign.[13] All around the picture was dominated by a growing economic stranglehold of Western imperialism.

This mounting dependence on foreigners brought the sharp turn around in official attitudes to trade unions. It partly accounted for the first big swipe at Weekes in 1963, when it was combined with another factor. The buoyancy of the economy collapsed. The year of the political high of Independence, 1962, was the year of an economic highfall. Between 1956 and 1960 economic production (as reflected in GDP figures) had grown on average by 11% each year.[14] The growth continued in 1961 by almost 10%[15]. But in 1962 growth stalled to a mere 1%[16]. When you take into consideration that population was increasing by over 3% per annum, it means that per capita growth actually fell in 1962. It was a drastic turn around.

In the depressed economic conditions, Government revenues were coming under extreme pressure. Current expenditure was catching up with current revenue. Put simply, the government had little left for spending on development programmes after they paid their fixed annual bills. Surpluses of revenue over current expenditure, which went into financing the development plan, had climbed to a high of $33 million in 1958. By 1961 the surplus had dropped back to $11.4 million, lower than the 1956 level. While the money available to spend on development, from taxes and other government revenues, fell so sharply, the cost of planned developments had escalated. The cost of the development programme in 1956 was $20.9 million. In 1961 it was $53.1 million.[17] Therefore much higher levels of borrowing were now necessary to finance development. Since the major sources of borrowing were external, the noose of dependence was tightening.

The masses were feeling the pressures of free wheeling capitalism and economic stagnation. Prices were rising and the ranks of the unemployed were growing. The economic optimism of the government, expressed in the early budgets, collapsed with the GDP indicators and a looming fear at the beginning of 1963 that Britain would enter the European Common Market that year. The government was desperately worried about the effect that would have on the country's external markets for oil, sugar and other products which depended largely on British importers. The mood of growing concern was expressed in the 1963 budget in a number of ways, one of which was a warning for labour.

In that budget, A.N.R. Robinson, the Finance Minister, quoted an ILO report describing the negative effects of high wages in the "modern sector" (oil and manufacturing in the case of Trinidad and Tobago) on overall economic development[18]. The story, with its mixture of truth, half-truth and misrepresentation, is one which was to become all too familiar. It went something like this.

74

High wages, wrenched by the trade union movement, were leading to capital intensive investment since investors preferred to use more machinery rather than pay the high cost of labour. The result — less employment in the modern sector.

Further, high wages in the modern sector were forcing government to pay higher wages in the public sector and so putting strain on government revenues. The result — government could afford to employ less people in the public sector.

High wages were jacking up prices to consumers, farmers and businessmen, jacking up costs of production and so making locally produced goods too expensive to compete on the export market. Again this was leading to less investment, less exports and therefore less foreign exchange, and greater unemployment.

High wages were leading to greater consumption of imported goods thereby draining foreign exchange and generating employment abroad rather than at home.

High wages were taking too great a share of the National Income at the expense of government revenues and profits for business to reinvest and create more employment.

The arguments seem logical. But they have nothing to do with the structural problems of the economy which were responsible for the failures of investment, for high unemployment, inadequate government revenues and poor export performance outside of the traditional areas. The economy really needed no assistance from so-called high wages to crumble at any time.

In fact the term "high wages" was really a catch phrase. Naturally, stronger union actions after 1960 extracted higher wages than the pittance paid in earlier periods for the few workers represented by unions, less than one third of the labour force. But high in relation to ridiculously low, is not necessarily high in relation to what is just and justifiable in terms of the prevailing economic situation. There were no arguments from the government to indicate that wage rates were in fact too high for existing conditions. And there were no arguments to substantiate conclusions that wage rates, such as they were, were having the dire effects on the economy stated in the ILO report and the 1963 budget.

The government itself must have known that whatever the impact of wage rates, there were far more substantial reasons why the economy was failing. Fundamentally the Trinidad and

Tobago experience was no different from that of other ex-colonies which remained tied in knots of economic dependence to the Western capitalist world. Everywhere the path of development chosen was creating conditions of permanent underdevelopment and recurrent economic crises, even where unions were weak or non-existent. The common underlying reason is simple. Corporations came to already ravaged and unsound economies to plunder, not to build. Whatever material benefits a subject nation gained were merely incidental, or, in some cases, extracted by the forceful actions of governments or unions.

Arguments in the 1963 budget, therefore, were very far divorced from the economic reality. However spurious the arguments though, the conclusions of the ILO report, quoted approvingly by the government, were very pointing:

... it is very important that there should be moderation and restraint in demanding, and in conceding, wage increases in the modern sector.[19]

The theoretical basis was laid for the restraint of trade unions.

All this might seem strange in relation to the attitude adopted against Weekes and the OWTU in 1963. Clearly the budget warnings were about wages and the strike in the oilfields was about jobs. Saving jobs!! The fact, however, is that what counted was not the specific arguments and logic borrowed by the government, but a developing negative attitude on the part of the Williams' regime towards trade unions, only hinted at in the 1963 budget. The concerns underlying the incipient hostility were disguised in economic arguments about wage rates. But the real anxieties of the government had far less to do with wage rates and far more to do with militant trade unionism on the whole. The question of wage rates was subordinate to the demand of investors for a docile labour force. This was clearly expressed by the Finance Minister at a later point, in December of 1963, when he presented the budget for the following year. In his diagnosis of the country's growing economic problems, he identified certain factors which he said were "tending to nullify the various incentives offered by the government to attract investment".

The negative factors were identified in the following order:

Firstly, there appears to be a developing 'strike consciousness' on the part of business which is

inhibiting the impetus to grow. Secondly, unsatisfactory industrial relations during the past two years
have struck at the root of confidence of investors[20] . . .

Only as a third factor he mentions that "rapid wage increases
are reducing the competitiveness of local labour"[21].

Obviously government's attitude to militant trade unionism
and strikes (no matter what the cause) was conditioned by what
the businessmen communicated to them. One could just imagine
the profit hounds whispering the message in the right ears,

"We would like to invest here, Joe, but those trade union boys
are raising hell. You got to stop them or we can't risk our money
in this country."

With a growing feeling of dependence on external aid and
investment, the government was a willing sucker, buying and
propagating the arguments of the multinational corporations.
The policy makers may or may not have been gullible enough to
believe that if they strangled trade union militancy for the
benefit of these parasitic corporations, the corporations would
have responded with adequate levels of investment, relevant
kinds of investment, appropriate technology and other measures
that would solve the country's economic woes. But, no matter
what they thought, or if they thought at all, they lacked the ideas
and the will to attempt any other course of development. And,
with the hungry mouths of the people in the hands of the
corporate lions, the regime was becoming increasingly prepared
to sell the national soul for any crumbs that might be offered.

Picture the intervention of an oil strike in this atmosphere,
with its potential effects on government revenues. It is clear that
the economics of the early 60's set Weekes up as a target for a
government that had lost its way.

But there was more to explain the sinister tone of Williams'
reproach and actions. Weekes was not playing the game by the
established rules. When Williams took him to London in
September 1962 as part of the national team to the Commonwealth Prime Ministers' Conference, Weekes did not respond
right. It was an important conference, important enough for
Williams to fix the date of Independence in haste just for him to
have the status to attend. The issue that gave the conference that
importance was the discussion of Britain's possible entry into the
European Common Market and its implications for the colonies

and former colonies. Williams sought to emphasise to Weekes how crucial his contribution would be in the discussion of how Britain's proposed move would affect the trade union movement. The loyalty Williams expected to gain from this ego-building did not materialize. The oil companies had a go at him too. Oil company representatives tried to bribe him. Weekes has always felt that Williams deliberately set him up for the offers that were made[22]. That failed. Weekes' honesty made him dangerous. A radical trade union leader, in charge of the most powerful union and outside of the ambit of manipulation either by the government or the big companies. That was a critical political factor.

The government over-reaction to the 1963 strike in turn had its own political repercussions. It marked the beginning of George Weekes' role as a bulwark of radical opposition to the PNM regime in Trinidad and Tobago. This is really something that happened without Weekes taking a decision for it to be so. It came out of the underlying factors in the 1963 confrontation. The seemingly inappropriate reaction of the government was the first reflection of a juncture in the country's politics where Williams, the front runner, stopped, and Weekes, the man behind, kept coming with nowhere to pass. It was the point of contradiction between a nationalism that had run its course and a nationalism spurred on by crossing another hurdle on the way to a more glorious end.

PNM nationalism reached its ultimate goal with political independence in 1962. Thereafter the objective of policy became consolidation of the perceived achievement. Given the route taken from 1956 to 1962, consolidation at that time meant accommodation with the institutional structures of colonialism, whose continued growth and dominance had been supported by government policy. With this new emphasis, any sense of conflict in the society was not just irrelevant in the official view, it was counter-productive. The conflicts Eric Williams and the PNM had spearheaded, generated and/or encouraged were aimed at lowering the British flag. Anti-imperialism was anti-colonial government rule, nothing more. Now that Trinidad and Tobago flew its own flag, it was time for a national partnership, including the traditional local elite and the transnationals, a partnership of "the octopus and the sardines", according to OWTU economic adviser, Bernard Primus.

Almost unbelievably, the psychology of accommodation would so predominate that the same Williams who proclaimed "massa day done"* in 1960, and the government he led, actually reconciled themselves with even the most offensive forms of racism and racial discrimination in the society. This contradiction was astounding even for the liberal nationalism the PNM preached and it sowed seeds of bitterness which would bear the fruit of Black revolt in 1970.

In the immediate post-Independence period, there was only one major obstacle to the PNM implementing its revised ideal, which was to secure from the masses a quiet acceptance of the very foreign domination, exploitation, impoverishment and racism they had fought against. The one major obstacle was the OWTU under the leadership of George Weekes. At the broad national level the masses were immobilised and largely unorganized. The only substantial semblance of national political organization was the PNM and the party's governing ethic was loyalty to the maximum leader. The other important units of popular organisation were the trade unions. But among the more powerful, the OWTU, the Civil Service Association (CSA), led by Oswald Wilson, and the manipulable All Trinidad sugar union, led by Bhadase Maraj, were the only ones not controlled by PNM loyalists, and, except in the case of the sugar union, only narrowly so. The margin of difference in the OWTU was largely the President General. With Weekes it was not simply a matter of opposition to the government. In fact he could hardly be accused of that in 1963. What made George Weekes the centre of organised resistance (which is what would develop) is that he was the only leader with a base of power who had a fundamentally different vision to that of the regime, and who had the commitment to struggle for the realisation of that vision.

The combination of ideology and character is what marked Weekes out from other trade unionists, not militancy. He was not the only militant trade unionist. From 1960 onwards, there was an upsurge of trade union militancy, no longer just tough talk, but a readiness to take positive action as reflected in the frequent

---

* When Williams used this phrase in a public address in December 1960, he was strongly attacked in the press and accused of racism. In response he made a biting anti-colonial speech on March 22nd 1961, entitled "Massa Day Done".

use of the strike weapon from that time. Militancy at the trade union level was therefore the prevailing spirit in 1963. The year's first strike indicated the sensitivity of unionised workers, which often forced the hands of leaders. Workers represented by the Seamen and Waterfront Workers Trade Union shut down the port for two weeks in January to demand an apology from the white managers of the Shipping Association for what they considered an insult to two of their grievance officers. The differences that could have been observed between unionists in 1963, then, would not have been at the level of tough talk and action. The visible differences lay in their political party affiliations and how they allowed such involvements to affect their trade union practices. Differences could be seen in their ideological statements. The difference in commitment to independent trade unionism was also there, but not obvious. Only when the state forced a polarisation in 1965, the differences and their significance would clearly show.

In reality, however, the gulf between Weekes' ideologically rooted and committed militancy and the ad hoc militancy of many other unionists, which could be compromised by political loyalty or co-opted by rewards, was there from the beginning. This was perceived by the government very definitely in 1963. That is why the subversive commission was aimed at George Weekes more than at any other trade unionist. He was not the only trade unionist it was directed at though, since others like James Manswell of the Public Service Association and Eugene Joseph, the Secretary of the National Trades Union Congress, were also considered nuisances at the time.

In the regime's opinion Weekes constituted the gravest political threat because he used industrial disputes (over real grievances) to further the ideological education of the workers in directions the government was not prepared to go. And he was strategically positioned to highlight the most fundamental contradictions in the nation's struggle for self-determination. The OWTU was in direct confrontation with the major imperialist firms, the oil giants who formed the core of the "government behind the government". In 1963, out there on the industrial battleground, Weekes was again raising the issues which had provoked cutting jabs from Williams after the 1960 oil strike, even in the midst of his overwhelmingly pro-union speech. For Weekes every opportunity was to be used to motivate the people towards controlling their destiny, which, in his concept, must at some stage involve nationalisation of the oil industry.

While he pushed consistently in the direction of this ultimate goal, he also pursued a minimum agenda in the 1963 strike. As always there was the objective to change the balance of power between the foreign corporation and the nation, as far as possible at the given stage of the struggle. This involved changing the perceptions of the workers and the people generally about the corporations and their role in the economy and attacking identifiable areas of exploitation.

In this context, during the 1963 strike, he had to fight on one level against the paternalistic image BP was trying to project, an image the government would have been glad for the workers to accept. The managing director of the corporation, Bennett, in a radio broadcast on the 22nd February, had made a most obscene effort to draw on colonial hang ups about the benevolence of Europeans, which he still expected to be operative, in order to persuade workers to resume their jobs:

> We (workers and the company) ... have to fight against the common enemy (other oil exporters) and not amongst ourselves as we are doing now
> ... it is YOUR future which is causing me most concern.[23]

The company was trading on the concept of the octopus and sardines partnership. But George Weekes' influence on the workers was too strong for that "we" talk to work. Weekes was very conscious of the inherent conflict between labour and capital in a capitalist society. He was very conscious of the conflict between national interests and the profit seeking goals of the multinationals. And he consistently dealt with these contradictions in his education of the workers.

Bennett's broadcast gave Weekes an opening to deal publicly with the economics of the multinational and indicate how national interests suffer in the global calculations of these corporations. He characterised them as "foreign interests solely guided by the profit margin"[24]. His analysis came in a radio broadcast on the 5th of March where he put forward the union's arguments against the claims of Bennett that British Petroleum in Trinidad and Tobago was experiencing such hard economic times that it made retrenchment indispensable to survival.

81

Apart from discrediting the claims of British Petroleum, with well researched information, reflecting the back up work of professionals retained by the union, Weekes struck hard at the company on a very sensitive issue of national concern, to which he returned in more detail in a press statement on March 21st. It had to do with offshore concessions granted to BP and other oil companies, operating jointly under the name of Trinmar.

The Gomes government had allowed the companies to begin exploiting the country's offshore reserves of oil on terms which amounted to naked robbery, through the mechanism of a special oil depletion allowance. It was an arrangement that Williams himself had poured scorn on, expressing the determination of the new government to renegotiate the terms. In fact, in his prepared statement, Weekes quoted what he referred to as Williams' "masterly expose" of the rip off in the 1958 Budget. Williams called the deal "the worst example of political irresponsibility in the history of Trinidad". Weekes used the information provided in the budget and other supporting data to accuse the companies of a billion dollar robbery, the estimated national loss from the way they obtained the concessions and continued to deny millions annually to the nation's treasury. At the time he thought he was backing the government in their efforts to redress an area of continuing exploitation by the foreign corporations.

These propaganda wars became a hallmark of Weekes' trade unionism. They went beyond the immediate issues of particular strikes, deliberately sought to influence the direction of national policy, and brought an ideological dimension to the basic questions of jobs, wages and conditions of work.

This was healthy for the budding nation. In the immediate pre- and post-Independence period there was a dysfunctional lack of debate about where the country or the Caribbean was going. There were a number of reasons for this. The main one was the dominance of the image of Eric Williams, which also meant the eclipse of the image of Butler, the only other prominent politician who offered any challenging alternative ideas. The marxist left, for various reasons, was on the periphery of the political process, at least since the mid 50's. A dynamic intellectual community, with a sense of purpose, to stimulate national debate about fundamentals, was lacking. The media was backward. British paternalism was in itself helping to smother any impetus for the nation to chart its own course. It made freedom look too deceptively easy and cut and dried.

When Weekes, therefore, used the medium of the trade union to communicate a radical vision of change, to challenge the status quo, he was playing a much needed role in the society. It was one however that was not appreciated by those in power. In fact, it drove a sharp wedge of alienation between him and the government of Eric Williams. Instead of the regime seizing the cues he provided as a basis on which to make further demands of the multinationals on matters where they themselves were being squeezed, they developed a greater preoccupation with stopping Weekes. He was "embarrassing" the government. They took up the sword on the question of subversion.

But political disfavour was not absolute in 1963. A hope was still held out by the regime that despite all the revolutionary rhetoric, maybe Weekes could be co-opted. There was so much history to indicate that militant and socialist trade unionists could be induced one way or another into an accommodation with capitalist enterprise and a capitalist-oriented state. So the sharp statements about who was out "to embarrass the government" and the threat implicit in the appointment of the anti-subversive commission formed only one side of the reaction in 1963. These were smoke signals of war all right. But they were soon to be mixed with smoke signals from a pipe of peace.

CHAPTER 6

RISE TO NATIONAL PROMINENCE

"This column names as the 'Most Outstanding Trade
Union Leader of 1963' — Mr George Weekes,
President General of the Oilfields Workers Trade
Union . . . ."

This tribute from *Evening News* columnist, George Alleyne, on
January 2nd 1964, is one reflection of the spectacular rise of
George Weekes to national prominence within his first year and
a half as President General of the Oilfields Workers Trade
Union. It is significant that the writer could have accorded that
honour without introducing any note of apology for his
judgement, two months after the Commission of Enquiry into
subversion in the trade union movement had completed its
sittings. The time was approaching when hardly anyone would
express a similar opinion publicly without some qualifying
statement like "despite his beliefs" or some other indication of
personal distance.

But Weekes had come through the propaganda skirmishes of
1963 with a very positive public image. The very issue on which
he was first attacked by Williams was the issue which most
impressed the *Evening News* writer. Alleyne praised him "for his
fight against retrenchment in the oil industry".

There was nothing singular about Alleyne's description of
Weekes as "the 'Most Outstanding Trade Union Leader of
1963'". At the time Weekes had emerged as virtual leader of the
entire trade union movement in the country. He gained this
distinction when he was elected as pro-tem President of the
National Trades Union Congress in September 1963. The
NTUC in 1963 included almost all the major trade unions in the
country. (The only exception was the National Union of
Government Employees which had not yet been granted the

84

admission it sought.) Weekes scored this victory without any backroom manipulation. The vote for him by members of the Congress General Council was just a tangible indication of the way George Weekes was able to establish himself as a prominent and powerful national figure in 1963.

The fact that he acquired this positive reputation against hostile public attacks from a number of quarters, is due to some extent to the ambiguity of Williams' attitude at the time. To an even greater extent it is a result of the practical achievements of Weekes himself, and his style. His approach to trade unionism harmonized with the needs and spirit of the time.

Williams' postures, his actions or inactions were important because there was only one force which could have stopped the rise of Weekes in 1963, and only with concerted effort — the PNM. But at this stage, Eric Williams, leader of the party and nation, was ambivalent about how best to handle the new trade union leader. He had his minions attack in various ways. His own stab in the back just as Weekes had exhausted the aggression of the alien company, British Petroleum, was certainly the unkindest cut in a year when daggers were drawn in many quarters. But Williams did not follow up with the kind of relentless attack which would have suggested that Weekes must be destroyed at any cost.

Where dealing with Weekes was concerned, the main thrust of the government in 1963, and this was continued into 1964, when he was sent on an official delegation to Geneva, was to co-opt him. Maybe he could be swayed or tempered by the prestige of high-sounding national office. So Weekes was nominated by the National Trades Union Congress to two national bodies in July 1963. One was a proposed Labour Advisory Council and the other the National Economic Advisory Council, which comprised representatives of government, business and labour. Its stated purpose was to discuss and advise on national economic policy. There is no record of any objection by Williams to Weekes' nomination to these national bodies. In fact, judging by Williams' pattern of operation and his influence with most trade union leaders, the names for the two councils would almost certainly have come from him in the first place. At the inaugural meeting of the National Economic Advisory Council on July 19th, Williams gave the opening address, a clear indication of his satisfaction with the nominees.

When the light maneuvers of 1963 are contrasted with the full mobilization of the machinery of character assassination, the wielding of the legal riot staff and the indecent interference into the internal affairs of the OWTU that were to come in 1965, it is clear that from Williams point of view 1963 was just a year of warning. He was still placing major emphasis on the hope of getting the OWTU President General decidedly under his influence.

With the direct PNM campaign against him at a low-keyed level and retarded by its own inconsistencies, Weekes was able to shake off other attacks with relative ease. However he knew from the signs of government's nervousness that he could not afford to ignore completely the campaign against so-called 'communist subversives' in the trade union movement, a campaign directed mainly at him. Weekes is convinced that this campaign was PNM inspired, though its most vocal advocate was Rojas, the deposed President General of the OWTU, who by September 1963 was also the deposed President of the National Trades Union Congress.

Rojas, who had been appointed to the Senate in 1962, did all in his power to justify the Commission of Enquiry into subversion set up by Williams. In fact, he, more than anyone else, set the stage for the enquiry when he launched his vicious campaign in the Senate in 1962 against alleged communist infiltration in the trade union movement. He said on August 7th:

> We must not flatter ourselves to believe that we in Trinidad are immune from the political philosophies which are overthrowing governments in South America, Latin America, in the Caribbean and other countries of the world, because right here in Trinidad at the present time there is no doubt that there are communist elements operating . . . There is no doubt about it that Marxists are operating in some of the trade union movements in the country, and some of the most powerful unions are now headed by Marxists.[1]

He identified a number of trade union leaders, Weekes chief among them, as agents of this "alien ideology" seeking to destabilize the country. He made charges of sinister communist plots over and over in the Senate and the press. He took his venom to the international arena, repeating his accusations in an article in *Petro*, the journal of the International Federation of Petroleum and Chemical Workers. He claimed in the article, that communists had captured key positions in the OWTU, Civil Service Association and NUGE. He said further that they had invaded the SWWTU and split the ATSE & FWTU as well as Congress. When Williams did set up the anti-subversive commission, under the chairmanship of a Nigerian Chief Justice, Mbanefo, Rojas was the chief witness during sittings which ended in November of 1963. Weekes warned:

> Our own Senator McCarthy, with his witch-hunting, is endeavouring to do as much damage to the people and the economy of Trinidad and Tobago as the infamous US Senator did to his country.[2]

Rojas and his backers calculated that because of Rojas' close association with the trade union movement since 1937, his accusations would have a ring of credibility. But that was not to be. Both at the level of the union and at the level of Congress Rojas had been forced to resign. In both instances he was succeeded in office by George Weekes. Therefore the first hurdle he had to cross was to make people believe that his attacks were not motivated by a personal vendetta. Secondly, while Rojas represented a discredited era of too much compromise from which unions were emerging in the early 60's, George Weekes' style of trade unionism reflected the spirit of the times. Trade unions were now shaking off the effects of a stifling British tutelage, which was preoccupied with stability and far less concerned about justice for the colonial worker. The new spirit was bold, militant, demanding. The self-assertive stream in labour, the legacy of the 1930's, was moving to the centre of industrial relations, coming out from the backwoods of the movement where it had been marooned, confined to sporadic strikes against the unjust and 'responsible' order.

Weekes, more than any other trade unionist, exemplified the new spirit. This was dramatically brought out by the way workers in the oil industry related to their new leader. On July 25th 1962, one month after he had been elected, he got thousands of workers to sacrifice a day's work and pay to attend celebrations for the 25th anniversary of the founding of the OWTU. The workers willingly responded when Weekes made a call because he fearlessly articulated their often suppressed thoughts and feelings. By words and actions he nourished their strength for the daily battle to hold on to their manhood. He bolstered their courage for the ongoing struggle for just rewards for their labour.

Weekes understood the psychological and material needs of the workers he led. When he stood at the podium in the Palms Club on July 25th 1962 and surveyed the audience before him, the white guests from the oil companies, government officials, union executives, the rank and file with their proud and hopeful black faces, waiting to hear what their new President General had to say, he knew exactly whom he had to talk to and whom he had to talk for, he knew what the workers expected and wanted. He felt the adrenalin flowing, the strength of the vibrations emanating from the assembled oil workers, and he began:

"Comrade Chairman . . ."

Years later the *Vanguard*, the official organ of the union, made a reference to the speech that indicated its impact:

One month after his election to office Weekes was in action at the 25th anniversary of the union making his first Official Black Power speech before guests that included Managers and their wives from all the major and minor Oil Companies doing business in Trinago. Workers still tell of how he spoke of the days of slavery when slave leaders found simple ways and means of communicating with their followers. They recall the example he cited of the slave leader who filled a calabash with black beans, placed a few white beans on the top and then shook the calabash making the white beans disappear. This was the first shocker the power structure received from George Weekes[3] . . .

Rojas' slanders were nullified by this new spirit Weekes was expressing.

Other anti-Weekes and anti-union forces, including ministers of government, who sounded alarms of communism and subversion, had no more success. They too failed to create any significant negative impression of George Weekes in 1963.

The forces hostile to Weekes and the new vibrancy of the trade union movement conducted their propaganda wars in the media. The media was open to their diatribes because this was a period of growing press hostility to trade unions, reflecting the fact that big business was reacting with alarm to the post-60 militancy of labour.

Naturally Weekes, like other trade union leaders, came under direct attack from the media in the process. The hostility to his influence and policies was strongest during the BP strike. To make matters worse, in the midst of the strike at British Petroleum, there came the report of the Honeyman Commission which had been appointed by the government to enquire into disturbances in the sugar industry in 1962. The Honeyman Commission report, released near the end of March 1963, further added to the justification for the Mbanefo Commission of Enquiry into subversion. Honeyman reported that "deliberate subversion" was at work in the sugar industry. The *Trinidad Guardian* quickly took up the cue, seeing the Honeyman report as confirmation of the claim by Deputy Prime Minister, Patrick Solomon, that "subversive elements, claiming a foreign ideology" were behind the labour unrest of 1962. The March 31st editorial alarmingly warned of communists at work in the unions.

Weekes was not involved in the sugar strike investigated by Honeyman. But the coincidence or design in the release of the Honeyman "revelations" at a high point of the longest oil strike the country had experienced, the follow up media hysteria about communists in the trade unions, and the climatic performance of the Prime Minister announcing he would appoint a commission to investigate subversion in the trade union movement, all pointed a finger at George Weekes.

Later the scare stories of Senator John Rojas would be extensively quoted, reinforcing the impressions. The image of Weekes kept looming in these accusations of communism and subversion, even without his name being called.

Overall though, the thrust of the media was broadly against the trade union movement. Weekes was targeted in specific situations but in general the media had not yet zeroed in on him as "Public Enemy No 1", the way it was to do in later years.

On the whole, during his first 18 months in office, Weekes was up against the efforts of an establishment to find ways in which he could be influenced, manipulated and controlled, if not bought outright. He was wined and dined at the beginning, a specially invited guest at official functions in celebration of Independence, where he could sip cocktails with Royalty*.

---

* Princess Alice represented the British Royal Family at the Trinidad and Tobago Independence celebrations.

There were enough offerings — a business trip to London with the Prime Minister, national appointments — to indicate to him that the door to acceptance in the hierarchy was open. And there were enough attacks to try to convince him of the dreadfulness of the alternative.

Weekes, for his part, moved decidedly to establish his strength and to demonstrate the battle readiness of the OWTU. He remained uncompromisingly firm in seeking the interests of the workers. But, at the same time, he was able to achieve a level of balance in his projection that probably postponed a final decision by the ruling corporate and political interests to go all out to crush him.

There was the George Weekes who took a hard line approach in his negotiations with Texaco in 1962 to extract a 40 hour week from them and a 19% wage increase for oil workers. And there was the George Weekes whose New Year's Message to oil workers in 1963 could draw favourable comment in a *Guardian* editorial.

In his first New Year's message, he addressed oil workers as "members of the most powerful union" having certain national responsibilities, as well as a responsibility to their own welfare. He called on oil workers

> to show by example and precept that collective bargaining, as an essential element of economic democracy, can work well in Trinidad and Tobago and serve industry and the national interest ...
>
> We owe it to our country to do all in our power to keep the oil industry efficient and competitive ... .[4]

The *Guardian* was pleased with the expression of such thoughts and especially Weekes' advocacy of "duty" to employers which entailed a "policy of wholehearted co-operation in the search for ways and means to boost the efficiency and productivity of the workers ... [5]"

Similar sentiments could well have been expressed by a Rojas.

It must have been very disturbing to the establishment when the same Weekes called a strike two months later. They did not realize how deeply George Weekes meant the proviso, that the workers must do their part, but "without abuse or exploitation".

From the very start Weekes indicated his opposition to imperialism. He also spoke out against domestic racism in the US. For example, when racist whites bombed a church in

Alabama in August 1963, the OWTU President General had the Executive send a letter of protest to the President of the United States.[6] But he took these principled positions without projecting implacable hostility to the United States. He even showed a very generous admiration for US President John F. Kennedy. Following the murder of Kennedy the OWTU Conference of Delegates in November 1963 observed two minutes of silence in respect. Weekes paid a personal tribute:

> The sudden death of President Kennedy in such tragic circumstances will be mourned not only by Americans, but by each and every human being who values the democratic way of life and the civil rights of the individual, for the late president lived solely in defence of both of these.[7]

In his fight against imperialist economic domination, Weekes was also careful to indicate that he was not advocating an absolute rejection of all foreign investment. What was important was the terms and conditions under which foreign firms were allowed to operate. In July 1963, on signing an agreement with Santa Fe Drilling of South America, he said that OWTU welcomed such foreign companies to Trinidad[8]. The company gained this credit for its policy of training locals to assume senior positions.

Weekes was very much aware of the nature of the political environment in which the OWTU was operating. He was sensitive to the stage of national development, the early phase of Independence. He wanted to influence the course of the ship of state, not to overturn the ship. That is why he was prepared to, and he urged workers to, take "cognizance of programmes of national economic development and policies for the economy as a whole".[9]

As subsequent events showed, Weekes' radical nationalist/socialist views of economic development could not really be reconciled with pro-imperialist national economic policies. And those views were bound to affect, firstly, the approach to negotiations and the resolution of disputes, and consequently, the economic and political environment. But the OWTU President General was making efforts to fit in with government strategies of development, however over-cautious and contradictory he saw them, once he felt that the basic direction was nationalist.

Even in the early period of his leadership though, it was clear to see those things in which George Weekes believed strongly. Whether in the concrete demands he made on companies and the way he fought for those demands, whether in the political perspectives he stated or in the positions he took in regional and international affairs, a radical identification was obvious. The marxist Premier of British Guiana, Cheddi Jagan, came to Trinidad in July of 1963 for a governmental conference. Weekes showed his identification by inviting Jagan to speak at a meeting at the OWTU Palms Club. In December, two members of a liberation movement in Venezuela hijacked a plane to Trinidad and Tobago and sought political asylum. Weekes publicly denounced the actions of the local government in returning the hijackers to Venezuela[10]. For Weekes it was a human rights, more than an ideological issue. Rojas later said accusingly:

> How well some trade union leaders of Trinidad and
> Tobago came out in open support of the Communist-
> terrorist hijackers who stole and landed a plane in
> Trinidad is well established.[11]

The saving factor for George Weekes at the beginning of his term of office was that political and ideological radicalism, at least at the verbal and symbolic level, were nothing new to trade union leaders. John Rojas, whom Weekes succeeded as President of the OWTU, had even visited Russia and praised that country's system of political and economic development. While Weekes' actions were arousing suspicions in the establishment that he might be a very different character to Rojas, he was also making some statements they could live with. They could envisage time and the realities of office tempering his actions, especially when backed up by 'guidance'. They would 'guide' by praising him when it suited their interests (or appeared to) and using psychological coercion (through threats and condemnation) when they felt he needed to be checked.

That was the hope. But the praise never swayed the practice of George Weekes. And, whenever and however they lambasted him, up to 1964 at least, the underhand jabs, the misrepresentations and false charges just did not have any telling effect on his public image. The attacks were negated by the mass perception of trade unions at the time as well as the strength of Weekes' growing projection. The masses had seen the benefits of economic buoyancy in the early years of the PNM filtering down to them through the militant efforts of the trade unions. The militant trade union was the assurance that wages and working conditions would continue to improve for the employed and their hope of protection against retrenchment in the period of economic reversal.

Weekes' tremendous success as a trade unionist was the solid rock on which his image was built. The 40 hour week, he secured for oil workers in his very first negotiation with the giant Texaco, was a revolutionary step forward for workers in those days. After establishing his reputation as a negotiator with the conclusion of this agreement in December 1962, he went on to triumph over the might of British Petroleum in 1963. The managing director, Bennett, had warned "you cannot stand up against a rising tide".[12] But George Weekes had done just that and dissipated the rising tide of retrenchment at BP, which had already claimed 760 victims between 1956 and 1962.

From these beginnings he went on to establish a new principle for contractors in the oil industry — they would have to bring their wages in line with those paid by the oil companies for similar jobs. This was laid down in an agreement with Wimpey in May. He even got a company, Santa Fe Drilling, to agree to amend an existing agreement to upgrade wages and conditions to match those he was establishing in the industry[13]. So while the slander and innuendo of his detractors were tailored to discredit, George Weekes was emerging as a hero of the working class on the basis of demonstrated successes.

If there was any "rising tide" in 1963, it was the rising tide of Weekes' influence as the dominant labour leader in the country. By the time he was elected pro-tem Chairman of the National Trades Union Congress in September, he had established himself beyond a doubt as the foremost trade unionist in the country. Weekes' enviable and envied record of success was secured by the ability and qualities he brought to the trade union movement. He was well read and he had a quick mind. He was an effective and commanding public speaker, which gave him the ability to motivate and influence people. He was totally dedicated and courageous. There was no taint on his integrity and he had the political independence which allowed him to seek the workers' interests first. He was not arrogant. He recognised the need for the union to hire the skills it was deficient in, such as legal advisers and trained economists to assist in negotiations, and he did so.

Against this background, and with the added advantage of being leader of the country's most powerful union, there were not many obstacles that could have stopped Weekes assuming the leadership of the National Trades Union Congress, once Rojas had been removed. The major obstacle though was George Weekes himself. His energy, his forcefulness and commitment kept placing him on the frontline. But there was always an inward hesitancy about taking up the mantle of leadership. He had to be nudged along to reach the level of President General in the OWTU. He had to be dragged into the post of President of the NTUC.

Weekes had been deeply involved in the struggle to remove the old executive of the NTUC led by Rojas. But he fought that battle on principle, not out of personal ambition. The executive was moribund, out of step with the new spirit of trade unionism in the country. One writer in the *Guardian*, under the penname of 'Quashie', referred to alienation as one of the major factors in the frustration with Rojas, Tull, C.P Alexander and other Congress executives. 'Quashie' saw the PNM rise to power as partly responsible for this alienation. Trade union leaders were on a high with the new level of recognition by the state. They could attend big functions and find themselves in the company of the Prime Minister. Rojas became a senator, Tull became a senator and was also appointed as a diplomat (representative to Guyana). Internationally they were gaining more recognition as well. This brought increased opportunities to travel. These factors led to the leaders distancing themselves from the grassroots of the movement and even the second echelon leadership. As the *Guardian* writer pointed out a major charge during the "purge" was "absenteeism" and another one was "lack of consultation on decisions". The OWTU example of union democracy, furthered by Weekes' presence and activity, was having some ideological impact at the level of the NTUC.

But when the General Council of the national labour body met on September 18th and formally dissolved the Executive, following the refusal of Rojas and most others to resign in the face of a vote of no-confidence three weeks before, Weekes left the meeting and went downstairs before they could elect a pro-tem executive. Nevertheless he was elected behind his back, gaining 26 votes against 15 cast for W.W. Sutton of Amalgamated Workers Union, who sought to contest the post. As soon as the voting was over and members came out to greet him, he knew what had happened. His response was, "I had an idea you wished me to be Chairman, but I was trying to avoid it. But it is your democratic right and I accept your decision".[14]

The tone of resigned acceptance in his reply was no indication of the type of leadership which he would bring to the Council. When Weekes urged oil workers in his New Year's message of 1963, as he consistently did, to recognise their duty to the entire labour movement in Trinidad and Tobago, he was not making any empty statement. For Weekes personally, that was a deep commitment. As President of the NTUC, he would involve himself totally in the struggles of member units of the Council or even trade unions and workers outside of the Council.

This policy, pursued with the zeal, idealism and fearless commitment, typical of George Weekes, was destined to be his downfall as President of Congress and to bring an intensification of political pressures and hostile personal campaigns against him so vehement that the fact he survived as head of his own union was an achievement. The fact that he not only survived but went on to new victories, expanded the base of the union and played a dynamic role as a mass leader at other points in the nation's history is a minor miracle.

CHAPTER 7

1965: DEMOCRACY THREATENED

Driving home alone at 2.00 a.m. on the morning of March 16th 1965, George Weekes was fully aware of the risk he was taking. The country was tense, rumors were rife and the feeling kept building that something was about to happen. But there was nothing unusual about a sense of apprehension in March of 1965. This was a time of war. For close to one month sugar workers had been on strike. A number of houses, the homes of activists in the sugar belt, had been bombed. In fact just a few days before, on March 8th, his close associate and fellow activist in the sugar belt, Krishna Gowandan, was lucky to escape unharmed with his family when, around this same hour, gas and gelignite bombs had been hurled into his home[1]. Gowandan, an officer of TIWU was also founder of the Sugar Workers Study Group, one of the rebel factions involved in the current struggle. To add to the tension, the dispute in the sugar industry had been magnified into a national crisis by the March 9th Declaration of a State of Emergency which was now in force in the affected areas. C.L.R. James was under house arrest in a bordering constituency[2], where the Emergency had been extended, apparently solely for the purpose of restricting the movements of the noted author and former political associate of Eric Williams. Just four days before, on Friday 12th, the government had tabled an Industrial Stabilization Bill in parliament, which in effect would outlaw strikes.

These were the very issues which had Weekes out of his house at that hour. He had been presiding over a meeting of the NTUC General Council discussing how to proceed at this stage of the sugar strike, to which the Congress had been lending official assistance. They were also discussing what stand to take on the proposed labour legislation. The meeting had run till around

1.00 a.m. With mounting tensions and signs of political polarization in the trade union movement, Weekes was coming under increasing pressure in his efforts to hold the NTUC on a course which he felt befitting of genuine trade unionists. Hostile union leaders in Congress shot verbal daggers at him, in and out of meetings.

However, hostile union leaders in Congress were not the source of physical danger to Weekes at this time. Before he left for home, fellow trade unionist, Clive Nunez of NUGE, had cautioned him. Nunez said he had observed suspicious movements of vehicles, with occupants identified by him as "Bhadase henchmen", along the Eastern Main Road in the San Juan area. At that time Weekes lived on the Eastern Main Road in Petit Bourg, San Juan. Nunez warning was just one among many during the period. The reputation of Bhadase Maraj, the leader of the All Trinidad Sugar Estates and Factory Workers Trade Union, the man against whom the anger of the striking sugar workers was mainly directed, was well known. Struggles against Bhadase always brought out armies of gunmen and arsonists, which is precisely what was being experienced in the sugar belt over the past few weeks.

George was very much aware of how Bhadase felt about him. The strongman of the sugar union had sent his own graphic messages via some workers. He had summoned them to his home, which he frequently did with different groups of workers, and, as George recounts the story they told him afterwards:

> ... Bhadase began criticising Eugene* and myself. He sat at a table at his home in Champs Fleur saying to the workers — 'All yuh gone and following Weekes, all you ungrateful!!' He then began to threaten them pulling out two revolvers, a small one and a big one. He told them the small gun is for Small Eugene, and the big gun is for Big Weekes.[3]

George was well aware of the real dangers. Hardly a day passed without threatening phone calls being made to his home. But he had a job to do and he was doing it. It demanded late hours and he obeyed the demands of the struggle.

Sometimes it was the problems of oil, sometimes the problems in sugar that kept him out. His wife, Theresa, and children spent

---

* Eugene Joseph, Secretary of the National Trades Union Congress.

many sleepless hours at night praying for the moment the car would drive up and he would walk in the door, mercifully alive at least one more day. They could not help worrying but they just had to understand. Though the union provided him with a driver, he could not see himself asking an employee to keep the consistent late hours, driving from distant areas like Guayaguayare, Point Fortin, all the areas of the sugar belt in Central and Southern Trinidad, night after night to get him to his home in San Juan in the North. So generally he drove himself and most times he would be alone as he was this morning. One night, earlier in the course of the strike, as he was on his way home, passing through Caroni, in the heart of the sugar belt, one of the frequent police patrols stopped him. When they saw who he was they detained him for a while — as a precaution. They explained that Bhadase had just passed with some of his men, so it was advisable that George, who was alone as usual, stay back till the coast was clear.

Such reflections were natural at an hour like this. At the time George knew nothing about the observations of his wife when he was leaving home the morning before. When the car was pulling out with the children, whom he would drop to school on his way to work, Theresa was convinced that a man she saw standing at a corner a few yards away was marking them carefully. She kept her eyes on the stranger's movements and saw him walk up the road and get into a waiting car with other men as soon as George drove off. George's long day had taken him to Fyzabad and other areas of the deep South of the country before he wound up at the meeting of Congress in the evening. In his usual preoccupation with what he was doing, he had not communicated with his home.

Now as he approached the house, he realized that something was strange. 2.00 a.m. and all the lights were on. However he reversed into the yard as usual. The next step would have been to walk from the back where he parked his car to the front of the house and let himself in with his house key. But as he got out of the car his wife opened the back door and called him. He heard the fear in her voice, saw it in her face. She was shaking, near hysterical. She tried to explain everything in a rush. She did not know what happened. She was sitting on her bed, too worried to sleep. At one point the dog was barking so much she looked out. She was in time to see a car back into a street close by. Then there was this sudden shout, more a scream. Soon after . . . She is not too sure how long after she had observed the car, she heard the scream. She knew with a dread certainty that the scream was from one of her children. When she jumped out of bed and went to look in the children's room, their seventeen year old son, Cyril, was missing from his bed. Her actions aroused the other children and she felt a chill, convinced that Cyril had been kidnapped . . .

"Call the police, quick!" Weekes felt as if the blood was drained from him.

But, by the time they were making a call to the police, Cyril himself walked in, clearly not recovered from the scare he got.

The barking of the dog a few minutes earlier had caused Cyril to look out through a louvre in the living room. He too was unable to sleep soundly, feeling anxious about his father not being home. He had seen the unknown car backing into Broome Street. His suspicions were aroused by the way the dog continued to bark. He stole quietly out of the house, trying not disturb anyone as he went to have a look around. There was a church next door. A shrub fence separated the two yards. Cyril saw what appeared at first to be a broom stick, jutting out of the fence towards the back of the house. But then the object moved and pointed in his direction. As the movement drew his attention, his eyes focused on a man hiding in the bushes, aiming a shotgun at him. He screamed. As he screamed he turned and fled around the house, through a neighbouring yard and up the main road. All the while he was picturing the armed intruder in pursuit, but he was too terrified to look back until he had run a good distance and turned up a side street. He remembers though hearing a car engine start up after he screamed[4]. By the time he returned home, via a back route, his father was there.

Weekes' vulnerability, which he himself had always been aware of, was brought dramatically home to him. Had he come home a minute or two earlier, the moment he stepped out of his car at the back of the house he would have been an easy close range target for the unknown figure waiting in the church yard.

The postscript to this incident would come many years later. One day a man came up to Weekes and Panday, while the United Labour Front was campaigning in the sugar belt in 1975. In shame and sadness he confessed that he was the man whom Bhadase had sent on an assassin's mission a decade earlier.

But the misguided men with guns did the least damage in 1965. This was the year of an all out effort to shackle the trade union movement, to destroy George Weekes, and strangle any potential political threat, real or imagined. It was a year of organised hysteria, vile character assassination, treachery by trade union leaders, repression, political retrogression, paranoia and betrayal, in a form and on a scale new to the independent nation. Within days after Weekes had almost paid with his life in the struggle for workers in Trinidad and Tobago, he was submitting his resignation as President of the National Trades Union Congress, in a chorus of condemnation from some other trade union leaders, barraged by sustained slander in the media, and persecuted by the political authorities. The trade union movement was divided, in disarray and in bondage.

The hardest blows for Weekes at this time were that workers themselves were mobilized to call for their chains and he was being portrayed as the villain who brought havoc and harness on the trade union movement. If there was ever any trade union leader in Trinidad and Tobago who genuinely believed in the freedom, strength and the unity of the trade union movement, it was George Weekes. He had shown himself prepared to take any risk, make any sacrifice to ensure that the strength of the trade union had to be respected. That did not only apply to the OWTU. Any union, any group of workers, who called on Weekes for help were guaranteed that he would take up their struggle, that he would be there on the picket line with them, there in the strike camps and on the demonstrations, there confronting the employer with their demands. He practised what he called in his letter of resignation "the fundamental motto of the Labour and Trade Union movement":

An Injury to One is an Injury to All[5]

Weekes was sharply critical of some other trade union leaders in the NTUC at times. But despite inevitable differences, some quite fundamental, he consistently pursued the unity of the movement which he felt was essential for it to be really strong. Long before he became President of Congress, long before he became President General of the OWTU even, he preached this theme. From his very first stint as a branch officer at Pointe-a-Pierre, he moved a resolution at the 1955 Annual Conference of Delegates of the union calling for the union Executive to take measures to bring about the unity of the national labour movement, because "division makes our enemies happy and weakens our struggle . . ."[6] At that time there were two national bodies, the Trade Union Council and the Trinidad and Tobago Federation of Trade Unions. He had exulted at the attainment of this unity in 1957 when the two bodies merged to form the National Trades Union Congress. It was a real triumph when in 1963 he had the honour to lead this united body as pro-tem President. He was confirmed as the President in January 1965.

Less than two months later, on March 24th 1965, he was resigning amidst more fragmentation and confusion. Once again there were two rival national bodies, the NTUC which he was giving up leadership of, and the National Federation of Labour, formed by unions which broke away from Congress in late 1964 — W.W. Sutton's Amalgamated Workers Union, Bhadase Maraj's All Trinidad Sugar Estates and Factory Workers Trade Union, Carl Tull's Communication Workers Union and the Federated Workers Trade Union. In addition the powerful Seamen and Waterfront Workers Trade Union had pulled out of Congress on March 11th, during the sugar struggle, the UCIW had pulled out on March 17th and the Cement Workers Union a few days later. A number of other unions — Communications and Transport Workers Trade Union (CATTU), Electricity Supply and Industrial Workers Union (ESIU) and the Port of Spain Branch of the Postmen Union — had passed resolutions calling for the resignations from Congress of George Weekes and Eugene Joseph, President and General Secretary respectively. They were threatening to withdraw from the national body if these executive members continued to hold office.

Weekes was deeply hurt by this situation and the easy passage of the Industrial Stabilisation Act, marking the end of his effort and sacrifice as leader of the NTUC. He could never forget March 18th, the day on which the bill was passed in the House of Representatives. On that day he sat in the public gallery of Parliament listening to Williams presenting the bill in the House. He was both angered and saddened by the performance of the diminutive man who was in the process of inflicting such a "monstrously oppressive"[7] law on the workers and the people of the country generally. His mind went back to the pre-election period in 1961. He marched in support of Williams then, in a demonstration organised by the National Trades Union Congress, only because he saw the Prime Minister well on course where the trade union movement was concerned. He thought of a speech made by Williams in Guyana in March 1963. Williams spoke about "the five articles of the political creed to which I believe all parties in the West Indies could subscribe".[8] He listed as article four:

> Each party would pledge itself to the promotion, maintenance, and above all, enforcement of proper and civilized industrial relations based on collective bargaining[9]

Williams went on to drive home the point:

> This is to stop all these idiots all over the place who say that Government must step in to interfere in the relations between employer and employee or a Government must pass laws to ban strikes etc[10]

Listening to Williams now, actually setting a precedent for restrictive labour legislation in the Commonwealth Caribbean,[11] the contradiction was astounding. He was sweeping away the basis of union strength in collective bargaining. Unions could no longer call strikes. Disputes were to be settled by an Industrial Court . . .

Suddenly all ears were drawn by the sound of marching feet and chants outside. Weekes felt a moment of elation. The workers of the country had decided not to take the bill lying down. There was a rush to the balcony to see what was taking place in the streets below.

The sight and sounds were crushing blows for Weekes. Hundreds of demonstrators were out there, holding aloft banners proclaiming the groups they represented — trade unions, Communication Workers Union and Amalgamated Workers Union; several youth groups, Laventille Youth Movement, North West San Juan Youth Group, Newtown-Woodbrook Youth Group and others. The marchers had been drawn from steelbands and government special works projects. Prominent among the organisers were trade union leaders, especially Carl Tull and W.W. Sutton. They had come not to bury the ISA but to praise it. The denunciations on the placards were aimed at Weekes and the NTUC.

It was a sad day for the President General of the OWTU and President of the NTUC. He felt his heart heavy as he thought: if only the trade unions could have maintained their solidarity and reached out as a body to get people to understand what a bill like the ISA meant for the country. United they could have mobilised the people against the dread law. He was seeing it clearly as "the prelude to the establishment of totalitarian fascism in Trinidad and Tobago".[12]

But he understood the "political forces" which were operating against such an effective public thrust, operating against him, and creating chaos in the trade union movement to divide and oppress it. In the days after March 18th, more and more he would realize the extent to which they had succeeded. And it genuinely disturbed him. He could come to terms with the antics of Tull and Sutton, for whom he felt nothing but contempt. But those union leaders from within the Congress who were wilfully breaking it up, who were denying and denouncing him at a time of crisis for the labour movement generally, they are the ones whose betrayal he felt. In reference to Daniel Reid of the SWWTU and Vas Stanford of the UCIW, whom he accused of abandoning Congress because he defeated them in the elections for the Presidency, he said:

> I marched for them in the J.T. Johnson strike. Now I
> am treated like Caesar was by Brutus — stabbed in
> the back.[13]

This is how he felt about all of them who deserted him. The betrayal hurt more because of the issue on which it came. The sugar strike. The most fundamental violations of trade union principles were involved in the 1965 strike in the sugar industry. The immediate issue was a grievance which Tasker Drivers in the Ste Madeline area had with the company, aggravated by the refusal of the union, ATSE & FWTU, to take up the matter on their behalf and a general dissatisfaction with the union. This led to the strike on February 21st. But on the morning after the drivers went on strike, the union leader, Bhadase Maraj:

> appeared on the scene of the strike and instead of
> speaking to the workers and taking up their grievance
> in negotiation with their employers, he proceeded to
> attempt to break the strike by placing strike-breakers
> he had brought with him (including his brother and
> his nephews) into the empty seats of the cane trucks
> before the eyes and under the noses of the striking
> Tasker Drivers, and with the full and open support of
> the Industrial Relations Officer of the Company who

ordered the strikers to leave the Company's premises
and allowed the strike-breakers to enter.[14]

Bhadase was protected by company police in doing this.
In Weekes opinion:

Such action on the part of a so-called Trade Union
Leader can only be regarded by any self respecting
Labour and Trade Union leader as high treason to the
cause of Labour and Trade Unionism[15]

This action by Bhadase drew Weekes totally into the fray and
caused the strike to spread throughout the industry.

Weekes involvement was to precipitate his downfall as
President of Congress. It became the rallying point of his
enemies. When the politicians gave the signal, the unionists who
were out to cut his throat all brandished excuses based on the
strike. Weekes had been "irresponsible". He had overstepped his
bounds by intervention in the sugar workers' dispute. He and
Eugene Joseph must resign from Congress because they had
"embroiled" the NTUC in the dispute. Their unilateral and
highhanded actions in the strike were responsible for the yoke
placed on labour.

When Weekes read the statements of his detractors in the press
and in the letters they sent to the Congress Executive, he was
pained by the sad truth they revealed. Individuals with whom he
had been working as leaders of the workers, were exposing
themselves as men so shallow in their convictions they could
deny the responsibility of their own decisions. These were
decisions they had taken not years before, not months before, but
just weeks before, and up to days before.

In the face of such "unbecoming and shameful behaviour"[16]
Weekes did not feel he could work with those men anymore.
Within his union he expressed the thought of resigning from the
Congress. The OWTU Executive, who were very supportive in
this period, shared the disgust of the President General. They
were prepared to accept any decision on his part to resign, in fact
they felt that would be the best decision. Reaction of the workers
was quite strong. If Weekes went to Fyzabad he could be sure
that loyal branch officers, like Doodnath Maharaj and Soogrim
Coolman, would be pleading with him to turn his back on those
"crooks" in Congress. They were very bitter about the pressures
to which Weekes was being subjected. If he went to the Pointe-a-
Pierre branch, the President, Oswald Johnson, would be sure to

raise the issue too. It was the same wherever he went among the workers, in branch meetings, liming with them in Palms Club, or in rumshops. They were saying:

P-Gee, them fellas is traitors, leave them let them cut up one another. You stay with we. We going to protect you.

There were, of course, some oil workers and supporters of the union who felt Weekes should hold on, but they were fewer in number. Lennox Pierre was one of those who felt that Weekes should not give up such an important base of influence in the society. He felt for Weekes to resign would be to give in to the reactionary forces. There were many trade unionists at the level of the Congress General Council who were also totally against Weekes considering resignation. They fought to the end against him taking that course of action and it was quite clear that if Weekes wanted he could have held on as President of Congress.

The decision was not an easy one to make. But in the final analysis, Weekes went along with his strong feelings of revulsion against further close association with those whom he felt had betrayed trade unionism. When he did resign, he made sure he recorded the treachery of their actions. In his letter of resignation he was careful to detail and document how the NTUC Executive had taken a collective decision to support the sugar workers and how they continued to take decisions about further support actions as the struggle developed.

The workers had first sent the Congress an SOS, in the form of a letter appealing for assistance in their dispute with their union and the company, on February 17th, before the strike. Following the strike and the action of their union leader, they strengthened their appeal for Congress intervention with a delegation. Weekes, who had previously been giving moral support to the workers, advised them on this approach. He felt that Congress would agree to support. With that authority, he would be able to talk with a collective voice on their behalf.

At an emergency meeting on February 24th, the Congress Executive decided to assist. On the basis of unanimous decisions, Congress acted.

They wrote to Caroni Ltd. seeking a meeting, prepared to use their influence to end the strike. All Caroni had to agree to was, no victimisation of striking workers, and that would have been the end of the strike. The workers agreed to that. No reply from Caroni Ltd.

They wrote the Registrar of Trade Unions to discuss the workers internal problems in the union. No response.

They informed the All Trinidad union of what they were doing.

When they couldn't get action anywhere else, they wrote the Minister of Labour. Letter acknowledged. Full stop. Up to March 10th, they wrote him again. No further response.

Weekes thoroughly documents this collective involvement of Congress throughout the strike, backing up his claims by extensive quotes from the minutes of relevant meetings.

The facts establish that the specific charges being made against Weekes by fellow trade unionists could not possibly be the real reasons for the extreme hostility they were expressing. But the fact they could even imply by their accusations, that Congress should have stayed clear in the face of Bhadase strike-breaking action, was too much for Weekes. He stated frankly,

> If there are trade unionists and trade unions in the country who feel that that sort of conduct must be tolerated and condoned, I and the Oilfield Workers Trade Union are not among them. And the fact that on this issue there are unions and trade unionists who are prepared to censure me and the General Secretary of Congress, Brother Eugene Joseph, for opposing this and throwing the full weight of Congress on the side of trade union democracy, against strike-breaking and in opposition to victimization has convinced me that I am the wrong man to head and lead this Congress.[17]

But Weekes knew that these trade union leaders were only repeating prepared lines. They were actors performing in a grand play.

The sugar strike merely provided the backdrop against which they would act out their treacherous roles. Weekes read through the play, but was unable to prevent the trade union movement, the masses in general and himself from falling victims to the choreographed crisis.

The play had national and international dimensions. In fact foreign interests were the hidden theme of the drama. This accounts for the command roles played by multinational corporations and the backstage work of the CIA.[18]

The major sugar producing company, Caroni Ltd, local subsidiary of the British multinational, Tate and Lyle, played a good lead. Caroni Ltd magnified the strike with stories of violence and outside agitators. They refused to meet with Congress because that was not part of the script. Meeting with Congress could have ended the strike immediately. Such an ending would have been completely contrary to the spirit and intent of the play.

Locals were not to be outdone in the production. The master director, Eric E. Williams, who had captivated a large audience with his earlier disguise as a messiah, introduced dramatic props. Like the March 9th State of Emergency and the nail-in-the-coffin climax, stunning, anti-labour legislation. The build-up to these high points was impressively handled. Against a background of timed stories of subversive plots, unnamed government officials fed "information" to the press about pending repression in the form of anti-strike and public order legislation, newsmaking "emergency" meetings of the National Security Council were held with mind-boggling frequency, at one stage three in two days, and police and troop movements in the sugar belt added greater suspense to the atmosphere.[19]

Public relations was well handled by the foreign-owned media. A classic example of purposeful sensationalism was provided by the *Guardian* of March 6th. The dramatic frontpage headline announced "TROOPS IN THE SUGAR BELT" and the picture immediately below it was one of troops marching in Vietnam.

The church blessed the performance with appropriate sermons. Reverend Father Nelson James Campbell, who was white and English, preached at the Holy Trinity Cathedral:

> Many social evils, many moral blemishes are to be found in every nation. But it is difficult to envisage a greater than the existence of the Trade Unions . . .
>
> It is an evil act, a thing completely contrary to the Divine Will for those employed in labour to 'down tools' and strike because of imagined injustice . . .[20]

Even the behind-the-scenes crews in the Chamber of Commerce, the Employers Consultative Association and in the Manufacturers Association, applauded heartily. They are the same ones who had been very suspicious of the director in bygone years, when he staged such blockbusters as 'Chaguaramas', an anti-American street play calling for alienated land (under long lease to the US military) to be returned to the people, and 'Massa Day Done', a cheer raising soliloquy against colonial values and a colonial social structure.

Weekes saw tragedy in the role of the star trade unionists. He knew the play acting had deadly aims — the real crucifixion of himself and the trade union movement.

There were many reasons why a number of trade union leaders inside and outside of Congress could have been drafted into roles Weekes found so reprehensible in 1965. The type of petty jealousy of which he accused Reid and Stanford was only one of them. For many of them there were party loyalties involved. They were members of the ruling Peoples National Movement. In the context of the times, Williams left little room for flexibility in the party — this was war demanding complete subordination and obedience to achieve the political objective.

Outside of party loyalties, and also helping to ensure already existing party loyalties, were the rewards for faithfully following directives. The regime could and did dispense so many things that bought support — senatorships, scholarships, appointments to boards and various committees that gave prestige, trips abroad. Trips were by no means to be considered minor. One of the top trade unionists once threatened to withdraw his union from the NTUC when he was not selected to attend a conference in Jamaica.[21]

On the other side of rewards, the government had clearly indicated there was 'punishment' for not toeing the line, which could come swiftly and suddenly as it did with Critchlow, the president of NUGE. He only knew of his removal from the Senate when he read it in the newspaper. He was convinced that he had been so ignominiously removed because he had opposed the government on the question of giving public workers 40% of their backpay in government bonds.[22] His rejection came at an appropriate time to be a lesson to those who had ideas of not conforming in the crucial period of 1965.

The trade unionists were up against a mobilization of the PNM party machinery which undermined their authority on the ISA within their unions as well. The example of St Elmo Gopaul, General Secretary of the Teachers Union and a loyal PNM member, illustrates this. His Executive had called for postponement of the debate on the ISA and criticised the "undue haste" with which it was being rushed through Parliament. A hostile reaction from the union's General Council forced Gopaul to clarify that the resolutions of the Executive Committee did not in any way mean that they were not in support of the bill.[23]

Similar membership pressures were reflected in a statement from the Civil Service Association condemning the "activities and utterances" of Weekes and Joseph during the sugar strike. The CSA statement, signed by James Manswell, the General Secretary, stressed they did not want any further fragmentation of the trade union movement, thus dissociating itself from the intent of other similar criticisms. The reason given for making the statement at all is instructive. It was made "in view of certain doubts which appear to have arisen in the minds of some of its members and the general public as to the roles and attitudes of the Association in the recent sugar strike".[24]

The PNM hierarchy was working hard, mobilising members and making it very clear at this time that battle lines were drawn.

In effect two things were being extracted from the trade unionists — support for the Industrial Stabilisation Act, which amounted to support for the government's aim to substantially paralyse the trade union movement, and support for the destruction of the President of the NTUC and President General of the OWTU, George Weekes.

On the question of the ISA, sharp divisions in official positions appeared between the National Federation of Labour and the National Trade Union Congress. However, a close examination of actions suggests that the differences were more rhetorical than real for many trade unionists.

The official position of the NFL was one of fundamental support for the bill, though they mildly expressed a desire to see certain amendments. Their public attitude to the bill is well represented in the words of W.W. Sutton who referred to it as "an Emergency measure to meet an Emergency situation". The "Emergency situation" predictably was the NFL's standard justification for every backward action, invoked this time to rationalise their acceptance of anti-labour legislation, the "threat of communist subversion in the Trade Union movement". They even recommended that the government extend the repressive trend to consider legislation to "exclude known communists from holding office in the trade unions".[25]

The extreme within the NFL was represented by Carl Tull, President of the Communication Workers Union, just returned from ambassadorial assignment in British Guiana and re-appointed to the Senate. Tull unapologetically acclaimed the ISA as "the most popular piece of legislation ever enacted in this country"[26]. Tull's position is made even more ironic by the fact that in 1961 he was the chief instigator of demonstrations organised by the NTUC in support of the PNM election campaign. Support for the demonstration was drawn on the basis that statements from the leader of the main opposition party, Dr Rudranath Capildeo, indicated that the right of workers to strike would be threatened if the DLP won the pending election. At the time Tull questioned what Dr Capildeo meant by the "ominous phrase 'stable labour conditions'", particularly as Capildeo had used the phrase in a context where he was criticising the labour movement for staging too many strikes.[27]

The official position of the NTUC was in stark contrast to that of the NFL. NTUC, while recognising the need for legislation to regulate industrial relations practices, soundly condemned the actual Bill presented before parliament as "undemocratic" and "unconstitutional". They asked for a postponement of the debate in the House to allow adequate time for study and comments by unions, business and the public.[28] NTUC even took their position to the public with a mass meeting in Woodford Square in Port of Spain.[29] Among the speakers highly critical of the ISA were prominent PNM party members such as John Hackshaw and Nathaniel Critchlow, whose Senatorship had recently been rudely withdrawn by the government in favour of Carl Tull.

In addition to the collective condemnation of the Congress, individual member unions took decisions for positive action to protest against the government rushing the controversial Bill through parliament. The T&TTU, led by St Elmo Gopaul, called on members to wear black arm bands, ties or rosettes in protest against the "undue haste" of the government in seeking to pass the ISA. The National Union of Government Employees took a decision to picket parliament on the day the bill was to be debated, March 18th. The OWTU General Council took a decision to call out all their workers on strike and march in full force outside the Red House from 1.00 p.m. on the fateful day.

Subsequent events made a mockery of all the condemnations, resolutions and decisions to protest. The mobilization of the

PNM machinery scuttled the plans of fickle and firm trade unionists alike. There were no black armbands, ties or rosettes; the NUGE picket was hastily called off; the blue shirted army neither responded to the call to strike nor made an appearance around the Red House.[30] In the case of the OWTU, where the leader (as distinct from the leadership) remained firm, some General Council members, who voted for strike action actually went out in the fields canvassing workers NOT to strike. Two of these General Council members, Lesaldo and Nelson, when called upon to explain why they voted for the strike resolution and were now advising workers against striking replied, "We were just giving Weekes enough rope to hang himself".

The most disturbing aspect of the story is that leaders in the NTUC, who had voted their opposition to the Bill, diverted all fury from the legislation and directed it against two individuals in particular — George Weekes and Eugene Joseph. Instead of "the ISA must go", the clamour became, "George Weekes and Eugene Joseph must go".

The deliberate corruption of priorities is exemplified in the statement of Stanford, president of the UCIW, when he announced his union's withdrawal from the Congress, the night before the bill was passed in the House of Representatives:

No self respecting trade unionist can be expected to support the act as presented by the government, but because of the action of these leaders (Weekes and Joseph) such legislation has become NECESSARY[31]

Stanford is representative of a number of trade unionists in Congress who managed to evade the responsibility to struggle to protect the fundamental rights of workers by setting up a greater enemy than the bill itself.

While, on the question of the ISA, many trade union leaders wanted to express verbal condemnation, or at least indicate some reservation, if only for the historical record, there were no such reservations in the attack on George Weekes. For some of them, the government was encouraging them to do what they would have been glad to do anyhow. Weekes seemed ideal in 1963 to bring maximum respect to the trade union movement, but now with a whole new world opened up to Congress Executives, even brighter than the one that had seduced the old Executive, Weekes was leading Congress in directions that were contrary to the ambitions and preoccupations of the times. His personal involvement with the grassroots of the movement in the resolution of their problems and his continuing militancy served the purpose of individual leaders at times. But basically they found Weekes' militancy more of an embarrassment. It was undermining to the new roles some of them conceived of for themselves as executives.

In reality a growing division was inevitable. Joe Young explained it on the ideological level,

> . . . there was this conflict of ideological viewpoint. There were on one side, TIWU and OWTU. On the other side Sutton, Stanford and the rest. Their whole concept of the role of the Trade Union was based on the view that capitalism was an eternal order and that their primary role was to negotiate every three years for more money for the workers. Our view was that we had to negotiate improved wages and for better working conditions. In fact we were determined to be more effective in this area than they were, but we also felt that the Trade Union had to politicize workers so that they could accept the view of a more just and equitable social order. Thus our tenure there, given the PNM capitalist sympathies of so many union leaders could never have been a comfortable one.[32]

There was ideology and there was more than ideology involved. Weekes acted the way he did because he had a different spirit from most of the leaders he had to work with. In the sugar strike the difference could be seen even when all were expressing support and taking decisions to support. In the first place support might not have come at all if Weekes had not brought up the uncomfortable matter, uncomfortable because it was an issue on which it was difficult to morally defend inaction, once it was raised directly. Without Weekes' forcefulness, Congress may well have stayed out on the pretext that the workers were represented by a non-Congress union.

Even when the decision for involvement was taken, it meant different things to different Congress leaders. For some the polite letter writing and passing resolutions were all that duty and the record for posterity required. For Weekes there had to be total personal involvement, total immersion in the struggle with those affected until the problems were resolved. Weekes' own descriptions give the picture:

I can remember during that same strike in sugar, Eugene Joseph and I . . ., we went campaigning throughout the sugar-belt and we were able to close down all the sugar factories.

We marched from Ste Madeline factory to the Brechin Castle factory — women, young and old, men, young and old, calling the workers at Brechin Castle who were still working to come out on strike. On the way to Brechin Castle, workers went and occupied the Headquarters of the Union (Bhadase union) which was on Mon Chagrin Street in San Fernando, all the while saying they wanted Weekes as their leader.[33]

The way the workers at the grassroots level related to Weekes is indicated by the way in which the sugar workers first addressed their 'SOS' to Congress. The banner atop the letter read:

S.O.S. CALL OF SUGAR WORKERS TO THE
T & T NATIONAL TRADE UNION CONGRESS
AND ALL ITS AFFILIATES - PARTICULARLY
THE OIL WORKERS' TRADE UNION[34]

Weekes did not have to contrive a close relationship with the masses. It was a deeply ingrained part of his personality. Referring specifically to the tense, demanding period of the strike in 1965, he said:

"It was very hard work but I loved it, I enjoyed it"[35]

Placed in implied judgement by the kind of leadership Weekes was offering, many other leaders of Congress did not find the ISA itself too difficult to accept, along with Weekes' resignation. Weekes is convinced that they wanted the law:

The Congress, although they claimed they were against it in talk, they were actually supportive of it because a lot of them saw the ending of strikes as something good for them. Now all they had to do was just talk with employers without fear of workers taking strike action on their own, which used to occur frequently . . .

Now with the law saying strikes were illegal I, as Leader of Congress, was not supposed to identify with that kind of action.[36]

113

Apart from the aspect of embarrassment by example, there is another aspect of Weekes' involvement which further alienated him from other Congress leaders. In giving reasons why they were in fact supportive of the ISA, he pointed out that with the new law, "the fear and embarrassment of having unofficial strikers calling on (George Weekes) was removed".[37]

Workers did frequently call on Weekes when they struck without the prior approval of their union leadership. The fact that they would seek his support was a natural outcome of Weekes' projection and it was one of the most delicate issues for him to handle, especially in view of his position as President of Congress. Weekes' predisposition to action, his strong sense of class conflict and his genuine feel for grassroots movement led him to support these 'unofficial' strikes. Even though he would try to get the relevant leaders involved, his interventions jarred the sensitivities of other leaders, thus helping to promote the desire for his downfall.

However, while such factors added to his problems with other Congress leaders, they were not the root of the problems. The fundamental ground of alienation was a difference in spirit, and nothing could have prevented that manifesting itself in a dynamic situation where political loyalties, personal ambitions and the tantalizing prospect of vendettas were all deliberately manipulated by the government in office.

When all is taken into consideration, therefore, it is not difficult to understand why the government could have achieved the de facto compliance of a number of Congress unions on the anti-strike bill, and a highly motivated response in its campaign to destroy George Weekes.

Largely as a result of this connivance, the forces of reaction tasted victory. They got their oppressive act in place. They were able to drive Weekes and Joseph out of Congress. They were all set to close a chapter in the industrial relations and the politics of Trinidad and Tobago which smacked too much of people's power.

But there was one more hurdle. George Weekes was still the President General of the powerful Oilfields Workers' Trade Union.

114

CHAPTER 8

"SUBVERSIVE ELEMENTS ... AT WORK"

Weekes understood the nature of the fight he was in. He had sensed the arrival of the fateful moment since January 1965, before the sugar strike. Addressing the 3rd Biennial Conference of Delegates of the NTUC on January 30th he said:

> I am satisfied, and the signs are there for those who want to see, that the powers-that-be have made up their minds and are even now preparing to 'deal' with certain trade unions, to 'discipline' the labour movement in this country. The first step is to divide in order to be able to rule. Further, to do this they perhaps need to have introduced, certain repressive legislation or disciplinary measures. And to do this in turn they need the excuse of the 'Communist infiltration' and the 'Communist plot' plus a few scapegoats.[1]

There was no clairvoyance in this accurate prediction. Weekes had seen the notorious zig zag course Williams was on, the progressive degeneration from an aggressive pro-labour stance to increasing ambivalence and incipient hostility to unions. The signs were all pointing to the draconian legislation which eventually came in 1965 and to the all out effort to destroy any trace of Weekes' influence in the trade union movement.

Winston Mahabir, a former Cabinet member in the PNM government, expressed the view that:

> Part of the answer lies in the area of Williams' ambivalence ... I speak not of flexibility and compromise, which are at the core of the art and science of politics. I speak of observable, documentable, recurrent, mutually contradictory pronouncements and operations.[2]

115

The ambivalence was more than a characteristic of individual personality. As C.L.R. James said in analysing the behaviour patterns of Caribbean leaders,

The more highly placed a politician is, the more you can expect his personality to have historical attributes or express the pressures of social forces.[3]

Williams' 'ambivalence' and the government's resort to the ISA were products of a particular historical process in the Caribbean. The region's prolonged experience of slavery, of colonialism, and of indentureship (which came in the tail-end of the horror) has left deep psychological scars and created cultural disorientation in the victims. Centuries of subjection to racism, powerlessness, material exploitation and all the dehumanising characteristics of imperial domination robbed Caribbean Blacks, like all colonised peoples, of their self confidence, handicapped them with inferiority complexes and a psychology of dependence. The psychological and psychic destruction did not end with colonialism. Powerful economic, cultural and political forces in the modern world, moulded and controlled by the former colonisers, re-enforce the damage to the personality of the former colonised.

One of the sources of tragedy in societies like the Caribbean is that the educated classes, who, naturally, tend to lead in politics, have been even more insidiously exposed to the cultural virus of colonialism than the masses. As a result, they are more affected by a near pathological dual personality.* Further, leadership roles in themselves heighten the contradictions in the colonial personality because such roles pit men and women suffering from diminished self-images against political and corporate hierarchies, which are in reality very powerful and whose psychology is the psychology of the dominant. Given the fact that the material odds are already stacked against the ex-colony, with its economy structured to be dependent, the psychological imbalance between the nationalist rulers and the former colonisers adds to the disadvantage of the struggling new nations. Another disadvantage stems from the fact that the new political elites can secure personal gains by compromising with the system of imperial domination. Therefore nationalist movements founder on the conflict between independence-

---

* Groups classified by some analysts as 'Afro-Saxons' and 'Indo-Saxons'.

oriented strivings and urges on the one hand, and colonial values and concepts on the other. The 'ambivalence' of so many leaders is that they clearly manifest both tendencies. Nationalism is more forcefully verbalised, but pragmatic behaviour increasingly reflects a colonial orientation.

Failure to break the links of dependence at the economic level is one of the primary explanations for this recurring political scenario. But the daunting problem of economic transformation, which defeats so many leaders in the former colonial world, is more than a challenge of economics, it is also a challenge of self-concept. There must be some level of triumph over negative self-images for leaders to place faith in the capacity of themselves and their own people, to take the bold and sacrificial steps necessary to move towards economic self-determination.

The ISA was a result of the failure of transformation in Trinidad and Tobago. In fact, the PNM regime never conceived of any real transformation in the first place. Consequently theirs was a necessarily losing confrontation with the fearfully entrenched economic power of the multinationals. Williams' strategy was to co-operate with the international giants and champion the cause of labour at the same time. He probably underestimated the depth of the contradiction. Weekes once made a statement to Texaco about the company/worker contradiction which existed at that company. But, in principle, the point is applicable to all the multinationals:

> The company exists to turn oil into profits. The workers work to turn oil into wages. It is the same oil.[4]

Williams probably overestimated the degree of control he could exercise from the level of government. Eventually he learnt that rhetoric could not intimidate the effective controllers of the economy into dealing fairly either with government or labour. The development of the inherent conflict between multinational interests, on one side, and labour and national interests reached a stage that forced him to unequivocally take a side. He chose within the limitations of his ideology, his emasculated psychology and his conception of what was in the best interest of the survival of the government. He could not conceive of an independent survival. The real problems of economic dependence and the self-disarming perceptions and

117

instincts of the colonised mind produced an alliance against progress and against labour.

The crisis point in 1965 had its economic origins in the elaboration of the same forces which were apparent in 1963. There was no significant growth of the economy between 1963 and 1965. Per capita GDP grew by a mere 2.1% in 1963 and 1.6% in 1964.[5] The harsh economic realities were making the government reformulate its concepts about wages and industrial relations. The ILO report, extensively quoted in the 1963 budget when the re-appraisal began, was again quoted in the 1965 budget to re-emphasize that the government was regarding increasing wage rates as a negative economic factor.

It is not surprising that even conservative unions had not taken a cue from the strictures in the 1963 budget. The direction of thought on wages, which appeared in a budget for the first time then, was in itself a reversal of what had gone before. Up to the 1961 budget, Williams, who was still Minister of Finance, was exulting at the effects of the rise in wage rates, which indicated the prosperity of the country:

Import of luxury goods testify to the buoyancy of the economy and the rising standard of living . . . Equally striking as an index of the rising standard of living are the imports of domestic appliances which, only a few years ago, were regarded as the hallmark of the well to do only.[6]

Such simplistic nonsense had to come to an end. But in going against it the government never took into account the expectations that they themselves had helped to create. They never engaged in mass education and open and frank dialogue with unions and workers. They just moved from technical references in the budget to heavy handed action. Worse, because the government analysis when it came was just as off the mark as its early perceptions, it led to concepts and proposals for a cure which were more dreadful than the disease. While every ill was being blamed on "high wages", a blind eye was turned to graver obstacles to economic growth.

Unionists like Weekes therefore remained unconvinced when A.N.R. Robinson, as Finance Minister, made annual complaints about wages taking too large a share of the national income, at the cost of government revenues. The unionists saw that government revenues were coming under far more strain from tax concessions, which were granted even to multinational giants like W.R. Grace & Co (owners of Fed Chem). Government revenues were reeling from the sacrifice of customs duties under the terms of assistance to pioneer industries, from the heavy expenditure on infrastructure to accommodate these companies which returned nothing to the economy — except the very wages that were now the focal point of government economic concern.

The unions could not accept arguments that "high wages" were encouraging capital intensive investment. From the very beginning, when wages were abysmally low, the pattern of investment by these foreign firms was capital intensive. They were never large employers of labour in relation to their investment. Why would they come here with anything but the same technology they used in the metropolitan countries which was designed to minimise the use of labour?

There was the same credibility gap in relation to the criticism that "high wages" were depriving the economy of money that would otherwise be available for investment. Clearly, profits going abroad, in many cases untaxed — either by law or by fraud — were the really big problem. The foreign firms consistently took out of the economy more than they put in. Their investments between 1956 and 1964 amounted to $712 million. The recorded amount taken out as profits was $1.34 billion.[7]

It was fundamentally capital-serving economic theory, therefore, that led to the trade unions being identified as the great enemies of progress in the country with their "**ruthless** policy of higher wages and salaries and other benefits" according to the 1964 budget.[8]

Ironically, the very businessmen in whose interests Robinson was voicing these ILO arguments, were soon to cut his throat. They aggressively sought and secured his removal as Minister of Finance after he introduced a Finance Act in 1966 which attempted to get more for the state and the domestic economy from the earnings of big business.

From the outset, Weekes had a different view of the problem from that of the government. Weekes was part of the radical left and the radical left never accepted the official analysis. Therein lay seeds of continuous conflict. An example of how concepts differed on the whole pioneer industry program and its

119

misguided philosophy is provided by an article entitled 'The Golden Myth' in *The Vanguard* of April 30th. The article shows up many of the shortcomings of the government's approach to development and sees the strategy adopted as "a pernicious policy which is milking the country dry for the benefit of foreigners". Coming from such a position the trade unions that had radical leanings regarded it as a national duty to wring what they could from the foreign corporations. This was a legitimate position, even though it also had its shortcomings.

With the right approaches it might have been possible to find some ground on which the opposing views could have met. The Williams' regime enjoyed enough goodwill in the first half of the 1960's to elicit some form of consensus in the national interest. But the kind of political initiatives, that such a truce would have required, were completely outside the arrogant psychology of Williams.

George Weekes' policy in the situation was to fight for everything possible, rely on tough action and hope that a militant trade union policy could push the government in more radical directions.

The signs that this approach would be repressed had been growing even before the 1963 "disappointment", though there were enough contradictory signals to lead one off the track. In the year of Independence for example, 1962, Williams had told a Woodford Square crowd (to quote the *Guardian* report) "that industrial unrest would only strengthen the forces restraining the country's development". And in this context he warned (Williams' words):

> Now that we are independent, we have to save
> Trinidad from Trinidadians.[9]

In that year, Williams gave serious thought to outlawing strikes in the civil service.[10]

The preoccupation with industrial unrest on the one side and high wages on the other would mount in the government's outlook, until, confronted by no signs of relief from their economic failure, they exploded with the ISA in 1965. They had run out of ideas. The budget that year reflected all the confusion and intellectual paralysis. Policies the government considered key to its economic strategy (evidently they could not conceive of development outside of a framework of dependence) had been pursued to the limits:

> In several respects, the concessions we offer go much beyond the terms offered anywhere else in the region[11]

Yet:

> A cause for serious concern is the sluggishness displayed by the rest of the manufacturing sector[12] (except for Fed Chem)

And the confession:

> All the indications are that the problem of industrialization in Trinidad and Tobago is becoming more complex and urgent[13]

Naturally the government sought to portray the ISA as everything except what it was, the backlash of this despair.

Williams laced his justification for the law with statistics that seemed very damning to the trade union movement. 803,899 man days lost, between 1960 and 1964, in 230 strikes involving 74,574 workers. The figures were particularly damning to George Weekes. More than one third of the man-days lost were in the oil industry. More than one sixth of the man days lost were in the sugar industry.[14] That implicated Weekes too since the firm impression in people's minds at the time was the image of Weekes at the centre of the recent strikes in sugar. (The fact, that twice as many days were lost in sugar when one of his chief accusers, W.W. Sutton, was involved in 1962, would not have been remembered then.)

The statistics laid the groundwork for the political deductions. Williams reinforced Sutton's early warning, since March 9th, on behalf of the NFL, that the unrest was "not a manifestation of accident, but of carefully planned moves, embodying well known communist strategy and methods of coercion, intimidation, subversion, ... to plunge the community in chaos and confusion as a prelude to the establishment of a communist totalitarian regime". Williams too was effusive about, "a recalcitrant minority ... quite obviously communist in sympathy, in persuasion, and in the tactics it contemplates and even advocates". This minority "has sought to operate principally by utilizing the trade unions and playing on working class discontent — creating such discontent where necessary"[15].

Once people could be convinced about the abnormality of the number and intensity of strikes, then it was easy to impute motives. The statistics made effective political statement, but far more truth was lost in their presentation than man-days were lost in strikes. The number of strikes per capita was not abnormal by international comparisons and the strikes were not abnormal in terms of conditions for workers and attitudes of employers in Trinidad and Tobago. On a per capita basis some of the metropolitan countries from which the firms operating in the Caribbean come, were far worse off in terms of man-days lost during the same period. Too much store cannot be placed on that alone as there are very different circumstances. But this fact indicates that industrial unrest such as Trinidad was experiencing was not necessarily unusual in a capitalistic environment. The unrest stems from what Weekes describes as "a built-in conflict" in the system:

> There is in the capitalist system as we know it a built-in conflict which militates against good labour relations. The workers have only their labour to sell and by the rules of the system they are entitled to sell as little as possible for as much as they can extort. Which is exactly what the employers do with the products derived from the workers efforts. But the higher the wage the lower the profits and vice versa, so that the employers for their part strive hard to get the most possible labour for the least possible wage. There is nothing morally wrong or reprehensible in either of these two attitudes. It is how the system is designed to operate.[16]

In the Trinidad and Tobago environment, there were factors affecting industrial relations that went beyond the inherent conflicts of capitalism. The economy was dominated by white imperialist firms, with a subordinate white local business elite; firms, as Weekes always classified them, from "former slave-owning countries" and a local elite who are "the descendants of former slave masters". The workers, on the other hand, were Black - the descendants of former slaves and former indentured servants. Against this historical background, with the attitudes it generated, no subversion was needed to explain high levels of industrial unrest.

When the government made an about turn with its decision to "save Trinidad from Trinidadians" instead of saving Trinidad from imperialist exploitation, it put its authority behind the corporations and their allies instead of behind the interests of the workers and the nation, thus giving the corporations the moral initiative to underpay, disrespect and intimidate workers and their representatives.

Where the issues involved in the strikes are concerned, the arguments for subversion also fall down. There were only two oil strikes of any consequence, the first in 1960, which Williams himself described as normal in the course of industrial relations. The other in 1963 was to save jobs. In sugar there has always been the greatest mass concentration of heavily exploited workers, and until the 1970's the question of representation always remained problematic, largely through the machinations of the company and well assisted by government at points.

The statistical arguments fall down in another area. There was no pattern of increasing unrest. The most man-days lost in any particular one of the years 1960-1964 occurred in 1960, the least in 1964.* Industrial unrest had shot up in 1960. It remained above the levels of previous years, when employers more or less had their way, but there was no pattern of escalating unrest in the subsequent years. What was escalating was official hysteria about strikes and official identification of strikes with political subversion, a deliberate strategy of the government.

The strategy worked. The forcefulness with which a political definition of the struggle was communicated is reflected in the fact that for the first time Weekes was not able to mobilise oil workers. Precisely because they were deluded into believing that trade union principles were secondary to a political choice on the question of the ISA.

Because of the over-dramatisation of the situation in early 1965, in particular by the government, its trade union allies, and Caroni Ltd, it is easy to draw a conclusion that the issues were only strategically politicised to facilitate the passage of legislation that had no more than an economic purpose. There are a number of factors however that suggest that under all the organised drama and manufactured hysteria, the political concerns and even paranoia were real. They were expressed in terms calculated to mislead the population. But though the government artfully misrepresented its political fears, there can be no doubt that Williams was seeing in Weekes a political threat

---

* Man Days lost 1960-1964: 1960 — 275,223; 1961 — 145,105; 1962 — 164,657; 1963 — 204,971; 1964 — 95,906

in the making. The very fury of the attack on Weekes, which did not let up after the ISA became law, and the underhand nature of attacks in which Williams became personally and openly involved, indicate this fact. The restrictions placed on the movements of the 65 year old C.L.R. James, when he landed in the country to cover a cricket test series between Britain and the West Indies, also point to a certain level of desperation in the actions of the government. Williams' own justification for what was done to James was incredibly fanciful:

> The subversive elements in the society, with James in
> the forefront, were at work . . .[17]

Weaknesses in Williams' personality were coming into play. The Prime Minister had a single-minded obsession with personal power and an accompanying tendency to paranoia. A statement he himself made summed up an important aspect of his character:

> I can say to any man, come and he cometh, go, and he
> goeth

He could not deal with anyone prepared to and capable of exercising independent judgement, whether in or out of the party. Where such an individual had some basis of power or authority, outside of his patronage or control, such as Weekes did, he quickly acquired the definition — political enemy. Jealously guarding his 'absolute'* authority, Williams saw threats behind every shadow. Even when Williams was at the peak of his political strength, as in 1960, when he could accommodate an oil strike, evidences of the paranoid tendency still showed up. In his speech after the strike he made the startling accusation that "the strike was aimed at the government and was fundamentally political both in its origin and nature". This backed up another statement, equally out of place in terms of what Williams himself had to say about the strike otherwise. He claimed that it was "dominated by the interference of union and companies in matters of government".[18]

Two further examples would highlight the tendency to panic reactions and paranoia which was part of the Prime Minister's personality makeup. In 1961, Williams quickly proclaimed a

---

* The term 'absolute' is very relative here. Williams could not exercise effective authority in relation to the multinationals.

State of Emergency in the San Juan area, a very heavy handed measure for dealing with some pre-election violence. By 1963 he was sufficiently preoccupied with ghosts threatening his power to appoint the Mbanefo Commission of Enquiry into subversion.

The trade union movement has consistently figured in Williams' panic reactions and George Weekes has generally been the centre of apprehension (the 1961 emergency being the notable exception).

Quite apart from individual personality traits, there were also factors that make for government insecurity in the very nature of the post colonial society. Trinidad and Tobago was trying to follow the path of Western-style democracy, but the society did not have democratic traditions. The social structure grew out of the worst forms of oppression — slavery and indentureship — and the political system was Crown Colony government, the most extreme form of direct rule from the colonizing country. Therefore the adoption, in the post colonial period, of institutions of government modelled on the British parliamentary system produced a very rough and capricious imitation. The country just did not have the kind of political culture to support the functioning of those institutions in a way that could give government and people a sense of confidence in them. This lent a distinct fragility to the system of government. The ruling party felt the fragility. It affected the way they perceived things.

The political system suffered the further hazard of standing on economic legs that were shaky, and worse, operated by remote control. With each tottering movement, therefore, the government sought the assistance of the outside and overseas controllers to steady the step and offered further concessions for their cooperation. In 1965 the controllers were calling for concessions earlier withheld by the PNM regime — the emasculation of the labour movement and the sacrifice of George Weekes.

Attention also has to be paid to the psychological framework of government, where the state was beset by economic problems, beleaguered by foreign demands and besieged by the rising expectations of the people in the era of Independence. In this environment sudden swings of mood and behaviour became the norm because of the inherent anxieties, despair and susceptibility to external influence.

FOR BREAD JUSTICE AND FREEDOM

In such a situation an individual like George Weekes, with a popular base, a radical ideology running counter to the kind of relationships the state felt were essential to its survival, and the courage to struggle for his beliefs, logically emerged as a threatening figure. When the multinationals, with their dominant influence, stepped in to reinforce the government's own urge to suppress such a "threat" the confrontation became stark. This is what happened in 1965.

Weekes did in fact represent a challenge to the status quo, though the ways in which the challenge was perceived by the political directorate and construed for public consumption were off the mark. What was fed to the public went beyond what was thought to be true by the political rulers and gossip merchants, but was not wholly in conflict with what they believed. For example in the sugar strike, the ploy of prolonging the strike and imposing an emergency was aimed at aborting, through repression, any possible alliance of oil and sugar workers, especially under the leadership of George Weekes. Williams portrayed his prevention of this "open attempt to link the unions in oil and sugar" as his "outstanding responsibility" in Parliament during the 1961-1966 term.[19]

The action had nothing to do with "communists" at work trying to take over the government by subversive or illegal means, as the official story goes. But the grain of 'truth' here was the real fear of the government that the political forces on the left, including the marxists, would have been strengthened by such a formidable combination of workers under a radical leadership. Whether or not the left would resort to subversive means to overthrow the government was not the point. It was a question of too much potential power for forces opposed to the PNM in ideology and likely to translate that opposition into political challenge.

The political methods used to fight this perceived threat were sinister, but there was nothing irrational about the perceptions. In the 1960's one would logically have focused on Weekes for the potential development of any serious challenge to the government from the left, whether or not Weekes saw himself playing such a role. Outside of Butler, organisations and individuals on the left had failed to make any substantive political impact on the country. And Butler himself did not belong to the orthodox or Marxist Left. There was an organizational vacuum where the Left was concerned and it was only natural that George as a formidable organiser at the trade union level, leader of a powerful working class unit, and possessing the appropriate ideological inclinations, would be regarded by radical thinkers and political activists as the central figure around which some sort of credible socialist, even marxist movement could be built. However not much building of any kind of political organisation went on in the 1960's for various reasons.

Weekes' ideological leanings definitely helped to draw government suspicions, and finally malice towards him. He readily admits to a socialist creed and he has repeatedly been labelled, especially by the establishment, as a "marxist" or, to have more emotional impact in the milieu of reactionary phobias they have cultivated, as "communist". On close study Weekes in fact defies any classical ideological categorization. He welded many strands of thought into his outlook in ways that would not fit any orthodoxy. The predominant influences came from Marxism, Garveyism and Butlerism. But, though Weekes was consistent in his advocacy of certain very basic ideas and ideals, essentially he was more of an activist than an ideologue. He drew ideas from his wideranging experience and reading and never indicated any undue concern about whether his assimilation and presentation of those ideas conformed with an established methodology.

The strong marxist influences on his thought and his marxist sympathies made him gravitate to political organisations which had this kind of outlook. As a result he developed relationships with individuals who were strongly committed to Marxism. Some of these relationships turned out to be quite fruitful for the union. His associations with Lennox Pierre, John La Rose and Jack Kelshall, whose commitment to their beliefs proved to be real over the years, are the three prime examples of such relationships which contributed important intellectual and legal resources to the union. It is precisely such relationships, however, as well as Weekes' own radical projection, which, given the position he held and the influence he wielded, made the Williams' regime fearful of him, even paranoid about his activities.

But the left was deficient in political organisation, and Weekes' strong hold on the workers did not extend to political loyalty. He sought to give them as much of a political and ideological education as he could, but he did not make the mistake, in the atmosphere of the early 60's, to try to weld the OWTU into a directly political organisation under the leadership of George Weekes. Quite apart from his realistic appraisal of the situation, with the overwhelming popularity of the PNM among oil workers and even in his own Rebel cabinet, there are factors in his own personality that would have militated against such an attempt, in particular a diffidence about leadership which he always revealed.

There were also very important questions of time and priorities when Weekes took office. It was necessary to give priority to the material needs of the workers. Attention had to be paid to the state of the union itself. As Weekes described it:

> OWTU was a divided and weak union when we took over. Many people were out of the union at the time. There were contractors who were not in the union and so on. We had a small labour force, maybe around 6000, and no sooner I became president people began to join the union expressing confidence and we had to do a number of things. We had a small headquarters, a small amount of funds. We had to look at the position Rojas left things in. We had people who were Rojasites . . . and were criticising the union leadership at Branch meetings. At Pointe-a-Pierre we used to have fights between the old guard and the new guard. So you had to consolidate your position then by winning over people, holding mass meetings, talking to the workers . . .[20]

Weekes saw as immediately urgent too the question of building up the union's finances with a strike fund after witnessing the experiences of the workers in 1960. In other words, improving the material conditions of the workers, uniting and expanding the membership and strengthening the union financially were far more important in the years 1962 to 1965 than questions of forming political parties or building clandestine organisation.

Weekes' political associates on the left, who were outside of the trade union movement, could not take up the task of political organisation within the OWTU or the trade union movement either. For a start they did not enjoy the relationship with the workers that Weekes did. They had far less chance than Weekes of coping with the strong PNM currents of the time. And they very likely shared his conception of the priorities. In addition, in the early 1950's, during the period of the Workers Freedom Movement and the WIIP, when their influence in the union was strongest, Pierre, La Rose and other radicals had not established a mass base of organisation in the OWTU. Their focus had been on the building of cadres.[21] The President General of the OWTU, John Rojas, was the Vice-Chairman of the WIIP. Some effective organisers within the ranks of the union, like Walter Annamunthodo, John Hackshaw, John Abraham and Fabien Lesaldo, were also members of the party. There were a few junior staff employees in the oil industry who participated as well. However, in the aftermath of the repression in British Guiana and the visit of Dalley in 1954, this process of building cadres lost whatever potential it might have acquired for transforming itself into mass revolutionary organisation. The task of organising on a revolutionary basis was far more difficult in the first half of the 1960's, a time of PNM-inspired political illusions, than it was in the period before Dalley.

There existed no mass organisation base for socialism within the OWTU, therefore, or within Congress when Weekes was President. So any supposed subversion from "communist" agents would have had to come from a more clandestine, military or para-military level of organisation. Subsequent history indicated that the PNM was able to remain in power for 30 years without confronting a serious threat from organisation of that kind, except for a short-lived army mutiny in 1970, which did not have organisational roots in the 1965 period.

Notions that linked industrial agitation in Trinidad and Tobago to some kind of international communist conspiracy were just as fanciful as those that ascribed them to subversion. Up to 1965, Weekes had the barest minimum of contact with representatives of any communist countries and he had not yet travelled to any of them. The fact that other former WIIP members had travelled to Eastern Europe was irrelevant to what was happening in Trinidad at the time, based on the dynamics of the local situation. The slander that travel to or contact with communist countries makes one an agent of those countries has been consistently fed to people in the Western-dominated countries to shut them off from objectively examining alternative political and economic systems.

The question of "subversion" in 1965 therefore was a product of a mixture of paranoia, systemic insecurity, calculated political strategy and purposeful fiction.

However, what the government believed to exist and what they chose to make people believe about Weekes and the OWTU were far more important than what did in fact exist in 1965, important enough to substantially affect the destiny of Trinidad and Tobago.

CHAPTER 9

DAVID WITHOUT THE SLING SHOT

When the Governor General, Sir Solomon Hochoy, signed the ISA on March 20th 1965, it marked a new era in the political history of the country. Very deep wounds showed up in the society during the course of the sugar workers struggle and the Act rubbed salt in those wounds. Anxieties and divisions cut through class and organisations. New directions of political thought were forced upon those who saw clear signs of danger in recent government trends.

The trade union movement was in the greatest disarray. The Trade Union Congress was reduced to just a limp shadow of its former self, depleted in numbers and rent with internal strife. Membership, which had peaked at 70,000 in 1964, dropped to 45,000 by the time UCIW pulled out in March of 1965.

Workers themselves were divided. The more perceptive were demoralized. Even among those who supported the Act, many were torn by self doubt. Their support was essentially an act of blind faith in Eric Williams, the political leader to whom they entrusted their destiny. But there remained nagging questions about what the Act really implied for their interests as workers. Were their acceptance of repressive labour legislation and their denunciations of the NTUC leadership a betrayal of themselves? What was the truth about George Weekes, the trade union leader who had never failed to respond to their cries for help? Whether it was bus workers fighting for the nationalization of public transport, J.T. Johnson workers on the picket line shouting "Don't buy", Lock Joint workers seeking some modicum of justice, Trinidad Cement workers dissatisfied with their representation, they all had called on Weekes. And he had responded to every call. It was hard to believe that his actions were all part of a master plan of subversion. But somehow a political war had developed between Williams and Weekes. The question of supporting or rejecting the Act had been posed in political terms by the government. Therefore there seemed no choice at the time but to decide on the basis of political loyalty.

At least one group of workers had no illusions about what the Act or other events of the time meant for them. The sugar workers, who were so mercilessly used by the government in its determination to heap more oppression on labour, had the backbone taken out of their struggle. Under the State of Emergency still in force there could be no mass meetings to keep up their spirits. Under the new law no one could express support for their strike or lend any form of assistance. To crown it all, Weekes, their main support, was now cut off from his Congress base and thrown into a battle for his own survival in the OWTU. The sugar workers had no option but to crawl back on the job, defeated by an overwhelming combination of forces, which sadly included opportunistic trade union leaders and other misguided workers.

The major opposition political party, the Democratic Labour Party, was divided. The Executive had taken a decision to oppose the Industrial Stabilization Act, which they described as "repugnant to a free society"[1]. The parliamentary group decided to go against the Executive. As a result, at the level of the House of Representatives, the acting leader of the party, Stephen Maraj, and one other DLP representative, Simboonath Capildeo, condemned the bill. The others voted in its favour. In the Senate, the four DLP senators also voted in favour of the bill.[2]

Sections of the middle class had become worried. Evidently the treatment meted out to James played an important part in mobilizing a response from this sector. A dozen lecturers at the University of the West Indies, St Augustine, some of them quite conservative, sent a letter to the newspapers expressing their deep concern about events in the society related to the State of Emergency and the restrictions on C.L.R. James. The letter appeared in the *Guardian* on March 20th, the very day on which the Governor General was signing his assent to the ISA. In the letter, the university lecturers*, highly critical of the treatment

* The lecturers who signed the letter were: Roy Thomas, James Millette, Alister McIntyre, Carl Campbell, R.W. Thompson, Henry Beissel, G.E. Seaforth, Victor A. Richardson, C.A.W. Deane, H.O. Phelps, H. Craig and L. King.

meted out to James, said that "a terrible burden of proof" rests with the government to establish that they had good reasons for imposing the restrictions. They saw the whole handling of the dispute in the sugar industry in a context where "rather extraordinary means were adopted to handle a rather ordinary situation". And they questioned whether the extension of the emergency way beyond the sugar belt and into the St Anns ward had not been done in anticipation of James coming.

These issues also occupied the attention of speakers at public meetings. The organisers of the meetings were citizens, disturbed by the emerging trends and asking the question, "IS THIS COUNTRY FREE?" The first of the meetings on this theme was held at Woodford Square on April 12th. Simboonath Capildeo of the DLP and Peter Farquhar, leader of the Liberal Party (another opposition party, which was a breakaway from the DLP), along with private citizens Max Ifill, an economist, and Clifford Sealy, a bookshop proprietor, addressed these meetings. A resolution was passed at the Woodford Square meeting calling on the government to justify with evidence their extension of the emergency into the St Anns ward and the detention of C.L.R. James "to reassure the citizens of Trinidad and Tobago that they are in no danger of losing their cherished freedoms enshrined in the constitution, the spirit of which was violated by the State of Emergency". An additional item on the agenda of these public meetings was the recently released Mbanefo report, which was severely criticized for its "defamation" of citizens.[3]

Even the businessmen, exuberant as they were about the controls on labour, were not seeing the Industrial Stabilization Act as an unmixed blessing. Senator Lange, a prominent spokesman of this group, represented one side of their response. He was effusive in his praise.

> Mr President, it is going to give me a great deal of pleasure and a great deal of satisfaction to support this Bill . . .[4]

The Senator congratulated the Attorney General and the government, expressing the view that they had given him the same kind of comfort the battleships of the British did in the colonial days:

> . . . this matter has been beautifully timed; it could not
> possibly have been handled better — whether we had
> warships outside or not.[5]

There was generally a more mixed response from the class of
interests Senator Lange represented. During the debate independent Senator Stollmeyer, one of the pillars of the local white
business elite, a prime target of Weekes' attacks on this sector,
supported the bill, for the same reasons Lange did; but expressed
fears about the abuse of privilege which it made possible. He
repeated a suggestion, which was first raised publicly in a
Guardian editorial on the 18th of March, for a periodic review of
the bill.[6] This group had got what they wanted with the ban on
strikes. But they were concerned about the pretence in the bill
that it would seek to control prices as well as wages. Tommy
Gatcliffe, another pillar of the local white business elite, at the
end of his term as President of the Trinidad Chamber of
Commerce in March 1965, reiterated the fears of the businessmen about price controls. The businessmen argued that
widespread price controls by the government would destroy the
country's free enterprise system.[7] On the whole the businessmen
had deep anxieties that the Act portended an intention on the
part of government to regulate the economy too much for their
liking.

The confusion and conflicts of the early 1965 period,
disconcerting to so many groups in different ways, made it
almost inevitable that new political alignments would emerge.
And it is no surprise that as the new realignments began to
emerge, George Weekes was a central figure in the process. The
Guardian, in an editorial, described him as "the epicenter of
rumblings in the industrial field". Williams had earmarked him
as the pivot of political opposition; there was no serious
parliamentary opposition. Williams had also stepped on his
corns in another way that was critical. He made the
emasculation of the trade union movement a cornerstone of
PNM political strategy. Any response by Weekes in this context
would have far-reaching political implications, whether the
response was primarily and intentionally political, or whether it
was motivated entirely by trade union concerns.

The fact is trade union activity in its own right became very
politicized under the conditions created by the government's
1965 measures. Of course there never was any such thing as non-

political trade unionism, though there was more than enough pretence at it. But there were important qualitative differences in the politics of pre-ISA and post-ISA trade unionism. For a decade before the ISA, interventions of the state against workers in industrial relations had virtually ceased. There was a near elimination of the conflict between state and workers, which had been a major factor in social upheaval during the first half of the twentieth century. In the early years the PNM government seemed to be taking the pledge they made in their 'People's Charter' seriously.

> The People's National Movement, resolute in its opposition to colonialism, places the interests and welfare of the workers in the forefront of its programme.[8]

Militant trade union activity, a necessary counterweight to employers who still lived in the past, was recognised as legitimate in government pronouncements.

All that changed in 1965. After the ISA, the trade unions entered an era where objectively, in at least one important respect, they were closer to the nascent workers organisations in the pre-1937 period than they were to the status they had acquired in the 50's and early 60's. The implicit confrontation of workers' organisations and the state, which characterised the colonial period, had returned. With strikes virtually outlawed, the trade union could exercise its major weapon only in direct confrontation with the government. The 'Independent' state, in this new regressive phase, unambiguously identified itself on the side of the multinational corporations and big business, in direct opposition to the people's interests, which were represented in the main by radical trade unions and progressive individuals. It was very much like the system the PNM had denounced. In their words:

> The Crown Colony system of government was designed to protect the interest and ensure the profits of the employers; it was based on the degradation of the workers, either by African slavery or by Asian indenture, and by the domination of coloured labour by white capital . . .[9]

Under the post-ISA PNM system, according to Weekes:

> Instead of foreign exploitation supported by a white minority (in government), they now have

foreign exploitation supported by a local Negro
Minority.

As much as Weekes welcomed the change in the complexion of
the state, he was not prepared to compromise with the colonial
contradiction the state was trying to preserve by legal repression.
He was not prepared, like many other working class leaders in
1965, to sacrifice the interests of the workers for the handouts of
the state and the companies. Therefore his position and that of the
OWTU reflected the stark reality of the confrontation. The ISA
had to be treated as a declaration of war on the labour movement.

The war called for strategic planning and action. The OWTU
President General, deeply entangled in the web of events, had to
rethink his political position, he had to consciously consider the
political nature of whatever move he made, and he had to
calculate the resources he had to fight with. It was a situation
where his very survival as a trade union leader and the survival
of those principles he stood for in the trade union movement
rested very much on his decisions. Apart from assessing where he
stood in relation to the government and the whole power
structure at this time, there was also the question of where he
stood in relation to other radicals. Some of them were pressing
him to take on a leading role in the fight for political change.
One of the options he had to weigh, therefore, one which would
appear almost mandatory under the circumstances, was the
option of deliberate political organisation to challenge the PNM
at the level of government.

Weekes felt his political instincts bristling, awakened by the
hurt and the disillusionment which he felt, despite his own
analyses and predictions of the government's moves. He was
enraged at being backed into a corner and dared by the regime
to strike back. Nevertheless he maintained level headed
judgement. He trod cautiously on the direct political front.
There were trade union issues that demanded urgent attention.
He knew that this was the arena in which he would either prove
his strength or be completely vanquished. His first emphasis,
therefore, was on the consolidation and protection of the OWTU
itself. As he told the Trade Union Congress:

> . . . all my services, all my energy, all my integrity, all
> my manhood are now needed to defend the standard
> of living of my fellow oil workers and the
> fortress of the Oilfield Workers Trade Union against

a combined onslaught by the calculated cunning of frightened employers, the military force of a Machiavellian government and the indefensible cowardice and unbelievable treachery of trade union leaders who serve the other side.[10]

In pursuing this course he had to protect his own position and that of the Rebel team he led. Naturally he was the main target of the anti-union forces. Already the government had brought the fight into the OWTU. One PNM general council member in the union was challenging Weekes for the leadership in the upcoming general elections, scheduled for May, 1965. On March 12th, Fabien Lesaldo had publicly announced his intention to fight for the presidency. It was a timely announcement at the high point of the manoeuvre to get Weekes out of Congress. The Emergency was on, the ISA had been tabled in parliament and the SWWTU had just announced its withdrawal from the NTUC. The climate was right for Lesaldo's first salvo against Weekes which was 'good copy' for a willing press.[11]

More ammunition from outside was to come the way of Lesaldo and his 'Free Trade Union Group' when the Mbanefo report, which had been tabled in parliament on the day of the ISA debate, was released to the public on April 8th. Weekes correctly said of the report:

Like every other Trade Unionist mentioned I have been attacked most bitterly in it. The only difference is that I have been attacked more often and in more virulent terms than the others.[12]

Weekes was condemned by the Commissioners who enquired into subversion for his struggles for oil workers:

There is evidence to support the allegation that since Mr Weekes took over control of OWTU affairs employer/employee relationships in the oil industry have progressively deteriorated.[13]

Special focus was placed on his membership in the long defunct West Indian Independence Party:

Mr Weekes' close association with the WIIP which was described as the only Communist organisation in the Territory and as having some extreme left-wing elements in its membership, supports the description that Mr Weekes is a Communist.[14]

Most of all he was considered dangerous:

As President General of the OWTU which is the
strongest and best organised Trade Union in the
territory, and by virtue of his further official position
at the head of the TUC (Pro-tem President), Mr
Weekes is in a position to wield considerable power
for good or evil. That fact, together with his past and
present associations, marks him out as a person to be
watched.[15]

Lesaldo and his Free Trade Union Group immediately seized
upon the report's defamatory references to Weekes to call for his
resignation from the leadership of the union.[16]

Mbanefo's aspersions were mild compared to some of the
attacks. Apart from a stream of outrageous pamphlets in the oil
belt, rumours started to spread within the union. They were
centered, in keeping with the national propaganda, on the hoax
of communist plots and subversion, but they also introduced
questions of integrity. All of a sudden the spending of union
funds and even the democracy of which the union has always
been extremely proud became issues of concern to those opposed
to Weekes and the Rebels.

The PNM thrust in all this was very clear. If anyone wanted to
believe that the party loyalty of Lesaldo, who was stirring up the
malice from within, was incidental, or that the attacks of
unionists like Tull and Sutton were independent, Williams own
participation in the anti-Weekes campaign removed all doubt
about the government's active interest in destroying Weekes.
Williams pulled his own stature down by the open part he played
in calling the integrity of Weekes into question on the spending
of union funds. In April, one month before the OWTU elections,
he declared in an article in the *Nation* that the misuse of union
funds was a "scandal which can no longer be tolerated". The
context of such attacks pointed unambiguously to George
Weekes. What bothered Weekes' enemies the most was the
special "strike fund" he had set up when he took office. The
purpose of the fund was to help ease the burden on workers when
they had to sacrifice income during periods of industrial strife.
When the ISA outlawed strikes there was a mortal fear that the
funds would be diverted to political purposes.

To add to the portrait of dishonesty being painted by
implication, Lesaldo was calling on the government to supervise
the OWTU elections, making signals to the public that there was

no confidence in the working of the machinery of elections within the union. In this call, ridiculous in the context of the kind of democracy introduced and entrenched by the Rebels, the sponsored opposition to Weekes was supported by the *Guardian* in its editorial columns.

These were very sensitive areas of attack to a leader whose proudest boast would remain, up to his retirement, the intactness of his integrity; sensitive areas of attack to a leader and a team whose collective pride was well founded in the level of democracy they brought into the union.

A *Guardian* editorial, which appeared a few days after Weekes resigned from Congress, unashamedly identified the purpose of the heavy progaganda artillery directed against the OWTU President General.

First the *Guardian* called Weekes' resignation from Congress "his major contribution to the union movement". But the editorial pointed out:

> This, however, is not the end of the story. Mr Weekes is still the head of the Oilfields Workers' Trade Union . . .
>
> . . . it is left to the judgement of Mr Weekes and the executive in the first instance, then by the oil workers in the second, to decide whether a changing of the guard is not also due in the OWTU.[17]

Weekes had to summon up courage in the face of such attacks. Ordinarily the challenge of a Lesaldo could be treated as a by-the-way nuisance. It was easy to come to terms with the role of the press, which represented identifiable vested interests. But the level of Williams' personal involvement gave the struggle a life-and-death character. Weekes was taken back by the Prime Minister's slanderous innuendos about the union funds. He could not miss the devious calculation in the timely release of the Mbanefo report, which they had sat on for well over a year. The report was in the government's possession since the beginning of 1964. He understood the threat in Williams' constant references to subversion in a series of articles on the ISA which ran in the *Nation*. These were unmistakable signs of the importance the government attached to the objective of removing him from the position of national influence he held as President General of the OWTU.

Weekes therefore had to put tremendous energies into fending off the attacks. He was not taking chances on what may or may not be believed in the existing atmosphere. He took up the challenge to counter allegations.

He sought to vindicate his position in the sugar strike by the detailed information he recorded in his letter of resignation from the Trade Union Congress. He saw the necessity to clearly outline the issues involved in the strike, since it had been used to foster suspicions among the workers that there was a hidden design of communist subversion behind his trade union militancy.

He also countered individual attacks. For example, he publicly challenged Senators Rojas and Tull to initiate criminal proceedings against him and others whom the Senators claimed, very definitively, were involved in a "plot" to overthrow the government.[18] They made these charges during their senate contributions to the ISA debate. Both claimed firsthand knowledge for their accusations.

He made a very extensive public reply to the report of the Mbanefo Commission. Rather than a statement by statement rebuttal of the Commission's charges, Weekes made a predominantly political response. He described the report as "easily **the most disgraceful publication which has ever been issued officially here.** The Commissioners appear to have regarded it as their function to degrade any person or organisation on the side of the down trodden workers . . ."[19]

Weekes suggested the government's underlying motives for appointing the Commission,

> The PNM government has as a matter of policy embarked on the dangerous course of breaking up the Trade Union movement.[20]

He identified OWTU, NUGE and CSA as the main targets of the state and he recognised that individually they were after him more than anybody else "because I refused to be a government 'yes-man' but put the interests of my union members first".[21]

Weekes knew that the propaganda was not only aimed at affecting the outcome of the union election. There was another critical factor on the horizon — negotiations with the Texaco oil company. These negotiations too became a part of the war because they would be the first after the ISA. Therefore they were meant to set an example for all future union negotiations.

They were meant to get the message to workers that the days of substantial wage increases were over. They were meant to establish that the multinational corporations had regained their former strength and that the power of the OWTU was broken forever. That is what it was hoped the negotiation with Texaco would accomplish, with or without Weekes being present. Of course it would be far more easily accomplished if Weekes could be removed at this time.

In its determination to see these goals achieved in the negotiations, the government made an unprecedented, anti-worker, anti-national and outright reactionary intervention in the process. They were not prepared simply to allow the recently introduced ISA to demonstrate its effectiveness. At the very beginning of the negotiations they introduced a most damning statement into the talks in the form of a letter to the company and the union stating government's position on the negotiations.[22] This statement, although in theory it was supposed to be a statement in the national interests, was in fact, and glaringly so, an added weapon in the hands of the multinational corporation in its negotiations with the OWTU.

Virtually every clause in the government statement gave the impression that any increase in wages granted to oil workers would "be contrary to the national interests". According to the arguments of the government, they were concerned that increased wages could "adversely affect the growth of Government revenues derived from the industry or the ability of the companies to maintain a high level of local investment". "Adverse effects" on government revenues would "militate against the implementation" of the Second Five Year Plan with its objective to create jobs. On the oil company's behalf the government was also suggesting that increased wages could lead to further retrenchment in the oil industry and to further declines in crude production by taking away funds for investment in exploration. They further argued that "wages and other conditions of work in the oil industry exert a considerable upward pressure on wages and other conditions of work in other industries both in the private and public sectors" with negative effects on employment and other important economic variables.

In the aftermath of the ISA, therefore, Weekes was totally absorbed in a grim struggle. It went beyond the question of his survival or ignominious defeat as President of the union. In fact, from the response of the workers, Weekes was confident that the PNM could not succeed at that time in removing him from the leadership of the union. The workers were loyal to their Prime Minister and they would not support Weekes in opposing him politically. But they were also loyal to Weekes as their trade union leader and enjoying the material benefits of his militant leadership. As a result they would not allow their Prime Minister to deprive them of his services so easily. One of the critical considerations in the Texaco negotiations, where the future of Weekes was concerned, was that if things worked out the way Texaco and the government wanted them to, it would undermine the confidence the workers had in Weekes where their bread and butter was concerned. Therefore if the immediate attack did not displace him in the union elections, but Weekes effectiveness around the bargaining table could be destroyed, then in the next round even the objective of ousting him from the OWTU might well be within reach.

Weekes understood what the greater battle, the Texaco negotiations, meant for himself, for the OWTU and for trade unionism in general in this country. A defeat around the table for the OWTU this time, any compromised and undignified settlement would be a serious blow to the entire trade union movement because it would be a blow to the most powerful and the most militant of the trade unions. It would be a one shot vindication of the ISA from the point of view of government and the capitalists.

Weekes entered the negotiations on April 6th 1965 very conscious of this fact. With so much at stake he had to win. The OWTU had to win the 1965 Battle at Beaumont Hill. For its own members and for all workers. The ISA, as he told workers months later, had taken away the "sling shot" of the union. They had to deal with that reality. "But although (the sling shot) has been taken away, the union should remain, like David versus Goliath, as it has been in the past".[23] With or without the legal right to the armory of the past, the OWTU had to fight the war.

An important part of war is psychological warfare. Weekes reached for that weapon in his opening statement at the Texaco negotiations. He began by saying:

> These negotiations may prove to be the most important in the long history of my Union's association with the oil industry ...

142

The critical importance of these talks results, of course, from the changed labour situation brought about by the passage of the Industrial Stabilisation Act.

In effect, this Act purports to remove the workers' right to withhold their labour if they are dissatisfied with the conditions offered to them.

For the time being I am merely pointing out that there is a great danger of the company officials feeling that with this ultimate power removed, the union has no bargaining power left.[24]

Weekes knew, that is exactly what the Texaco officials were thinking. The leader of the company team, the Manager of Employee Relations, E.G. Stibbs, in his opening statement had referred to the changed situation. Behind the mild tones of Stibbs warning that the union was asking for too much and the company was prepared to offer very little, Weekes could see the confidence of a team who felt they had all the trump cards. They had the government on their side. Stibbs hinted at this. They had the law on their side. And, to add to their assurance, less than three weeks before, they had seen oil workers stay on the job, ignoring the call of the OWTU General Council to strike and demonstrate against the ISA.

Weekes would not allow himself to be floored by the thought of that humiliation. George Weekes had an unshakable faith in the "blue shirt army". Williams had immobilized them on the ISA with a political pincer attack, marshalling fears of communist subversion on the one side, and fears about the racial implications of Weekes' politics on the other. The move was so lightning fast, it left little time for union officers to counter attack. A Trojan Horse was already inside, increasing the problems for the union.

However, in the fight against Texaco, the question was directly about the bread and butter of oil workers, no confusion about that. There was more time to mobilise, more time to educate workers about the ISA, more time to identify and deal with the traitors within. Weekes was prepared to stick his neck out. In this situation, he had no doubt, the oil workers, with their militant tradition, would not let him down, they would not let themselves down, they would not betray their class interests and national responsibility.

Armed with this faith, he let the company and the country know:

> In this fight the workers have only one weapon. Their ability to cut off completely the flow of profits which is the single reason for the company's existence. For if the workers refuse to sell their labour then the profits will stop.
>
> What I fear today more than anything else is that the company's representatives may feel that the Union cannot strike and therefore has no real bargaining power. There may be a tendency to feel that these negotiations are really only an academic exercise that must be gone through before the matter can be taken to the industrial court.
>
> I want to give a warning as soberly as I can and with full knowledge of the implications of what I say that it will be a grave mistake to take this view.
>
> For my union hesitates to recognise the validity of the Industrial Stabilization Act, and also hesitates to submit to the jurisdiction of the Industrial Court.[25]

Observing the reactions of Texaco representatives to such remarks, Weekes reminded them:

> ... I noticed that some of you looked shocked. You are not really justified in this reaction because after all if we break the law, you have set us the precedent in this. For years whenever we have had to bargain, we have sought to get information as to your profits. Despite the fact that the companies Ordinance calls for you to file annual accounts, your company has consistently refused to do so, and apparently you are above the law, for no prosecution has ever been instituted by Government against you.[26]

Finally he let them know that:

> ... almost the entire membership of my union is in a fighting mood. There is wide dissatisfaction and if these negotiations do not result in something satisfactory to my members there will be no controlling them ... The OWTU are in the mood to fight.[27]

Such statements in the context of the period must have seemed like just bravado. But Weekes was remarkably able to keep up the militant image and spirit of the union and himself even in the very trying period of 1965. During the negotiations he was able to mobilise the workers to demonstrate against the slow pace and intransigence of the company. But despite the rhetoric and the marches, including a symbolic trek to Charlie King Junction on July 24th, the power of the past was not there. Because to go a step beyond marching and shouting would mean direct confrontation with the law. This was a trump card in the hands of the company and Weekes had to carefully calculate his options and assess just how far the workers were prepared to go to get the monkey of the ISA off their backs and make Texaco respect the power of organised labour.

Despite Weekes' skilful brinkmanship, which was very unsettling for the company and the establishment generally, the shifting balance was reflected in the length of the negotiations and the failure to resolve the issues around the bargaining table. On October 5th, after six (6) fruitless months of talk, the matter went to the Industrial Court. Weekes and the workers were now only the rearguard of a battle fought out in sterile halls between high-powered lawyers and economists representing union, company and government.

While the union's professional team — Jack Kelshall, lawyer, Bernard Primus and Max Ifill, economists — argued with technicalities and figures in the court, Weekes kept up the morale of the workers. He never let them lose the sense of battle. But he was feeling the psychological pressures of not being able to fight his kind of fight in the tradition of Butler, except in ways too symbolic to be satisfying. The workers were mobilised and because of their confidence in the leadership they were not cowed into taking things lying down. But, in the absence of the strike weapon, the answer of the workers was not on par with the level of contempt Texaco showed for workers. It did not match Texaco's defiance of the nation by defiance of the Industrial Court. The defiance came on the same issue of providing necessary information that Weekes had chided them on in his opening statement.

Texaco had bluntly refused to produce figures about its production costs ordered by the court on the request of the union, eventually forcing the court to go back on its own decision. The illogic in the new status quo, emphasized by Texaco's high-handedness, and the sense of outrage it brought were well expressed in the newspaper *We The People* edited by C.L.R. James:

If for the traditional rough and tumble of Industrial warfare, there is to be substituted the scientific examination of the court room, then it goes without saying that the only starting point on any issue is the facts.

Either the Industrial Court has the power to get at the facts or it does not. If it does then nobody, not even Texaco, must be allowed to flout its orders. If it does not, or if Texaco can flout its orders, then the Industrial Court is a hoax, a farce, a mockery.[28]

When the Industrial Court finally made its award on December 10th 1965, the reaction of the union leadership indicated their understanding of the dilemma facing trade unions under the new order. The award of the court itself, as far as wages and working conditions were concerned, was not considered unjust. In fact, though they felt that "in some respects" the union got less than they would have got on their own, substantially they saw the court arriving at "what they would have got under normal circumstances".[29]

The problem then was not the content of the judgement, but the process leading up to the judgement by the court. There were new difficulties for unions and workers. The agreement took longer because of the court, it cost a great deal of money which could not be recovered (a problem all the more serious for smaller unions) and the award was not the end of the matter as the parties would have to go to court from time to time to have certain matters clarified. According to *The Vanguard,*

The shadow of the Industrial Court now hangs over all industrial agreements like the skeleton at the feast.[30]

But what was even more fundamental than any problems of time, cost and inconvenience was the fact that to all intents and purposes it seemed, "The court has taken the place of the union". The real distress being experienced by Weekes and other officers of the union stemmed from the fundamental alienation involved in battling by proxy, a method that went against the grain of a leadership with a tradition of direct involvement in the forefront of the struggle.

It is one of the most traumatic adjustments George Weekes had to make in 1965, a year in which he was forced to fight two of his major battles, in part at least, by proxy. Apart from the Texaco entanglement, there was the legal thrust to have the ISA declared unconstitutional. Weekes was responsible for this action and the OWTU had to bear the costs alone as the NTUC, despite its anti-ISA statements, refused to get financially involved in the exercise. OWTU retained a British QC, John Platts-Mills, on the recommendation of Jack Kelshall. Eventually this battle was lost in the courts.

However Weekes did not just sit back and allow high powered lawyers to argue and judges to decide. He spearheaded a political and propaganda war against the ISA, which began the essential process of opening the eyes of the people to the growing predicament of the labour movement and therefore the welfare of workers and the ordinary people in the society. He launched an intense campaign of public meetings on August 10th at the historic Charlie King Junction, followed by meetings at Barrackpore on the 11th, and Guayaguare on the 12th. The next week it was Point Fortin, Cedros and Couva, and so the campaign built up with support for the OWTU team coming from the Transport and Industrial Workers Union, the National Union of Government Employees and the Sugar Workers Trade Union. There was an impressive response at the meetings to what Weekes and the other speakers had to say. Some individuals came out to heckle and disrupt, but in meeting after meeting they were silenced by the information coming from the platform.[31] The state had had its say, befuddling the minds of the people with red herrings about red plots. Now for the first time the masses were being exposed to the truth about the ISA, actually hearing provisions of the Act read and interpreted, and understanding their dread significance.

A consistent campaign against this atrocious law was also waged in *The Vanguard* newspaper, the official organ of the OWTU. The revival of this paper in April of 1965 (after it had been defunct for years) was one of Weekes' achievements in this period when he was under increasing pressure from the establishment. The question of reviving the union paper had been one of those issues uppermost in his mind from the time he assumed office in 1962 but it had been deflected by other preoccupations, including the effort to get a national labour paper going through the instrument of the National Trade Union Congress. One issue came out on the ISA. After that events ruled out any hope of a progressive labour paper emerging from the Congress on a continuing basis and Weekes moved with a greater sense of urgency to re-establish *The Vanguard*. He got Bernard Primus, a legal adviser of the union, to stand in as editor until the arrival of George Bowrin, returning from legal studies in England, to take over the editorship.

The Vanguard with its educational, worker-oriented content and militant tone was one of the early signals that Weekes was not going to be silenced or intimidated by the many pronged attacks he was being subjected to. *The Vanguard* became a weapon in the post-ISA fight back and a very important weapon in a situation where the established media suppressed truth, consistently slandered or misrepresented Weekes and promoted anti-trade union propaganda.

It was just one aspect of a fight back that saw Weekes overcome all the attempts to destroy him, a fight back that grew stronger after he resoundingly defeated his enemies in the union elections of May 17th 1965*. It was a constructive fight back. Weekes did not compromise his program of building the OWTU and taking up the struggles of other workers. Far from such efforts being thwarted or suppressed by the hostile onslaught of opposed forces, they gathered momentum as he responded with greater energies to the challenges of the establishment.

Weekes tried to make his own union, whose membership had grown to 11,500, more prepared for battle by educating the leadership. A major step in this direction was the introduction of in-depth leadership training seminars. These seminars were well planned serious educational projects. The first in November of 1965, for example, lasted from November 21st to November 27th. It was held at Mayaro, away from the distractions of the city. This became the pattern for subsequent seminars.

Weekes used the seminar as a gesture to indicate his concern for unity in the trade union movement. He invited other union leaders, some of whom had denounced him, especially in the most trying period of early 1965, and stressed his commitment to unity in his opening statement. He suggested that the OWTU consider sponsoring similar seminars for all NTUC affiliates and even consider the award of scholarships to members of other trade unions. This was the vision of a man totally committed to the development of the trade union movement as a whole,

---

* The enitre Rebel team won.

looking at ways in which his union, with its ample resources, could assist the educational development of other unions in the absence of the long promised national labour college. And he proved that he was not just saying things that would sound good. He soon put promise into practice. By the time the OWTU returned to Mayaro for another seminar in 1966, there were participants from other unions.

Weekes proved that he was prepared to continue to struggle with non-OWTU workers and other trade unions. In October, the P.Gee, as he was popularly known in the union, was out in the field, side by side with Joe Young in stormy public meetings, trying to regain recognition for the Transport and Industrial Workers Union as the bargaining agent for bus workers. After a long and bitter struggle, TIWU won this battle.

Weekes was also involved with the workers of the cement company who were dissatisfied with their union, the Cement Workers Union, and were seeking representation by the OWTU, a struggle which was drawn out for years before eventual victory, because of legal technicalities having to do with the OWTU constitution. Until changes were made to this constitution in 1969, the OWTU could only represent oil and chemical workers.

The most telling involvement of Weekes in this period was his continuing struggle with sugar workers. This is the involvement that the establishment most feared, the involvement that had triggered the wave of repression, attempted assassination, and efforts to purge Weekes from the trade union movement. The sugar industry remained an area of industrial turmoil. Sugar workers had to continue fighting internal battles in the union, battles against the company, and, in the wake of the ISA, battles against the Industrial Court. The leader they turned to for support and guidance in all these battles was George Weekes. And he took up their cause without fail.

In displaying the same resolute defiance that Butler had done before, Weekes saw himself following in the footsteps of the father of the labour movement. He always acknowledged his personal debt, the debt of the labour movement and the masses of people in general to the ageing Chief Servant. He always made Charlie King Junction, where the spark for the 1937 uprising was lit, a focus of struggle. In meeting after meeting there, fighting various issues, on the piece of ground that for him was a shrine, he reminded the people of the sacrifice and victory symbolized by that spot where the people had risen to defend their leader and burnt to death the policeman who had dared to try to arrest him. He reminded them too of the man himself, Butler, who was still alive, cast up on the political periphery by Eric Williams.

Weekes was determined to use his position as the head of the OWTU to keep alive the memory of Butler and the martyrs of 1937 and their struggle. As an individual Butlerite, he had always joined the Chief Servant on his annual pilgrimage in the small town of Fyzabad from the historic Charlie King Junction to the grave of La Brea Charles, who was killed when he was mistaken for Butler. As President General of the OWTU, he dedicated himself to making that annual June 19th ceremony, grown small in the 1960's, into a memorable national event. He broke significant ground towards this goal when he got the participation of the union in the event in June 1966.

That was the beginning of the restoration of the glory of Butler Day and the memory of Butler. By his unflinching determination Weekes was able to keep the memories of a heroic struggle and a heroic figure vibrant in the minds of an older generation and to stimulate a new generation to appreciate an important chapter in the nation's history and to revere a freedom fighter who made an unparalleled contribution to the struggle against colonialism in the English-speaking Caribbean in the first half of the twentieth century.

Weekes also internationalised the struggle against the ISA. As part of this effort, he travelled to Cuba where he addressed the Tricontinental Conference in January 1966 on the question of the ISA in Trinidad and Tobago.

The trip to Cuba, to address a conference on trade union affairs, was the symbolic combination of Weekes the trade unionist and Weekes the ideologically committed politician. As a trade unionist Weekes was political, daring the political establishment by his style of trade unionism and the content of his rhetoric. But he did not confine his defiance and challenge to the trade union field as the struggle evolved in the wake of the ISA. As he told students at UWI in December of 1965:

> We have all recently seen the violent rape of democracy by means of which the ISA was passed . . .

Just as the Taff Vale case brought about the birth of the Labour Party so do I expect that the ISA will usher in a new approach to Politics by the Trade Union Movement in Trinidad.

Just as Lord Halsbury's portrait might well hang as the man who brought unionists into politics in the UK, so might Eric Williams portrait hang as the man who did the same in Trinidad . . .

I am all the more strengthened in my belief that it is necessary for Trade Unions to enter the political arena, because as I have shown it seems that our political difficulties stem from a breakdown of democracy. It has been said that the only cure for bad democracy is more democracy. If our salvation is to come from an extension of the process of democracy among our people, then I search in vain for the medium through which this may be done if not through the unions.[32]

What Weekes outlined here as general principles, he was at the time seeking to put into practice. While his main focus after the ISA was on the trade union movement, he was also involved in preparatory work for a plunge into the arena of electoral politics. He had established that David without the slingshot, though at a disadvantage in conflict with the industrial Goliath, was far from defeated. He now had to prove to himself that David could confront the political Goliath and take back the slingshot.

CHAPTER 10

A PLUNGE INTO CONVENTIONAL POLITICS

"The time has come ... for trade unionists in Trinidad & Tobago to push their own leaders in the forefront of the political battle. And who should be the first in line? Why George Weekes of course?" (George Bowrin)[1]

When George Weekes rose to address the inaugural conference of the Workers and Farmers Party (WFP) at the Palms Club on November 7th 1965, the size and nature of the audience provided no indication that the time had come when workers had accepted the responsibility outlined by Bowrin "to push their own leaders in the forefront of the political battle". On the opening day of the conference, Saturday November 6th, C.L.R. James had quoted Shakespeare:

"We few, we happy few, we band of brothers"

However, a few, no matter how happy, was not an auspicious launching for a movement which would have to defeat the might of an entrenched PNM regime, in an election one year away, to fulfil its mandate: "It must form the next government", said Party Chairman, Stephen Maharaj.

The time had not come either when George Weekes could be pushed into the forefront of the political battle in the conventional sense. At least that could not be accomplished by those doing the pushing in 1965. Weekes was 100% supportive of the goals and ideals of the WFP and its leadership. And he was involved. In fact he was among the founders. He was an active participant in the discussions of the early days initiated by James and including individuals like Stephen Maharaj, Lennox Pierre, George Bowrin and Jack Kelshall, which shaped the party and its philosophy.

Before the final decision to go full speed ahead with the new party there was discussion about C.L.R. James taking up an offer

152

from Stephen Maharaj to lead the opposition Democratic Labour Party to help overcome its communal identification, the 'Indian Party' image. Weekes was part of those discussions.

He identified openly with the WFP, with its mildly socialist manifesto, when it made its formation public. He made it possible for them to use the oil workers' club for their inaugural conference. He addressed members at the conference on the question of the need for a labour code and the necessary ingredients of such a code. He made his house in San Juan available for fund raising ventures. But the Executive that was installed consisted of Stephen Maharaj — Chairman, George Bowrin - 1st Vice Chairman, M.A.S.A. Khan — 2nd Vice Chairman, C.L.R. James — Secretary, Dalip Goopesingh — Assistant Secretary, Clive Phill — Treasurer, J.M. Dube — Public Relations Officer, Lennox Pierre — Education Officer and Basdeo Panday — Youth Director.

Weekes had declined the offer of C.L.R. James to serve as Chairman of the party and he did not make himself available for any other office.

Weekes opted for a relatively low-keyed role although he had a clear analysis of the political situation and he understood theoretically why trade unions should be in politics, particularly in the post-ISA period. In a speech delivered at the University of the West Indies, St Augustine campus, in the month after the convention, Weekes demonstrated how clear his perspectives were on these issues. He saw the country as poised on the brink of social and political upheaval, basically because the social and economic aspirations and hopes of politically conscious young people during the preceding decade had not been fulfilled. This was a generation who had directed their energies towards the defeat of the colonial system, which was the essential promise of the PNM. As Weekes saw it:

> The movement for national independence crystallised around the PNM and its main driving force was the intense dislike of the local coloured people for a system which allowed the white people to dominate, irrespective of their merit, and to reap an unjustly large share of the wealth in return for protecting foreign interests. This was the real driving force behind the PNM crusade.[2]

These politically conscious young people expected that under a national government there would be an end to the white dominated system, they expected "foreigners to be cut loose from the wealth they were extracting". Instead, in Weekes' judgement, PNM policies had "consciously made" economic exploitation worse.

> Instead of using the power vested in him for the destruction of foreign exploiting interests, Dr Williams has preferred to side with these foreign exploiting interests and 'stabilize' them to use a word now popular.[3]

He had seen the development of what he called "inner racial conflict", conflict between Africans and Indians. He was appalled at the PNM's manipulation of this:

> In the second general election fought by the PNM, it became clear that the real issue was now whether Negroes or Indians will dominate the political scene and this deep cleavage is now the main question.[4]

Further he drew a picture of the dangerous course the country was on. One of the critical signs of this was the way the government was overriding the will of the people. He drew instances of the 'Solomon Affair' where the people were completely dissatisfied at Williams' handling of the matter in which the then Minister of Home Affairs, Patrick Solomon, had used his authority to have a family member released from a prison cell. He drew other instances of the Industrial Stabilisation Act, the Education Bill (which was opposed by the Catholic hierarchy) and the Civil Service Bill, all measures seen as forced upon the society without proper consideration for opposing interests. He saw the attempts at the destruction of unions as particularly dangerous, drawing parallels with what happened during the rise of fascism in Nazi Germany. On the basis of his analysis he drew the conclusion that only through the trade union movement could democracy be restored.

The further conclusion he did not draw was that if the trade union movement was to be involved, the task automatically fell on him to lead the movement in the right direction. Bowrin was right about Weekes being the person to play that role. His whole life almost was like a preparation for that role. He had been sensitised about oppression, about social and political issues from his vision of his father, the exploited headmaster, from his early observations of racial inequality and the political talk he sometimes heard in his home town, even though it did not mean too much to him at the time. As a teenager, international issues of racism and Nazism made a firm imprint on his consciousness and his participation in World War II opened up a world of ideological perspectives that were to remain with him. The radical ideas which crystallised in his mind during the war were to drive him, on his return home, first to be an ardent on-looker and follower of socialist-oriented organisations, and eventually, to join the West Indian Independence Party. His subsequent critical support for the People's National Movement was constantly undermined by the contradictions of Eric Williams until it was completely shattered by the ISA. By the time this occurred the political slant of Weekes' trade unionism had established him as a more effective force in national politics than any figure in opposition party politics.

Weekes had his express reasons for not taking what seemed the next logical step in his participation in national affairs, even when the initiative for the formation of a political party came from C.L.R. James. Weekes' own interpretation of why he "never initiated any political organisation", is that he "wanted to concentrate as much as possible on the trade union front, to develop that popular base".[5] This line of thought is credible and even rational in the subversive ferment of 1965. He is right when he says, "I knew that taking any initiative in forming a party would affect that development, so I avoided it". The fact that he "succeeded to a large extent" in his goal of expanding and consolidating the union is well recorded.

However, by the time the Workers and Farmers Party was launched Weekes was totally identified with it. Because of his beliefs in what the WFP represented, he was prepared to take the risks of involvement, ". . . as President General, I knew that I would be in conflict with members of the union who were sympathetic towards the PNM and even the DLP. Nevertheless, I thought this was the best thing to do . . ."[6]

Strategic considerations within the union therefore, important as they were in the early 1965 period, did not weigh heavily enough on Weekes to explain his decision to decline leadership of the WFP by the time the party was being publicly formalised in November. Weekes' self-perception was the real issue:

I never saw myself as leader of the country, contrary to what people said. I was most reluctant to be in that position of leadership, to be head of the country (which is what leadership of a political party implies if the party is successful) . . . I did not feel I was the person for that . . .[7]

Weekes points out that it is the same position he had taken with leadership of the union, which he only accepted "after a lot of pressure" from the Rebels. "But on this occasion, which is a higher office politically, where you are dealing, not with just an industry but the whole country, I was **very insistent** in not wanting to do it".[8]

A certain level of self-consciousness about an academic background, that did not include graduation from college or university, is probably a key factor in explaining Weekes' tendency to impose upon himself feelings of inadequacy about leadership tasks. Williams' impact on the political culture, which implanted in people's minds a myth that academic achievement was a major criterion for fitness to lead, could have had some negative effect here. It is something Weekes failed to overcome, despite his remarkably successful trade union leadership. At this level he was successful because, once he crossed the hurdle of an inbuilt psychological resistance to assuming leadership, his natural leadership qualities, fired by his unswerving commitment to ideals, drove him to achievement.

One of the most misrepresented characteristics of Weekes therefore is the widespread belief that he is a man driven by a burning ambition to take over leadership of the country. Weekes' life certainly demonstrated ambition, strong political beliefs, and actions to foster those beliefs. But there are two important considerations in assessing Weekes politically. One is his self imposed psychological handicap where national leadership is concerned. That has made him confine his vision of himself to a person "who could assist politically, and use my position to support"[9] as he said of the way he saw himself in the WFP. The other factor is that Weekes' political involvements have been guided by principle. At the time that Tull was being assigned to Guyana and Critchlow was brought into the Senate by the PNM, Weekes could have secured that senatorship. Tull had raised the question with him and he had refused. He refused because he just had too many doubts about the direction of the

PNM. He was not a member of the party and he did not want to have that 'fixed'; which could easily have been done. In later years Weekes was again to turn down offers to enter the Senate, where they were inconsistent with his political principles. He refused to be a DLP Senator when approached by Jamadar because he did not support the DLP. In the period after the 1971 election, when two PNM members in the all PNM House of Representatives, defected to form an opposition, he again refused a Senatorship. The issue was raised with him by Panday, whom they were about to appoint to the Senate, and who wanted Weekes with him. Weekes declined because he saw Richardson and Charles, the Members of Parliament who had crossed the floor, as PNMites. He was convinced that they were just playing games to give the impression of an opposition in parliament.[10]

C.L.R. James' approach, in his all out efforts to persuade George Weekes to take up the challenge of leadership in the WFP, indicates that he was aware of the basis of Weekes' reluctance. Apart from his efforts at a personal level he made use of lectures and articles in *We The People* the organ of the WFP, even before the party was formalised, to build Weekes' self-image. James consistently pointed out the significance of Weekes contribution and analysed the importance of his position, as leader of the OWTU in the emerging social forces.

The essence of James' position is revealed in an article in *We The People*. At one level in this article he deals in the most flattering terms with Weekes the individual. James calls on the peculiar political culture of the Caribbean where the "idea of personality" is dominant, to justify the eulogy of Weekes which he incorporates in his analysis of the prevailing political conditions. James saw in Weekes the qualities which he felt were essential to a political leader. In the article he praised his political insight. He saw this demonstrated in an interview he had done with Weekes which appeared in a previous issue of *We The People*, of which James said:

> We venture to say that nowhere in the local journalism of the last few years will you find so penetrating, so unambiguous and so balanced an analysis of the contending currents in Trinidad politics.[11]

He praised Weekes for his anti-imperialism and his confidence that "the forces of democracy could defeat the imperialists and their alliance with local reaction". He praised Weekes for his oratory, referring to the President General's address at the 28th Anniversary celebrations of the union. In fact he described Weekes as "the only [orator] in the country" at the time. He praised his "sincerity and honesty of purpose, the rock on which he stands".[12]

On the whole James couches his personal praise of Weekes in very flattering descriptive language. He is consciously building up the personality of the man, trying to woo him to the idea of playing a leading role in the emerging political thrust and at the same time establishing to his audience the bona fides of Weekes for national leadership. In the end James failed on both counts. Weekes predictably emerged as a leading target for the attacks of the media in the 1966 election campaign but could not be convinced to assume leadership of the party. The masses of the people could not be convinced to switch their traditional allegiances to vote for Weekes or those with whom he was associated. In the national elections held in November 1966, all the WFP candidates lost their deposits.

The fact is the WFP was fighting against strong currents in the 1965-66 period. James was over-optimistic in his analysis of the political situation in the post-ISA period. This is demonstrated in a political analogy of Weekes and Williams which he used to illustrate his concept of the relationship between the working class and the middle class at the time:

> George Weekes has knocked out Eric Williams, knocked him out flat. That is a dramatisation of the fact that the bid of the middle classes for political leadership that they made in 1956, is now irretrievably lost.[13]

James was envisaging

> the final defeat of the middle classes of Trinidad and Tobago by the organized labour movement for the political leadership of the country . . . to lead, that is to say to have a preponderant political influence and above all a moral influence, in the future of the country, that is now the possession of organized labour and nothing on earth will be able take that possession from it.[14]

It is very likely that here James was not so much interpreting the political situation as trying to influence it by an ideological intervention. He was after all writing not as an academic observer but as a political activist.

At the time there were undeniably objective factors which could be seen as a basis for change. Factors, such as a serious chronic unemployment problem, the resort to anti-labour legislation, the ever increasing economic dominance of foreign corporations with their racist policies, the continuing visibility of whites in positions of influence, among other things had undermined the popular base of the PNM to a noticeable degree. Eventually this would be reflected in the voter turn out in the 1966 election. While 88% of the electorate had cast their votes in 1961, only 66% did so in 1966. The growing alienation of the traditional PNM support was mainly responsible for this marked decline in popular participation in the election.

But, important as the indicators of potential change were, there were also contrary indicators, both in terms of the entrenchment of the existing government and in terms of the persistence of traditional political attitudes and perceptions which would affect the electoral chances of Weekes and the WFP. The fact is, despite murmurings, the PNM still remained the predominant political force. Furthermore the disaffection which began to develop with them did not reveal itself as a disaffection for the political leadership of the middle classes. It even less signalled a more self-conscious participation of the working class through which it could assume a "preponderant political influence".

It is important to note these points because the ideas expressed here by James form an integral part of the ideological platform on which the political thrust of the WFP was built.

The WFP was born into a political situation where, to some intellectual observers, class issues seemed sufficiently stark to influence political perceptions along class lines. Central to this conception of the political situation was an assessment of the social significance of the ISA. La Rose, who was London-based but maintained a close ideological and political relationship with some leading members of the party, described this piece of legislation as "the cornerstone of the constitutional coup d'etat in Trinidad" and "the catalyst which is bringing matters to a head". He saw the government's resort to such methods as evidence that "The back of the middle class bid for power has been broken. It has suffered a telling defeat".[15]

The situation was therefore deemed to be ripe for a class based approach to politics, right in James' assessment for the national acceptance of a true leader of the working class like George Weekes. A class ideology also recommended itself as strategic to counter the traditional voting patterns which had polarised around the division of Africans and Indians.

Though the WFP campaign did not work, it cannot be said that this ideological approach solely accounted for the party's defeat. For various other reasons, which would be examined, the organisation had little chance of electoral success. But the course of national events during the 1966 election campaign, the voting pattern which emerged and subsequent political history, do indicate deficiencies in the WFP's analytical premises which made their framework inadequate for practical political involvement.

The ideology of the WFP embraced an important aspect of the material reality, class contradiction, but treated it too much as the only politically significant aspect of reality, if not virtually the whole reality. In the real distorted world of Trinidad and Tobago politics the election campaign provoked high levels of racial tension between Africans and Indians, on which neither Weekes himself nor the WFP could impact. The conflict reached such levels that in some parts of the country, Indians living in predominantly African populated areas had to move out and find temporary shelter with relatives or in community centres and schools and vice versa. Such exacerbation of racial tensions in an election period was nothing new. In 1961, the government, in a characeristic over-reaction, had declared a state of emergency in limited areas in response to incidents of communal violence. The actual voting patterns in 1966 reflected this division which allowed no space for the WFP. Or for the Liberals, the fourth party in the elections, which openly represented the interests of big business.

One can look further down the line and see that what manifested itself in 1966 was nowhere near dying at the time. The racial confrontation was not as apparent in 1971 because the electoral system broke down following the popular revolt of 1970. But the old patterns re-emerged in 1976 and 1981, though with less open hostility.

Only in 1986 there appeared to be change in the established racial voting patterns. In the December 1986 General Election, the tradition of Africans by and large voting for a perceived 'African' party and Indians voting for a perceived 'Indian' party was broken. However this did not come about because of a new non-racial political perspective in the society. In a large measure it had to do with the nature of the National Alliance for Reconstruction, the party that emerged victorious in the election. The NAR was a pragmatic coalition of racial interests. More significantly, by absorbing the Alliance,* it removed the factor of a perceived Indian party. The contest therefore became one between the 'African' PNM, and the race coalition NAR. This, coupled with the extremely high levels of national frustration with the PNM and conditions of economic crisis, accounted for a shift in voting patterns, large enough to be decisive.

An analysis of the election results indicates that the NAR, which absorbed the dominant 'Indian' party, gained overwhelming support among Indians. The support for the NAR among Africans, who could still perceive the PNM as an option for them as a racial group, was widespread enough to defeat the PNM, but nowhere near as overwhelming as it was among Indians. Logically, it would seem that both the level of Indian support and the more marked caution of African support occurred for some very traditional reasons. The NAR victory therefore represents more a triumph of maturity for the leaders, who realistically manipulated the racial factor, than a triumph of the national political psychology over racial division, which in fact has not happened. This is a very telling commentary on what the WFP was up against when they hoped that the debilitating African/Indian political schism would have been killed by the pressures on the working class since the mid 60's.

It is also significant that the party that eventually caused some shift in the established voting patterns, represented, in its own propaganda, an all-class alliance. In terms of image it was even more removed from the working class than the PNM it defeated. Except for the presence of Basdeo Panday, a prominent trade union leader, on the platform, the National Alliance for Reconstruction did not project a working class image and it

---

* The Alliance was an electoral alliance of Panday's United Labour Front, of which more is said in later chapters, and Lloyd Best's Tapia. These organisations combined to fight the 1981 general elections.

evaded the most fundamental issues facing workers. Yet it attracted a massive working class vote.

Twenty years after the WFP's bid for power and their expressed belief in the emerging political ascendancy of the working class: the NAR victory pointed to a continuing middle class hegemony in the country's electoral politics.

With the advantages of hindsight, looking back at how the political history unfolded for 20 years after the WFP bid, it is possible to appreciate the shortcomings of WFP idealism in 1966 and the problem of tackling the political power structure with the vision they did. The analytical abstraction of class was taken too literally and in too orthodox a perspective to be functional in terms of predicting political behaviour and guiding effective political strategy in the Trinidad and Tobago situation. Theoretical biases led to a mis-reading of the middle class/working class political relationship as one of confrontation. For historical reasons, this particular class relationship did not evolve in practice or appear in the people's perceptions the way it was conceived in WFP theory. 'Class' was also defined out of context with other prevailing realities in the society, which needed to be seen, not as subordinate elements in the social structure, but as integrally related components of it. In the main, the tools of analysis put the racial realities out of focus instead of creatively seeking to come to terms with their implications.

Weekes' experiences in the election campaign made him very much aware of the forces he and his party were up against. He knew that in the oil areas of his constituency it would be no easy task to translate his overwhelming popularity as leader of the OWTU into votes for him as a parliamentary representative or government leader. He could easily perceive the still dominant PNM influence among oil workers, an influence he was aware of even on his Executive in the union.

Past traditions in the society did not favour the OWTU leader in any special way as a trade unionist entering the political field. The relationship between politics and trade unionism did not evolve in Trinidad and Tobago the same way it did in other Caribbean islands. Writing in 1954, after the experiences of the first two general elections in Trinidad and Tobago based on universal adult suffrage, Dalley observed:

> Trinidad voters . . . do not, at this stage, give substantial support to trade union candidates as such.[16]

A PLUNGE INTO CONVENTIONAL POLITICS

In the post 1956 period, trade unionists per se became even less prominent in the political hierarchy than in the period of Dalley's observation. The point is not that trade unionists did not have any success at the polls in 1946 and 1950. Some did. Albert Gomes, for example, who was set up as a Premier of sorts by the British government after the 1950 election, was President of the Federated Workers Trade Union. But there was no consistent pattern where workers would vote for their trade union leaders and the electoral defeats of trade union leaders suggest that other factors were more important than trade union leadership in attracting votes. Rojas, while he was virtually unchallenged President General of the OWTU, failed to win elections in predominantly oil areas. He was defeated by the influence of Butler. McDonald Moses was wiped out in elections in Central Trinidad while he was head of the All Trinidad Sugar Estates and Factory Workers Trade Union. One of the factors which probably affected the development of a tradition identifying union leadership and political leadership in Trinidad and Tobago was the divorce of Butler from the trade union movement. As the pre-eminent working class leader he attracted political support away from the elements who worked within and led the trade unions. Another factor was the sensitivity and volatility of the racial psyche. Chauvinist Indian sentiments were deliberately invoked in the campaign to defeat Moses in the sugar belt.

As a result of these peculiarities, though politicians of whatever persuasions sought support through identification and association with the labour movement and working class issues, a pattern did not emerge where, as in say Jamaica, the struggle for political office would be a battle between competing trade union leaders.

Weekes was therefore fighting without the psychological support of tradition and against some very specific influences of the PNM. The PNM and the media were systematically cultivating the feeling that trade unionists should stay out of politics. Weekes reacted strongly to such lines in the *Guardian* of February 14th:

> You go on to criticize because I act 'politically'. What
> is wrong with acting politically?

... My aim is to get a fair share of the wealth of this country for the workers of this country. I will never abandon this crusade and I will certainly act politically to attain this objective, so do not be mistaken.

I would point out to you that the present government of Great Britain is formed by a party which arose directly out of political action by the labour unions. This is a fact that you conveniently forget in your continuous effort to persuade the workers of this country that there is something disreputable in their using their own organisation to alleviate the servile conditions in which they still live by political action.[17]

It was a theme often taken up by C.L.R. James, Bowrin and others in the campaign. In one article Bowrin pointed to the current situation in the rest of the Caribbean where trade unionists held political power. In Jamaica, Bustamante the Prime Minister had emerged from leadership in the trade union movement. Trade unionists were Chief Ministers in Antigua, St Kitts, St Vincent and Grenada.[18] Nevertheless it was tough countering the propaganda of the establishment in Trinidad and Tobago.

Weekes was also openly confronted with anti-Indian sentiment in his campaign among the mainly African oil workers. He was up against a well organised race campaign among the oil workers, who otherwise felt a strong loyalty to him based on achievement. For instance, in the Plaisance Park area where, as a result of union demands, Texaco had built houses, the workers felt a sense of gratitude to Weekes and the union. But they were affected by the subversive line of the PNM agents that he "wanted to bring in an Indian Prime Minister". This amounted to an accusation in the warped political perceptions created by the deliberate racism and divisiveness of colonialism and the opportunistic manipulation of politicians. Stephen Maharaj's chairmanship of the party was being used by the PNM elements to play upon deep seated fears and anxieties among Africans.

Initially, Weekes main base of political support was among Indians. He had never abandoned his fight for sugar workers. In the latter period of 1965 he helped them to struggle against the sellout of Anthony Geoffroy to Bhadase Maraj. Geoffroy, behind the backs of the sugar workers had struck up a deal with Bhadase to merge the rebel Sugar Workers Trade Union, which had just been through such intense struggle against Bhadase terrorism, with the rejected All Trinidad union. Weekes joined with Annamunthodo, Gowandan and others in mobilising the sugar workers against this betrayal, a deal which was eventually frustrated by Bhadase himself. In 1966, Weekes was in the forefront of the sugar workers' militant struggle against an unsatisfactory award of the Industrial Court. In fact he was coming under heavy fire from the press and other forces in the society, including some trade unionists, for his speeches at protest rallies denouncing the Court award and for leading vociferous demonstrations against it. Weekes therefore was working from a firm base he himself had developed among Indian workers. The fact that Stephen Maharaj, an Indian, was leader of the party was a decided political advantage in the sugar worker dominated sections of Weekes' constituency.

But he was to see this political base dissolve as the campaign heightened. The turning point was the return of Dr Rudranath Capildeo, the leader of the opposition Democratic Labour Party. Dr Capildeo, a Trinidadian physicist and mathematician lecturing at the University of London, had been prevailed upon to return to Trinidad & Tobago in 1961 to lead the fight of the DLP against the PNM. He was built up by his supporters as the Indian Doctor to fight the African Doctor. His presence in 1961 raised the academic image of the DLP and for a time, as his reputation in his field spread, he seemed to be building national appeal. After being elected into Parliament as Leader of the Opposition, he returned to his university job in England. When he was brought back in 1966, there was a widespread belief that Eric Williams had been influential in getting him to return to bolster the DLP with its 'Indian' image, the effect of which would be to split the voting population into ethnic camps and squeeze the WFP (and the Liberals) out of the picture.

There was justification for believing that there was collusion between the PNM and Capildeo. After all, the government had seen to it that he received his income as a parliamentarian, contrary to parliamentary regulations, while spending virtually the entire term abroad. He had also been quoted in the press as making statements in favour of Williams' policies which could come from any PNM fanatic. To take a sample from the *Daily Mirror* of 30th July 1965:

> (Dr Capildeo) complimented the government for maintaining law and order in spite of the situation.
> He said he wanted the people of Trinidad and Tobago to have peace and opportunity for advancement. And if it meant 'that the present government had to stay in power for 20 years', he would subscribe to it, so long as there was such peace and opportunity for advancement.

Collusion or not however, Capildeo's return had the desired effect. Weekes saw the numbers of his campaign workers rapidly dwindle. Some of them moved very apologetically out of the WFP camp. They rationalized it this way: oil workers were not supporting Weekes and if they (the sugar workers) supported him they would just be splitting the opposition vote and causing the PNM to win. "We would like to support you Comrade Weekes, but this seat is a DLP seat."[19] Traditional loyalties were stronger than trade union ties.

Weekes knew the die was cast long before the results of the polls on November 7th 1966 confirmed the defeat of the WFP. As objectively as he could, he weighed the pros and cons of his bid for political office.

On the positive side, he knew the advantages he had come into the fight with, his talent as a speaker, his record of achievement for labour, his popularity as a union leader among African and Indian workers, his commitment, the drive, energy and idealism which he brought to his task. Weekes had a clear picture in mind about the kind of representation he would bring his constituency, if elected:

> Not that I thought by going into parliament itself I would change anything. But I could use my position as an elected representative to organise the constituency, in a way that would radicalize the whole approach to the political situation in the country, through the example of living in the constituency and working among the people.[20]

He was impressed by the example of Cheddi Jagan in Guyana, who from a position of sole representative of his party in Parliament from 1947 to 1953, was able to so build an image of a different politics that the PPP which he organised was able to gain electoral victory.

Weekes saw himself establishing a permanent constituency office to service his constituents. His plan was to use the salary he would get as a parliamentarian to pay people to work there on a full time basis.

But there were too many forces acting against him, for him to cross the hurdle of gaining a seat in parliament through the elections. Despite the fact that he had not accepted the position of Chairman of the party, a lot of the image of the WFP revolved around his person. His reputation and the machinations of the media saw to that. The publicly expressed fears of established interests in the society preceded his announced entry into politics. As early as July 1965, the *Guardian* editorialised:

... The Government itself speaks of the need for a genuine opposition. But not all conservatives are equally keen to see a resurgence on the left. One of the specters haunting them is of Mr Weekes getting sugar workers, as well as oil workers behind him and shifting from wage demands to active politics. Such a phenomenon is deeply feared among businessmen.[21]

His enemies revitalized the communist bogey. Williams, always eager to take up the pen or the verbal dagger where Weekes was involved, wrote in *The Nation* of July 15th 1966:

A specter is haunting the trade union movement, especially active among the Oilfields Workers Trade Union, and concentrating in the sugar belt. The specter is the political ideology of MARXISM dressed up in the white robes of purity.

Williams went on to state:

The Oilfields Workers Trade Union has already been bought and sold in the auction without a murmur at the cheapest price. Cheaply because they have allowed themselves to be drugged into believing that the activity of their Executive, or a section of it is honestly and truthfully directed against the Industrial Stabilisation Act.

He portrayed the OWTU membership as "pawns" and "lambs", in contrast to the images of a "section of their Executive", "ambitious Marxists" who want to bring about a revolution in Trinidad and Tobago "under the boot of the Russian soldier and the tracks of Russian tanks".

He tried to make other workers and unionists feel threatened. Oil gone — sugar going, as he put it and identified dock workers as the next target, with electricity workers to follow.

Even though Weekes often made verbal replies to criticisms, when he spoke on platforms, or sought to reply through the daily newspapers or *The Vanguard*, by and large he was not the wily politician, the type of individual who would systematically cultivate an image to suit his involvement in conventional politics. He continued to act in the same way and do the same things which his enemies seized on to create a negative image of him. For example, in his involvement with the protests of sugar workers in 1966, he never concerned himself with how the attacks in the press, to which he was opening himself, would affect him politically. A good example of how he put ideals before any strategic calculation was his decision to attend the Tricontinental Conference in, of all places, Cuba, in January 1966. He was under pressure from accusations that he was a "communist", meaning all the things that American propaganda wants it to mean. The WFP was under attack as being a communist party. Predictably the newspapers seized upon this "evidence" of Weekes' links with communist subversion. Weekes was unapologetic. He stated his position very unambiguously in response to a *Guardian* attack on February 14th 1966:

> ... my visit to Cuba has given me added strength and added enthusiasm for my own just cause. I have found that it is indeed possible for the working man to get a fair deal if only he can find leaders of courage and honesty.[22]

Williams was to lambast him on political platforms for the visit as well. To quote the Prime Minister in his autobiography:

> I issued my own warning to the Castroites ...
>
> Go out and finish up with this Marxist ideology, which goes to Havana, Cuba and dares to sit down and take part in subversive resolutions against the legal government of Trinidad and Tobago.[23]

In a thoroughly miseducated society the "communist" image has been a "specter" "haunting" Weekes probably far more than he realizes. It has been a key factor in the dualism of the country's reaction to him. The radicalism is fine for securing better wages and working conditions but anathema for government leadership.

In 1966 Weekes was also fighting within a party that lacked material resources and the government was using the resources of the state to campaign. Williams embarked on official 'Meet the People' tours, raising his profile in the media. He hosted elaborate state visits, Haile Selassie, to play on racial sentiments and the Queen of England, accompanied by her husband the Duke of Edingburgh, to draw out every colonial instinct in the population.

Looking back in 1986 Weekes calmly assessed another factor that operated against him in his first and only bid in the conventional political arena. Inexperience. He admits that an election campaign in the wider society was a different ball game to what he knew in the union. He went into the election "without any type of plan" where the campaign was concerned, and relied on achievement to recommend him to the electorate.

This is a reflection of the organisational weakness and inexperience of the WFP as a party as well. Stephen Maharaj was a seasoned campaigner. But the party lacked enough people with this kind of experience. C.L.R. James had a wide ranging international experience, but in organisation and political activity of a different type. His experience in the PNM did not take in any of the general elections. The party therefore had the benefit of James' theoretical insights but that was not combined with enough of the practical on-the-ground know-how for an effective electoral campaign.

Another reality of 1966 which affected the WFP is that there were no organizational structures in place on which to build a working class political thrust. The OWTU could superficially have been regarded as the most important unit in such a political movement. But that is not the basis on which even its Executive was organised. Weekes points out that the Executive was not selected based on ideology and there were in fact, not just PNM but anti-socialist members of the Executive. That even created a problem for the education of the workers. The Assistant Secretary at the time Jeremiah Antoine, who was in charge of education, was a PNMite who in no way shared Weekes' vision of politics and society and in Weekes' judgement used the position more opportunistically than anything else.

Difficulties for Weekes within the union went even further. There was a resurgence of deliberate attempts to undermine his leadership during 1966. It reached a level where he was moved to say to the Annual Conference in April 1966:

> This may be the last Annual Conference I will attend as President General. There are intrigues in high places in the union to remove me from office.[24]

Operating within a political culture which did not in itself produce the kind of class conscious orientation to government on which the WFP pitched its appeal, there was no way to make serious inroads into the politics without a solid organizational base. The new orientation could not be created by ideological statement and circumstances did not exist which would galvanize organisation under WFP in a short period of time. There was no atmosphere of upheaval like 1970 would bring, or disillusionment profound enough to upset the psyche of racial politics.

Once the election results were out, and it was known that all the WFP candidates had lost their deposits, Weekes' enemies began to smile. Inside and outside of the union.

> The PNM was now saying that I had lost the election. I was rejected by oil workers and sugar workers. So what could I claim now.
>
> Even those Executive members who were quiet before the elections were now looking at me in a way as though hoping I would lose whatever popularity I had so they would be able to take advantage of the situation.[25]

They thought that George Weekes was down and out this time. They knew the man. Yet strangely enough they did not know him.

CHAPTER 11

THE EVE OF THE STORM

On the evening of May 12th 1969, as George Weekes ascended the narrow wooden stairway leading to the headquarters of the Transport and Industrial Workers Trade Union, his head was bowed deep in thought. TIWU, now the center of a national storm, shared the space atop the Trestrail Building on Broadway in downtown Port of Spain with another militant union, the National Union of Hotels Foods Beverages and Allied Workers. Weekes knew a decision would be taken that night which would have far reaching implications. He was mentally prepared for what was to come. The Transport union, led by Joe Young, had confronted the government head on with a strike by bus workers which was now at the end of its third week. This was the most open defiance of the ISA. The prolonged, massive and successful bus strike was really saying, to hell with the law. It was saying, to hell with the Industrial Court, since the strike was provoked by an award of the Industrial Court on the question of wages for bus workers. It was saying to hell with the government which was supposed to uphold the backward law and its institutions. And everyone knew it. Everyone realized that fundamentally, no matter what the rationale for the strike, these were the implications of the action taken by bus workers. The fear of the establishment was:

> Once let it appear that the law can be trampled upon
> with impunity if a sufficient number of people set out
> to do so, and the last state of this country will be a
> thousand times worse than the first.[1]

The government, faced by growing signs of rebellion in the late 60's, was cautious about resorting to open force. They were gradually undermining public support for the bus workers by a superior propaganda thrust. Their trump card to break the strike

171

was skilfully canvassed sympathy for the "poor school children" who could not get to school with the buses not running. That was the effective line to justify escorting the first buses through the picket lines, driven by scabs under armed protection. "Exclusively for school children", the Government claimed. Police protection was also extended to the homes of the scabs in order to reassure workers who might weaken as the strike wore on and the situation became more politically charged and tense. Therefore, as the school bus service built up, the trickle back to work became more pronounced. Workers retaliated by stoning some buses, gelignite was thrown into one, and some strike breakers received scares from molotov cocktails thrown into their homes. But the few bold acts of violence against buses and scabs, carried out despite police protection, were not effective enough to hold back would-be strike breakers. A limited general service was introduced — pity on the suffering public was the theme now. For every bus that rolled the corporation spoke as though there were ten, further demoralizing some workers.

The state was becoming more decisive in its fight back. They started to lay charges against workers on strike. 200 had already received summonses to appear in court for offenses under the Industrial Stabilisation Act. The union and those supportive of the bus workers had to do something urgently to stop the inevitable erosion of the strike, no matter what the risks. The alternative was to weakly concede defeat and face the consequences which could be anticipated for breaking the law. Without a doubt the government would want to set an example to preserve the notorious ISA.

These thoughts had the OWTU President General preoccupied as he climbed step by step to a fateful decision that evening. He was reflecting against the background of a meeting he had just held trying hard, but not successfully, to get oil workers to give their full support to the bus workers. He really felt he could resign at that point if members of the OWTU were not prepared to give their total support, to go as far as to strike on this critical issue. Even as such thoughts whirled around in his head, every stairway of imagination led to one point — the first bus scheduled to leave the Port of Spain terminus at 6.00 a.m. the next morning, the bus that would be the focus of attention at the meeting he was about to attend.

172

THE EVE OF THE STORM

When the meeting was assembled Weekes looked at the faces around the table. Here was a combination that in itself spelled change in the society. There were the trade unionists — a TIWU team led by Young, Nunez (formerly of NUGE) and Gowandan; Beddoe and other officers represented the National Union of Foods, Hotels Beverages and Allied Workers, and he himself was there from the OWTU. There were the politicians — Vernon Jamadar, official leader of the opposition in Parliament* and fellow DLP parliamentarian, Alloy Lequay; Peter Farquhar, leader of the Liberal Party. There were the university lecturers — Lloyd Best, an economist, James Millette, dean of the History Department. On the very morning before the meeting the Public Transport Service Corporation had refused to meet the union negotiating team accompanied by these two lecturers as advisers. There were lawyers — Basdeo Panday, Lennox Pierre; university students — Geddes Granger**, Syl Lowhar, Dave Darbeau***, David Murray****, Kelshall Bodie. Except for Lowhar, the students were there as representatives of the National Joint Action Committee. (Lowhar and Lloyd Best were members of Tapia). A number of other NJAC members were there too, among them Gerald Bryce, a young building contractor, Abdul Malik (Delano De Coteau), later to emerge as one of the country's top poets, Earl Lewis, an engineer and small proprietor. Darcus Howe was there too, a Trinidadian resident in London and closely associated with C.L.R. James.

This meeting was a continuation of a similar one from the night before. More to confirm decisions taken then than anything else, to work out the mechanics of time and other aspects of strategy for when the first bus was due to roll in the morning. Everyone seemed to share that feeling, everyone except Lloyd Best that is. As the meeting began, he asked to present his carefully considered views. He placed in front of him an academic text, which must have had him up all of the previous night, following the meeting. He started to read. It was

---

* Jamadar took over leadership of the Democratic Labour Party (DLP) in 1967 when Dr Capildeo forfeited his seat in Parliament by missing seven consecutive sittings.
** Granger later changed his name to Makandal Daaga.
*** Darbeau later changed his name to Khafra Kambon.
**** David Murray later changed his name to Aiyegoro Ome.

all about the "Options", in typical Bestian language and style —
academic terminology interspersed with popular phrases, folk
sayings and sports analogies (whether to carry Williams the full
distance and beat him on points or to go for a quick knockout).
As Best turned page after page, Weekes sat quietly through it
observing the growing restlessness around the table. He could see
Panday heading for explosion. Panday did explode. He jumped
to his feet and proclaimed, "Brothers, I did not come here for this.
We took a decision last night. If no compromise by the
Corporation or the Government this morning, we going to block
buses. Either we going or we not going. Who decide we going?"
He received ready approval for putting an end to Best's out-of-
context, and, in the circumstances, paralysing analysis. The
meeting sat down to discuss the business on hand. The buses must
not continue to roll so easily. The strike must be turned, by a
dramatic gesture, into a more serious political confrontation.
Everyone to report to TIWU Headquarters at 5.00 a.m . . .

Weekes made the journey from Marabella, on the outskirts of
San Fernando, where he was now residing, to Port of Spain on
time that morning. With the time to go down to the bus terminal,
a short walk away, rapidly approaching, it seemed there would
be some notable absences. Earl Lewis picked up the phone and
called Millette at home. He promised to be on his way shortly.
The group made its way down to the point of confrontation. The
riot squad was out in full force. The Black Marias* stood heavy,
sullen and silent in the semi light of the dawn. The police
inspectors in their khaki uniforms were rapidly exchanging
communications on their walkie talkies. Shocked workers, on
their way to their jobs, in the normally peaceful hours of the
morning, started to gather as they disembarked from taxis on
South Quay and were confronted with the unusual scene of guns,
riot staffs and shields, helmets and tear gas masks. The sun's rays
gradually grew stronger as the time approached for the first bus
to leave. Joe Young and other union officials were conferring
with striking workers who had set up camp at the terminus. The
workers were not to get involved. Weekes stood quietly at the
exit of the terminus with the small group who had marched from
the TIWU headquarters.

---

* Police vans for transporting prisoners

THE EVE OF THE STORM

Six o'clock was near on the morning of May 13th 1969. Tension was mounting. The police were being deployed into strategic positions. Clive Nunez took control of a microphone system which the workers had set up on the opposite side of the road. The plan was for Clive to stay out of the fray. Without a doubt there were going to be arrests and it was decided that he would have to hold the fort on the outside.

The rumblings of the bus engine could be heard distinctly from on the pavement. Notable absentees from the previous night's meeting, including Vernon Jamadar and Alloy Lequay, remained absent. Weekes remembered Granger's knowing insistence after the meeting the night before to let everybody sleep at the union headquarters. This suggestion had not found acceptance.

It was time for the bus to roll. The protesting group and the riot squad faced each other from opposite sides of the exit. The senior police officers stood in-between. They gave the signal for the bus to depart. Weekes steeled himself for the encounter. The past few years had been filled with many demonstrations for him. But he knew that this one was different. It was different from the marches of 1967 or 1968.

In 1967 oil workers, in a major battle against retrenchment at Shell and British Petroleum, held several militant demonstrations. The mood was bitter. They felt that they were not just fighting the oil companies. They were also up against the government, the Labour Congress and the nefarious ISA. That year, in an early meeting with the government, following BP's announced intention to lay off nearly 1500 workers, a union team led by Weekes had received an assurance of government's concern from Williams. But as the situation developed and BP commenced its layoffs, the government was silent.

As for the Labour Congress, their behaviour was even more reprehensible. OWTU threatened to withdraw affiliation in the face of the repeated refusals of the national labour body to at least issue a statement of support for the oil workers in their battle against retrenchment. The law also hung like a millstone around the necks of the workers. The ISA made the Industrial Court the centre of the confrontation. With all these frustrations adding to the dread prospects of massive retrenchment in the oil industry, Weekes had the oil belt on the boil with demonstrations.

Despite the heat of those times, the ever present threat of physical conflict between demonstrators and heavily armed police, the tension charged atmosphere did not equal the suspense of this moment. In the angry days of 1967, the oil workers were out in their thousands. And the demonstrations were legal.

In June 1968, when five unions combined to lead a massive demonstration, a 'March of Resistance' against retrenchment (which was hitting hard in the oil industry and on the docks) and unemployment, Weekes walked at the head of over ten thousand protestors. High levels of frustration over joblessness and social ostracism created a potentially explosive environment. The marchers sang their own version of the chorus of Calypso Rose's "Fire in yuh wire" giving it dire shades of meaning. The city echoed with the chanted slogan of H. Rap Brown, "BURN BABY BURN". The mood was menacing. But the demonstration was legal.

Now as the bus was heading for the exit, the group of protestors stepping forward to block its path was small, and the demonstration was illegal. The stakes were high. In the words of the *Guardian*, a few days before:

It is obvious that this strike, ... has resolved itself, despite assertions to the contrary, into a political confrontation with the government, with the ISA as a rallying point, using the strike as a political weapon for the repeal of the Act.[2]

In fact the strike was seen as more than a political challenge to the government and challenge to the ISA. It was seen as a challenge to the rule of law itself as it obtained in the society. A debate was sparked on the question of the primacy of justice over law and order. When those branded as 'radicals' in the society, like George Weekes, raise such questions it is one thing. Such individuals are considered "iconoclasts who would pull down laws, institutions and the very fabric of society in one fell swoop"[3]. But when those considered to be responsible voices, echo such sentiments, it causes more alarm. The support for the strike and suggestions for government intervention of a nature that would contradict the court ruling, on the grounds of justice, came from such quarters as the official parliamentary opposition and, quite surprisingly, the *Catholic News*. The *Trinidad Guardian*, for ever the ideological arm of the system was moved to comment:

The workers and the country generally must make up
their minds as to whether we are going to accept the
rule of law or not. This is the main principle at stake.[4]

Weekes looked at the approaching bus. He looked at the riot
squad at the ready to defend the position of the government, to
defend the ISA and to defend the rule of law. And he thought
about the relative position of weakness from which the union and
its associates, those who put justice before law and order, were
fighting.

TIWU was in fact out on a limb where the labour movement
was concerned. On the very first morning of the strike, W.W.
Sutton, then Acting President of Congress, had found himself at
the bus terminal, along with Vas Stanford, whose union
represented a minority of bus workers, trying to influence
workers to go back on their jobs[5]. Despite some verbal
expressions of support, which came later, Congress leadership
was not prepared to do anything practical to help. In fact they
seemed determined to demotivate workers of the Congress
unions from supporting the strike. They had even come close to
calling off the May Day demonstration on the pretext of
"tensions" caused by the strike. Critchlow and the NUGFW
team had led an internal struggle to save the May Day
demonstration. But all it had done was to demonstrate the
growing bitterness and division in the movement over the strike.

There were two May Day parades in Port of Spain, in
addition to the OWTU parade in San Fernando. One of the
parades in Port of Spain was passive and hypocritical — the
official Congress parade. The other was angry, positive and
militant, combining TIWU, National Union of Foods and
NJAC. The militant marchers invaded Woodford Square and set
up microphones a few hundred feet away from where Congress
was conducting their meeting from the bandstand. Thousands of
workers turned their backs on the Congress leadership to listen to
the leaders of the 'rebel' unions and NJAC, forcing Congress to
wind up their meeting early.[6]

The bus was drawing closer. Some of the policemen were
nervous, uncomfortable about what they were now called upon
to do. But there was hate in the eyes of others. They had been
heat-primed for just such an occasion, caged day after day in steel
can vans in the hot sun. Inwardly they had snarled as they

sweated through the torturous hours, silently cursing "lawbreaking strikers", the "trouble makers" and "agitators" - Joe Young, George Weekes, Geddes Granger and the rest. For their cause (whether right or wrong; who cared in a sweltering van after all these weeks!), the senior cops (strategically) made them sit and sweat and burn . . .

Weekes reflected on the fact that he too was out on a limb, unable to get the kind of support from his union that he felt the situation demanded. Now was really the opportunity to get rid of the ISA. The Labour Congress was calling for repeal. Several groups of the ruling PNM were calling for amendments and the party's General Council had mandated its labour committee to study the issue. Cabinet itself had set up a committee to study amendments. They were reacting to the pressures. But with the bus coming one way and the police another, Weekes knew that the struggle over the ISA was caught up between those who were afraid to fight and those who would put loyalty to the PNM before anything else . . .

An inspector, shouting on his megaphone, commanded the demonstrators to get out of the way of the bus. Another one called the bus on. The driver looked at the advancing human wall in his path and uncertainly edged the bus forward. Men and machine headed for each other. The men determinedly, the machine haltingly. The bus came to a stop with the protesting bodies pressed against it. The police were given the order and charged. Some of the protestors were just held and flung into a waiting Maria, backed close to the scene. Blows were rained on others as they were dragged from in front of the bus. Weekes and Young were among the last clinging on to the front of the bus being backed step by step as the driver kept edging the bus forward, urged on by a police inspector.

Weekes was the last man holding on to the bus in a drama that looked more and more like it would end with him under the advancing tons of metal. The inspector was becoming more insistent that the driver drive the bus, and the driver himself was coming forward with increasingly threatening jerks. But Weekes would not let go. Some policemen, mindful of the oncoming bus, were striking blows from a cautious distance. Others were trying to pull the OWTU President General away. The bus was almost in the centre of the street with Weekes pushing against it as though he had the strength of Sampson. He had become oblivious to the danger, the expressions of horror on the faces of onlookers, oblivious to everything but his determination not to yield voluntarily as he shoved and leaned on the bus with all his might, doing what he had come to do.

A fatal end seemed imminent.

But on the verge of what looked like certain tragedy, a group of policemen were able to drag him away and throw him bodily into the van along with the other men, but not before an exulting policeman got in a blow to his chest while his hands were held behind his back. The policeman blurted out that he had long awaited the opportunity to do that.

As the arrested group were being driven off to the cells at Police Headquarters on St Vincent Street, the voice of Clive Nunez could be heard clearly on the microphone, condemning the actions of state and police in the whole affair.

It was too much for the pent up frustrations of the police. They pounced on Nunez with an unbridled ferocity. The crowd around hardly had time to gasp or voice protest against the brutal punishment being inflicted by several robust policemen on one small man, now sprawled in the middle of the street. The police, who pointedly wore no identification numbers, charged madly into their midst, swinging riot staffs indiscriminately. An old man coming to take up work at the terminus, dock workers disembarking from taxis, women on their way to work, striking bus workers, dazed witnesses to the morning's earlier excitement, who had simply stood by as onlookers when confronted with the unexpected drama, all felt the weight of the riot staffs. A stunned country was given the first taste of open police brutality against a mass of unarmed and peaceful citizens in the era of Independence.

The first bus of May 13th was off, with armed police riding shotgun. Second and third and fourth buses would follow. Weekes knew at this point that the establishment had won another battle. But he had a strong feeling that the people were winning the war. Within this small group he could sense the turning tide. No one was overly bothered by the blows they had received. Even when they were thrown into the stinking cell, spirits remained buoyant. This was Weekes' first experience of a cell. It was a first experience for almost everyone else. The over used toilet that could not flush in one corner, the many signs scratched on the walls, some hand painted in human excretion by demented former inmates, the cockroaches crawling under the two dirty sleeping boards, the unswept concrete floor, all these sights and the stench were new experiences.

When Nunez was dumped in with everyone else, he was badly bruised, hurt and shaken by his experiences. But generally, the way the various individuals had adapted to the morning's events, coming as they did from various backgrounds, pointed to a tough edge developing in the social consciousness.

Weekes had seen something like it before in the many trade union battles he had fought. For example, when the determination of oil workers had for a second time forestalled BP's retrenchment plans. In 1967 the union's success was not as complete as in 1963. There was now the ISA to contend with and there were some divisions in the union leadership. 582 workers went out. 236 of them were directly sent home by the company, with agreement from the Industrial Court. The other 346 accepted the company's offered concessions for voluntary retirement.[7] But nearly 900 jobs had been saved, mainly through the forcefulness of Weekes' leadership. At a later date, the Court eroded this position by agreeing to allow the company to send home another 173 workers by January 1969. For those who went home, the compensation packages secured were very reasonable in terms of the times. These achievements had come because workers had shown their steel in the battle for jobs.

What was striking Weekes as significant now is that the people in the cells were not bus workers. In the main they were not even people directly affected by the fate of the bus workers. Unionists were present of course. There was Young, the President of TIWU, and there were other TIWU officers — Nunez, Gowandan, Sylvester Mondesir and Carlton Rosemain. Weekes himself and Francis Beddoe were fellow trade unionists giving their support. But the unionists were actually outnumbered by non-unionists. You had Panday, who could have stuck to making a professional contribution as a lawyer. The same applied to Lennox Pierre. You had Granger, up until just recently president of the Students Guild at the University of the West Indies, St Augustine, and president of a very middle class group, Pegasus. There were other university students, Dave Darbeau, on the verge of his final exams, David Murray, Kelshall Bodie. Weekes looked at Stephen Maharaj, a friend and political colleague from since the Butler days. They had been through

ht: Corporal George Weekes
(standing right) with fellow soldiers
[o]f the 1st Batallion Caribbean
[Re]giment at the town of Suez, Egypt,
1945. *Below*: At a United Nations
[Co]nference on Trade and
[De]velopment in Geneva, 1964. His
[next] child, a daughter Genieve, was
[bor]n while he was there.

Above: A meeting of the OWTU being addressed by Adrian Cola Rienzi, who was the union's first President General and served from 1937–42. *Right above*: Early Rebels: Walter Annamunthodo (1st from left) and George Weekes; with Cyril Gonzales (2nd from left), George Bowrin (4th from left) and Theresa Weekes (seated). *Right below*: George Weekes on a demonstration with three of his children. From left to right: Genieve, Gail and Christopher. *Below*: Signing and celebrating the Texaco-OWTU agreement in June 1963, the first major negotiations carried out by George Weekes as President General. The photograph shows from right to left: Cyril Gonzales, George Weekes and E.G. Stibbs.

Above: Raffique Shah being greeted by friends and supporters leaving the Royal Jail.
Left above: Workers' demonstration. *Left below*: Theresa Weekes welcoming A.N.R.
Robinson, Prime Minister since 1986, at the T&TEC
Sports Club in Port of Spain
during the State of Emergency.
S. Ali and Doodnath Maharaj,
the present General Secretary of
the OWTU, are standing on the
left. *Right*: George Weekes being
greeted by Lionel Beckles,
General Secretary of the OWTU
from 1968–73, who tried to
subvert Weekes' leadership in the
union in favour of PNM policy
in the early 1970s.

Labour Day 1974. *Above*: The lorry leading the demonstration carries Errol McLeod, the present President General of the OWTU, standing on the left; George Weekes, standing on the right; and T.U.B. Butler in front. And *Right*: T.U.B. Butler addresses the crowd at the spot in Fyzabad where La Brea Charles was killed by the police, who mistook him for Butler and shot him dead. *Below*: T.U.B. Butler being decorated by George Weekes.

Right: Weekes with Lionel Bannister, who was General Secretary of the OWTU from 1973–82. Desmond Allum, Attorney-at-Law, who defended Shah after the 1970 February Revolution, is standing on the left.

Above: George Weekes addressing the crowd from the OWTU headquarters at Paramount Building before the start of the march for 'bread, justice and peace' on Bloody Tuesday, March 18th 1975.

Left: Weekes gassed and arrested on the Bloody Tuesday march.

Above: Leaders of the United Labour Front on a Labour Day demonstration in the mid-1970s. From left to right: Joe Young, Basdeo Panday, George Weekes, Raffique Shah and Clive Nunez.

Right: Labour Day demonstration, June 19th 1977. Left to right: C.L.R. James, at that time living in Trinidad in an OWTU house, George Weekes and John La Rose.

The OWTU National Demonstration on the debt crisis in Woodford Square on October 23rd 1985. *Right*: George Weekes addressing the crowd. David Abdulah, the present OWTU Treasurer and Education Officer, is sitting on the right. *Below*: The listening crowd.

Above: The **CIDWIC** (Committee In Defence of West Indian Cricket) demonstration in 1986, against the presence in the English test team of Graham Gooch and other cricketers who had played in South Africa, being attacked outside the Queens Park Oval by the Tactical Force of the Trinidad and Tobago Police Force. *Right*: demonstrating against apartheid. Horace Scott, the present 2nd Vice President of the OWTU, is on the far left.

Above: Striking workers outside the Texaco headquarters.

Left: Dancing with his wife Theresa at an OWTU ball.

Right: Greeting the winner of the OWTU 50th Anniversary cycling race, June 18th 1987.

Below: Labour Day June 19th 1987, the march to Fyzabad. Leading the march: Bennett Berkeley, Boodram Jattan, Chris Lawrence, Basdeo Panday, John La Rose, George Weekes and Sam Maharaj.

Above left: Presenting a long service award to Thelma Williams. *Above right*: Walter Annamunthodo pays tribute to George Weekes.

George Weekes retires after 25 years as President General in the year of the OWTU's 50th Anniversary celebrations.

Below left: Greeted by Lennox Pierre. *Below right*: Doodnath Maharaj decorates the retiring President General with a specially created OWTU Labour Star.

Above: Handing over his gavil and the keys to his office to the incoming Acting President General, Errol McLeod. McLeod was later elected President General in the national union elections. *Below*: Receiving the Trinity Cross, the highest national honour awarded by the Government of Trinidad and Tobago, from President Noor Hussanali on August 31st 1987, the 25th anniversary of Independence Day.

VANGUARD

PRICE ONE PENNY   —ESTABLISHED 1939—   PRICE ONE PENNY

VOL. 8   VANGUARD, SATURDAY, AUGUST 2, 1947.   No. 436

TENTH ANNIVERSARY CELEBRATED IN FITTING STYLE

The Oilfields Workers' Trade Union celebrated its tenth anniversary at the Palm's Club, San Fernando, in fitting style last Sunday. From early members and guests wended their way to the club premises to be on time. The hall was suitably decorated.

His Excellency the Governor and Lady Shaw and party journeyed to San Fernando by railway special coach to identify themselves with the celebrations. They were met at the railway by Mr. J. F. F. Rojas, President-General and Mr. Ralph Mentor, General Secretary. The Governor's party consisted of Sir Errol Dos Santos, Colonial Secretary and Lady Dos Santos, Miss Joyce Burnham, Social Welfare Officer, Mr. R. Allan Ross, Industrial Adivce and Mrs. Muller, Mr. Perkins, General Manager of Railways and Mrs. Perkins and Major A. Bolus, the Governor's Private Secretary.

At the Club House, a group of ushers led by Mr. McDonald Moses, Assistant General Secretary, Ralph St. Lewis, First Vice-President, Cyril Gonzales, Second Vice-President and John E. Commissiong, Treasurer, received the guests and conducted them to their seats, whilst Mrs. Vera Moses at the piano entertained them with musical items.

After delivering his address of welcome Mr. Rojas, on behalf of oil workers, presented His Excellency with a miniature oil derrick as a memento of the occasion; whilst Miss Elvina Rojas, daughter of the President General, presented Lady Shaw with a lovely bouquet of flowers.

Mr. McDonald Moses read the congratulatory messages received; Mr. Ralph Mentor gave a review of the Union's activities after which Mr. T. Malcolm Milne, Commissioner of Income Tax and former Registrar of Trade Unions, conducted the unveiling ceremony re the portraits of Messrs. Adrian Cola Rienzi J. F. F. Rojas, Ralph Mentor and McDonald Moses.

His Excellency then addressed the gathering after which all lustily sang Labour's song "We are Comrades and Brothers". Cock-tails followed and the crowd dispersed with the singing of God Save the King.

In opening the proceedings Mr. Rojas spoke as follows:
Your Excellency, Lady Shaw, Ladies and Gentlemen: I wish to extend to you a cordial welcome to

JOHN F. F. ROJAS

this celebration of the tenth anniversary of the Oilfields Workers' Trade Union. As President of the Union I wish on behalf of the workers to particularly thank His Excellency and Lady Shaw and our distinguished guests for accepting our invitation and taking time off from their multifarious duties to associate themselves with us on this happy occasion. I assure Your Excellency and Lady Shaw that we appreciate this gesture of goodwill and sympathy and are profoundly grateful to you.

Ten years ago the Oilfields Workers' Trade Union was founded. Trade unionism was then very new to the Colony. Employers as a whole, were jealous and suspicious of any encroachment on their rights of individual bargaining. All associations or collections of workers were looked upon as subversive and any member of the professional class who dared to associate with a trade union was looked upon as a Communist and revolutionary. Under such conditions it is not surprising that at first our Union met with hostility, then subjected to severe trials and criticisms but finally accepted and recognized as the sole bargaining medium of the workers in the oil industry.

At the time when the Union was founded, working conditions and wages in the industry had not kept pace with modern trends and conceptions in progressive and civilised countries, and the demands formulated by the pioneering leaders were stoutly opposed and the leadership had to face misinformed criticism and hostility. But the honesty of purpose and the selfless devotion to duty and the sacrifices made by the leadership in those early days won recognition and both conditions of employment and wages were substantially improved and today the Union can boast of the industrial relationship with the employers which is second to none in Trinidad and for that matter in the British West Indies.

Today we can recall with pardonable pride that while ten years ago the minimum wage in the industry was as low as seven cents per hour and the maximum was only twenty-four cents, at present the minimum wage has increased to fifteen cents per hour while the maximum has also increased to thirty-six cents plus eleven cents hour war bonus.

Housing conditions were in many instances an eyesore and a disgrace to a civilised community. As a result of trade union presentation, housing both the industry and have been considerably proved. While this problem has not yet been completely solved, it is encouraging to note that both industry and Government are endeavour

(Continued on page 2)

Above: 10th anniversary edition of OWTU newspaper *Vanguard*.

many a mass campaign together. Stephen could have stuck to his drugstore and confined his politics to the conventional arena. There was Earl Lewis, a very emphatic speaker who was associated both with Millette's newly-formed Moko organisation and NJAC. He was there talking as usual and taking his lock up in stride. Darcus Howe, another non-unionist who was London-based, was no stranger to the rough side of the police. He had previously experienced arrest in Trinidad in his early days of association with the Renegades steelband, and in London, where he was involved in the Black Movement.

Most telling of all Weekes felt was the presence of Peter Farquhar. Three years ago, Weekes was branding Farquhar's Liberal Party as the instrument of big business, with ample justification. He pictured Farquhar in the 1966 election run up starring in a Madison Avenue-style, packaged campaign. Farquhar's platform appearances were preceded by films in which he was featured. His calculatedly late entries at public meetings were heralded by blasting music and lusty standing cheers, led from a rostrum dominated by white businessmen. Here was Peter now in prison on a workers' issue, shrugging off the licks he received on the way to the police van.

Farquhar was backing up by actions, statements he had made during the course of the strike. Seven days before the blockage of the bus he had said:

> The time for propaganda of words is over and the time for propaganda of deeds is here.[8]

The philosophical positions Farquhar had expressed reflected the ideological currents that were overturning traditional views in the society:

> What was it the Transport and Industrial Workers Union has taught the people of Trinidad and Tobago for the first time? They have taught them that law that does not bring justice was no law. They have taught them that order that means hunger was no order at all. They have taught them that law was not the prized property of Dr Eric Williams, Mr Justice Hyatali or the Police, but law was the property of the people of Trinidad and Tobago.
>
> There are some people who got frightened when the people took the law into their own hands, but there is where the law belonged — to the people.[9]

There had to be some fundamental stirring in the society to elicit such a conceptualization of the law from the leader of the Liberal Party, some stirring far deeper than the traditional politics to bring a group like this out of their beds at 5.00 a.m. to illegally block buses, face heavily armed policemen, and risk injury or imprisonment, if not death. The effects the demonstration would have on the strike, if any, paled into insignificance next to the message of the times it conveyed. The law was the property of the people. That was the abstract idea. In concrete terms the sense of justice in the society was coming into conflict with the practice of the book law. But no longer just at a conceptual level. At least some prominent individuals were prepared now to take direct and positive action to put the law into the hands of the people.

Here was an unmistakable sign. Winds of change were blowing with an increasing spiritual force. There were new and real humanistic concerns growing in the society, not limited to the radical core that had always been motivated by such ideals. These concerns were subversive in post-colonial Trinidad and Tobago. The society was very capable of rejecting aspects of its make up that those in control would have preferred to think were fundamental and unshakable — such as its vaunted 'respect' for 'Law and Order'.

Rejection was an ever present possibility because the people had been robbed of an essential feeling of coming in to their own at Independence. They had not gone through a process that would create a harmony of people and institutions. The dominant characteristics of the environment did not change to reflect the people's uniqueness, the ideas, aspirations and needs flowing from their heritage and peculiar experiences. The people had no input in devising new institutions of government or law. They were not mobilized to play any part in shaping or reshaping economic patterns and relationships. Culturally, the society remained enveloped in colonial values and ideas.

At the heart of the problem was leadership. The new political leaders were seeking to shape the society's destiny within the framework of imposed/borrowed institutions and ideas. Such institutions and ideas could not sink deep roots in the social consciousness. They held sway partly because of the manipulation of minds through constant propaganda which ascribed sacredness to profanity. They held sway partly by default, preserved by the absence of critical self-consciousness. They held sway partly by the reserve of force. Such institutions and ideas did not have the foundations to withstand the ideological ferment of the Western world in the late 60's. The debates that were stirred up by the bus strike were only dramatising this reality.

This was a unique period. Weekes saw it as having an ethos different to anything that he had ever experienced. In the industrialized countries there was a search for a new morality, especially among the young, a search that had a mesmerizing intensity, whether it branched into escapism, in movements of flower people or other counter cultures, or it branched into political confrontation as in the student protests on campuses in the United States or student revolt in the streets of Paris.

Weekes felt a strong sense of identity with the struggles and protests of the young all over the world, their sense of idealism. He had a sympathetic understanding, but no admiration for those who went the route of escapism, who in his outlook "have given up the battle, and, sickened by the difference between what they have been taught and what their teachers actually do, have decided to abandon society". His profound identification was with the students, especially, who were "fighting back and they were right. They may be futile in their efforts, ill-organised, but in the right and I am with them". The students made him wish that he was "20 years younger. The students of the world are my sort of people. They are young enough to be idealistic, poor enough to have little to lose and educated enough to understand the issues and to know wrong even when it is called right".[10]

In the developed Western world, students were in the vanguard of revolt against the old order. Western societies were convulsed by the moral overflow from a tidal wave of nationalist and revolutionary political upheaval in the colonial world in the 50's and early 60's which had swept independence movements to power. The Western societies were further shaken by the rise of the contemporary Black movement in the United States. The Black civil rights movement had become increasingly widespread and aggressive under the leadership of Martin Luther King Jr before he was assassinated in 1968. Out of the civil rights movement more radical ideological strands had emerged, even before the death of King, in particular Black

Nationalism as represented by Malcolm X (murdered by the state in 1965) and Black Power proclaimed by Stokeley Carmichael.

Youth were in the forefront of the radical white middle class reaction. Conscience was rekindled by the weight of guilt. The imperial guilt, fanned by the images of oppression and struggle, as the peoples of Asia, Africa and Latin America held up their bloodied hands like banners; the guilt of internal exploitation and racism against now vocal victims. These were burdens that overwhelmed the consciences of white youth. The jolt to the collective conscience and perceptions in white societies transformed itself into the new morality of its youth eating away at the hypocrisy, the lies and the anti-human values of their exploitative societies.

On the other side, Black societies, the homelands of the hundreds of millions of victims in the world of the colonised and the neo-colonised, were being propelled by a mutual recognition of their common condition. This recognition had expressed itself a decade before at the level of states in the Bandung Conference of 1955. Sukarno called it the "first intercontinental conference of colored peoples in the history of mankind"[11]. With more developed communications, Black societies were hurting with the pain of each other's suffering, echoing each other's cries, inspired by every act of courage, emboldened by every victory, and even further emancipated, psychologically, by the breakdown and turmoil in the oppressors' homelands. Black peoples felt re-awakened pride and rightness and rage, went through their own process of self-examination, re-defined their place in the world, and they were seeking to make that re-defined place a reality.

All around there was a rejection of norms, of which the law as it stood was just one. There was a near universal probing after fundamental truths, a reaching inward for self-discovery, an exorcism of the Western and Westernized soul. Young people were rattling words and shaking fists and setting fires after the corrupting demons of capitalism and colonialism and racism and materialism.

Farquhar's words on the law and the strike, and now his deed, were symbolic. The new moral force was irresistible. It gave a sense of spiritual renewal to a man like Weekes whose life had been a struggle for ideals. It could reach into the hearts and minds of those who had been aligned to the power structure, but were not of it. For those who were of the power structure, those who were its willing beneficiaries and guardians, the unfolding ethos was the fearful night cry of the death bird.

Long before this eventful day Weekes had felt the mood that was building. He was part of it.

... as the struggle for Independence intensified throughout the colonial world ... I felt very happy because for the first time we were taking our rightful place in the sun.

In the United States of America which is the heart of the Imperialist forces, when a Trinidadian, Stokeley Carmichael, introduced this question of Black Power, I quickly identified myself with that. I said, here I am President General, having this strong feeling about the oppression of Blacks and there in the United States a Trinidadian was campaigning to give the Black man power ...[12]

The tug at the soul that Weekes felt was part of a widespread motivation triggered by the rise of the Black Power movement. The ideological surge of this new movement was seeping into the conscious layers and the unconscious depths of the local society as a catalyst of moral upheaval and revolutionary demand. Trinidad and Tobago, where the years of Independence were dragging by without Blacks (Africans and Indians) feeling any new sense of dignity coming out of the social order, where there was visible discrimination in jobs based on race and colour in certain sectors of private enterprise, where foreign economic domination continued unchecked, where widespread poverty persisted and unemployment was an ever growing monster, Trinidad and Tobago was fertile ground for the seeds of Black Power. Brothers on the block, especially in the African dominated urban areas, were responding spontaneously to the militant music coming out of Black America and, more significantly, to the messages of Malcolm X, coming through more strongly years after his death. They were responding to the words of Trinidad born Stokeley Carmichael, who was leading the current round of revolt in the US. The images of the struggle fired the imaginations of the most downtrodden. Word images; "We shall have our Manhood, we shall have it or the Earth will be levelled by our attempts to gain it". Action images: Black

Panther Huey Newton patrolling the streets of racist America with a high-powered rifle in his hand, in defence of Black human rights.

George Weekes' very strong sense of identity with the movement in the United States came out of his own experiences. He was up against white power every day in the form of the giant multinational corporations. He witnessed and struggled against their racist practices, especially in areas like hiring senior staff and managerial personnel, and in the contempt they showed for Black workers. He was acutely conscious of the way in which these parasitic enterprises were sucking the lifeblood of Third World countries. Apart from his direct experience of their operations he would read and talk about the effects of their plunder. In his 1965 address to Congress he quoted a 1962 report indicating "that with 69% of the world's population, the underdeveloped countries were now receiving only 18% of the world's income". He also pointed out that "quite recently the United Nations Economic Commission for Latin America (ECLA) published a report which disclosed that foreign investors in Latin America took out of the area $3.17 for every $1.00 invested there during the period 1946-1956".[13] They were managing a global system designed for the permanent underdevelopment of non-white former colonial territories.

Weekes played his part in helping to spread the message of the Black movement:

> ... as far as possible, wherever I addressed people I would speak in support of that movement. I influenced people to listen to whatever records I could get, like speeches of Tom Mboya of Kenya talking about the oppression of his people: Martin Luther King Junior talking about the oppression of the Black Man ...[14]

In 1968 he placed huge posters on his car proclaiming "BLACK POWER". The establishment was upset, seeing this as having inflammatory implications. The media launched its predictable attacks. Even Weekes' friends and political colleagues were upset. For different reasons. Associates like Lennox Pierre felt there were dangers in the race line. Weekes was not a man to be arrogant in the face of advice, especially from those whom he respected. But in the final analysis he relied on his own judgement, especially in matters on which he felt very strongly. The slogan stayed on his car. Two years later, Pierre would readily concede that Weekes was right about what he had intuitively perceived and analytically justified at that time.

There were other notable signs of a changing consciousness in the late 60's. Weekes had actually seen oil workers developing a belief in the concept of a nationalised oil company. Every President General of the OWTU had preached nationalisation in the industry. But the doubts among the workers themselves and at the level of government leadership had always made such a goal seem an elusive dream. Now Weekes could feel the elation of triumph. Just the year before the government had announced that it would acquire the assets of BP and it would set up a National Oil Company. Even as George Weekes, the prime moving force for the formation of a National Oil Company and the nationalisation of British Petroleum, sat in a grimy cell, negotiations for the purchase of the oil company were underway. The fact that he could have motivated oil workers to mount the kind of campaign they did and the fact that the government could have responded, however reluctantly, indicated a welcome change for the society. It indicated a significant step on the rocky road to Black Power and Socialism.

Some very serious national developments, touching on the immediate self-interests of oil workers and government, had helped the movement to reach this point. The issue of retrenchment at BP and Shell sparked the consciousness of oil workers. The frightening combination of OWTU and SWWTU in the battle against retrenchment forced the government to be receptive to bold ideas. But the direction the struggle of the workers took indicated more than self-interest. It indicated a new way of looking at things. Because if the self-confidence of the workers had not been built up, if the conviction had not grown in their minds that Blacks could own, could manage and control an oil company, then things could have gone another way.

BP really had no further use for its Trinidad operations. The company had come here for a particular reason. The island was attractive as a safe haven for its investment when the Suez Crisis of 1956 made companies uncertain about the future of their operations in the Middle East. With those apprehensions gone, BP wanted out of what was for them a very marginal operation.[15] Without the intervention of OWTU and oil workers, that would simply have meant sale to another foreign company. In fact Texaco was the most likely taker. The national victory that came was the result of the massive campaign led by George Weekes with the memorable slogans:

N.O.C. YES: TEXACO NO! NOT A MAN MUST GO!

On the surface it seemed as though the decision to nationalize would be the fulfilment of Weekes' expressed commitment, "We shall not rest until BP means Black Power". But, as it turned out, the new developments did not bring only joy for the OWTU leader. There was personal agony in the triumph. In announcing that the government was setting up a National Oil Company, Williams announced that George Weekes would be appointed as a Director. The OWTU General Council accepted the appointment of Weekes on stated conditions, a major one of which was that he would function as a representative of the union. It was a decision that Weekes felt was necessary. He felt that he "could not do otherwise" than accept the proffered appointment "having fought so long for this socialist enterprise, and for reasons of strategy and tactics on the question of retrenchment".[16]

But it was a decision for which Weekes was to pay dearly in terms of his radical political image. For the first time he knew what it was to be seriously accused of having "sold out" to the system. One of the most vicious attacks was to come later from a former associate, Walter Annamunthodo,[17] who for personal reasons had turned against Weekes and the OWTU.

Some adverse reaction was bound to come once Weekes accepted the appointment from a government with which he was greatly at odds. What made his predicament worse though, was the subsequent backpedalling by the government. The PNM regime lacked conviction about the decisions they had announced on oil. In December of 1968, therefore, so shortly after raising national expectations, they disclosed that they were going in to a joint venture with an unknown petty American oil corporation, Tesoro, in order to purchase the assets of BP. At that time no National Oil Company, with the power to make policy decisions on the country's petroleum assets, even existed in law, far more to be a body meeting and discussing or deciding on anything. Nevertheless, in the public eye, the government decision to once more transfer the nation's precious assets to the hands of foreigners reflected on Weekes.

In the middle of what was in a sense a major triumph, therefore, agitated for over long years (the OWTU had submitted a memorandum to a 1963 Oil Commission recommending the formation of a National Oil Company), Weekes was giving thought to resigning from the proposed NOC. This he would later express to the union's 32nd Annual Conference in July 1969. In that speech he would express the hurt he felt at the accusations that he had "sold out". He also pointed out that he contemplated "retirement" not as an "admission of guilt but a result of my discovery that the NOC is not really a socialist enterprise at all — but a vehicle to further exploit our resources by foreigners . . . I have not become President General of the OWTU to preside over the sale of our mineral rights to foreigners"[18].

The irony of it all, however, which was eventually to reveal itself to George Weekes, was that there never was any National Oil Company to resign from. Government, after months of shadowing, passed a law providing for setting up a National Petroleum Company, but such an organisation never saw the light of day.

Nevertheless Weekes was right to see the developments taking place in oil in a positive light, despite whatever personal agony he endured and whatever disappointment he felt that the government had not decided to go it boldly alone in acquiring the assets of BP. His source of inspiration was the response of the oil workers who he always felt had a historic mission to lead the struggle for socialism in Trinidad and Tobago. Their actions in the campaign reflected the mood of the 60's. At the end of June 1969, when BP was finally going, the workers were to prove to him that a deep feeling against the outgoing imperialist enterprise and for the incoming national enterprise was running through the industry. They burnt the BP flag outside the administration building in Santa Flora, cheering as the burning flag fell to the ground, an exhilarating moment for Weekes who said that whatever tears they had to shed for BP were tears of joy and not sorrow. He also recognised the impact of the workers on government policy:

The workers are now forcing the government to go
Left or be left behind[19]

On the whole, new forces were developing in the society which were pushing left-ward. There was an intellectual thrust in

189

Trinidad and Tobago and the Caribbean which was giving further theoretical support to the struggle of OWTU for nationalization. Public conciousness on the issues involved was stirred by an extended debate in the *Trinidad Express* newspaper in the early months of 1968. The debate was between Dr James Millette, history lecturer at the University of the West Indies, St Augustine campus, who was advocating national ownership and control of the commanding heights of the economy, and Tommy Gatcliffe, an outspoken representative of the local white business elite, who was preaching the virtue and necessity of continuing multinational control. Apart from being a university lecturer, Millette was a member of a group of Caribbean intellectuals, based in the region and abroad, who were trying to define theoretically, new, radical strategies of development for the Caribbean. The group was called the "New World" group and its insights generally helped to orient at least certain sections of the intellectual community towards the ideals for which an organization like the OWTU was fighting.

OWTU was not the only union whose struggles reflected the spirit of the late 60's. Joe Young, one of the trade union leaders sharing Weekes' initiation into prison with him, had borne the brunt of the battle in the field against the ISA, even before the current Bus Strike which earned them the morning behind bars on May 13th 1969. The Transport and Industrial Workers Union had made industrial history when the union and 45 of its members were the first to be charged for violations under the ISA following a strike at Sissons Paints in September of 1967[20]. The union was fined $3000 but this did not stop Joe Young from calling a much broader strike, involving several companies and including bus workers, on June 20th 1968, to protest against the attitude of British multinational, Lever Brothers, which rejected the Minister's count in a recognition claim by TIWU. The fact that there was a substantial response to the strike call, despite the ISA, in companies not directly affected, showed a remarkable level of revolutionary consciousness among workers. This show of worker solidarity and defiance brought out the war cannons of the businessmen. The ECA hastened into emergency session and called on government to take action in a statement where they expressed some of the very ideas that would be expressed more forcefully in 1969:

(1) The strikes and attempts to force strikes that have been caused by certain trade unions are not truly labour disputes.

(2) The actions of these few trade union leaders and those who follow them are in full disregard of law and order and if continued will rock the very foundations of democratic processes in Trinidad and Tobago . . .[21]

The stocky Francis Beddoe, who had been through the wars in the sugar belt with Weekes, had also been charged for contravention of the ISA in connection with a strike at Cooperative Citrus Growers Association in 1967.

Bit by bit workers were chipping away at the ISA in the run-up to the major confrontation of May 1969. OWTU workers had been part of the process too. There was a brief strike at Fed Chem on November 14th 1967 for which charges were also laid. Here and there in the oil industry, issues would provoke shortlived, wildcat strikes. Up to March 11th 1969 Texaco was faced with such a strike in protest against acts of racism (an issue on which workers were very sensitive) and victimisation by a company manager.

The revolutionary fall-out from the growing social discontent of the late 60's had been enough to get some Congress unions involved in organising the March of Resistance in 1968.

Then, three weeks before the bus strike, 19 unions, including the OWTU, met in Tobago and decided to give the government a seven-day ultimatum to re-introduce the right to strike. They had not yet delivered the ultimatum and Weekes thought they were certainly not living up to its intent either, or more unionists would have been in prison with him on the morning of May 13th. But it is significant that they could even have made and publicised such a decision, obviously a response to strong anti-ISA pressures coming from the workers themselves.

On the blocks* in the urban areas, where several militant grassroots organisations were developing, there were more telling signs of rebellion. As the message painted large on a wall on Quarry Street in the East Dry River area said:

"WITHOUT EQUAL RIGHTS, BLACK IS DANGEROUS."

---

* Areas in communities where the unemployed and the underemployed, in particular, habitually gathered ("limed").

191

The revolutionary cry of Black Power could be heard even within certain areas of the church. One month before Weekes and others blocked buses, a minister of the Susamachar Presbyterian Church, significantly enough an East Indian, Reverend Albert Baldeo, came out strongly in support of Black Power, which he said, in a speech at the San Fernando car park, was "like Christianity, something of God".[22]

Students at the University of the West Indies also became part of the social ferment — at the St Augustine campus, as well as at other regional campuses in Barbados and Jamaica. At St Augustine the students acquired a more radical image when the president of the Guild of Undergraduates, Geddes Granger, led a student march in Port of Spain against the ban imposed on a university lecturer at the Mona campus of the UWI in Jamaica. The lecturer, Walter Rodney, was prohibited from re-entering Jamaica after he had attended a Black Power Conference in Montreal, Canada. This was in October of 1968.

During 1969, the mood was expressing itself more and more in action, with a new organised force developing on the scene. That new force was the National Joint Action Committee. Geddes Granger was its chairman. Weekes had played a part in the formation of this organisation. In February of 1969, he had discussions with Granger, Darbeau and other representatives of the Student Guild. They had come to seek his support for a movement to raise funds and whip up public support for West Indian students who had been arrested in Canada and charged for conspiracy to burn down the Computer Center at Sir George Williams University. Weekes and the OWTU Asst General Secretary, Lionel Bannister, who also attended the meeting, agreed to seek Executive approval for the union to be represented at a meeting called by the Students Guild to discuss and decide on what action could be taken on the issue.

Weekes felt immediately inclined to support the group of students who had come to the union. Apart from the fact that the issues involved in the Canada affair centered on racism and injustice, issues on which he could not turn his back, the students who came to his office represented a Guild that had been reaching out to the wider society, developing links with grassroots organisations, depressed communities and trade unions.

THE EVE OF THE STORM

Lionel Beckles and John Commissiong were sent to represent the union at what turned out to be the first meeting of the National Joint Action Committee. It was originally christened Joint National Action Committee that night by James Lynch, representing the Action Group of 100, one of the many groups who had responded to the call of the students. These groups included other trade unions, NUGFW and TIWU, youth groups and community-based organisations from throughout the country.

The first meeting of NJAC took place on February 26th 1969. It was a very auspicious night. During the day the Students Guild had organised a protest against the visit of the Canadian Governor General, Roland Michener, to the campus at a time when Caribbean students were being subjected to racial abuse in Canada. The protesting students, led by Granger, who was outgoing president of the Guild, had blocked Michener and his entourage from entering the campus to the shock and dismay of government officials. Shock waves in fact travelled throughout the society as a result of that demonstration.

In the weeks that followed, George Weekes became one of the principal speakers on the platforms of the National Joint Action Committee, of which the OWTU was a member organisation. There was a very militant campaign throughout the country, dealing specifically with the issue of the students in Canada, the blocking of Michener and the reaction to it which included calls for the expulsion of at least three students — Granger, Darbeau (publications officer of the Guild) and Augustus Ramrekersingh (Guild secretary). The events in Canada and at home were handled within the context of wider themes which included imperialism, with special reference to the operations of Canadian companies in Trinidad and Tobago, and racism, at home and abroad.

This was the beginning of a new tempo in the political history of the country. NJAC's focus quickly broadened to encompass other local, regional and international issues. There was a sense of purpose, seriousness and dedication in this group that made Weekes feel at home. In it he sensed in embryonic form the germ of a new order. The social combination, the combination of academics, trade unionists, community organisers, harmoniously integrated in a common struggle, portended well for the future.

The unconventional approach to social action, the revolutionary and daring spirit, these factors attracted Weekes.

The potential for struggle was clearly revealed by a dramatic demonstration on April 12th 1969 which highlighted the many concerns the National Joint Action Committee had been voicing, about the students in Canada, British action in Anguilla and non-action in Zimbabwe, racism, foreign domination of the economy and other issues. Weekes remembers, with a wry amusement, how he was used by Michael X for a publicity stunt at the start of the demonstration. As the demonstrators were about to get going, a number of leaders stood with their arms linked across the front of the demonstration. Michael X, mis-labelled as a Black Power leader in London, but whose unsavoury reputation was well-known to Weekes and others gathered for the march, stepped from the pavement with perfect timing and linked his arm with Weekes. He walked the first few steps murmuring some meaningless greetings, long enough to get pictures taken, and he left.

The real drama of the demonstration however had nothing to do with Michael X's little con-game. It was in the spirit of the thousands who turned out to march. It was not a bread and butter demonstration. It was not a demonstration against some action of the government of Trinidad and Tobago. Yet thousands of people, mainly young, had come out on the streets indicating a concern for non-personal causes, for principles and for some relatively abstract issues. The beating of traditional African drums, for the first time Weekes could remember in a demonstration, added a quality of vitality to the very disciplined, defiant and determined march through the streets of Port of Spain. There was a liberating force in the march. Whether it was the symbolic power of the drum, some telepathic communication in the eyes of the angry young people, an all pervading feeling of self-awareness and pride, or whatever, there was something, some indefinable but distinct something about that demonstration, that chanting, boldly striding throng of search-ing, protesting, hoping young people that was permeating the atmosphere with a new mood, a new, militant, dynamic, irrepressible, positive, Black rebellious mood.

No doubt it was out of that same mood then prevailing that the transport strike had come, out of that mood that small farmers of Montserrat village in Central Trinidad could be motivated to come into Port of Spain and bring food for the striking workers. It was the same mood that had brought together individuals from so many varying backgrounds to meet and plan ways and means of supporting the actions of the bus workers, the same mood that precipitated the actions which had now landed Weekes in jail with a group that would have been considered unlikely one year before.

As that unlikely group was taken to court around midday on May 13th, it was clear that the establishment action had only further heightened the mood of struggle. Thousands of people were outside the court house; bus workers, supporters, OWTU members who had journeyed from the South, the curious onlookers getting the feeling that something important was taking place. The flags waved impressively in the wind. Red flags and the black and green flags of TIWU. It was as if some psychic force was bringing the historic red, black and green of the Garvey movement together again to be the symbolic colours of another generation's awakening. In the court there was a weighty line up of lawyers most of whom had come voluntarily to the defence — M.A.S.A Khan, Theodore Guerra, George Bowrin, Clyde Crevelle, Desmond Allum, Allan Alexander, Jack Kelshall, Oswald Wilson.

Loud voices sent inspiration to the defendants in the court house, singing "We shall overcome, we shall overcome . . . some day". And even as bail was granted, against the objections of the prosecution, and the cases of obstruction postponed, Weekes felt deep in his heart that "some day" was close.

CHAPTER 12

REVOLUTION!!

"And then suddenly it sweeps on you 'like a thief in the night'. What? Not elections, but Revolution. And the 'Wretched of the Earth' stand up, realise that though they don't have bread, or enough of it, they have feet and two of them. And they start to walk about the place; and they realise that though they don't have guns or tear gas . . . , they have fists. And they start to clench them and throw them in the air; and they realise that though they don't have walkie-talkies nor even one good microphone they have voices. And they start to shout Power! Power! Power! Power to the People . . ."[1]
(George Weekes)

On February 26th 1970, George Weekes and Winston Leonard, who worked in the Education Department of the OWTU, were sitting in a room at the PSA Guest House in Scarborough, Tobago, listening eagerly to the radio for a report on the planned demonstration in Trinidad. They could hardly contain themselves when they heard the news. The demonstration, comprised mainly of university students, but including supporters from trade unions and various units of NJAC, had entered the Catholic Cathedral on Independence Square in Port of Spain. Instinctively they could feel the earth-shaking dimensions of that development, and, as men committed to struggle, they felt left out. That is where they were supposed to be. But union business had taken them to Tobago.

What stroke of fate, Weekes wondered, could have led the marchers into the church? There was no doubt about the connection between the Catholic Church and the issue which was responsible for the demonstration. The trials of West Indian students, accused of burning down the Computer Centre at Sir George Williams University, were underway in Canada. The Catholic Church in Montreal was one of the institutions that had condemned the Black students before they were even tried and helped to foment the racist hostility to which they were being subjected in that white city. Psychologically, the Catholic Church in Trinidad was linked to the one in Canada. Guilty by association. Not just the association of being Catholic, but the association of similar ideas. Eric Williams had once blasted the Catholic Church as "the last bastion of colonialism" in Trinidad and Tobago. It was closely allied with the white business elite and tainted with elitism and racism. It was a domineering symbol of cultural imperialism.

Ordinarily the marchers would have made their protest outside of the Cathedral. But destiny was on the march. Just listening to the news, Weekes could visualize the pattern of events that led almost inexorably to the conquering penetration of the Church's sanctimonious veil. The radio announcer spoke about clashes between police and demonstrators inside the offices of the Canadian High Commission. The news spoke about further clashes between demonstrators and police, this time inside the Royal Bank of Canada. Clouds gathering.

Then the demonstration had taken another kind of turn. Politically, it looked inward. In a swoop that further raised the pores of the listeners in Tobago, the marchers had turned on the local power structure. A department store belonging to the family of the 'sociologically white' Minister of Home Affairs, Robert Montano, had been invaded and they were forced to close their doors. Symbolically this was a strike at the political heart of the country, and at its colour and class hierarchy. Gale force winds hit the barometer of political perception.

Then it came. To the ears of the faithful listeners, the annunciation. As the taut body of the mobilised masses withdrew the collective projection of fury and rising excitement from that brash encounter, it thrust again with a greater psychic force straight to the altar of the Cathedral of the Immaculate Conception. One demonstrator covered the stare of the marble white virgin, with a black cloth, as the penetration took place and the revolution was conceived. A placard hung on St Peter's hand, outstretched with the key to the Kingdom, simply said, 'FREEDOM NOW'.

Weekes and Leonard suddenly felt imprisoned in Tobago. There was no choice but to stay. Weekes had to address an upcoming seminar of T&TEC workers in Tobago over the weekend. They could feel the trauma and the liberation of the moment. There would be a flood. There was. The blood red flags were streaming from deep inside what seemed before an impregnable canopy of mysticism and spiritual servitude, outpouring at the open entrance; the black flags, the symbol of the new strength and unity, stood upright and entrenched from aisle to altar while the black faces were haloed by an indefinable triumph; intermingling were the green flags that were the green of the liberated land beckoning, the elusive destiny of reclaimed resources, harmony in production and growth, man and land and technology and thought in fruitful bonds generating the New Society.

The news would later confirm the generality of the stirring Weekes felt in his soul, an irresistible urge that would have drawn him to Independence Square, to the imposing colonial architecture of the Cathedral, if the barrier of the sea did not lie between. But while he and Leonard were bound by flight times and prior commitments, the hills of Laventille, African-dominated concentrations of material deprivation on the city's edge, had erupted. The womb of suspended time had been ruptured and the suppressed hurt and pain was emerging, transformed into a rebirth of identity and pride with a cutting edge of explosive anger. 200 turned into 2000 in a flash like the news itself, and the number was growing as the demonstration now headed for the centre of the city of Port of Spain. All establishments, except those owned by African or Indian businessmen, soon got the message. The marching throng was not simply passing by. They were passing through. Store clerks welcomed an unsolicited timeoff as doors were hastily shut in deference to the approach of the "Black Steamroller"*.

It was hard for Weekes to have to settle for this information second-hand. As a perceptive observer and participant, who had strong intuitions about what he was involved in, he had seen it coming. In his New Year's message to mark the dawn of 1970, he had said:

---

* A term often used by NJAC to refer to the mobilized masses on the move.

REVOLUTION!!

The exploiting businessmen, big and small, have been quick to adopt for sale the slogan of 'the ROARING 70'S' ...

Brothers, we are certain that the roar that the businessmen are hearing comes from the warning winds of the impending Black hurricane that will blow them from the seats of economic power and privilege during the REVOLUTIONARY 70'S.[2]

He was out of effective range when that first howling wind blew. But thereafter he would march in stride. The first direct involvement to draw the blood to his head came on the Thursday after the historic demonstration of February 26th. That was Thursday March 5th. That morning, as Weekes sat in court, he could feel the tremendous sense of excitement that was gripping the country. Thousands of people were gathered outside of the court house. The police, out in full force, were struggling to keep the agitated crowd away from the precincts of the court. On trial inside were university students, Geddes Granger (former president of the Guild and Chairman of NJAC), Carl Blackwood (current Guild president), Kelshall Bodie, Winston Smart and Russel Andalcio (all NJAC members as well). Other defendants were NJAC member, Dave Darbeau (a recent graduate of UWI), as well as Errol Balfour of the Workers Educational Association and Earl Lewis of Moko (whose name was subsequently dropped without explanation from the list of those charged). A battery of lawyers, including Allan Alexander, Basdeo Panday, Lennox Pierre, M.A.S.A. Khan and Charles Tyson stood voluntarily for the defence, sensing the historic nature of the moment.

But the defendants had not left justice entirely up to lawyers and the courts. The most formidable line of defence could be heard from the streets outside, the mobilized masses.

Weekes admired the lightning mobilization that had taken place. After February 26th everything had just escalated with a breathtaking momentum. The first item of news on the morning of February 27th was the pre-dawn arrests of those identified as leaders of the protest the day before. The magistrate had bowed to the police request and denied bail to the arrested NJAC men. Bail was however granted by a Judge in Chambers the following day. As the men emerged from prison, the mobilization began. A series of meetings, concentrated mainly in the North of the

199

country, drew a response that shocked the establishment and shook like an earthquake in the soul of the nation. On Wednesday March 4th a demonstration in support of those arrested on February 27th drew on the seething depths of alienation and rebellion in the society and spelled out a formidable threat to the old order. No witness could be in doubt that some fundamental transformation was taking place. One could hardly walk in Woodford Square, where the demonstration was to begin. There were thousands of people, including school children in their uniforms, placards with revolutionary slogans, an atmosphere of love and struggle, brotherhood and determination. Striking to the eye were the visible symbols of an awakened African consciousness in clothes and hairstyles. The demonstrators walked with a military discipline. The *Express* newspaper described the demonstration as "mammoth and peaceful". It was peaceful. Not with the peace of passivity, but the peace of a contained explosion.

When he arrived in Port of Spain on March 5th, and as he sat in court observing the proceedings, Weekes could still feel the reverberations of the mass pilgrimage to Shanty Town, the country's most squalid slum at the time, which had taken place the day before. The headline he read on the *Express* newspaper before coming to court had captured the effect of the events. It proclaimed "BLACK POWER MARCH STUNS THE CITY". The people had answered the NJAC call. The *Express* said there were 10,000 in the march to Shanty Town. There could have been twice that number. Now thousands were gathered again outside the court. Inside, Weekes was becoming increasingly agitated. The sounds from outside were reflecting a growing restlessness and conflict between the people and the police. Eventually the noises became the noises of calamity. Running horses, running feet, shouts. The scene inside was a maddening one too. The charges themselves were enough to get one mad. Laws from just after the days of slavery were dug up to lay the charge for example of 'Disorderly Behaviour in a place of Public Worship', along with conspiracy to cause a riot. Apart from these charges laid collectively, there were individual charges. One was an assault charge laid against Dave Darbeau and this is the hearing that was actually started. The evidence being presented here was the last straw for Weekes' patience. He felt like dragging the stocky inspector out of the box as he sat there describing how, without rhyme or reason, and despite his kind and gentle words, he was physically assaulted by Darbeau.

Weekes managed to hold back the explosion in court that morning. But once he had left the court, following the postponement of the cases, and he had gone to nearby Woodford Square with the defendants, his anger let loose. Weekes has always been a user of strong language. But strong in a political sense, harsh adjectives condemning a harsh system of oppression. As Weekes addressed the crowd in Woodford Square that day, in a fuming moment, with all the images of the society's wrongs dramatised by the happenings in court and outside of court playing on his mind, he literally cursed. He cursed the police, who had driven the crowds from around the court building, he cursed the system of justice and he cursed the government.

The atmosphere was now an atmosphere of violence. Before Weekes and the defendants had emerged from the court, police provocations and rumours, in particular one that said the defendants had been sentenced to three years in prison, had sent the crowd, forcefully driven from around the court, on a rampage of selective destruction. Tempers were high in the square that noon as the assembled masses listened to the words of Weekes, Granger, the charismatic leader of the blossoming mass movement, Nunez, Darbeau and others. Nervous bankers and businessmen in the surrounding area hastily boarded up their broken show windows and glass fronts. Most stores in the city, all those owned by whites, closed their doors. Children were sent home from schools. From here on there would be a peaceful mass of protestors in the day, at least most times, but after dark the flare of anger would become the flare of the molotov. The exploding lighted bottles of gasoline sparked fears in targeted households where they rudely awakened the inhabitants but did little physical damage. The main targets in the pre-dawn hours were property not individuals. Several buildings, symbolic of oppression, met a fiery destruction.

For close to two hectic months Weekes would go through one of the most memorable periods of his life. Through the sixties he had carried the burden of an isolated prominence in the leadership of the radical and only meaningful opposition to the PNM regime. After 1966, the DLP, the official opposition in Parliament, headless once the election campaign was over, deteriorated from being ineffective to being completely silent (in protest over claims that the election was rigged*). Most trade unions were co-opted by the regime. The others, outside of the OWTU, were relatively minor. Weekes' party, the WFP, disintegrated. New grassroots organisations, the most prominent being the Black Panthers, led by Aldwyn Primus, and Young Power, led by Michael Als, lacked the clout to really challenge the status quo in any measure close to the threat presented by George Weekes from his trade union base. With the rise of NJAC this would change. The oratory of Granger in particular and that of the other leaders; the consolidation and spread of the organisation as it transformed itself from being a federation of groups into a unitary body in close liason with progressive trade unions; the zeal and the courage of the predominantly young NJAC leadership and membership, and their harmony with the ideas and spirit of the times; created a new dynamic force with the power to bring the establishment down. Weekes could now function as an integral part of something that was drawing on a wider social base than the few progressive unions, but including them, something that had the potential to evolve into a genuinely national mass movement, which is what it was rapidly developing into in 1970.

Weekes was an active and leading participant in the various stages of growth of the movement which consciously set out to transcend its mainly Northern, urban, African base. NJAC had done some significant mobilization outside of that environment in 1969. They had gone into the Central, mainly East Indian area of Montserrat, organising small farmers and effectively preserving their lands against the encroachment of Tate and Lyle, the British-owned sugar company. Small units of organisation were scattered throughout the country, extending to Santa Flora in the deep South. But the dramatic upsurge after February 26th 1970 had come predominantly from the North. The mood and the organisational depth had not taken a hold in Central or South at a comparable level. Weekes saw the march to Caroni, to the heart of the sugar belt, as one of the most dramatic moves to redress this, to draw not only regions together but to

---

* All the parties which opposed the PNM in 1966 had been clamouring against the use of voting machines (first introduced by the PNM regime in 1961). After the election there was an outcry from the parties, including the WFP, that the PNM won by rigging the machines.

build an essential revolutionary unity between the two numerically dominant races in the country, Africans and Indians.

On the morning of March 12th 1970 he left home with some unease, but with great hope that this would turn out to be a historic day for Trinidad and Tobago. The Caroni March was coming off under threat and the threat had to be taken seriously. Bhadase Maraj had openly threatened violence if NJAC tried to take the demonstration into the sugar belt, where he wanted to remain god. Karl Hudson-Phillips, the nation's Attorney General, had gone on the radio and television the night before and there were threatening innuendos in his speech. Weekes himself had been approached by pretended well-wishers who wanted him to use his influence to get NJAC to call off the march.

The rumours were thick that morning. The most persistent story was that Bhadase had gunmen hidden in the canefields, waiting for the demonstrators. As Weekes drove up along the route the demonstrators would be taking through Caroni (from the opposite direction), official fears about the outcome of the day were apparent. A police helicopter persistently circled overhead. Weekes finally came in sight of the marchers just as they were approaching the Caroni Bridge, on the edge of the canefields. The huge banner stood out in front of the demonstration with the poignant message:

INDIANS AND AFRICANS UNITE NOW

You could see purpose in the stride of the thousands of people approaching the iron bridge. The purpose in Weekes' own eyes inscribed meaning on every girder. The narrow bridge was heavy with the symbolism of the marchers' cause. If they could build a bridge of iron bonds between the oppressed Black races it would be the fulfilment of a dream for which Weekes was one of those who had fought untiringly and risked his life. The marchers, mainly young people, had the faith and the determination to accomplish that goal. Mindful of the threats and the heavy propaganda in the Indian community before the demonstration, Geddes Granger, the NJAC leader, had committed the marchers to an oath at two points. In Woodford Square in Port of Spain, and at the Curepe Junction, just on the border of the Caroni area, they had repeated:

> We pledge to create Brotherhood and unity between
> brother and brother, between the two Black races of
> Trinidad & Tobago . . .
> We pledge not to retaliate against our Indian
> brothers and sisters in case anyone was used to create
> antagonism, but to hold responsible those forces at
> work to divide the two races.

There were mainly Africans, the Northern urban dwellers,
making that long pilgrimage. But out front there was a
significant group of Indians. Most of them were members of the
Society for the Propagation of Indian Culture, on the St
Augustine University campus. They had liaised closely with
NJAC during the days before the demonstration, moving
through the cane belt countering as far as they could the
saturation of anti-Black Power propaganda - Black Power was a
"nigger thing", the "niggers" were out to take away Indian
businesses, they were coming to rape Indian women. Up to the
very morning Weekes became aware of the continuing
propaganda, and it was not limited only to Bhadase and various
racists who felt threatened. The police were moving around
before the arrival of the demonstration, advising people to close
their shops because the demonstrators would raid them.

Near the front of the demonstration, Weekes could see some
priests too. But not the Archbishop, Anthony Pantin. The
Archbishop's statements, following the invasion of the Catholic
Cathedral in February, had shown a sensitivity and
understanding of the deep-rooted grievances in the society and
the negative image of the Church in the minds of the oppressed.
He was invited by the leaders of NJAC to make this historic
march with its most sacred purpose. He accepted, after talking it
over with God. But more influential forces intervened on the
night of April 11th, between his announcement that he would
participate and the time of the demonstration, forcing the
retraction of his inspired decision. To Weekes and others,
Archbishop Pantin's embarrassment was a clear indication of the
power of the white business hierarchy within the Church.

Weekes, Bannister and other union officials fell in with the
march. And it was an unforgettable experience. Despite all the
attempts to terrorise the Indian community, teachers and
principals brought out school children to line the streets and

welcome the marchers, households provided barrels of chilled fruit, water and juices along the way. All shops remained open and it was remarkable to see African brothers and sisters, complete strangers to the Indian proprietors, giving assistance behind the counters to deal with the huge thirsty crowds seeking service.

Much later that evening there were other indications of the beautiful spirit of unity which prevailed that day. There was an overwhelming response to African and Indian speakers at the final meeting in Couva, 26 miles from where the march started. Geddes Granger committed NJAC to ridding the sugar workers of the burden of Bhadase Maraj. Dave Darbeau reiterated the Black Power concept of racial unity based on mutual respect and understanding. Weekes repeated a call he had made several times for government to take over the sugar industry from the British owners, Tate and Lyle. Panday had arranged for some workers to bring two of the heavy chains that sugar workers, including frail women, have to drag from central heaps to the points where they use them to tie the canes they cut. The chains, an uncomfortable reminder of the slave past, most graphically demonstrated for the Africans who made the march the common bonds of suffering between the races at the mass level. After the meeting, as though in recognition that both groups were chained together under the system, people showed an outstanding concern for each other. Trucks and other vehicles were mobilized to take people back into town. Strangers became guests in the homes of local residents. And those who neither found transportation nor accommodation had coffee, tea and snacks brought for them.

The message that held the day was the revolutionary message, as earlier expressed by one of NJAC's Indian leaders, Chan Maharaj. In a public reply to Bhadase's public allegations of racism, levelled against the Black Power movement, Chan had said,

> The fight is not an African against Indian fight. It is a fight against exploitation and the political oppression upon the Black peoples of Trinidad (and Tobago).[3]

George Weekes left Couva late that night after the leaders of the march had sat conferring and assessing the gains of the day. He realized that not since the times of Butler were there such dynamic possibilities of African-Indian unity. His experience of 1965 had strengthened his conviction, based on history and a faith in the oppressed generally, that the Indian masses, especially those most downtrodden workers in the sugar industry, would respond positively to revolutionary struggle. The limitation in 1965 was that there was not a mass African response to the struggle of the Indian workers. Other African trade union leaders, like Joe Young and Francis Beddoe, were out there with Weekes in those turbulent days. But there was no mass involvement of the workers in their unions with the struggles of that time. In the oil belt in fact, the PNM agitators were playing upon backward racial sentiments to make oil workers resent the amount of attention their P-Gee was paying to a group of fellow workers. But in 1970 Weekes, by his intimate contact with the sugar workers, knew before the demonstrations started that they were ready for action. He had written the Labour Congress in early February about a meeting with a delegation of sugar workers following which he said:

> we are convinced that another crisis, almost identical to the one of 1965 is coming to a head, but with one significant difference. This time, the workers, rankled by the memory of betrayal and temporary defeat they experienced in the 1965 debacle, are grimly determined to prevent at all costs a recurrence.[4]

Now that the Caroni Bridge had been crossed, Weekes' next preoccupation was with the South, and naturally, oil workers. In his vision of the revolutionary 70's, the OWTU leader had pictured, "the Black proletarian warriors led by the blue shirts of the South and North (OWTU now represented T&TEC in the North)" acting "to dictate the political destiny of our own cosmopolitan nation". Weekes saw oil workers, whose occupation put them at the lifeblood of the nation's economy, as critical to the struggle. He always recalls Williams saying to him, "Industrial peace in Trinidad & Tobago depends on peace in Oil". The nation's fortunes in fact rose and fell with oil. In the 1950's petroleum revenues grew by 12% per annum, the national economy grew by 10% per annum. From 1962 to 1965 petroleum revenues grew by a mere 2% per annum. The national economy grew by a mere 4% per annum.[5] The nation's economic crises of the 1960's reflected the downward trend of world oil prices. If oil could make or break the economy, then oil workers could make or break the economy. That was the political significance of this group.

Ideologically, as well as strategically, they were on the frontline. A major part of the crisis of 1970 was caused by the foreign stranglehold on the nation's resources. There were some $2 billion (T&T) in foreign investment in the country. Over half of it was American capital, and over $500 million of that was in the oil industry.[6] Oil was the key to the alien domination of the economy which overall included banks (the seven major commercial banks were all foreign), manufacturing (where 80% of the investment was foreign), land ownership (nearly 50% of the acreage in estates over 200 acres was alien owned and over 300,000 acres were under leases to the oil companies), construction (where 43% of revenue was earned by foreign firms) . . .[7] The crisis over foreign economic domination had to do with more than the practical debilitating effects, real as these were, since foreign investments drained the country of some $200 million every year. Resentment against this domination had a fuller ideological dimension. External control of the economy clashed with re-defined concepts of Independence, which included, fundamentally, economic independence. As Weekes expressed it:

> . . . whether the Black worker lives under Shearer and his JLP in Jamaica, under Bird and his ALP in Antigua or under Williams and what remains of his PNM in Trinidad and Tobago, his situation (the black worker's situation) remains substantially what it was before the farce of political independence was enacted. The Union Jack has gone. "God Save the Queen" is played no more. The Governor General may have Yoruba blood, Madrassie hair or Mongolian eyes. The Prime Minister and his party may profess Nationalism, Labourism, even Socialism, or any sort of 'ism', the British and American capital and profits are as safe as they ever were under colonial rule. To understand this, the central fact we workers have to grasp is that it is economics, the economic structure of a society that determines its politics and the political system. So that if when you achieve the political power that spells national independence you

do not aspire to the economic power that ends colonial dependence, yuh just spinning yuh national top in the same old colonial mud: and the workers particularly come to realise that the more we (the Black nationals) perspire with the help of Williams, the more they (White imperialists) achieve . . .[8]

Foreign economic domination was in conflict with the new, healthier self-perceptions, nourished by the concepts of Black Power. People were putting that domination in historical perspective, they were rebelling against the negative cultural and psychological concomitants of the continuing control of the nation's economic destiny by the former slave-owning countries. To break that, it had to be broken in oil and the oil workers had to be ideologically persuaded to make the break successful.

In 1970 Weekes saw and felt the response of oil workers to the messages of Black pride and dignity. He knew they too felt that yearning for respect, for power, for Black Power. After all they had to deal with white racism on the job. Like all Black peoples, they experienced the prejudices about colour in the society, they too were caught up in the self denigration among Blacks, especially Africans. Weekes himself had always opened their eyes to the need to purge the society of these enslaving patterns of behaviour and ideas. He never failed to remind them of the gross material inequalities between racial groups in the society, a visible fact of life that had impressed itself upon his mind from childhood. The truth of inequality was documented in government's Central Statistical Office Survey of Household Income in 1961 which revealed that median income for whites was $500 per month, compared with $104 per month for Africans, and an even more abysmal $77 per month for Indians.

But Weekes recognised the problem of getting the total involvement of oil workers in this kind of political battle, despite their militancy in defence of their bread and butter interests. His own struggles in oil had achieved contradictory effects. He had shaken the complacency of the imperialists about Black workers. But in the process he had contributed towards the development of an "aristocracy of labour". As he put it "success . . . in the oil industry . . . brought changes in the lifestyle of oil workers . . . they had just begun to enjoy and reap the benefits of successful leadership and negotiations which previously they were not accustomed to".[9] In addition to higher wages, one of the benefits insulating oil workers from the social ferment was the Texaco housing scheme, one of the gains secured by the union, which was settling many of them in their own comfortable communities. Confusion was also deliberately added by the well-entrenched myth-makers, resorting tirelessly to the old ideas — the union should not be involved in politics, Weekes was trying to get them into another communist plot, or, the play on the reactionary fears about race, the talk about unity was really a ploy to remove the "Negro", Williams, and put an Indian in power.

Weekes devoted a lot of his time to educating the oil workers about the movement, gradually motivating them towards involvement. He was reaching them at meetings in branch halls, he was meeting them in groups where they lime and drink together, he was holding spot meetings. They were also being influenced by the national mood which was growing with all the reports in the press on regular mass meetings and demonstrations attracting numbers like 20,000, pounding the streets daily, pausing pointedly to identify institutions which symbolized oppression, whether the Parliament, the US Embassy, the foreign banks, Chamber of Commerce offices or other oppressive establishments, carrying placards that were an education in themselves. The roles of the most hallowed institutions were being called into question:

WHAT HAS THE CHURCH DONE FOR   (A) BLACK PEOPLE   (B)   SUFFERING   PEOPLE   (C) UNEMPLOYMENT[10]

The focus of protest was no longer just on individuals but on the system. Individuals were identified in so far as they functioned as an integral part of the system:

WILLIAMS IS KEEPING US IN CAPITALISM AND SLAVERY[11]

The response of the masses was indicating to Weekes that the people were beginning, with the education of 1970, to think in terms of the system, not merely government, not merely the 'goodness' or 'badness' of particular leaders or parties. For years he had been trying to get people to recognise evil inherent in capitalism itself, to see the shackles on the country's progress in terms of imperialism and neo-colonialism. Now, in the context of Black Power, the message was communicating at the mass level with an effectiveness which was only possible in a revolutionary environment.

The main slogans spoken and written everywhere carried powerful messages of uncompromising nationalism and people's power:

WE DO NOT WANT CRUMBS; WE WANT THE WHOLE BREAD

put in a nutshell the people's demand for control over the nation's resources.

POWER TO THE PEOPLE

was given all its philosophical weight as a call for fundamental political change, for the creation of a system of people's involvement in the decision making process, symbolized dramatically by the People's Parliaments of 1970. In 1968 at the end of the March of Resistance, Weekes had rechristened Woodford Square, which Williams called the University of Woodford Square, "the Parliament of the People"[12]. On March 6th 1970, as if to demonstrate how the same spirit moved in that time, Granger, with no conscious reference to that history, proclaimed Woodford Square, "the People's Parliament".

From the turmoil and the tumult of ideas, the feedback was strong, but not strong enough in San Fernando and the South in the early days of the uprising. In the beginning NJAC was leaving the mobilization of the Southern areas up to a San Fernando based group, United Movement for the Reconstruction of Black Identity (UMROBI) led by two young university graduates from the Mona campus, Winston Suite, an engineer, and Wayne Davis, a school teacher. The absence of the direct involvement of NJAC caused a lag in the impact of the movement in the South, which made the battle somewhat harder in the oil industry. When this was corrected with meetings and demonstrations coming from Point Fortin and Siparia to San Fernando, the Southern capital, the response began to grow. On the 21st of March, after a long walk on a demonstration he joined in La Brea, Weekes spoke outside the home of the Minister of Home Affairs, Montano, in San Fernando condemning his use of the police to try to suppress the "legitimate protests" of Black people[13]. By this time, incidents of police abusing people were mounting. Individuals were being picked up in isolation, brutalized and then released without charge, as a warning to the movement. Even a school boy had been victim of this practice. But worse was yet to come from the police.

REVOLUTION!!

On March 24th Weekes was late in reaching to Port of Spain for a demonstration, which included five of the students whose trials in Canada had triggered the chain of events now unfolding with such cataclysmic force. Two nights before he had been at the airport when they returned to a hero's welcome, with chanting crowds and flags and drums, after the government, under duress, had paid the hefty fines they were charged by the court in Montreal. He did not want to miss the demonstration, but he was delayed holding a press conference, responding critically to the first statements Williams had made publicly in the period of crisis. When he reached Port of Spain, tear gas in the air still irritated the eyes. The town was in a state of agitation. On Charlotte Street, sides of shoes were strewn about the place, shattered fragments of show-windows littered the street at points, with bags, umbrellas and other paraphernalia separated from owners who had obviously left in a hurry. A snowcone cart, with a microphone mounted on it, was lying on its side at the bottom of the street. The scene itself told the story of the first police attack on a Black Power demonstration since February 26th. Weekes met several participants in the demonstration who had managed to escape without being overcome by tear gas or mauled by riot staffs, who told him of the attack. From what he learnt, it had come when provocation by a store owner caused a demonstrator to hurl a stone through his shop window. The most distressing story however was that the police had shot and killed a ten year old boy. This put Weekes in a rage that came out clearly when he ascended the platform in Woodford Square where people were re-assembling.

It turned out to be only rumour. There was in fact a police shooting, but the victim was a young man, Stanley George, and miraculously the shooting was not fatal. Stanley George had been on lower Charlotte Street. A policeman asked:
"Aye, yuh in this Black Power business?"
"Yes, I am Black Power"
Bam! And blows followed too!
Weekes had to use a lot of persuasion to get the people assembled to disband and go home that afternoon. Ironically he would be attacked in the media for inciting violence by "irresponsibly" repeating the rumour that a boy was shot.

He had become accustomed to such accusations. A recurring issue the leadership of 1970 had to deal with was the official and

211

media condemnations of "violence". The condemnations started early. "IT'S TIME TO STOP THE VIOLENCE" screamed the bold headline of a front page editorial of the *Express* on March 10th. "Black dignity in the context of Trinidad and Tobago has nothing whatever to do with terrorism". "Terrorism" referred to small scale but ideologically slanted attacks on homes and business places, largely with molotov cocktails, that took place at night, after the demonstrations. The establishment was particularly incensed at the time of this article because the attacks on the weekend before had included the official residence of the US Vice Consul, Frank Hagen, which suffered minor damage. Stepped up police patrols were unable to stop the work of the elusive fire-starters some of whose targets were razed to the ground.

The state, the business community, the media and other such interests were troubled by the fact that on the NJAC platforms there was no indication of abhorrence to this creeping use of anonymous, individual acts of violence as a political weapon. They fearfully read meanings into the statement with which Granger closed meetings:

"Go home, lock your doors, and then . . . and then . . . and then"

But neither innuendos against the leaders, appeals for "sanity", direct attacks in the media nor else had the desired effect. The leaders of the Black Power movement absolutely refused to go on the defensive about the incidents the establishment chose to define as "terrorism". The acts were politically defined acts of rage and protest against forces which ordinarily had the protection of the law and its agencies in exploiting, discriminating against, and trampling the rights and dignity of the people.

Even the government was admitting that the employers abused the provisions of the ISA to deny workers their rights.

White racist institutions spit on the national anthem ("Here every creed and race find an equal place . . .") with impunity. For example, following the embarrassment of a Black American couple at the notorious Country Club in Maraval (the visitors were debarred from using the tennis court because they were Black), the government set up a Commission of Enquiry to investigate whether there were practices of racism at the Club. The Commission, instead of coming up with a condemnation of

212

the Country Club, chastised a Black witness, Tony Martin, a scholarly witness who later emerged as the major biographer of Marcus Garvey, for having "a chip on his shoulder".

So, in the atmosphere of 1970, when feelings of pent-up hurt were released, when shunned cries for justice and the absence of legal redress gave way to tangible expressions of anger, these were basically understood by the NJAC leadership. Huge sections of the society could identify with the mood and the reactions. The acts were considered minor compared to the wrongs inflicted on the people and the potential for violence at the time.

Weekes typified the response to the accusations of the establishment. In talking to a conference of Catholic teachers on March 9th he said:

> From quarters that are rich and feel well secured, there are now calls for 'Law and Order' and an end to 'violence'.
>
> Sisters and brothers, who can honestly doubt the unemployed and their families are the worst victims of violence . . .
>
> Is there anything more violent against a man than for him to be an eye witness to his wife and children suffering day after day hunger and want, his children unable to go to school or they become ill, and he cannot afford medical treatment for them; thus causing them to die. Is there anything more violent than for a mother, because of the above, in order to survive being forced to sell her body to keep her children from suffering . . .[14]

Weekes spoke with such emotion about social and economic violence that some listeners interpreted his words as "preaching violence". But his exposure of 'hidden' violence was a theme of 1970, a theme urgently addressed by other leaders of the mass movement as well.

Weekes knew from experience the effects of social and economic violence, effects that could destroy the soul or impel the mind to fury and the arms to strike. He knew the reaction this insidious, institutionalized violence could produce, not only in the victim, but even in the observer who was sensitive, especially when observation was combined with the illumination of ideology.

The ideas of socialism he had absorbed in the war had given him the conviction that something better, a social and economic order that was wholesome, that was equitable and just, was possible. He kept measuring the reality of poverty and exploitation against that vision and it transformed him into a permanent soldier on the political and industrial battleground. It gave him a restlessness about those procedures termed 'democratic' which did not seem to be working.

That is why he could empathise with the young people in revolt in 1970, the victims whose despair had been lifted by hope and who were now fighting against their social and economic debasement. He could identify with those other young people who were not themselves materially stranded, but who, by their identification, felt the spiritual wretchedness of a society which allowed a few to thrive on the backs of the many, a 10% minority to consume 40% of income, while the 20% on the bottom of the income ladder had to subsist on 2.2%. He knew these young people, in a predominantly young society*, felt the same restlessness about the system he felt, the same feeling that it was a maze of dead ends for anyone seeking liberation:

> Young people in search of truth and real freedom are saying exploiters will not easily relinquish their privileges, will not calmly hand over the reins of power to the exploited. For the exploiters not only dominate the economic resources, they dominate the means of communication. They control television, radio, newspapers, most educational and cultural institutions and the armed forces. I ask you teachers what peaceful means can be used to gain true freedom? The voting machine? The Ballot Box? Peaceful demonstration? The young are saying that they have tried all that before but to no avail.[15]

Weekes was talking against a material background where depression was so deep, the problems seemingly so intractable, that revolutionary struggle appeared as the only way out. The economy wound down to marking time in 1969 — zero growth, literally. But prices had not stagnated. Following the devaluation of the Trinidad and Tobago dollar in November of 1967, prices rose by 3% in the first month and then by "an

---

* 60% of the population was under 25 years of age

unprecedented" 9% the following year. In terms of the official index, price increases had continued at a slower rate into 1970. But the index hardly represented the reality with which consumers were faced because of the ineffectiveness of price control mechanisms. Even the PNM Women's League was calling on the government to probe the "indiscriminate rise" in prices of food, drugs and building materials, the very essentials.

In the face of all this there was massive unemployment. It was the government itself that confessed that the unemployment problem had proved to be "intractable", holding fast at around 14% in the late 60's, backed up by a further 14% underemployed. And it is the young who were hardest hit. As the Minister of Finance said "the unemployed are confined mainly to the younger age groups".[16] In human terms that meant a virtual army of some 50,000 young men and women, the unskilled, the technically qualified, the secondary school graduates holding impressive academic certificates, all growing weary of the futile search for jobs and dignity, bitterly joking they should cut off their hands because everywhere they went the signs said, "NO HANDS WANTED", from the banks and insurance companies where no one working looked like them, except the doorman, to the offices of the foreign corporations and local white conglomerates where the same applied (if yuh black, stay back), to the government ministries where they wanted to fire, not hire, to the construction sites where you could not even see the boss, to the shut and guarded gates of the factories that only opened to the transport trucks, to the lengthening lines outside the docks where fewer and fewer temporaries received the call on mornings . . .

The army, tired of marching in fragments to job sites, gathered in scattered and informal units on the blocks. There was a mood in the air, universal, dynamic, revolutionary, black; and the blocks now included educated voices. They were measuring their distress and social exclusion against new, emancipating self-concepts. Some units became formalised and they took on names. Then elements from the university reached out and pulled the disjointed units together, united them with the unions and organised the unorganised. With structure, and more vision and clarity, the seed was ready. By 1970 the season had come and it had sprung forth out of the soil of oppression and violence, the seed of the jobless transformed into a forest of

215

marching feet, clenched fists striking the air to the shouts of "Power", the war cry of Freedom Fighters. They were no longer looking for jobs, but for the control and salvation of their country.

This is where the potential for real violence lay, the potential for bloody revolt, not the pin pricks that were causing panic. An army 50,000 strong, young, energetic, motivated, daring, and with no hope outside of the Revolution was on the march.

Leaders who could not address their psychology, who were not themselves deeply moved by the pain and the frustrations of their lives, and the ignited hope of something to reach for, had no place in the ferment of 1970.

Weekes' life of struggle had prepared him for this phase of involvement. It had prepared him to fit himself comfortably in with a much younger generation (many of them less than half of his age) that came into political consciousness at that turning point, tuning in to events of the recent past that some of them were hardly conscious of when they occurred. Now they were gripped in the spiritual tow of those events. They relived Lumumba's agony in the Congo. They triumphed at the Bay of Pigs with Castro. They felt the courage, dreamed the dreams and suffered the frustrations of Che Guevara in the Bolivian jungles. They were fired by the anti-colonial hate of the Mau Mau in Kenya. They read Fanon on the Algerian revolution, on the psychological disorientation of the colonised and on the cathartic effects of violence. They shared the experience of descent into decadence and rebirth into revolution of Malcolm X. His autobiography became a collective confession, a sum of personal statements of all those who lived under the scorn of a society that was predominantly Black in numbers but hated Blackness, a society that de-classed and denigrated the hardest-hit Black victims of its exploitation, discrimination and aspirations to white values. They felt the way he felt about achieving Freedom, "BY ANY MEANS NECESSARY".

A generation, nurtured on the lives of these heroes, living in the shadow of the horror that was the Vietnam War, drew its own harsh lessons from history and Weekes was at one with them:

> History has shown that for an oppressed people to progress and win true freedom, they cannot go on bended knees or place their necks in a yoke. They

216

> must struggle to their death if necessary. People are
> forced to struggle not because they like to spill blood
> or go to war but because they are faced with
> SACRIFICE or SLAVERY[17]

The movement of 1970 did not turn to the violence of armed revolution. There was a real effort to change the system by mass action and resistance, and there were real possibilities of this being achieved. But the movement did not exclude armed revolt or any form of revolutionary violence in principle; it did not give away the right to respond in kind, if the defenders of the system met legitimate claims with violent repression; it never sought to disarm the people psychologically for the state violence which could be unleashed at any time.

Weekes himself admits that at times he had given thought to the question of whether the decaying political situation in Trinidad and Tobago needed an armed response, thoughts he has openly voiced in speaking to his members. In fact, he often wondered at the choice of the name, 'President General' for the office he occupied. Why did the founding fathers include 'General' in the designation of the office? Did it imply that they conceived of the union as a liberation army as much as they saw it as an instrument to deal with the day-to-day problems of labour? He thought about violent solutions. But with the weight of responsibilities as President General of the OWTU, and some lingering hope in the democratic options open in the society, he never turned his energies in that direction.

While the victims striking back were blamed for violence, the violence of the state grew. Shortly after the shooting of Stanley George, another young man, Irwin Faltine, of Belmont would be shot for raising his voice against the police harassment of brothers on the block in his area.

Weekes felt an increasing urgency to get the blue shirt army fully involved. Obviously the government was hoping they could solve their problem by repression. But they had reason to have serious doubts. The powerful appeal of revolutionary Blackness had infiltrated the country's military. Soldiers in uniform, on the army trucks passing demonstrations, openly identified with the struggle, raising their fists and shouting "Power". The police force was divided. Soldiers and police came from the very areas of the society that were erupting, the hell holes of unemployment, poverty and social neglect.

The fire, sparked by the combination of university students and the unemployed and underemployed in the main, was spreading through all levels of the society. In the Caroni March Weekes had seen many public servants, some of them in fairly senior positions, who had taken the day off for the event. He recognised some PNM (or maybe formerly PNM?) stalwarts. He was hearing of situations where businessmen, giving in to the reality, were offering workers time off to demonstrate. There were rumblings in significant areas of the work force. In WASA, on the docks. In fact dock workers, were able to secure a 40 hour work week in March 1970 and win what the Acting President General, Clive Spencer, hailed as "the largest increase we have ever had . . ."[18] T&TEC workers were very much a part of the prevailing mood, having just won their struggle for recognition by the OWTU. One of the main organisers of the T&TEC workers in the recognition battle was Winston Leonard, one of the OWTU men who was also a leading figure in the National Joint Action Committee. Secondary school students were caught up, participating in the mass demonstrations and beginning to challenge the education system to which they were subjected. The people of Tobago had torn down a barrier that excluded them from one of their best beaches.

This spread of the movement and increasing activity in the South was giving Weekes more leverage within the union. He felt strongly that there were members on his Executive who, even though they had little option but to voice support for the movement, deep down inside they were against it. However he was beginning to get things moving. On the 26th of March the union hosted a reception for the students who had returned from Canada - Teddy and Valerie Belgrave, Hugh Forde, Kelvin "Shaka" Robinson - and by April 4th he was able to get the General Council to commit the union to total support of the Black Power movement. In a statement issued a few days later, it was boldly stated:

> The question on the order of the day is — ARE YOU AGAINST THE REVOLUTION OR ARE YOU FOR THE REVOLUTION?
> The General Council of the Oilfields Workers' Trade Union with a full sense of the responsibility for leadership entrusted to it and on the basis of the democratic confidence reposed in it by the rank and

file of its members enlists our Union into the ranks of the revolution.[19]

The lengthy statement strongly reflected the sentiments of the union's leader:

> Let it not be said of the organised labour and trade union movement and particularly of us of the OWTU that in the finest moment of our country's history we soiled our blue shirts and other uniforms by failing (because of the reasonable but ever uncertain comfort of a relatively bigger pay packet than that of other workers) to rally to the revolution which was begun by our black brothers and sisters, the majority of whom have no pay-packet at all. Rather let it be said of us that, by providing the reinforcements they now in turn need and standing by, if called upon by them or when and if necessary, to lead the revolution on a new front on to a new stage, we too, like them changed the course of the inglorious destiny even now being further charted for our country by the enemies of the revolution.[20]

With this triumph, George Weekes set his eyes on May Day 1970. To dramatise the battle of the workers on that day when there would be a combined demonstration of NJAC and the progressive unions (which were then affiliated to NJAC), Weekes was calling on oil workers to wear their hard hats. He now had the General Council's official backing for an intense campaign of meetings in the oil belt. He had with him in the union two senior members of NJAC, Winston Leonard of the NJAC Central Executive, and Nuevo Diaz, Chief Labour Relations Officer of the OWTU and an area chairman of NJAC. Geddes Granger, the NJAC leader, also spoke at strategic meetings in the campaign. Weekes could feel the spirit of Butler, the spirit of the revolution moving in the oil fields again. He saw the glorious light of May Day shining up ahead.

Events moved very quickly in April. A young man of Barataria, Basil Davis, pleaded with a plain-clothes policeman, Joshua Gordon, not to take down a "brother", explaining that he was not too well mentally. Gordon pulled a revolver from his pocket. Basil turned to run. He was shot in the back at point blank range and sprawled dead on the pavement outside the Anglican Cathedral in Port of Spain, in front of scores of shocked eyewitnesses. The revolution had claimed its first martyr. A nation mourned for a young man it had not known, but who came to represent the yearning of the tens of thousands like himself, and the tragedy of a state that would murder men, women, children and their aspirations, if given a chance, rather than do justice. Davis' act of brotherhood, in a plea of loving concern for a victim of state violence, solidified the brotherhood of the nation. Some 100,000 people marched five miles in silent anger and dignified tribute from Woodford Square, the People's Parliament, to a cemetery on a hill in San Juan where his body was laid to rest.

The martyrdom of Basil Davis added to the momentum of the revolution. When the people buried Davis in the ground, they buried the murderous regime in their hearts. In their increased numbers they sensed victory. A *Vanguard* editorial on April 18th proclaimed:

> The end of the old order is in sight and the Black masses can sense it. No force on earth can stop this movement now.

The Labour Congress was shaken into making a statement pretending to be in support of Black Power[21]. They too spoke of May Day, saying its emphasis "shall be on the recognition and furtherance of Black Awareness" and calling on all organisations to demonstrate in the "interest of overcoming oppression of the masses". However they betrayed their hidden fears of the real movement for Black Power that was out there on the streets when, mindful "of what was going on in the country in the last four weeks", they urged all concerned to pursue Black "aspirations in a manner that is not repugnant to the rights and freedoms of the individual".

Even if their tone of accusation did not rankle, their identification was too late. Weekes had prophesied that many of them would be swept aside in the revolutionary 70's which would see "the 'retirement' from our movement of the tried and trusted lieutenants of the capitalist class". And it seemed his words were coming to pass. Workers at the Water and Sewerage Authority went on strike and they chased away the officials of the Congress-affiliated NUGFW, their official representatives, who went on the scene to discuss matters with them. The workers elected their own committee among themselves to handle their negotiations, which sat and discussed its intended proposals with

REVOLUTION!!

Clive Nunez, Public Relations Officer of NJAC and an official of TIWU, and Dave Darbeau, another NJAC leader. As the month of April advanced, workers' grievances were exploding all over, in small and big establishments and the workers were coming to one source, the National Joint Action Committee and its affiliated unions.

On April 19th a delegation of sugar workers went to the NJAC Headquarters in Belmont to seek assistance. Bhadase Maraj, their union leader, had kicked a worker, among other things. On April 20th a group of telephone company workers, officially represented by Tull's Communication Workers Union, approached NJAC members. They were planning to strike on April 21st and they wanted the representation of the organisation. Bus workers, retaining confidence in their leadership, were planning to strike and demonstrate on April 21, in dissatisfaction at the Public Transport Service Corporation's continued refusal to re-employ hundreds of workers who were kicked out following the bus strike one year earlier. On April 20th Geddes Granger and Winston Leonard led demonstrations of sugar workers in several areas of the sugar belt, closing factories and bringing the industry to a halt. In a mass meeting the sugar workers decided that the meaning of the march to Caroni must be completed by the march from Caroni to Port of Spain. Workers from the sugar belt, mainly East Indian, would march to the town to symbolise the realization of the unity of the struggle.

On the night of April 20th George Weekes met with Geddes Granger and Winston Leonard at the home of Leonard in San Fernando where they had a lengthy appraisal of the situation. Then he left for his home. The pace of events was quickening.

Weekes could hardly sleep that night as he lay in his bed. He didn't need to try. He didn't have much time . . .

CHAPTER 13

"A TEST OF ... MY MANHOOD"

The phone rang shortly after 4.00 a.m. on April 21st 1970. At that hour, it was either a threat or trouble. Somehow Weekes knew it was trouble and he was involved. Lennox Pierre, at the other end of the line told him, they had just picked up Darbeau. No need to explain who "they" were. Weekes got himself moving as quickly as he could and drove to Leonard's home. Was it something Darbeau did yesterday? Or was this the anticipated State of Emergency? This was the trend of discussion as he met with Granger and Leonard. It was wiser to treat it as the Emergency unless or until it could be determined otherwise.

Weekes and Leonard went to the OWTU office while Granger waited behind. He asked them to arrange transportation to get him out of San Fernando to the North where the base was stronger. By the time Weekes and Leonard reached the Paramount Building, a police car pulled up behind them. The sergeant asked Weekes to accompany him to the station. The superintendent wanted to talk to him. Weekes told him his office would be a more convenient place. When the police continued to press him, he insisted that if they did not have a warrant he was not going.

They left the premises and radioed the station. Weekes went in to his office. He picked up the phone and alerted Kelshall. Kelshall was packed and on the next plane to England that day. At his age prison was no place to be. But Weekes and Leonard would not get a chance to leave the OWTU office on their own. The police outside were soon joined by reinforcements and they needed no warrant. Thirty six armed men sufficed. Leonard was also given an invitation he could not refuse to join the "talks". There was no point arguing over legal details at 6.00 a.m. in an empty OWTU office.

At first the police were taking them to Staubles Bay on Trinidad's North Western peninsula, where the coast guard is based. But they were turned back at the Chaguaramas gate. It was too dangerous to go down there — rebellion in the army. This news brought joy to the hearts of the detainees. Back to town. To Police Headquarters on St Vincent Street. To cells full of prisoners, many of them injured and bleeding. From the chaos here, the sounds of bedlam and confusion, and the stories of prisoners, victims mainly of a raging war on the streets of Port of Spain, it seemed the country was being turned upside down. Police morale was obviously low. Discipline had disappeared. Junior ranks were cursing senior ranks, refusing to obey orders. Guns were dropped by nervous hands and went off accidentally. Weekes realized he was in the middle of a war zone, but he was a prisoner of that war. He was lifted, however, by the fact that the masses had obviously responded to the leadership call and were defying the Emergency. This they had been repeatedly advised to do by the NJAC leadership in the preceding days, in the event of such a declaration.

April 21st 1970 turned out to be a day of heroism for Trinidad and Tobago, the full story of which would emerge for Weekes and other detainees, only over a long period of time. More snippets were added to what they picked up in prison, after he and Leonard were taken to Nelson Island by coast guard boat at about five o'clock that afternoon. Weekes had now landed on the same island where his hero had been brought in 1939, like him a prisoner without charge; only, Butler, in his time, was fighting the colonial authorities. Weekes could not dwell then on the historic connection. His first preoccupation was with the present, the stories some detainees had to tell, those kidnapped later in the day, who were part of the fray in the city before it broke up. Over the coming days he would learn more as others were detained.

They spoke of running battles between youth and police in the city on the morning of April 21st, of bottles being rained on policemen from upstairs clubs in the downtown area and from rooftops on the city's edge. They spoke about shooting by the police, but did not know casualties. There was a story that a young girl had been killed on Prince Street. They spoke about a fire at the Bata shoe store in the heart of Port of Spain adding to the melee. The fire engines, with their screaming sirens, could hardly get to the scene because of the milling crowds. Frustrated firemen were having their hoses cut, which by then they had become accustomed to, when trying to out fires in Port of Spain. Thousands of people gathered on the scene cheering and jeering. The police were almost helpless in the situation.

At some point the police were withdrawn from the town and the mobilised youth demonstrated freely through the streets, peacefully at first. Eventually an incident on Independence Square triggered a rampage of destruction, which started with the glass fronts of the Trinidad Express Newspapers Ltd. Both daily newspapers were identified as part of the tyranny. The violent parade in Port of Spain left at least 52 business places damaged in the downtown area.[1]

Speakers and listeners felt proud of the fact that the people of the country had refused to just bow to the armed suppression of their fundamental rights and freedoms. The Emergency was regarded as highly unjust and a dangerous reaction to political problems. Except for the provoked incident on Charlotte Street, where the police over-reacted, demonstrations had been peaceful and highly disciplined. No one drank any alcohol, not even a beer, on a demonstration. The forceful impact of the uprising came, not from threats to order in the society or to the rights of the majority of the citizens, but from the popular nature of the struggle. There was no example of order in the society that could compare with the phenomenal order exhibited in the demonstrations, an unparalleled insight into the kind of discipline, dedication, effort and sacrifice the people are capable of. The Emergency, therefore, was not to protect the society, but to protect those elements in the society accused of exploiting the society mercilessly. It was to protect those elements who had found themselves on public trial, from public platforms transformed into People's Courts. The protected ones were the ones on trial for corruption, for legislating industrial slavery, for self-seeking collaboration in the destruction and destitution of thousands of citizens, for actively encouraging, aiding and abetting brutality and murder. In this situation those detained saw resistance, by any means possible, as a right and duty of everyone who cherished freedom.

Those who had the fortune to walk the streets on April 21st also spoke with pride about the manner in which the masses, even at the height of the action, did not lose sight of the lessons of the struggle, in particular the lesson of African-Indian unity. Prominent East Indian-owned business places remained untouched in the midst of the shattered windows all over the town.

They explained too that the break down of the resistance on the streets was less in relation to the actions of the police than in response to news that the army was coming over the hills. There was in fact truth in this. At the Teteron Bay Headquarters of the Trinidad and Tobago Regiment, soldiers had indeed rebelled under the leadership of army lieutenants, Raffique Shah, Rex Lasalle and Mike Barzie, on the morning the State of Emergency was declared. The army assumed the role of a People's Army in defence of the people's rights. The first convoy of soldiers leaving Teteron on trucks was stopped when coast guard boats, shelling from the sea, brought down a part of the hillside blocking the only road out for the army. Some of the men then took to the hills on foot. It is possibly this rebellion that caused the police to be withdrawn from the streets. Word of it also led to the demobilization of the people on the streets. One or two of the young men detained in the days after the Emergency were among those who, feeling there would now be a more decisive force with guns to confront the guns of the police, deserted the city streets and headed towards the hills of the Northern range. Others returned to their communities in the foothills, to await the People's Army.

Weekes would get his first insight into another area of resistance when Granger was brought in, after eluding the police for about three days. When he and Leonard were held, Weekes had left his driver, Titus Martin, with instructions to pick up Granger and drop him wherever he wanted. They drove to the area where the demonstration was supposed to begin in Central Trinidad. The workers were already gathering, but with the heavy police presence it would have been suicide for Granger to try to join them at that point.

Just to know that the sugar workers were responding to the call of the revolution brought joy to the hearts of the detainees. Months later, the imprisoned men would learn about the tremendous courage shown by sugar workers on that day. The men and the women refused to disperse when ordered to by the police. The march was forcefully broken up by the riot squad. Not once, but several times. After each clash they regrouped at further points down the road. This resistance continued until, just outside of San Fernando, a fully mobilized force put an end to the demonstration.

Many of the 59 people who would be detained during the State of Emergency were picked up in the swoops on that first day. Others would be brought in over the following two or three days. That 59 included OWTU members who also functioned in NJAC. It included the entire Central Executive of NJAC and all but one of its area chairmen. Hundreds of other NJAC members, group leaders and supporters of the organisation were arrested and thrown into prison, some just arbitrarily held in cells, others charged for various offences, trumped up or otherwise, under the Emergency regulations. The extent of the arrests left the people leaderless, in terms of any recognised leadership of the mass movement, during the critical days of the Emergency.

A really mixed group of detainees were thrown together on Nelson Island. It included members from the intellectual group, Tapia, university lecturers, students, individuals of various political persuasions, grassroots activists. Two women were held elsewhere. A few of the detainees were men with very violent backgrounds and long strings of convictions from the days before they were motivated by NJAC to give up lives of crime and fight for the people. Weekes knew it would take tremendous qualities of leadership to maintain reasonable harmony in a group like this confined together for an indefinite period of time.

Drama began on the first night. The men decided it was time to sleep. They shut off the lights in the dormitory where they were detained. The reaction was instantaneous. To Weekes as an old soldier, the rapid cracks of the rifles as bullets were loaded into the chambers were familiar sounds. Running feet surrounded the building. The door to the dormitory was violently flung open. Lights flashed on. Pointed gun barrels gleamed in the sudden light. The command was barked:

"Don't move".

Weekes looked at the panicking coastguardsmen and he knew the danger of that panic with nervous fingers on the triggers of cocked sub-machine guns, self loading rifles, and, in the hands of the commander that night, a massive bren gun.

In the tense atmosphere of April 21st, the outing of the lights was misread by the guards as part of a plan to escape. The error nearly had fatal consequences.

Thereafter, the detainees understood; at least some lights had to be left on at all times.

The first night's incident set the tone for a period that would have many physical and psychological tortures including, for Weekes, at least one other even closer shave with death.

Weekes was allowed to spend only the first few days of his seven month detention on Nelson Island. From April 22nd, he and other leaders began to organise classes and discussion sessions for those detained to maintain their revolutionary consciousness and strengthen their ideological understanding of the process they were involved in. This level of organisation disturbed the authorities. Shortly after Granger's arrival on the island they decided to move out those whom they apparently identified as the ring leaders within confinement. Weekes was transferred to a cell at the Royal Gaol, along with Granger, Nunez, Darbeau, Chan Maharaj, Brian Chen (an enigmatic figure whom George remembered publicly explaining how to make a molotov cocktail to anyone who would listen during the Bus Strike of 1969), Bayliss Frederick (a lawyer in whose house an NJAC team from Trinidad, including Granger and Leonard, had stayed, while mobilising the people in Tobago), Victor Marcano (a county councillor who had dropped out of the PNM and independently defeated its candidate in a local election), Winston Leonard, Nuevo Diaz and Errol Balfour. Winston Suite was later brought up from Nelson Island to join this group. The detainees were placed in individual cells in a block directly below men condemned to die for murder.

Here, as on Nelson Island, no radio was allowed, no books, no newspapers, no contact with families who were not informed about where their kidnapped members were being held, and the prison guards were strictly forbidden to communicate any information about what was taking place. At least on Nelson Island, the men could communicate with each other and learn from each others observations and experiences in the few hours or days of freedom some had enjoyed during the Emergency. In the Royal Gaol this was no more and there was no fresh news coming. Weekes had to endure the agony of knowing that the country he fought for was in deep trouble. But how deep he could not tell. The clues were frightening. He had heard from other detainees of the military aircraft circling overhead on the morning of April 21st. Later he would learn they were

Venezuelan. Before he was removed from Nelson Island he had had the opportunity to see the troop-laden American ships anchored in the country's waters, and observe the liaison with the ships of the coast guard.

It was a chilling experience to stand imprisoned on a small island, guarded by Black men with guns, and watch the forces of American imperialism, against which he had been an uncompromising fighter, setting up to invade his country.

With all this in mind, the lack of information was torture. What had happened to the army revolt? Had the US troops landed? Who was dead, who alive; he knew nothing, had no indications. To make it worse he had to keep the torment bottled up inside. It was impossible to communicate his deepest thoughts with anyone because the only form of communication possible was shouts across the cells. All of a sudden he was living in a nearly wordless world, or where the few words were necessarily meaningless or tortuously veiled. There was no pencil, pen or paper to even write a thought, no printed line to read and relieve his restless imagination. The only time he could leave that cell was to take the walk of a few feet to the toilet at the end of the block, almost across from where he was. There he had to sit on the bowl with the prison guard standing in the open door. Even that privacy was gone.

One day he knew something had gone dreadfully wrong. The sounds at the back of his cell, where the entrance to the prison reception was, indicated that soldiers had been brought in. The leadership was among them, because he distinctly heard the names "Shah" and "Lasalle" shouted in the crude manner which typified the admission officers when men were placed in their charge. Detainees shouted from their cells at the men and they shouted back, but little could be said or understood as the thick walls muffled the sounds, legislating conversation between blocks in short distinct syllables. From here on, hope for any imminent triumph of the revolution would be an act of faith.

The soldiers' rebellion, it turned out, had come to a very lame end. The advance guard of soldiers who had left the base on April 21st were ordered by the rebel leadership at Teteron to refrain from any military action. The leaders had entered into almost immediate negotiations with the government. Out of these negotiations, and possibly influenced by the visible presence of the American forces, came the eventual decision to surrender and hand over all army weapons to the police. The decision brought tears to the eyes of some of the soldiers outside. In the circumstances, with the masses already off the streets and waiting vainly, the surrender signalled the end of effective resistance to the State of Emergency.

Weekes did not know this background at the time the soldiers were brought in. But he recognised the depressing implications of the fact that obviously quite a large number of soldiers, including the leaders, were being locked in cells.

Something had gone wrong. What? Through indirect contacts, Weekes had heard before April 21st that there were elements in the army planning some kind of move against the government. It was a prospect he was not too sure how to relate to. On the positive side, the army could be a decisive line of defence for the people in case of an emergency. A coup was a more hazardous thing. An army coup under the right leadership and committed to a revolutionary civilian base of government could be one way of dealing with the oppressive Williams regime. It could also lead to a backward step — military rule and the end of any semblance of democracy. Weekes was being assured about progressive leaders in the army. He did not doubt this, but he did not know the men personally. He was troubled that a development of this magnitude was taking place without collaboration or co-ordination with the civilian leaders of the mass movement. Unfortunately everything 'came down' before he had had an opportunity to meet with the army leaders involved, hear their opinions, make his assessment of them and deal with any of the issues which he considered critical.

Now, whatever they might have planned, whatever they may or may not have done, clearly that was a phase that was all over. The why and the how he could not fathom because, for some time to come yet, he would not be able to communicate with them or with anyone else.

Lawyers provided the first opportunity for Weekes and a few of the other detainees to feel the sunlight and see a fleeting glimpse of life outside the prison walls. They filed writs of habeas corpus which forced the prison authorities to take the men to court. Those who got this opportunity made the maximum use of it to expose through the court the harsh conditions in prison, including the atrocious meals. This public exposure brought the first bare improvements. Like daily sunlight for half an hour each day. One detainee at a time in the enclosed prison yard, guarded by prison officers and a policeman with a high powered rifle standing at the top of a stairway.

The writs of habeas corpus and legal challenge to the detention orders also had a different kind of effect. The lawyers established that the orders contravened the law. The judge saw the point but deferred his judgement while the detainees were in court, to hand it down a few days later.

One morning the prison officers came and ordered Weekes to gather all his things. No explanations were given. They escorted him to the first of the heavy iron gates leading outside of the prison, opened it and bade him goodbye. But there was one more gate and it was closed. Legally he had been released from prison by this gesture, in response to the judge's order. The police were waiting by the gate to the street to slap another detention order on him and escort him back through the gate from which he had just come, into the hands of the waiting prison officers. It was just a game, played with the rights and freedom of men, and it was played with each detainee in turn that day.

The other aspect of the reaction to the writs was that some of the detainees were charged for sedition and granted no bail, just in case the new detention orders did not hold. In addition to being charged with sedition, Weekes was charged with using obscene language on March 5th.

The first morning they came to take him to court on the charge he refused to go to a court that was mocked by the very authorities it served. That caused the first strong physical protest in prison. The officers went for reinforcements and with a tremendous clamour coming from other detainees, lifted him bodily out of his cell to take him to court. Amidst the shouts and the loud pounding on the doors, Weekes heard the distinct sound of a heavy wooden cell door breaking as he was taken away . . .

At least one good came out of the court hearings. Detainees now had to be provided with pen and paper to prepare statements in their defence. Weekes seized this opportunity to put his protest and his feelings in writings. In his first letter to the union on June 9th, which he was able to smuggle out of the prison, he said:

> I protest the fact that we are not allowed to read the news or listen to the radio or talk to fellow detainees face to face, even for a brief moment. If this act is not

meant to send us mad or break our spirits, I don't know what it is intended to do. I can assure you that such a plot will not succeed with me . . .[2]

Over the months, the protests in court, hunger strikes and other forms of protest at the prison would bring somewhat better meals, the right to once-a-week visits by family or friends, open cells during the day so that detainees could communicate with one another, the right to books approved by the prison authorities, paper and pens.

Weekes saw the period in prison as a test of his manhood. He had to fight in some way every day. There were no guaranteed rights or standards. A violent reaction to hogwash today brought better food tomorrow and possibly the next day, but three days or so down the line, the meal would be hogwash again. Weekes would turn his back in anger and disgust. There were other detainees who would fling plates across the yard and shout for the world to hear exactly where Munro, the Prison Commissioner, came from — at birth. (It is notable that Weekes, the man who in the final analysis had sullied his public reputation by cursing in Woodford Square, never once, no matter what the provocation, uttered a single obscene word either during the first or the second detentions.) Weekes and other detainees had to fight for visitors not to be separated from them by two walls topped by wiremesh fences, four feet or so apart. When they got this changed, they had to fight to maintain the more satisfactory arrangements. They had to fight for supplements to the prison meals to be allowed in and fight to keep it so . . .

But the best way to understand the experience is to have it told in the words of the man. In his first letter to the union, Weekes said:

> . . . I regard my imprisonment as my greatest test yet. Indeed it is a test to my courage, honesty, dedication and my manhood. Only time will show the result . . .
>
> I have conditioned my mind and body for a long and bitter struggle as I do not expect to win my freedom soon . . .[3]
>
> Living under the gun, I have learnt not to panic when one is fired even behind my back, as was done by the white Commissioner of Prisons when he gave us a warm welcome to the Royal Gaol, I have learnt

not to stop protesting in my cell when shots are fired outside the prison walls to terrorize me. I have learnt to walk towards guns pointing straight at my chest as I clench my fist and puncture the air above my head shouting the popular demand of our people — Black Power — Power to the People! Power to the People! Power to the People![4]

In those dread and uncertain times he had his thoughts not only on himself, but on the OWTU, the trade union movement and the people. He held firm in his confidence in the people:

... the Trade Union Movement and their leaders, like the rest of the people are facing a similar test, but unlike the uncertainty regarding the results of my own test, I am confident that the workers and the people generally through this great test will come out with honours.

... as I have said so many times before, I believe in and trust the members of the Oilfields Workers Trade Union, the working class of the country, and the people of Trinago generally. Never forget that united we stand, divided we fall, and if our backs should ever be against the wall, we must be together, you and I. Therefore it does not matter how hard they try, they cannot stop us now.[5]

The more personal emotions of the times, influenced further by the effects of a second, longer detention, come out strongly in a sermon delivered by Weekes in October 1972 at the Mount Moriah Spiritual Baptist Church in California, Central Trinidad, where the union's Assistant General Secretary, Lionel Bannister, was the pastor. He referred passionately to the 1970 experience:

Why ... we who were never charged with any crime were LOCKED in 'Death Row' block of cells? Was it not to at least send us mad and so create a situation that will provoke incidents, to give an excuse to the power structure to have us shot or brutalised for ATTEMPTING to escape their mental torture?

Why did no one detained, not even myself, go mad during that long stay housed in 'Death Row' on the ground floor locked in separate cells with men condemned to die on the floor above us?

"A TEST OF ... MY MANHOOD"

Night and day we felt their presence and heard the singing and praying of those CONDEMNED MEN FACING DEATH. We heard their naked feet on the concrete floor above us as they marched round and round in their cells as they prayed and sang to God to help them wash their sins away before they die. I saw those condemned men coming forth for sunlight and airing with their skin discoloured after months without any, and which only became a reality after strong protest by political detainees against the inhuman treatment meted out to men facing Death. I saw in their eyes both desperation and sadness, and I understood deeply their plight and suffering.

Why was I not shot when on a Sunday like this and in the presence of an American Black Preacher we heard the crack of a rifle bolt held by an advancing but unknown and unnumbered policeman, who shouted at, and abused Clive Nunez? As Clive retreated behind me, I saw the safety catch of his rifle released and, with his finger on the trigger, I saw murder in his eyes as he pointed his rifle straight to my heart as he abused us. Why then did he not pull the trigger?[6]

Weekes had really come perilously close to death at the hands of a police guard. The cop, with his SLR directed at Weekes' heart, was in a trembling, inexplicable rage. He appeared to be on drugs and so out of control that he could have murdered even by accident, though there was enough purpose in his eyes. Addressing the church congregation two years later Weekes attributed his escape to prayers, the prayers of his congregation and all those outside who had prayed for the detainees, "It was the work of God and the voice of the people". At the time of the encounter, only the look of strength in Weekes' eyes as he confronted the policeman face to face must have defused something inside his deranged mind, a fraction of a millisecond before he would have pulled that trigger at close range and sent a deadly shell straight through the bodies of Weekes and Nunez.

In prison in 1970, Weekes had enough inner strength to shake off the occasions of physical danger and overcome the mental anguish, which was especially hard in the days of not knowing, the prolonged period during which he could get no information

233

even about his family, from whom he had suddenly been cut off. Weekes was concerned about his wife and six children (four boys and two girls*) for whom he could do nothing, from whom he could hear nothing during the early period of incarceration. Alone in his cell he thought about the pressures they had had to endure. His wife Theresa was really strong. He was aware of the kind of frustration she had to overcome in the early years of their marriage when she hardly understood his involvement. Often when he came home in those days he was too mentally exhausted to sit calmly with her and give her the explanations she wanted. He felt pride when she was able to rise above initial hurt and anger and join Christina Lewis's Caribbean Women's National Assembly so that she could learn more and share in his involvement. He tried whenever he could on a weekend to take the family on outings, especially to his old home town, Toco. But such occasions, though important for the love they showed, could not make up for all the days and nights of worry and loneliness, as more of his time was consumed by the struggle and danger lurked ever closer in his life.

He thought of the way duty had sometimes taken him away from his family in the most difficult of times. His last daughter, Genieve, was given that name to mark the fact that she was born while he was away in Geneva in May 1964. Apart from his wife being pregnant and ready to deliver at any moment when he left for Geneva on a government mission, his last son, Christopher, was in hospital at the time, recuperating from a motor vehicle accident. The family had borne a lot. What were they bearing now?

When communication was re-established, it was a joy and relief for him to learn that this area of personal concern had not been ignored in the time of need. When the risks to Theresa and the Weekes children appeared grave, Lionel Bannister and members of his congregation had taken them to temporary shelter at a home in California for their safety and comfort. Other union members, in particular Doodnath Maharaj, kept close to the family throughout the Emergency.

The protection and care of the family was one of the very personal ways in which members of the union and other

---

* Cyril (22), Kenneth (21), Keith (18), Gail (17), Christopher (11) and Genieve (6).

concerned people were able to demonstrate to the P-Gee their appreciation for his contribution to their lives, his contribution to the thousands of families who benefitted directly from his struggles and sacrifice and the many thousands more who benefitted indirectly. Such actions lifted his spirit behind bars.

On the whole, once the barriers to communication with outside had broken down, there was a lot to occupy Weekes' concern and sustain him spiritually. A man of the struggle gets his nourishment from the struggle. Once it is continuing he is strengthened. And in 1970 the struggle never stopped. Its most effective forms were suppressed. The presence of six American warships offshore in the early days of the Emergency, the airlift of sophisticated weapons to the police by the US, Venezuela and Britain, the collapse of the rebellion in the army, all contributed to this suppression. Many people who had shown courage before were undeniably cowed. But there were strong indications of a resilience and preparedness to continue the struggle in many pockets of the society.

The reports reaching Weekes about the OWTU strengthened his faith. The two organisations bearing the brunt of the attack in the Emergency were OWTU and NJAC. The OWTU had much more in terms of physical structure to attack and the establishment had the police going all out to strike telling blows. On the night of April 21st an attempt was made to burn down the Paramount Building, the headquarters of the union, and gasoline bombs were thrown into the offices of *The Vanguard.*

What impressed Weekes, when he finally could get news, was the response of the union leadership to the attacks. Executive members and branch officers decided it was their duty to protect the property of the union and they started to sleep in the building at night. This protective action almost cost Doodnath Maharaj, a trustee of the union, his life. On the night of April 24th shots were sprayed at the building from a passing car and one passed so close to the head of Maharaj that he was lucky to be alive after the incident. *The Vanguard* too was attacked again that same night by petrol bombs and Palms Club was fire bombed. *The Vanguard* was also invaded by the police and accounting records, invaluable historical documents, important photographs and other priceless items were seized.

It is not surprising that there would be this kind of attack on *The Vanguard* which had played a critical propaganda role during the days of upheaval. Weekes, who had a feel for propaganda, had approached Wally Look Lai, whose articles in the *Express* impressed him, and he got Look Lai to accept the job as editor of the *Vanguard* in 1969. He had also obtained the part time services of Dave Darbeau to write for the paper. Together they built the paper into an organ of the developing consciousness. In the hectic months of 1970, when Darbeau could no longer write for the paper, Weekes got Darcus Howe to join Look Lai and the *Vanguard* continued as a major voice of the revolution. Look Lai fled the country with the declaration of the State of Emergency and was not to return for almost 17 years for reasons having to do with his guarded contacts in the army. The *Vanguard* however remained a thorn in the side of the establishment and, despite the attacks, Weekes had the satisfaction of seeing the paper published during the State of Emergency.

These small but significant signs of resistance were important to Weekes psychologically. Ideally he would have liked to see a mass response of oil workers to his arrest and detention and the State of Emergency. But he could understand why that did not come.

Not since 1937 had the society experienced the level of repression unleashed in 1970. People were being indiscriminately, individually and en masse, swept off the streets, brutalised and imprisoned in ghastly overcrowded cells with or without charges. All symbols of the revolution were being savagely attacked. Women wearing their hair natural were being dragged into police stations and having their hair crudely cut before they were thrown back out on the streets. Young men with long hair were suffering a similar fate. Even a bulletin board, NJAC had set up in Woodford Square, was pounced upon by enraged policemen as though it was a living enemy. Those policemen, who were uptight all along about the Black movement, forced to swallow their bitterness as they worked the extra hours imposed by the demonstrations, and those who cringed with their fears when they heard of the army rebellion, were now taking out their rage on any person or object which to them represented the hated Revolution. Curfew hour at six p.m., which resulted in the fatal shooting of an old man by the police on the first morning after it came into effect, added to the sense of dread in the society. Five deaths on the first day of the Emergency created the atmosphere of a state under martial law.

The violent attacks on the union itself bred fear in the ranks. Weekes took into consideration too that the union had not yet been fully mobilised and involved before the declaration of the Emergency. So there was no momentum to keep going. The involvement had just been developing when the Emergency was declared. Against this background, and with the dispersal of mass resistance by the circumstances of April 21st, it would have taken tremendous courage for any group to take serious action challenging the establishment. It would have taken dynamic leadership for there to be any hope of stimulating that courage to resist, the kind of leadership which only Weekes himself could possibly have given to oil workers.

Understanding this, Weekes could deal with the real world where less dramatic gestures could indicate the continuation of the struggle, by showing that the will to resist was not broken even if the capacity for resistance was limited.

This was shown in the society generally in the highly-motivated campaign mounted against the Public Order Bill. The campaign expectedly involved radical organisations like NJAC, which had been held together by a second line of leadership, and the more militant unions, like OWTU. But it also included conservative lawyers, the church, conventional politicians, individuals of various persuasions and a wide range of institutions. They all stood up to be counted when the horrendous provisions of this Bill, presented to Parliament on August 7th, became known. The name of the then Attorney General, Karl Hudson-Phillips, became a symbol of dreadness from that day.

Again Weekes was satisfied with the response of his union. They organised an anti-Public Order Act campaign, which included jerseys, posters, stickers, leaflets, streamers and indoor meetings. With proud exaggeration the union, in its annual report for 1970, boasted of its mass meeting of members, families and supporters on September 12th against the Act, as one "the like of which was never witnessed in the history of the OWTU7". Invited speakers at that meeting included Allan Alexander and A.N.R. Robinson, formerly regarded as Deputy Prime Minister in the PNM government, who resigned first his ministerial post and then from the party, justifying his resignation as a response to the government's handling of the crisis. The Annual Conference report summed up the union's part in the defeat of the Public Order Act in these words:

> The Oilfields Workers Trade Union's special con-
> tribution to this defeat and withdrawal was one of our
> finest moments in the history of the union.[8]

The Bill was in fact withdrawn by September 14th. The PNM government had set up its own party General Council to meet on September 13th and call for the withdrawal. The pressures for withdrawal were more than the government could withstand. What made the victory outstanding was that a campaign, sufficiently effective to force the government to back down on a critical bill, could be mounted by various sections of the community during an emergency. This in itself indicated at least one legacy of the recent Black Power upheaval. It had left an imprint on the manhood of the society generally. Recognition of this brought pride and inspiration for all those who could only receive the news from behind prison walls.

Weekes' greatest satisfaction was to know that his imprisonment was not just taken for granted by oil workers. Psychologically this was important. The establishment and even, he believed, certain Executive members would have liked him to be forgotten in prison. But the majority of oil workers, whether confused about his politics or not, whether prepared to take a political stand or not, wanted their President General to fight their battles. Therefore the leadership of the union, including those who preferred him behind bars, had no choice but to seek his release. As part of this effort, the OWTU supported NJAC in a heavy campaign it mounted to free all political detainees, which revealed the capacity of that organisation to paint and poster the country on a wide scale despite the State of Emergency. In addition the union mounted its own campaign to free Weekes and the other detainees.

A significant development in the campaign was that it produced another institution in the union which strengthened its democracy, the Conference of Shop Stewards and Branch Officers (COSSABO). Another element of democracy which became institutionalized in the months of crisis was the Mass Membership Meeting (MMM). The first meeting of the COSSABO on September 16th 1970 took decisions on steps to be taken towards securing the release of George Weekes and other detainees. One decision was for the membership to begin wearing red armbands as a sign of protest against the continued detention of their President General.

"A TEST OF ... MY MANHOOD"

Another aspect of the campaign was to seek a meeting with the Prime Minister on the question of his release and that of the other union officers. As it turned out the Prime Minister used the occasion for another propaganda stunt to justify the continuation of the State of Emergency. He informed the union that the very day before their appointed meeting (quite coincidentally of course), the police had discovered a cache of arms so huge that if he were to tell them the quantity, they would "hit the roof".[9] Many such arms caches, which neither the press nor anybody else but the finders ever saw, and about which no one was ever brought to trial, had been discovered previously, just like "Cubans" were sighted in the hills, and Cuban or Russian ships would often mysteriously turn up off the coast, somewhere. Already accustomed to ghosts, ghost ammunition and ghost ships, visible only to those with the gift of power-at-all-cost vision, the union team was unimpressed enough to ask what was the connection between the "arms cache" and the continued detention of Weekes. To judge by his response, Williams could no more see the connection than ordinary mortals could see the arms. He would keep Weekes locked away anyhow. If Weekes wanted his freedom, let him apply to the tribunal set up under a lawyer named Lionel Seemungal to review the cases of detainees who wanted to be released.

There was no way that Weekes was going to apply to this tribunal, which had been condemned by himself and the entire imprisoned leadership of NJAC, a commission which they had advised all other detainees to boycott. A few disagreed with the boycott and some others weakened and went before it, grasping at any hope of freedom. But Weekes was too convinced by the justice of his cause to put himself through the humiliation of a mock hearing by a tribunal, which was a gimmick to start with, and powerless too. In his own mind he was vindicated by the sincerity and objective good of his struggle. The only other vindication that mattered to him was the vindication in the hearts and minds of the people for whom he fought. Ultimately they, and not any advisory court, must decide on whether or not he should be free to live in the society for whose freedom he was paying a price.

One of the realities that Weekes had to face in prison was that the attacks of the establishment on the union were in the end directed at him. First they were meant to drive a wedge between himself and the union through sheer terror — scare the workers and other Executive members away from him by identifying him as a source of danger to themselves and the union. Then the attacks became more pointed. Given the nature of the PNM government, they could not bring themselves to believe that George Weekes, head of the powerful Oilfields Workers Trade Union, negotiating with the wealthiest corporations in Trinidad and Tobago for eight years, and head of the richest union, with millions of dollars in assets, was not corrupt. Williams took the unprecedented and utterly shameless step of using special emergency regulations to have the police search the personal bank account of one man - George Weekes. To their utter disappointment they found only $4.81. They could not publish it. Instead, on May 14th and 15th, they invaded the union's headquarters and carried away all the accounting books and records along with other material. Again they failed to find anything to taint the integrity of the man.

These were indeed some of the most disgraceful acts of persecution of an individual carried out by the PNM government. They only reinforced Weekes' commitment and his image in the union, because they were attacking him where he was strongest. Jack Kelshall, who has worked along with Weekes for many years, in the union and in politics, says about Weekes:

You cannot beat the man's integrity. It is simply amazing for a man in his position in this society.[10]

Though the state sought to crucify and destroy men like Weekes and Granger in 1970, many of the statements (such as the Prime Minister's National Reconstruction speech[11]) and actions of the very state stood as concrete testimony to the fact that those whom the state castigated were right. While the men were held in prison and their thoughts condemned as sedition, Williams reshuffled the government more thoroughly than he had ever done before. The *Express* referred to the re-shuffle as "the most drastic cabinet-parliamentary surgery since the Peoples National Movement took control of government 14 years ago".[12] And, as if to reinforce this de facto admission of the government's incompetence, Williams changed existing constitutional practices to draw on new personnel outside of elected members to reform and hopefully upgrade his cabinet. Among those thrown out were the two Ministers most criticized by the Black Power movement, John O'Halloran and Gerard Montano.

The country got a National Commercial Bank and a Workers Bank. Pressure was being gently applied to foreign banks to "localize". The state bought shares in the sugar company, Tate and Lyle. Government encouraged the formation of cooperatives.

The hasty implementation of changes that presented themselves as consistent with Black Power were not limited to the state. Private sector businesses offered shares to workers. Banks gave business loans to formerly excluded African businessmen. Petty level jobs in banks and other private institutions, formerly denied to Blacks, were now open to them. There was even a deliberate tokenism at higher levels, conferring managerial titles, though not management responsibility on Blacks. The church confessed its guilt and sought to get itself more involved in dealing with the real problems facing the poor in the society.

Weekes was not naive to think that the state or other institutions of the power structure had been ideologically persuaded. There were critical areas of difference between what was being officially projected and done, and what the movement preached. The concept of a people's economy for example was watered down to a people's sector in the economy. But it was obvious that the masses of Black people had been ideologically persuaded enough to exert political pressures which could bring reactions that were a significant advance, despite their limitations. This was the essence of the victory. All the reactionary forces could and would in time gang up to undermine the directions indicated at the height of the consciousness, to defeat the purpose of new institutions and activities which sprung from the actions of the people. But the fact is, they had to acknowledge that this direction, the direction of national control of resources and people's involvement, was the ideal. They had to acknowledge the existence of and the need to correct the evil spectre of discrimination against Black peoples. These were worthy achievements in themselves.

In such a situation Weekes could not be overwhelmed by any depression in prison. He was able to overcome the low and testing moments, though at times he had to dig deep within himself. After all there is no substitute for freedom. Weekes would walk around and around the prison yard for exercise, others would walk, some would jog and run, do other exercises, pull up on the bars of the shed. But walking around and around in confined walls, cut off physically from the masses, is not the same as walking in the excited, hopeful throng of a demonstration. Or even the same as walking down the road alone. The monotony of the routine, the knowledge that your life is so totally controlled by others from day to day, the absence of any indication of when it will all end, such factors do exert mental pressure.

Then there would be constant reminders of ever present danger. One such occasion came when the prison authorities organised to teach a lesson to the soldiers who were held on charges of mutiny, and in some cases, treason. That day, from the detainees section, Weekes could hear all the buses pulling up at the prison, bringing officers from other stations. He could hear the unprovoked attack on the soldiers, many of whom did not stand up like soldiers when faced with the overpowering number of prison officers. It was not easy for Weekes and the other detainees to hear the commotion close at hand as fellow prisoners were abused, or even to witness the subsequent look of defeat on the faces of men who had roamed the prison at will and were now confined and regimented in their every activity.

The attack almost spilled over into the detainees section. Nunez took the bold step of spitting on the Commissioner, Munro, when he came too close to the gate of bars that separated the yard where the detainees were from the remand yard. Nunez lost his temper at the sight of the white Commissioner arrogantly beaming after the attack on the soldiers. Somehow there was no physical reaction to this insult. Maybe the very hate that was radiating from the detainees on that day stopped Munro from ordering an assault on the small but vocal group at that point. Weekes knew there would have been resistance from his companions and the resistance would have been violent, no matter how ultimately futile.

Such were the trials that would sap the nourishment of the triumphs if Weekes only gave in to them. But he never did. He set his eyes on his people, his union, his fellow detainees who had to endure the same tortures, his country, his dreams. Battles that seemed formidable a few months before had suddenly been won. The workers had repealed the ISA. Bowrin put it very accurately in *The Vanguard* in October of 1970:

> The workers have now taken over. They no longer
> ask government to repeal the ISA. They have

repealed it for themselves nationally. They go slow, they go on strike, they call sympathy strikes with impunity. For them, whatever the government may say, whatever the Industrial Court may do, the ISA, in so far as it hinders their freedom of action in 'industrial matters' is repealed.[13]

There were in fact 64 strikes in 1970 and 99,600 man days were lost.

Politically, Weekes did not see the people as having lost:
The power structure has won a battle by the force of arms but they cannot win the political war. The masses will win.[14]

Weekes also set his eyes on the Caribbean reverberations of the struggle that he was a part of in Trinidad and Tobago. Allister Hughes had commented that Eric Williams had a fire on his hands so hot that it could jump from island to island. And it was doing precisely that. The stirrings of Black Power were manifesting themselves right through the chain of English speaking islands.

West Indians abroad, in the United States, Canada and Britain, were moved to play their part. For example, at the beginning of the Emergency students at Howard University in Washington had demonstrated calling on the US government to keep its troops out of Trinidad and Tobago.[15] There were demonstrations in New York, Canada and London as well. Some groups raised funds to assist.

Every act of struggle, every affirmation of the rightness of the goals of the Revolution, every demonstration of support was a mitigation of the test that was the 1970 detention. Therefore, though it was a test, which some failed, for a man with Weekes' fighting spirit, ideological commitment and experience, it was not such a grave test. When he was finally let out of the prison doors on November 17th and he walked down Freedom Road (as Frederick Street was unofficially renamed), he had every right to feel satisfied that he had passed this test. But the real trials were yet to come.

243

CHAPTER 14

FROM CRISIS TO CRISIS

When Weekes was released from prison on the evening of November 17th 1970, he returned to a society that was torn between fear and defiance. As he and the last small band of detainees walked down Frederick Street they could see and feel that mixture of emotion in the greetings. There were warm and open greetings. Some people boldly thrust their clenched fists into the air and gave the Black Power salute, "Power". There were others along the way whose clenched fists, hugged closely to their bodies, could not rise higher than their chests, whose heads bowed with the weight of seven months of terror.

Weekes had a conception of the task that lay ahead of him:

> The revolution has not ended; and it is not going to
> end until the working class . . . rises to the historical
> task, which it alone is capable of performing, that is,
> to intervene in the continuing crisis and take over and
> 'hold the reins' of the economy of Trinago. And this
> goes for the entire Caribbean up to Jamaica.[1]

One major area in which the revolutionary ferment had certainly continued was in the field of industrial relations and from prison Weekes was walking straight back on to the battlefront. A hot zone had developed a few weeks before his release. In late October, OWTU workers employed with an oil contracting firm, Halliburton Tucker, went on strike protesting the dismissal of two fellow workers. They were out there now on the picket line. They were fuming that an American racist management thought that Black workers could once more be trampled on because spirits were broken by Eric Williams' State of Emergency. A bitter experience during the strike had brought this home to them:

> Once during the picketing, Haynes (the most
> offensive of the managers) came out of his Company's

244

offices and raising his fists in the air, he shouted
arrogantly that Black people were seeing and feeling
the effects of real power — White Power[2]

When Weekes joined the workers he was garlanded. He had
returned as leader, and also now, a hero.

His release so inspired the brothers that they began
fighting back with a confidence that could have only
ended in victory.[3]

In this battle, Weekes led the first demonstration through the
streets following the State of Emergency.

The Halliburton Tucker struggle turned out to have some
revolutionary significance for the union. Texaco workers
responded to the cries of their fellow workers. In the
Guayaguayare field they struck in protest against working
alongside Halliburton Tucker scabs. They immobilised
Halliburton Tucker trucks. The workers out on Marina 1 (an oil
rig) also refused to work alongside Halliburton Tucker scabs.
The workers' action forced Texaco to take a decision to refuse
jobs to Halliburton Tucker until the matter between the firm
and its workers was settled. Workers and, significantly, their
families, kept all night vigils by beating drums and patrolling the
"occupied areas". By December 23rd Halliburton Tucker was
forced to reinstate the dismissed workers. They were not only
forced to re-employ them, but to re-employ them without break
in service, and — to pay strike pay to the workers who had
stopped work in support of them. *The Vanguard* celebrated the
historic victory:

> It is the first time such a secondary boycott by OWTU
> was successful as members of the union came out in
> strong support for their brothers in another firm. This
> marks the beginning of a new era in the Oilfields
> Workers Trade Union[4]

And the editorial added:

> . . . the credit must go to George Weekes, the man who
> fresh from a seven month term of imprisonment in Dr
> Williams political prison showed that he has not lost
> any of his old fire.[5]

The OWTU General Council did not want the return of the
P-Gee to be all work immediately, to have him once more totally
absorbed, cut off from his family without at least some short
respite. They decided that he and his wife should have a break

together, wherever they wanted in the Caribbean. His efforts to spend some time in the other English-speaking islands taught him that for him the world had grown smaller. As he describes the experience, the authorities in the islands "had me and my wife going from island to island like tic-tac-toe stones".[6] First Barbados said he was not welcome. Grenada let him in and then threw him out after three days. St Lucia would not let him in. Antigua turned him back at the airport. Eventually he had to leave the familiar language zone and settle for 10 days in the French colony of Guadeloupe.

The experience had its rewards. His reception at the points where he touched ground indicated the positive responses of the Caribbean people generally to the "February 26th Revolution", as Tapia leader Lloyd Best christened the 1970 phase of the struggle. He was embraced as a father figure of the trade union movement in the Caribbean and as a heroic representative of the common revolutionary struggle. In Grenada he and his wife were welcomed by the Trade Union Council and his reception among the people was such that it must have prompted Prime Minister Gairy to get him out. Maurice Bishop, a young lawyer just returned from training in England, who on his way back to Grenada had passed through Trinidad and Tobago in the heat of the revolt, sought unsuccessfully to have the order for Weekes to leave rescinded. When the Antigua Workers Union heard of his difficulty at the airport in Antigua, representatives went out there to welcome him and his wife. The customs and immigration officers, bound by instructions to keep him out of the country, were nevertheless very supportive and helpful, making efforts with every other English-speaking island (except Jamaica) to see if they would accept George Weekes. When this failed they made the Guadeloupe arrangements for him.[7]

His brief, relaxed sojourn in Guadeloupe was just a recharger for the OWTU President General. Things were moving so quickly for him outside of prison that events had to be heading somewhere. He could feel it. Not too far down the road the mass struggle would erupt again or the state would strike again, a pre-emptive strike this time.

Official nervousness was obvious on December 12th 1970, a day proclaimed Re-dedication Day by NJAC. The build up to a demonstration planned for that day was remarkable, given the nightmare the people had just been through with curfews, police violence and the suspension of constitutional rights. A familiar militancy was coming back into the atmosphere at huge preparatory mass meetings. It looked as though Re-dedication Day would be the government's nightmare.

But the government struck at the eleventh hour. On the morning of December 12th the newspapers and the radio carried the news that by special proclamation of the Governor General, demonstrations were forbidden in defined areas of Port of Spain. The prohibition was in fact limited. The demonstration would have to skirt the heart of the town but there was nothing to prevent the marchers from visiting, as planned, the grave sites of all those who were killed during the course of the struggle. However the effect of the proclamation, well-timed so that it could not be countered, was to give the impression that the demonstration was banned. The four or five hundred who turned out and marched anyhow, made up in spirit for what was lost in numbers because of the government's move. The demonstration was constantly harassed by the police, eager to take advantage of its relatively small numbers while they were out in full force. The face of terror was naked and ugly. But the red, black and green flags stayed high in the air, the clenched fists reached for the sun, the voices were full of fervour. The people won the psychological battle on that day.

However, there were byproducts of Re-dedication Day which had repercussions on the course the struggle would take. The use of the special proclamation gave a clear indication that the government would use all authority vested in it to prevent political demonstrations of the type that rocked the country earlier in the year. That, and the menacing behaviour of the police on the day, strengthened a growing conviction in many young people that peaceful demonstration or any form of peaceful protest was a waste of time. This direction of thought led, among other things, to tensions about strategy in NJAC. Eventually these tensions, combined with other factors, resulted in some members breaking away to take a path of armed fightback. That was a development of late 1971.

In the post-Emergency period, Weekes had to pay considerable attention to the union with its escalating demands. Its membership, standing at over 11,000 in December 1970, had grown by some 1000 during the course of that year alone. The change in the constitution had opened the doors and T&TEC

workers, agricultural workers, workers in various industries, like Dunlop for example, had come marching in. Hundreds more were waiting in line, hundreds that would grow into thousands. Apart from the multitude of individual issues to deal with in servicing the greater membership, serious attention had to be given to questions of national policy which were impacting on the welfare of workers generally.

In late 1970, one of the major national issues where workers were concerned, was the proposed National Insurance Scheme. Since the plan was first introduced in 1969 Weekes had written to the Prime Minister, seeking clarification on how it would affect existing private plans which were, in the case of OWTU workers, far superior. He had only received an acknowledgement. Much had intervened. But the issue was still relevant and still vexing workers.

The OWTU was not objecting to a National Insurance Scheme, whatever the specific reservations about the actual proposals. Such social legislation was necessary. More than two thirds of the workers in the country were not unionised. Of those unionised, many were in unions not worth the dues and some had employers who, no matter what, could not afford adequate sickness benefits, pregnancy leave arrangements, pension plans and such benefits as the NIS was designed to provide. The OWTU concern therefore was that the NIS must not pave the way for big companies, like the oil companies, to merge their plans into it in ways that would take away the benefits already won by the unions. This simple concern remained unanswered by the authorities.

By February 13th 1971, Weekes was marching the streets again with oil workers in protest over this unresolved issue[8]. The matter finally came to a head in 1972 when Texaco and Shell actually tried to merge their pension plans with the National Insurance Scheme. Resistance by the union finally settled the question in the workers' favour. They would not lose any of the benefits they were entitled to under negotiated plans.

The increasing demands of the union and union related matters did not make Weekes forgetful of other national matters and he made sure that the union continued to see its wider responsibility. A United Labour Front* was formed with the

---

* A completely different organisation to the ULF which was formed later, in 1975.

OWTU, other unions and non-union organisations which it was hoped could develop into an effective political voice for labour. Weekes had some strong concerns about political unity on the left at this time. A number of political organisations mushroomed in the post-Emergency period as people sensed the imminent demise of the PNM. The unity moves did not succeed in building a solid political front out of these diverse bodies. The only serious threat to the PNM regime from an unconventional political organisation continued to be the one posed by NJAC.

On the national front, Weekes also felt deeply committed to doing what he could for the imprisoned soldiers. He had the union participate in a campaign organised by NJAC, which included the wives and families of soldiers, aimed at building up public support to free the soldiers who were on trial for mutiny. Some of them were also slated to face trial for treason. Jerseys printed for this campaign were worn by many demonstrators on Re-dedication Day. Secondary school students were playing a high-profile role in this campaign. In fact the growing turmoil in the secondary schools, led by a student arm of NJAC, the National Organisation of Revolutionary Students, was a telling indication of the state of unsettlement in the society.

The convictions and sentences of many of the soldiers to long prison terms brought another flashpoint in the struggle. Raffique Shah and Rex Lasalle, identified as the leaders of the mutiny, received the harshest penalties. Shah was sentenced to 20 years imprisonment and Lasalle to 17. Secondary school students organised their most massive demonstrations. They walked out of their schools throughout the country and marched in protest against the judgement of the military tribunal, a tribunal which was comprised mainly of foreigners — a Judge Advocate from Ghana and military officers from Ghana, Nigeria, Uganda, Malaysia and Guyana[9]. OWTU's General Council met on March 5th 1971 and strongly condemned the trials and convictions.

While Weekes was fighting national battles and the battles of his union, a war of a different but familiar kind was being waged against him. In the public mind, the old bogies about him were being re-ignited. A fairly wide spread whisper from this campaign was that everything was going good in 1970 until Weekes (the communist) came in, or the variation would be until Weekes and Nunez came in. Among those who fell for these lines were people who, if they only tapped their own memories, would remember that neither Weekes nor Nunez "came in", both were there from the start; and "everything was going good" until the momentum was broken by one single factor — state terror. All else followed from that. There was no indication prior to April 21st 1970 that people were drawing back from the movement in disenchantment at the presence of Weekes, whom they were lustily cheering on the platform. In fact the movement was growing. But such is the effect of propaganda. It worked against Weekes because of so much that had gone before; essentially because he had been publicly opposing Williams since the 60's, a period when Williams' moral authority, and therefore his ability to tarnish the image of an opponent, were too high. Williams' cutting jabs left many people with an overhang of fears where Weekes was concerned, fears based on the indoctrinated dread of communism, or just undefined fears that they themselves are unable to pin down rationally if asked to explain.

It is only Weekes' strengths that saved his public reputation from complete annihilation and in fact allowed him in large measure to triumph over the negatives. He has had to live with the image of hero and villain, not just hero to some and villain to others, which is part of it, but often hero and villain in the minds of the same people. Weekes' success as a trade unionist, his integrity and the sincerity with which he comes across when speaking are his strengths. People are drawn by his achievements for workers and find him believable when they listen to him speak.

Another of his strengths is the fighting spirit which he communicates. This motivates people to fight against exploitation and to place confidence in his leadership in such a fight. But, in a contradictory way, the same inspiring aggression also acts as a negative. Not because it is negative in itself. But it turns out that way in the context of all that has been said about Weekes. On the one hand the masses of people, in their oppressed state, identify with the sentiments. But in the areas of the subconscious where the propaganda lies buried, something is triggered identifying his forcefulness with a mythological communism (the violent, warlike images of American indoctrination). This is what sets up the political barrier. It agitates the lingering negatives which are like a settled dust that can always be stirred up by propaganda in the right environment.

The post 1970 period was such an environment. It was a time of shattered dreams for many people. Re-dedication Day was an attempt by leaders to reunite the scattered fragments of hope that had kept the dream alive, to reaffirm the direction of those whose faith and courage preserved the manhood of the revolution in pockets of resistance and saved the morale of the society from dying under the gun. It was also to rejuvenate spirits that had been daunted. For just as there were those who had overcome, there were those who had succumbed. In the disappointment and disillusion there was a search for scapegoats, especially by those who were disappointed by the failure of their own will. The sorcerers of the system presented them with the already branded scapegoat, George "P-Gee" Weekes. Meanwhile they were heating the irons to scar the other principals of the February drama, who were fortunately without imposed taint from the past. It would take a little time to conjure up a history of discredit for them because they had to make over the history of 1970 for that. But they were working at it, smothering the truth with lies, killing the memory of the substance and painting shallow media images that would lean more and more to violence, to tension, to hatred, to fear; and further and further away from the liberating ideas and ethos, the love and brotherhood, the dedication and sacrifice, the very soul of the Black Revolution.

The practical effects of the stigmas versus the reality where Weekes is concerned is probably the sharpest dualism in the relationship of the people to an individual that has existed in Trinidad and Tobago. The conflicting images in people's minds are not simply between Weekes, the trade unionist, and Weekes, the radical politician. It exists within the image of him in politics. Obviously there is something in the man beyond his pull as a successful trade union leader that draws people to him. In 1976, for example, a group of pollsters at UWI conducted a survey to find out who people saw as the "most respected public figures" in Trinidad and Tobago. George Weekes ranked seventh, ahead even of figures like A.N.R. Robinson and Lloyd Best.[10] If the vote was related to power, it would change dramatically. The contradiction is visible. Weekes sits on a platform on a political issue, and politics is where the doubts are. The crowd wants to hear him. They call for him to speak. It has happened over and over, in the 70's, in the 80's. There is warmth in the reception.

The listeners are moved. Yet when they huddle and talk the fears come out. His words are right, but there must be some hidden motive somewhere. This is the Achilles heel in the social mind that the establishment stabs all the time, through agencies like the media, publicised criticisms by high profile political and corporate personalities and the whispering field agents.

Throughout Weekes' struggle for a better society, they have been able to sap his full political potential this way. He was at his strongest politically on a national scale in 1970 because he was part of an environment in which it was possible to communicate a radical message without it getting lost or distorted in anti-communist propaganda. This had to do with the movement's language, the rootedness of its concepts and their expression, its timeliness and the consequent difficulty to label its unlabelled leaders. Precisely because Weekes reached such a political pinnacle in 1970, as part of a movement that came within close range of toppling the PNM regime, the propaganda machine ground harder at him in the aftermath of the upheaval. They could not alienate him from the NJAC leadership though, who dealt with the person and not the myth. This turned out to have more political significance than the doubts stirred up at various levels in the society by anti-Weekes propaganda. Because the politics that mattered in the 1970-1971 period revolved around the OWTU-NJAC axis. Industrial battles were at the heart of the struggle in that period. And the OWTU, led by George Weekes, was at the heart of the heart, reinforced by an active NJAC presence.

On the industrial front even the nastiest of campaigns failed to shake the faith of workers in Weekes. Union membership tells the story. The union picked up a surge in the 1970's, a decade during which its membership doubled from 10,000 (at the beginning of 1970) to 21,000. This leap in membership had nothing to do with any significant growth in the labour force or growth in the bargaining units already represented by the union. In fact there was a decline of jobs in the major oil companies. The growth was a general, nation-wide vote of confidence in the leadership of George Weekes, trade unionist, and it came from white collar workers and blue collar workers, it came from industrial workers and it came from agricultural workers. The oil workers, the original base of the union, restated their confidence in May 1971, when they returned Weekes and his entire Executive to office in the union election. Oil workers would defy Mammon to follow Weekes, but halt dead in their tracks if you shouted, "politics".

The confidence shown by the workers was important to Weekes. But not all his supporters were happy. One day shortly after the election, he sat in the union's Palms Club with his Executive officers. They were having lunch with some of NJAC's leaders after a joint meeting. The two organisations had maintained a close liaison despite efforts to break the links. An old oil worker, named Bell, came up to Weekes to congratulate him on his victory, but with hurt in his voice he said:

> Yuh see you P-Gee, for you we will do anything. But
> you see them (pointing to Edwards and Beckles), you
> have to get rid of them fellas.

In the eyes of many workers, Weekes had made a big mistake going in to the elections with men whom they felt were dangerous and at heart against the President General. Weekes had calculated that in the few months he had outside of prison he did not have the time to shake up his team and replace men who were, in his estimation, popular with their branches. This is one time he did not show enough faith in the membership, whose overwhelming confidence in Weekes would have given him the mandate to go into a new term with a more positive Executive.

The result of this compromise is that the union entered what was to be its most trying period for the 1970's with internal tensions and possibly treachery. After being arrested in July 1971, Doodnath Maharaj said the police were able to accurately represent to him sensitive, highly confidential discussions that took place at the level of the Central Executive of the union.[11]

It is remarkable the battles Weekes was able to fight from this difficult position. Problems for the union were mounting with such intensity, and employers were proving so recalcitrant that the union leadership came to the conclusion that there was a systematic, organised plot by the government and the "White Power Structure" to destroy the OWTU. Companies seemed to want strikes and to want to prolong them. It happened with Dunlop, where the workers were fighting an entrenched racism that excluded Blacks, no matter how qualified, from senior positions on the company's staff. The salary scales showed a disparity between Whites and Blacks that would be acceptable in South Africa, which is where some of their management came from. Controversy over the appointment of yet another expatriate at the company, over the head of a fully qualified and experienced local, led to a strike. The company's attitude was totally uncompromising.

Soon, unyielding tactics in negotiations, provocations and harassment of OWTU shop stewards at Federation Chemicals Limited opened up another war front. The company dismissed eight workers and a strike was called. Federation Chemicals' attitude was as uncompromising as Dunlop's.

During these strikes the whole mood of the country underwent change. First it was the atmosphere in the strike camps themselves. No conflict in 1971 could be separated from the perceptions or the conscious and unconscious ideas and emotions trailing from 1970. In opposition to the multinationals, emotions were especially charged. The tensions exceeded tensions that had to do only with worker/management confrontation. It was a confrontation between managements that were white, foreign and arrogant, and workers who were Black, proud, self-knowing and nation-conscious. The management knew that more than its industrial relations and wage policies was being questioned. It was their very presence that was being challenged, their right to alienate and profit from the nation's resources. The sub-layer of the fight was the contention for who would control the country's economy. For Weekes personally that had always been the fight. The mass movement had now generalized such concepts.

Both the state and employers recognised this element in industrial struggles in 1971 and they reacted to it. The police presence at strike camps became more hostile and intimidating. The inevitable clashes and arrests followed. Employer organisations, such as the ECA (to put it in the terms used by the workers) "called for blood". Managers directly involved reacted with venom and provocation. Hildebrant at Fed Chem would stop his car near the picket line, heavily protected by the armed police, and taunt the workers, calculatedly trying to escalate confrontation into violence, hoping the police could win his war by breaking heads if he could not break wills.

The mood of the strike camps was spread to the other parts of the country by propaganda on both sides. Weekes, in addition to using the *Vanguard*, drew on NJAC's resources for preparing and distributing the views of the union. Mass meetings and demonstrations in areas of the South complemented the union's propaganda thrust. The public was informed of the national rip-off that these companies were getting away with, through extended tax holidays and other concessions, including extra cheap utilities. The public were informed about their racist and anti-worker practices and their South African links, a point Weekes was always very vehement about. There were physical attacks on scabs and the homes of scabs, who crossed the picket lines under armed protection. From Savonetta to Point Fortin the pre-Emergency feel of 1970 was coming back.

That mood would envelop the nation when on July 1st 1971 the continuing refusal of either company to budge forced Weekes to take the struggle further. By this time there were some leaders in the union who wanted to back off. They were seeing danger and they felt the visible presence of NJAC was making matters worse. Weekes built up the pressure from the workers to hold them on course. Mobilization was going on apace among oil workers to get their support for the Dunlop and Fed Chem workers. Worker turnout to general meetings at Paramount and Palms Club gave Weekes the indication that they were ready. They not only packed the halls but spilled over into the yard. They were angry and calling for action. June 19th had come like a build up for the July action. A statue of Butler was unveiled outside of the Fyzabad branch hall of the union and the hall was re-named the Butler Hall of the Revolution. Thirty three years of struggle were invoked by the main speakers on that historic day — Butler himself, threatening to lead his forces again and sounding as though he could do it; George Weekes, who had brought militancy to the conventional trade union movement and stood unquestionably as its foremost leader; Geddes Granger, who had led the most dynamic mass uprising since the time of Butler; A.N.R. Robinson, who had caught national attention with his break from the PNM. On July 1st Weekes called on the spirit of June 19th and the oil workers responded. The frightened media tried to underplay the response to the strike call, but it was effective. Next step would be to call out electricity workers. They were ready. The whole nation was on the brink of expectation.

At the very point of total confrontation, a confrontation that could have led anywhere, the companies compromised and so did the union. Grave matters, including dismissals, were left for possible resolution by talks.[12] Just as the scale of the confrontation had frightened the employers into coming back around the table to talk and talk seriously, it had also put fear into some of the union leaders who were anxious for any opening to withdraw from the brink of further escalation.

But then Weekes had to face the state. The union's headquarters was raided one more time by the police on July 12th and the books again seized. On July 15th the police made early morning raids at homes and detained five members of the union. Three were members of staff — Maniram Dubay, the accountant; Hilda Harris, bookkeeper; and Iola Charles, a cashier. They also held two Executive officers — Doodnath Maharaj, trustee, and John Commissiong, education officer. Psychological pressures were brought on all five of them to sign statements prepared by the police. The union lost its accountant who resigned on July 16th, unable to take the harassment anymore, fed up with the aspersions on his character implied by the repeated police seizures of the books and repeated checks on the books by auditors which were ordered over and over, no matter how many independent firms cleared them. They were trying to get at Weekes but others were suffering in the process.

The upshot of these raids came in September. The day was the 25th and the General Council was in session. A police party led by Superintendent Ignatius McPhillip entered the building and McPhillip indicated that he wanted to speak to Weekes. He was asked to wait until the General Council meeting was over. He did. At that stage warrants were read for the arrest of Weekes, Bannister and Irving Noel, charged for "conspiring with persons known and unknown to defraud the union of five thousand dollars".[13]

It was the kind of charge to make George Weekes see red. In court he suddenly drew a razor blade, held up his left hand, and, to the blood curdling shock and horror of union members who had come out in support, lawyers, magistrate and spectators in the public benches, he furiously slashed at his own hand until he was restrained. They wanted his blood. He shed his blood in protest against this vicious blow at his most cherished reputation, shouting as he did so:

> In the name of the Black Indian and African masses
> and as a mark of protest against the corrupt regime
> and the oppressive power structure . . . blood! I shed
> my blood![14]

Weekes' reputation for honesty survived the charge, which was never seriously pursued by the courts. He was made to appear in court several times along with the other defendants, but not a word was ever read in evidence against any of them. A public hearing would only have undone the damage intended.

The charge was part of a larger build-up too. Throughout 1971, the atmosphere in the society was heavy with repression. Apart from excessive shows of force on picket lines or when workers demonstrated, frameups against young men identified with the Black Power movement were increasing. Large scale swoops by police on blocks where there were 'limes' were commonplace. Armed terror was even directed at secondary school students. Schools were occupied by armed police. Young students, including girls, were arrested and beaten by the police. Whole scale expulsions of students were encouraged. At one time, 100 students were expelled from Woodbrook Secondary.

It was clear that the establishment was deathly afraid of the continuing militancy in the society. What worried them the most was the continuing connection between OWTU and NJAC. They were disturbed by the high profile of Leonard and Diaz in the union. They were disturbed by the distinct presence of NJAC members, men and women, on the picket lines, in the strike camps day and night, at the meetings, sometimes speaking on the platforms, in the demonstrations. PNM members of the union made efforts to get Weekes to debar NJAC members, even those who were officers of the union, from speaking at some meetings. The government could not rest until this relationship was broken, until Weekes was destroyed or discredited and deposed, until NJAC was crushed, until labour legislation could be enacted to do what the ISA was meant to do (since the ISA was in fact dead), until the framework of laws gave the government tighter control over mass forms of protest and action. Emperor Williams was naked without an ISA or a Public Order Act and Weekes was pointing at him on the street.

With each passing month of 1971, it was clear that the desperation of the establishment was growing. It had to because all tokens of appeasement thrown at the people crashed against a solid wall of consciousness and shattered the government's hopes of regaining control of the situation.

Government attempts to co-opt the spontaneous co-operative movement by financial assistance, which eventually destroyed this healthy development, met with only partial success and was not on a scale to deliver the political peace wanted.

The government engaged in discussions about permanent and prestigious relocation with young craftsmen and women who, stimulated by the new black consciousness, had drawn on their own creative resources to set up mini industries on the pavements of downtown Port of Spain. They were producing sandals, pendants, necklaces and a range of other personal items. In October 1971 a decision was taken to build booths for this group on Independence Square. This measure could not buy widespread support or loyalty.

The government compelled businesses and high income earners to pay a new Unemployment Levy which was used to expand the programme of public works, creating thousands of temporary 'jobs' for the unemployed. These programmes were concentrated in the areas considered to be most explosive. To their dismay, brothers and sisters held on to the concept that they were not fighting for crumbs. They were hungry enough to eat the crumbs but politicised enough to continue fighting for the whole bread.

The government pinned a lot of hope on the General Election in May. They wanted an election victory to restore some semblance of legitimacy. But psychologically people had withdrawn from the system of conventional politics. To add to this a 'No Vote' campaign developed. A number of organisations, including UNIP, UMROBI and WEA (the Workers Educational Association), which had come together in late 1970 under the banner of the Union of Revolutionary Organisations (URO), initiated this campaign. It was later joined by the coalition ACDC/DLP (an amalgam of A.N.R. Robinson's Action Committee of Democratic Citizens and Vernon Jamadar's Democratic Labour Party), which decided against contesting the elections. Their decision not to contest was an about turn. The party had already started election campaigning. But they felt the freeze in popular attitudes to the polls. Weekes was personally supportive of the 'no vote' campaign, and he attended meetings though he did not speak on the platforms. The OWTU General Council officially advised members not to vote. The result of it all is that Williams only managed to get Bhadase Maraj to put up a token opposition group in a few seats in the elections. Bhadase's party had no credibility. They did not win a single seat. A mere 28% of the registered electorate went to the polls to return the 36 candidates of the PNM to office, with full legal powers but not a shred of moral authority.

When the election exercise failed, the regime tried to re-define the revolutionary crisis as "Constitutional" and to assuage the demand for people's participation in the decision making process. A Constitution Commission was appointed under a former Chief Justice, Hugh Wooding, in June 1971. It was mandated to hold public sessions throughout the country, inviting citizens to submit memoranda, present and debate their views on a new constitution before its members. Public response was not even lukewarm.

They tried the participation gimmick with the students as well, staging a massive Education Convention down at Chaguaramas. The Convention did draw valuable ideas and critiques but the student organisations were convinced from the start of its futility. They rejected it as a diversion and militancy continued to increase in the schools.

By September 1971 Williams had had enough. He had endured a full decade of opposition from Weekes. The political potential of this opposition had grown with Weekes' participation in the mass movement of 1970. Now the combined opposition of NJAC and OWTU was making the country ungovernable. Williams decided on a do it or die approach. On the one hand he hinted at resignation, using the words of a then popular song, "like a bridge over troubled waters, I will lay me down."[15] On the other hand he "let loose the dogs of war".

Williams got his party machinery working. They produced a report which spoke about the existence of "an extremist anarchist element dedicated to the promotion of murder, mayhem, kidnap, hijacking and violent revolution".[16] The report was presented at a weekend convention of the PNM on September 26th, one day after Weekes was arrested on fraud charges. The report made specific claims of NJAC involvement in the indoctrination of the unemployed and the security forces with the intention of promoting armed revolution. It was a heavy propaganda strike.

Next Williams turned to his natural allies, others who, like him, would welcome the end of Weekes' national influence, others who felt threatened by the revolutionary upsurge led by

NJAC; he turned to Texaco and the Trinidad and Tobago Labour Congress. The Emperor wanted a screen behind which he could put on new clothes.

Texaco obliged. The company was in the process of erecting a desulphurisation plant. OWTU had gained recognition for workers employed by the main contractor, Badger Pan America Limited. The union secured higher wages for the workers employed directly by Badger than those paid by a sub-contractor, Wimpey, to men who worked side by side with the Badger employees, performing the same tasks. This naturally led to industrial problems and Wimpey workers struck for equal treatment. In the spirit of the revolutionary struggle Badger workers also struck in support of their fellow workers. The militancy of the strike reflected the spirit of the times, an aggressive search for justice, a consciousness about exploitation and sensitivity to white employers using divide and rule tactics against Black workers, and disrespecting Black workers. At one point angry workers, in the course of protest, did some minor damage to a company office. This was conflagration point number one.

The Labour Congress was equally ready to do its part. This was not surprising. Members of its Executive, led by the then President, Clive Spencer, had run secretly to Williams in 1970, begging him to declare a State of Emergency to save them from losing the majority of the workers they represented.[17] Now they were under pressure again. Workers from Tugs and Lighters Ltd, who were represented by the Seamen and Waterfront Workers Trade Union, had gone to the OWTU to seek representation. The reaction by the SWWTU, and subsequently the Labour Congress, to this normal development in industrial relations was nothing short of phenomenal.

First the Seamen's union made a grand announcement on September 22nd that their Acting President, Vernon Glean, had held discussions in London and New York seeking a possible boycott of tankers plying the Trinidad and Tobago route. The episode reeked of CIA involvement through the AIFLD and AFL-CIO contacts of Congress unions. The union further claimed that its members would refuse to handle all goods consigned to companies in which the OWTU had representation. On the 29th of September the Labour Congress not only endorsed the decisions of its affiliate but took a decision to extend the scope of the announced boycott if OWTU did not respond to an ultimatum to cease its "poaching" within seven days from the 11th of October. According to the Congress threat, published in several full-page advertisments in the daily newspapers, seamen would boycott goods at the docks, CATTU workers would boycott goods at the airport, postmen would do the same with mail addressed to the companies where OWTU was represented, and telephone workers (members of the Communication Workers Union) would stop installing and servicing phones in the targeted companies.

The lame justification for this incomprehensible extremism was that Congress had to stop Weekes from building a power base to destroy "industrial peace" and the "investment climate", to create unemployment, discontent and the "fomentation of political strife . . . thereby making the country fertile ground for the propagation of an ideology of which he is a local protagonist".[18]

The Congress threats, which if carried out would have virtually shut the country down, were nothing but unvarnished bluffing. They had no purpose beyond creating an atmosphere of hysteria. This was conflagration point number two.

By the time Congress was making its statements the OWTU had cooled off conflagration point number one through skillful negotiation with Badger and talks with that company's workers, who resumed their jobs. In early October the union attended talks with the Labour Congress, which from first reports were progressing well, though Weekes and the OWTU remained firm that the workers at Tugs and Lighters must be free to choose their representation. That was a sacred principle of trade union democracy. Peace, it seemed, was on the horizon.

But in a flash, like the lightning before the storm, the horizon disappeared. On October 11th, Badger officials suddenly blew the whistle and announced that work would be halted. There was a predictably violent reaction by the workers, which resulted in injury to a security guard and to the Badger Project manager, who had to receive six stitches following a blow to the head. Within 48 hours the company, behaving as though a civil war had erupted, had flown all its executives to Miami on a chartered BWIA flight. That was only the beginning of the drama.

Within another 48 hours, the Governor General had banned public marches in San Fernando (by proclamation), the National Security Council had met in emergency session, the Labour Minister had announced supposedly alarming strike statistics for the past few months, the Employers Consultative Association had met hastily with the Labour Minister, panicking over "anarchy" in industrial relations ... While all this was happening the media was charging the atmosphere with sensationalism about the racism and violence of workers. Then to crown it all, the SWWTU announced on October 15th that it was embarking on its threatened boycott against companies where OWTU was recognised.

Weekes had seen it all before. When the police arrived at his office on the afternoon of October 19th, his question was only a formality:

"Do you have a warrant?"

CHAPTER 15

THE INTERVENTION OF FAITH

There is an extra irritation to this State of Emergency to start with. It is such a shameless and transparent fraud. People's right to liberty is being taken away, guaranteed constitutional rights are being suspended on the pretext of grave national crisis, and in the same breath this is announced, the Prime Minister assures the country there would be "parang as usual" for Christmas and there would be "Carnival as usual".[1]

Weekes can hardly get the dangerous implications of this cunning manipulation out of his mind. It is plunder by seduction. He knows what the state is after — to rob a sedated public of their fundamental freedoms, permanently. But there must be no panic, none of the nightmare atmosphere of 1970 with curfews and widespread restrictions. Take the minimum number considered necessary to achieve the purpose off the streets — Weekes, Granger, Leonard, Darbeau, Diaz, Nunez, Suite, Kelshall, Stanley Antoine ('Tiger'), Leslie Ramdoo, Tony Ayoung, Dedan Kimathi, 'Salim', Allan Campbell, Michael Joseph ('Scobie') and Alvin Adams.

Conspicuously absent, of course, were Nathaniel Critchlow, President of the Labour Congress, Vernon Glean, Acting President of SWWTU and all the other union big shots who were making the grandiose threats, which supposedly became so grave when combined with a cut on a foreigner's head, that the government's response was to declare a State of Emergency.

Weekes knew they would strike hard at him within the union too. He had given Beckles and Edwards a new lease on life in the union election in May. He did not realise he would be taken away again so quickly to give them room to manoeuvre. It was too late for regrets. He had opened the gates to the Trojan horse. Now he must bear the consequences. His heart sank early. It was just the beginning of a sad and tortured period.

The environment in gaol was one of constant stress. As in 1970, there were the regular protests about food, prison conditions and detainees' rights. But there was a new, more dangerous development. 1970 had seen some loud verbal clashes and at a few points physical clashes between individual detainees and officers, which were quickly defused by other officers and/or detainees. Such incidents were rare because when detainees protested, the protests were directed at the authorities. Officers on duty were not abused, and they did not get involved beyond reporting detainees's actions or complaints to those at the top. The few incidents which went beyond shouting were provoked by officers who seemed to bear personal hatreds against what the detainees stood for. The harmonious general relationship between prison officers on duty and detainees did not change in 1971-1972. Nevertheless, for different reasons, full scale physical confrontations developed.

Ironically the first one came at the height of the season of peace. Christmas 1971 was going to be George Weekes' first Christmas in prison. At one point it looked as though for him, and others detained with him, it would never reach. On the eve of Christmas 1971, preparation in Cell Block H was as feverish as Christmas preparation anywhere. But there was no spirit of cheer. No stockings were being hung for Santa. Detainees were ripping legs off of tables with which to arm themselves. They were setting up barricades at strategic points in the narrow corridor between the cells in the block they were locked into by a barred iron gate. They were wetting pillow cases and other pieces of cloth in case of tear gas attack. They were preparing for the return of the Acting Commissioner of Prisons, Phillip, who would either compromise with a protest that led to detainees deciding cells would not be locked that night or he would employ force to suppress the protest.

The Acting Commissioner's return was accompanied by a now familiar sound. The riot staffs clunking and dragging outside the cell block. Inside the men were as ready as they could be. Hands tightened their grip on makeshift weapons. The sound of the key in the gate to the exercise yard echoed in the waiting night. The officers, led by the Acting Commissioner, approached the outer gate of Cell Block H, visible through its iron bars. Within seconds there would either be an attack or there would be a truce. Phillip opted for averting confrontation. He sought an

264

assurance that this would be the only night of the protest. That was agreed, and the riot staffs were heard clunking away from Block H.

That turned out to be only part one that night. A few minutes after agreement had been reached the sounds of sirens and heavy vans pulling up outside the prison were heard. Shortly afterwards there were footsteps and voices outside the Cell Block. Tony May, the Commissioner of Police, was pressing Phillip for the authority to launch an attack on the detainees, claiming he had information that they were planning an escape. The tension returned. But the Acting Prison Commissioner held to his word and the crisis passed.

This incident brought back home to Weekes, what his experiences had taught him in 1970. In prison, under the given conditions, you walked a thin line between life and death and ever so often the option to risking death would be to allow those in authority to walk on your manhood.

On another occasion he would get a very personal test within the collective struggle. That day in 1972 is one Weekes would never forget. In the course of the afternoon, a senior prison officer named Halfhide came into the section of the yard where detainees were allowed out in the day and ordered,

"Everybody, inside!"

That had to be a joke. It was 3.00 p.m. Prolonged struggle had earned detainees the right to remain outside the cell block until 6.00 p.m. Those who were inside, including Weekes, came out. Refusing to advance any explanation for the strange order, Halfhide left. Detainees had to prepare with the limited resources available for his return. There weren't enough table legs left. Some ended up bare-handed. The officer on duty cautiously let himself out of the gate to the section. Everyone knew there would be no negotiations this time.

The speed with which Halfhide returned with the prison riot squad said something. This had been planned. They were on standby.

On his return with some 60 to 70 officers, Halfhide stood with his hand on his holstered gun and barked his orders. Detainees took up positions with their backs to the Northern wall. Weekes and two others sat quietly on a bench. Others stood around with whatever they could get their hands on. Alvin Adams stood erect against the wall, fire in his eyes and an iron bar he managed to wrench from a bed, jammed between his back and the wall.

The prison officers lined up against the Eastern and Western walls and in front of the detainees. Others stood at the gate in the adjoining prison yard. Once more Halfhide ordered the group of detainees to get into their cells. When he could not get collective obedience, he decided to pick individually, beginning with Weekes. He anticipated that Weekes would be his easiest target. Weekes was over fifty and he was sitting quietly. This was not his kind of fight. So Halfhide thought.

"George Weekes, go into your cell!"

"For what?"

"George Weekes, I said go into your cell!"

Halfhide's voice hit a higher, harsher note. The prison officers gripped their staffs and looked uncertainly at the greatly outnumbered group who were determinedly standing their ground in front of them. When Weekes refused to move, they knew the next order that was coming.

"Take him in!"

Feet shuffled forward. No one wanted to reach first. There was no doubt about the violent battle that would ensue. The fourteen* men would eventually have been massacred, but not without blood on both sides. The officers saw it and they did not know why they were being called upon to start this. Many of them had a respect for several of the men whose heads they were now being called upon to bash ...

"I said take him in!"

Halfhide's voice trembled with rage. Feet shuffled forward again. The group of men confronting the prison officers did not believe in senseless violence, but they would not give up their manhood inside or outside of prison. The prison system was designed to break wills. If they did not fight this issue, there was no telling what tomorrow's imposition would be, and what would come the day after, until they would be robbed of all self-respect. Weekes decided there was no way he was going to walk on his dignity by taking those steps into his cell.

In the end it is the will of the detainees that triumphed. The prison officers would not obey Halfhide's command. Instead of the evening ending in bloodshed, it turned out to be an evening

---

* Detainees Jack Kelshall and Allan Campbell were in the infirmary.

of enlightenment for the officers. They stood leaning on their riot staffs for over an hour listening to Granger 'rap' to them on the meaning of the Black struggle. Those from the adjoining yard crowded through the gate to listen. A deflated Halfhide had to stand crestfallen through the session. In his closing remarks, Granger invited the officers to come again the following week to listen to George Weekes speak on labour.

The close calls with violence were one thing, but there were other severe psychological pressures on George Weekes during the second emergency. One of the greatest hurts for him was the deliberate and cruel persecution of Jack Kelshall. There were close bonds between the two men. Kelshall had given tremendous service to the union for many years as legal advisor. He was more than a lawyer working for fees. Kelshall was the kind of ideologically committed individual who packed his bags and went to help Cheddi Jagan in Guyana in 1963-4, based on his belief in marxism holding the solution to Caribbean problems. To Weekes he was advisor, comrade in struggle and trusted friend. In 1971, Kelshall was not a young man and already his role with the union was declining because of his health. Prison conditions were a trauma for him. Although he was a radical in his beliefs, Kelshall, then in his late 50's, had come from the white upper class of the society and had been accustomed to physical comforts all his life. It was difficult for him to make the enforced adjustment. He pleaded with fellow detainees that he be allowed to apply to the tribunal, to which there was still general objection. Realising his problem in coping with prison life, which was taking a visible physical toll on him, and considering that in fact he had been inactive where the struggle was concerned, it was agreed that, if he felt strongly enough about it, he should apply to the tribunal.

It turned out to be a mentally tortuous and physically debilitating experience for Kelshall. Weekes, looking at his pain, felt it as though he was undergoing the torture. Seemungal, a fellow lawyer who chaired the tribunal, was merciless with Kelshall, for no apparent reason. There was no substance in the accusations against Kelshall, basically that he had planned certain violent actions with leaders of the Black Power movement. Apart from the accusations being untrue, Kelshall was easily able to establish that he was not in Trinidad on the dates cited. Therefore the question of truth was irrelevant to the manner in which he was crossexamined and the matter prolonged. Seemungal could see the effects the proceedings were having on Kelshall just as the detainees could see. He collapsed at hearings. The prison doctor was concerned about the way his pressure was going up. He had to be kept in the infirmary. Each time Kelshall recovered sufficiently the hearings continued, probing every area of his life. Kelshall was desperate enough for his freedom, and growing more desperate as he declined physically, to keep going. Weekes felt like he would go mad just watching the way in which they were slowly but surely killing Jack. And there was nothing he could do. The pressure was kept up on Kelshall until he suffered a paralysing and near-fatal stroke.

The other deep wound for Weekes in the 71-72 emergency was the betrayal he suffered at the hands of two Executive officers of the union, Verne Edwards, the 1st Vice President, and Lionel Beckles, the General Secretary. Instead of mobilising the union to fight against the detention of its President General, who, on this occasion was detained in the midst of an industrial confrontation involving the union, they were manoeuvering to depose him as President General. One of their early moves, defeated by the General Council, was to try to have his salary stopped on the basis that he could not serve the union while in prison. As the most senior officers of the union outside of prison, they were actually resisting calls from branches and the General Council to "condemn (Weekes') arrest and detention as an open and provocative attack on the union". They were inferring that he had been detained for "personal political activities which had nothing to do with the business of the union". The General Secretary had to be forced to reply to correspondence from the President General in prison. It was even reported that "the 1st Vice President deliberately sabotaged the recognition dispute between the OWTU and Tugs and Lighters".[2]

As the months went by, Weekes saw the union, already under siege by the state, and now debilitated by treachery, too weak to take up the cause of his own freedom with any effect. Eventually a delegation, including those who wanted his office, went to the Permanent Secretary in the Ministry of National Security and then came back to him with the advice that he should apply to the very tribunal that had destroyed Kelshall.

He saw them too weak to put up meaningful resistance against the laws, whose introduction the emergency was declared to facilitate. He saw the police get the power to enter and search homes without warrant under the amended Firearms Act. He saw free speech curtailed by an amended Sedition Law. He saw peoples right to hold public meetings and to march taken away by a Summary Offences Amendment Act. Finally he saw them pass an Industrial Relations Act to replace the debunked ISA with only token protest by his union. The IRA idea had been broached since 1970 at tri-partite talks to which his union and others outside of Congress had not been invited. At the beginning of 1971 he had warned:

> ... I think it is my duty as President General of the OWTU to warn the Government and those Lord Protectors and Witch Doctors of the Capitalist System in the Labour Congress that the OWTU, the Union in which I have the honour to lead, is going to resist with its blood any attempt to replace the Pig Law, ISA, by the Sow Law, IRA ...[3]

The OWTU reaction when the time came made his words ring hollow.

This was doubly tragic as there was a section of the IRA specifically geared against the OWTU. It was a clause which prohibited a union from representing workers in more than one essential industry. The purpose of this was to keep Weekes and the OWTU out of the Water and Sewerage Authority, which was classified as an essential industry. Workers here had been clamouring for some time for OWTU representation. The concept of essential industry would widen conveniently later on. The most absurd example was when the government set up a small steel mill, ISCOTT (the Iron and Steel Company of Trinidad and Tobago), and declared it an essential industry when the workers sought representation by the OWTU.

Weekes saw that the union was too weak to put up effective resistance when Badger, on its expected return to the country, introduced a most pernicious condition for employment. All applicants would have to qualify by presenting a Police Certificate of Good Character. It was a dangerous precedent (soon followed by other companies) and a contempt for the nation that weighed heavily on the spirit of the old soldier. He saw Edwards and Beckles over hastily accept what he considered an undignified settlement in the wage negotiations with Texaco which had opened days before he was detained.

George Weekes had to dig deeply into himself to keep his calm as he was forced to sit helplessly in prison while men with whom he had worked closely for years were undermining all the principles for which he had sacrificed. They were seeking to undermine him too. Lionel Bannister was leading a fightback. Some workers were getting aroused and Beckles and Edwards received physical threats. But the longer the indefinite detention wore on, the more uncertain Weekes felt about his position in the union.

He bore much of the burden in prison himself, not wanting to make his problems the problems of others. He would sit quietly, pensively, trying to plan, trying to will things to happen. He would hold his balding head and feel it get literally hot to the touch. He would write letters to various members and smuggle them out trying to influence the course of events. But he was a caged onlooker, and, in fact, an onlooker with a very limited view, at the drama that was unfolding and would decide his fate.

The outer calm Weekes achieved masked the torture of his soul. He never exploded either with other detainees or prison officers. He always seemed to be the coolest person when tensions ran high in confinement. He got into no arguments and squabbles. In fact he was consistently the level-headed peace-maker. His nervous system must have paid a high price for his unreleased frustration and tension.

Weekes suffered from growing fears of assassination during the second emergency. For years he had been warned of possible assassination by various people, some claiming to have inside information. Friends, who looked at the manifest hostility to Weekes of the state and other powerful forces, themselves fomented these fears each time serious political tensions gripped the island. One day in May 1972, he strongly protested against going to court in San Fernando and was taken barefooted and in his nightclothes. His reason for refusing to go voluntarily was a "whispering voice", as he characterised the warning:

> Had I not responded to the whispering voice that advised me to write a protest to the Magistrate in San Fernando giving reason why I was not prepared to leave my cell, for fear of being assassinated, their evil plot to kill me might have become a reality.[4]

The warnings, valid or not, took on a more ominous character in 1972. There were no examples of the state degenerating to the assassination of prominent political opponents. But shootings and killings of an obviously political nature were becoming a feature of life in the society. The rape of democracy by emergency laws, politically motivated frame-ups of young men on charges of possessing arms and ammunition, the reign of terror on the blocks and other abuses of official force that increased throughout 1971, had borne bloody fruit. By late 1971, several young men, and a few women too, had turned their backs on peaceful means of change, got their hands on guns, raided banks for funds, and tried to establish an armed opposition to the regime. Early signs of this new development had come in August of the same year when Commander Bloom of the Coast Guard and Theodore Guerra, one of the prosecuting lawyers at the soldiers' court martial, were shot and wounded in close succession by unknown assailants.

The armed offensive against state targets was limited. An attack which damaged a major communications satellite receiving system was the budding group's most attention-getting political strike. By their very nature though, the actions of NUFF, the National Union of Freedom Fighters, had tremendous psychological impact on the society. The state embarked on their massive anti-guerilla campaign, with the emphasis on killing whoever they caught, or defining as a guerilla whoever was killed.

Over a period of three years there would be the murderous elimination of many of the young men and one of the women who took this course. They were too small in number and completely outmatched by the fire power of the police (shotguns and pistols against powerful modern weapons — long range rifles, machine guns and other effective military hardware). They were lacking in any military training and not nearly well enough organised. Some of them were bright young people, educated in the leading high schools, from middle class homes, victims initially of police frame-ups, who decided against facing the courts in which they had no confidence and who felt enough was enough. They formed the National Union of Freedom Fighters to fight fire with considerably less fire.

In May of 1972, with this kind of conflict escalating, Weekes felt strongly it was the right kind of environment for them to attempt his own assassination. The possibility seemed all the more real because attempted political assassination had already reached the neighbouring country of Guyana which had a similar history and political culture. On October 5th 1971 Dr Josh Ramsammy, a lecturer at the University of Guyana and an open opponent of the Forbes Burnham government, was shot and seriously wounded while he sat in his car on a Georgetown street. The practical effect of such fears was to turn the mental pressure gauge up a few points higher.

On the whole, in 1972 Weekes did not feel the same vitalizing forces that buoyed his spirits in 1970. It was not that there was no struggle. There could hardly be greater inspiration for a fighting man than the courage and idealism displayed by the brothers and sisters in NUFF, even though there was a sadness in the futility of their efforts. By their sacrifice they were making a powerful and moving statement about an unquenchable thirst for freedom that defied repression; they were pointing to a reborn manhood and spirit of selflessness that were the hope for a brighter future. The revolution had not died.

Middle class groups were still making militant reactions to situations too. Lawyers for example went on a one week protest strike when the police searched and ransacked the home of a magistrate, Neville Clarke.[5]

Two days after the declaration of the State of Emergency, death had taken Bhadase Maraj off the backs of sugar workers, just as he was reigning terror on another group trying to remove him.

On the personal level, Weekes was not forgotten in his time of need. Even when the spirit of carnival infected the society, his memory and his plight were recalled. The country was hit by an unusual amount of flooding. The calypsonian, 'Tangler', raised questions in his song about the floods:

"Is it a message to the Premier
to release George Weekes and Geddes Granger?"

Weekes knew it. But his mind could barely draw from such sources of nourishment, the inspiration that would ordinarily have sent his spirit soaring. When the OWTU was in trouble, the very centre of his existence was under immediate threat. Enemies had penetrated the citadel. Demons were claiming his soul.

At night he would lie quiet and alone in his cell and hear the sad songs from the cells of the condemned above. There was an indescribable sadness and pathos in those voices, the voices of men singing in their own wake. In each fateful Thursday to Tuesday* period, there would be one voice knowingly singing its last songs. One man with infinite certainty was counting the days and hours to a precisely timed end. When the voices sang "nearer my god to thee" it was with the most literal belief. And in the great sadness, wasn't there a lining of hope? Faced with the certainty of death, man could find hope. Weekes did not live in such morbid and measurable time. There was no prearranged appointment with destiny. At 7.00 a.m. on the Tuesday morning after the wake, he would not be the victim at the end of the rope. He would be alive to experience the eerie stillness of the prison on the fateful morning. In the silence his ears would discern the muffled slap of the trap door. He would sense the finality of death for another human being. But he would have life and he would know that man who was no more had walked with hope in his last hooded steps through the narrow corridor to the unknown. There was something in faith when there was no knowledge and no power over fate.

In 1972, Weekes too drew on faith, not just the revolutionary faith he had always lived with, but a religious faith. It was not a conversion. He had been brought up as an Anglican and never abandoned his essential Christian beliefs though he denounced the white images the Christian churches imposed on Black peoples. The change in 1972 was a change in the intensity with which Weekes practised religion and a shift towards the Baptist faith. The total experience of this incarceration made him receptive to the many letters he received from the faithful, informing him they were praying for him, the psalms that were copied and sent for him, the bible verses quoted. He was made to feel a part of a concerned spiritual community. Members of the Women's Auxiliary of the union, journeyed to many churches in many parts of the country on many a Sunday offering prayers for the protection of detainees and their families and their release from prison.

The re-affirmation of religious faith reflected the fact that Weekes was drawing deeply on inner reserves to cope with the effects of what he saw taking place. The way he felt about

---

* The customary procedure is to notify a prisoner on a Thursday that he would be hanged on the following Tuesday.

OWTU, that deep spiritual bond between the man and the organisation, had been a source of strength through many trials. It threatened now to be a consuming angel of destruction. If George Weekes was not possessed of considerable inner strength, he would have crumbled in that second State of Emergency.

CHAPTER 16

THE ROAD TO BLOODY TUESDAY

". . . when tomorrow you may point your guns straight at the hearts of oil and other workers we will, with our last ounce of courage, clench our fists above our heads and even die for justice." George Weekes.[1]

Whatever sense of normalcy was communicated by "parang as usual" for Christmas 1971 and "carnival as usual" for early 1972, was deceptive. Trinidad and Tobago was still a battlefield when Weekes and other detainees emerged from prison on June 16th 1972. But it was not a battlefield like 1970 or mid 1971. In 1970 the fall of the ruling PNM regime seemed imminent. In 1971 everyone could sense a national upsurge welling up just below the surface, precariously dammed by walls of fear and caution, walls however that were visibly cracking with every hammer blow of industrial defiance and mass protest.

In 1972 something was missing — the feeling of a critical point. It was not that the defiance had gone. The industrial relations environment never settled back down. The IRA had nothing like the effects of the ISA in 1965. Workers acted as though it had never been enacted. Industry by industry they continued to dare the fully mobilised forces of the establishment and the power of the law. An even more significant sign of continuing battle was the increasing confrontation between the police and the armed elements of NUFF. The existence of this arena of struggle was having powerful psychological repercussions on the blocks where more and more police terror had been concentrated. At this level there was strong identification with those who operated from the hills. The blocks also provided practical support and new recruits. The wider society, in its post-1970 incarnation, did not reject the turn to armed resistance. If there wasn't a general embrace of NUFF, there was considerable understanding and empathy. Real hostility to this radical departure from the adopted rules of politics came only from limited quarters.

Overall though the impact of continuing struggles was fragmentary and non-threatening compared to what had gone before. Part of the problem was the national mood, overcast by recent setbacks. Hope as a collective phenomenon, trounced by repression in 1970, barely resuscitated and trounced again, slid into protective recesses, outside the realm of easy mass recall. Not many dared to bear the potential pain of revolutionary hope.

In this psychological environment industrial conflicts lacked political firepower, despite the political implications of striking in defiance of the law. They represented something important, a refusal, individual and collective, to lie down and be walked on by the employer class or the state, a refusal to surrender rights. The strikes were acts of resistance but an essential factor was lacking — a milieu which could transform them into positive acts of revolt.

The armed fightback might have held the key to the restoration of a fuller revolutionary consciousness. But its political statement got clouded over. The drama wavered between spectacular raids for necessary funds and evasive action which forced the society to pay attention but did not have the same effect that more of a political offensive would have had. Massive police reaction, which later escalated into combined police and army operations, forced the small armed group into defensiveness. Victories were escapes and the people shared in these victories. As the calypsonian, 'Lord Kitchener', mocked:

> They looking for Jericho
> Jericho ent dey
> They looking for Jericho
> Jerry slip away
>
> They looking in Lopinot
> Jericho ent dey
> They gone down in Mayaro
> Jerry slip away
> Ooooooh! Oooooooh!

But evading the police for a time was not the essence of revolutionary struggle. NUFF could not accomplish its goal of armed revolution or get a feel prevailing in the society that there was an armed revolution in progress. It was protest with guns. And it would look increasingly futile as casualities started to mount for the ill-equipped and infiltrated group.

Coming out of prison in the midst of this ongoing struggle Weekes had to make a decision about which way to go. He admired the courage and idealism of the National Union of Freedom Fighters, but on the practical level he did not see their course of action as a feasible one.

He pondered the question of making militant workers struggles more viable, more sustainable, more politically meaningful. Part of his questioning came out of his experience of embarrassment, frustration and deep hurt at the relative inaction of his own union members when he was torn from them while clearly fighting union causes. The troubling thought of the kind of inertia that could pervade if he is removed brought into his mind calculations of risk that had hardly disturbed him before. The idea of a workers' party took root again. That however could not be his first move.

He had come out to face problems, serious internal problems in the union for a start. But he had also come out to an immediate celebration of victory. For the first time Butler Day was a national holiday, recognised as Labour Day. Weekes was one of the few stalwarts who never gave up Butler on the observance of this day. When he became President General of the OWTU he got the union involved in building it into a truly powerful national observance. Now the regime was recognising it.

This glory was long in coming. Since 1939 some politicians led by Roy Joseph had campaigned to get official recognition for Butler Day. Cipriani fought against the proposal then and defeated it. In the Captain's* view, June 19th was a day of shame, a day that would best be forgotten by the colony.[2] Weekes in his own efforts to drag a deserving tribute to Butler out of the mud of historical slander and distortion provoked strikingly similar reactions in the 1960's. A feature writer in the *Guardian*, under the pen name 'Civicus', upset by the emphasis OWTU was placing on June 19th in 1967, referred to the "events" of 1937 as "a chapter of the exploitation of man's lowest mob instincts which no one can celebrate". He offered the

---

* Cipriani was often referred to as the Captain

opinion that the OWTU emphasis on the anniversary was an indication that "the leadership of the union lives still in the mentality of 1937".

The government had done worse. To their eternal shame they had jailed Butler for squatting in 1966. Years later, in 1971, they were forced by public pressure to award him a national medal. Now June 19th had been proclaimed a public holiday in tribute to the struggle Butler led in 1937.

Weekes did not agree with the official projection of this day as a substitute for May Day. This is what some other long-standing advocates of a June 19th holiday, like W.W. Sutton wanted. Weekes knew the importance of the international workers' day, May 1st, as well. But on June 19th 1972, this was secondary to the pride and joy and triumph he felt as he addressed the thousands of people gathered at Charlie King Junction, the mecca of the revolutionary in Trinidad and Tobago.

Observers would have noticed that Weekes sounded more like Butler now than in the past, in one respect — the integration of religion into his political perspective. The more profound religious convictions that he had developed in prison stayed with him. Along with the Women's group, he went to several churches in different parts of the country where the women had been while he was imprisoned and where prayers had been said for his release and the release of his companions. When he delivered a message at the Mount Moriah Spiritual Baptist Church, on October 15th 1972, Lionel Bannister, pastor of the Church, commented, "It is the first time George's prayer was loud and clear for all to hear in the last 12 years". Weekes' own words brought out the transformation:

> So when I come here today and go on my knees, something that I found hard to do . . . in the manner in which I have done it in open and in a loud voice . . .[3]

Weekes' sermon however dispelled any thought that the solace he had found in prayer, in a very trying period, might have turned into escape. It was a message of cultural self-emancipation:

> If therefore, we believe and accept that God made man in his own likeness and image and it is a sin to worship false Gods, it is therefore logical to conclude that when we Afro Blacks pray to God and to Christ we must see and picture him in our likeness and

image, just as the Indian followers of the Hindu religion see and worship God in their own likeness and image.[4]

It was an affirmation of pride in his union. He spoke about feeling,

closer to the blue shirt of the OWTU which I proudly wear today as on so many other occasions. Whenever we see the blue ocean or the blue shirt of the OWTU we must know what it means, what it symbolises and why as the leader of the OWTU, I attempt not just to preach but to practise what the blue shirt represents . . .[5]

The OWTU . . . was born out of struggle, blood, sweat and tears, to defend the poor and oppressed[6]

He preached about greed and exploitation, about sacrifice and the need to struggle. There was no divorce between praying and fighting the war that had to be fought:

Any man who informs others that he serves God but to hell with the people . . . is either a hypocrite or a fool.

We in OWTU do both. We struggle and we also pray, we pray and struggle. We serve God and the people . . .[7]

It was not surprising that in October Weekes would be expressing everything in terms of the OWTU,

Whether some like it or not it is the OWTU in the main that today prevents our limited democracy from moving into complete Dictatorship[8]

Whatever frustrations and disappointments Weekes suffered during his eight month long nightmare in the Royal Gaol, though they would have lingering effects in the subconscious, they could not separate Weekes in spirit from the OWTU. For at least nine years of intense struggle and sacrifice the union had taken precedence over family in his life. The extra pain he felt was the pain that only love can bring. Once he was physically reunited with the union he was once again completely absorbed in its concerns and his vision of what it ought to be.

The establishment had failed once again to dislodge Weekes from the union. By October he was saying triumphantly:

We are ending the rot in the Union, the enemy within is on the run, we are again consolidating the

Union and we are again marching forward on the
road of progress.[9]

Weekes had wasted no time when he came out of prison in
dealing with the internal betrayal. After Executive meetings on
the issue, the matter was brought before the General Council on
July 29th. After several hours of discussion and debate the
General Council passed a motion of "No Confidence" in Beckles
and Edwards, the General Secretary and the First Vice President
respectively. The officers refused to resign and fought back with
long-drawn-out battles in the court.[10] But the membership spoke
decisively. While they were doing legal battle they could not
even sit in their offices.

Though the machinations of those in power to get Weekes out
of the OWTU had failed again, all their efforts were not
completely fruitless. They created internal problems within the
union. And they did manage to break an alliance which had
played a significant role over the past three years. The close
liaison between Weekes and the OWTU and NJAC fell apart.
There was not a complete break. NJAC leaders and members
were prominent at the Butler Day observations on June 19th,
three days after the detainees were released. Weekes continued to
use his influence to unfailingly make OWTU halls available to
NJAC for rallies, cultural shows, meetings and lectures. But the
close working relationship that had brought fear to companies
and government was no more.

Within the OWTU, Weekes was also to suffer some critical
losses of personnel. Winston Leonard, who worked in the
Education Department; Allan Campbell, president of the
Badger Branch at the time of the crisis; Nuevo Diaz, Chief
Labour Relations Officer. These three men were all militant and
radical organisers, three of the most politically dynamic
associates Weekes had within the union. Diaz was also invaluable
as a negotiator. None of them left out of any direct conflict with
Weekes. The problems had to do with other Executive officers.
But it was Weekes who would feel the loss most.

The union had to go through some agonizing years to regain
strength despite the purge of Beckles and Edwards. And it had to
do with leadership. Weekes had a more loyal Executive, but it
could not be considered revolutionary by any means. It is really
Weekes in his rapport with the workers who bore the
revolutionary image of the union, with very few of the men at

the top around him sharing his vision. The support they gave over the years came largely from personal loyalty and the practical appreciation of the importance of Weekes to their survival and the strength of the union. They could cope with militancy in the strict trade union framework. They had come out of the militant Rebel tradition. This was fortunate. But with the political pressures on the union and the fears abounding after the beating taken during two States of Emergency, the times demanded much more. Weekes confessed to the workers,

> The cause of my worry and my fear stems from the fact that in spite of the many successes we have won against the corrupt enemies within and the fraudulent forces of law and order without, I still feel that I am surrounded by (that I am a victim of) too much apathy on the part of those in important and responsible positions of trust.[11]

Where was his own spiritual sustenance to come from? He got a lot of support and encouragement from his political colleagues outside of the union. But Weekes' political colleagues, who were closer to him in ideological vision than most of his union officers, men like Allan Alexander, Lennox Pierre and John La Rose, at the same time they had not undergone his revolutionary experiences. Weekes was not therefore in an environment where both vision and experience combined in a spiritually uplifting whole. In a profound sense he had a lonely task to dig within himself to rejuvenate his fighting spirit from the psychological exhaustion and trauma of living on the edge of death and being rewarded by betrayal. His task was not only to overcome his own experience but to put the union in a state of battle readiness. The fight was far from over.

In the consolidation period Weekes and other officers of the union held a series of meetings throughout the union, revitalising its branches, re-establishing the necessary rapport between members and leaders. A new education thrust was launched at the 33rd Annual Conference of delegates. A special Conference of Shop Stewards and Branch Officers (COSSABO) met in regular weekend sessions from July to September 1973 for an education process termed "Dialogue". The programme was aimed at giving OWTU members a greater theoretical understanding of working class struggle generally, a greater understanding of the concepts of socialism, and of the struggle that they were involved in, in unsettled Trinidad and Tobago. It was also aimed at improving their knowledge of the critical oil industry and other matters considered relevant. Among the lecturers were Trevor Farrell, an oil economist from the University of the West Indies, and two legal advisers to the union Lennox Pierre and Allan Alexander.

This was taking place against a background of turmoil and repression in the society which would eventually engulf the OWTU once again.

Weekes could feel the way the mood of the society was changing again since the end of the last emergency. He could see all the signs of another approaching political storm.

Signs were there on the industrial scene which continued to be a disturbed one. In all, strikes resulted in 98,149 man days being lost in 1973.[12]

The unemployed were fighting back too. On July 5th 1973, Lasana Kwesi, NJAC Vice Chairman, mobilised about 400 unemployed workers from sections of the economically depressed area east of Port of Spain known as East Dry River and they staged a march through the streets to Whitehall, the office of the Prime Minister.[13] It was a period of growing economic hardship. To add to the pressures caused by joblessness, prices were rising at a staggering rate, 23% in 1973[14], due partly to increases in the prices of food and other commodities produced by the developed Western capitalist countries. The police rushed to try to stop the demonstration for which they were not prepared and for which no permission had been sought. They tried to persuade the people not to march by reading the Summary Offences Act, but they were told:

"We cannot eat Summary Offences . . ."

The demonstrators occupied the pavement outside of Whitehall, virtually imprisoning the Prime Minister inside. The police were very reluctant to use force against the demonstration because of some of the people involved. Efforts were being made by the political authorities to draw influential individuals with a history of violence away from the mass movement to defuse the tensions and potential for explosion in the critical Northern urban areas. A police attack here could precipitate a train of events they would rather avoid. Word was sent from inside Whitehall that projects would be opened immediately to meet the demands of the demonstrators.

Then there were the more overtly political signs. NJAC, still the most influential force at the grassroots level, was finding ways to re-establish its political voice despite the restrictions imposed by the new laws, under which they would have had to notify the Police Commissioner of any planned outdoor meeting or seek permission to demonstrate. A series of indoor cultural rallies, which featured progressive artistes and raps by the organisation's political leaders, helped to pull people back together again. Direct community involvement through People's Parliaments, block sessions and meetings without formal announcements or loud speakers also added to the build up.

The result is that popular acts of defiance were motivated, very often in ways that reflected the spirit and thought of the 1970 revolution. For example, in East Port of Spain where the government had announced a massive Re-development Plan, without any consultation with the people, they ran into serious problems. At a series of People's Parliaments, the masses decided that no plan could be implemented unless residents were involved in the discussion of the plan. Numbers that were painted on the houses by government to identify units for particular phases of the program were painted off by the people and a halt put to further painting until the relevant authorities agreed to consultation. The people were able to force the planning authorities to come and have dialogue with them.[15]

Even in the prisons the unrest was escalating. On August 9th 1973, several prisoners climbed up on to the rooftops of the Royal Gaol protesting against prison conditions. They held up prepared placards for the public to see and raised their voices pleading their case with the gathering onlookers. One of the placards carried the message:

"VOICES OF THE OPPRESSED CRYING IN THE WILDERNESS"[16]

The political detainees who had taken part in protest on behalf of the prisoners during both emergencies, who had publicized the plight of these forsaken men behind bars, and raised their self-image with the new consciousness, had left their mark. The prisoners were defining themselves in political terms.

The rekindled mood was not only experienced in North Trinidad. In Central and South Trinidad rumblings were beginning that would grow into an earthquake. Once the rumblings were moving southwards, they were moving towards George Weekes.

The route to Weekes was slightly roundabout. Rampartap Singh, successor to Bhadase Maraj as leader of the All Trinidad union in the sugar belt, had made the error of inviting Basdeo Panday in as President, changing the union rules to ensure that Panday would be a powerless, figurehead president.[17] In late 1973 Panday was in the process of laying the groundwork to turn the tables on the old Bhadase clique. Quietly he was organising from branch to branch, mobilising a force that would not only upset the old leadership, but help to bring the country to its hottest point since 1970.

In the other area of sugar, among the canefarmers, an intense struggle had already broken the surface, led by Raffique Shah and Winston Leonard. Shah and other soldiers had been released from prison in 1972, shortly after the detainees. The court martial convictions for mutiny could not hold, and there was no way the government could face the political consequences of death sentences for the soldiers, which would have been mandatory if they pushed ahead with the treason trials and succeeded in getting convictions. Shah formed the Island Wide Cane Farmers Trade Union (ICFTU) to rescue cane farmers from the clutches of Norman Girwar and others, the company-approved leaders of the existing union, Trinidad Island Wide Cane Farmers Association (TICFA). The new union quickly gained the support of the majority of cane farmers, but the law, Act 1 of 1965, was against them. It entrenched TICFA. While the battle against the Act was fought in court, violent clashes developed between factions of cane farmers over union loyalties and strategies employed by the new union to disrupt the flow of farmers' canes to the factories. In many areas of the South, where cane farming was concentrated, the atmosphere of a war zone was developing.

In the secondary schools the revolutionary spirit continued to be strong. Students were now bringing out their own militant organ, *The Voice of Revolutionary Students*, dealing with issues in schools, analyses of the education system and political concerns in the society at large.

Similar developments were taking place up the other Caribbean islands.

Repression was also becoming more murderous. Many people in the society, including conservatives, were recoiling at the slaughter of young people associated with NUFF. There was tremendous bloodletting, under the guise of "shoot outs". The bodies and in some cases eyewitnesses, told tales of murder. When hideouts were raided, anyone disabled by injury from making their escape, was summarily executed by the police. When friends and families turned up at the mortuary to identify bodies, they found them riddled with more holes than they could count. A grotesque pattern also emerged on raids that involved Randolph Burroughs who was later to become Commissioner of Police. The bodies consistently turned up with their groins shot up.

The physical elimination of NUFF which was taking place was just the most extreme form of a general repression which was making invasions of privacy and the searches of homes of political opponents of the government routine. Police brutality against innocent civilians had become endemic in the society. What had already begun with Weekes in September 1971 was becoming more general, the frameups on criminal charges of leaders of radical political organisations opposed to the government. This had long been practised with lesser-known members.

A desperate government was hitting back, because it was seeing economic collapse staring it in the face and political resistance had refused to die. In August 1973 in fact, while the OWTU COSSABO met in "Dialogue", the government assessed its foreign reserves and realized that what was left was the equivalent of four weeks of imports. For the previous two years they had been engaged in negotiations with the oil companies to raise the posted price of the country's oil and so increase the government's tax take. But there was no success. The picture looked so bleak that Eric Williams actually threw in the sponge. He resigned on September 28th condemning ministers, party and people.

Weekes felt the resignation had to be a bluff. People were feeling the economic pressures but there was not an awareness of just how precariously perched the economy was. Weekes interpreted the move of his arch-foe as a game, maybe to identify and cut down anyone who seemed too ambitious to succeed him as political leader of the PNM; maybe to gain a political truce by hopefully scaring the people that if they did not "behave" they stood to lose the "indispensable doctor". When the expected cry "Don't go, Doctor, don't go" (as the calypso by 'Mighty Cipher' put it) started to develop from within the party, led by the women's group, and from some supposedly non-partisan quarters as well, including significantly the Inter Religious Organisation, it seemed the game was following the anticipated course. However, developments overseas confused the picture. OPEC quadrupled the price of oil. Trinidad and Tobago was in for a bonanza. Williams came back in glory, so he thought. Was it the money? Or was it that the pre-planned end of the game coincided with propitious fortune?

If the resignation and comeback formed a strategy to bring peace or a political truce, it failed. If indeed Williams was only recalled by the prospects of the new wealth, they were prospects that could not buy peace either, not for a long time. In fact the oil wealth, which allowed the government budget to jump from $400 million in 1973 to over $1 billion in 1974, had the reverse effect. It led to an escalation of demands by workers and trade unions. The strain workers had to bear in 1973 with the leap in prices, continued to increase in 1974, when prices rose another 22%.[18] Given those very real pressures, the image of a wealthier country and the breakdown of moral and political authority, there was no holding back on the demands for higher wages or the intensity with which the demands were pursued. 1974 was to witness a total of 478,941 man days lost due to strikes.[19] One effect of the sudden boom, that was to have far more serious consequences than just the number of days lost to strikes in 1974, was that it gave some measure of credibility to an OWTU demand for a 147% increase in wages in the new round of negotiations with Texaco.

There was a whole train of events which led to that point, to a demand that was as much political as it was economic. Panday had triumphed in sugar, with the reluctant blessings of the PNM regime. He himself was very aware of their reasoning, which he gleaned from meeting with a senior government Minister, Errol Mahabir — better the sugar workers have Panday than they turn again to George Weekes. What the government did not anticipate, because they had failed to read Panday right, was that the sugar workers would have Panday and they would have Weekes.[20] Worse. There would be a significant difference from

1965 when they had Weekes, but they did not have oil workers. This time they would have Weekes and they would have the support of oil workers.

The die was cast in September of 1974. Panday had won a 100% increase in wages for sugar workers and guaranteed employment. He went to Weekes, whom he had avoided for the past months, while he was fighting to get into a position of control in the sugar belt.

> George, we have a job to finish. Now is the time to continue what we started in 1966. We have to unite the workers of oil and sugar, get rid of the racial antagonisms . . .[21]

Panday met a receptive Weekes. The OWTU leader was in a fighting mood and Panday was re-igniting his most precious dream.

Throughout 1974 Weekes had been continuing his efforts to restore the fighting spirit in the OWTU. He defined 1974 as "the first year of the future". He could feel a momentum in the people building to another climax. On March 10th 1974 he addressed the 34th Annual Conference of the union against a background of mounting tensions. He expressed how he felt at a time of hope and anguish, hope at examples of idealism and courage and anguish at the bloodthirsty ruthlessness of the dying regime. From deep within he paid tribute:

> To students and youths whether they be in the hills now as our black, beautiful and courageous sister Beverly Jones was, or in a river swimming as the gallant Guy Harewood was, or on a street drive as heroic Brian Jeffers was when they all were killed and/or murdered by the forces of 'law and order' while in valiant struggle for justice, democracy and liberation. Of them I say, these martyrs are more alive today and their examples of courage, dedication and self sacrifice are more meaningful at present and will be more so in the future than when their bodies visibly walked this good earth.[22]

He was caught up by another area of the struggle as well. As a trade unionist who held strongly to the concept that "an injury to one is an injury to all", as a firm believer in the unity of African and Indian workers, as a leader who felt a personal commitment to sugar workers, as a revolutionary drawn by militant struggle,

George Weekes was deeply moved and motivated by the renewed struggle in the sugar industry, this time involving cane farmers as well as sugar workers.

He had "worried feelings, perhaps even fears" about the state of readiness of the union he led for the times upon them, at least their preparedness to play the kind of role which he always conceived it was their duty and historical destiny to play. He had tested the militancy of the oil workers in December of 1973 with a call for a march from the Palms Club to the Roman Catholic Church on Harris Promenade in San Fernando. He had gone ahead with the march despite a refusal of permission by Police Commissioner, Tony May. That day he felt let down by the poor response from officers as well as members:

> ... when I realise that our failure stemmed from fear of breaking an unconstitutional law which we have on paper condemned as wicked and unjust and rejected, and further, when I witness sugar workers and cane farmers in their thousands marching the said streets of San Fernando without police permission, protesting against injustice and for the release of their leaders from prison, I bow my head and cry silently.
>
> Comrades, it leaves me no choice but to ask delegates to consider whether we are still worthy to be called and to be regarded as a revolutionary union and respected and feared as such.[23]

When Weekes surveyed some of the significant events of the time, and touched on the Caribbean, especially Grenada (Unison Whiteman was present representing those involved in a tremendous struggle there at the time), when he spoke about the conspiracy against the OWTU, he was trying to communicate to union members how strongly he felt about their need to be involved:

> Unless I can feel that you are as much if not more concerned than I am about what I have mentioned, I am going to find it most difficult to remain and be effective as your President General, personally directing and negotiating on your behalf in any meaningful manner in the near future.[24]

When Panday spoke to Weekes in September of 1974 the "near future" was virtually upon them. Negotiations with Texaco were due to begin in November. They decided on a mass rally of oil and sugar workers for December. Despite the victories Panday had already secured around the negotiating table, he was still holding out for an agreement on profit sharing for the workers. In itself it was a very valid demand, but the determination and aggression with which it was pursued in the existing context suggests strongly that for Panday this was the plum to keep up the struggle of sugar workers in support of Shah's union. Weekes was tabling proposals to Texaco for an 80% wage increase. This was later raised to 147%. All the unions were going to carry the fight. At least until ICFTU, which had the least clout, was recognised by Caroni Ltd as the representative union for cane farmers.

The rally did not come off in December. It came off on February 18th 1975 at Skinner Park in San Fernando. When Weekes surveyed the crowd that day, he felt the fires of Butler burn in him again, he felt the spirit of 1970 possessing his soul. 25,000, maybe 40,000, people. Workers, their families, Indians, Africans, a demonstration of racial and class unity so passionately longed for, so relentlessly fought for. In 1970, when sugar workers were about to head for Port of Spain to establish such a demonstration of unity, Williams had declared a State of Emergency. Five more years of bitter struggle and here it was. Weekes could see himself like Butler in 1937. This was an angry crowd, a determined crowd, vanguard representatives of a people at war. They responded with a mighty voice to the denunciatioins of the multinationals and the government for acting as their puppets. Deep down inside, Weekes would have liked to think they were saying "Death to the multinationals". He wanted to believe that deep down inside they were forming a resolve to do battle for this country to belong to nationals, a resolve to purge it of the corrupt who had hijacked the authority of government in a non-election and held office by terror and murder — Guy, Beverly, Brian . . . Weekes did not know them in life, but they lived in his thoughts . . .

The unity was on the platform too. Prominent along with the OWTU President General were Basdeo Panday — the man who more than anyone else had made this day possible — Joe Young, President of the Transport and Industrial Workers Union who had pledged his full support for the battle at hand and Raffique Shah, whose struggle for cane farmers was central to what was developing here. Together they stood, labour leaders, representing collectively some 50,000 workers and farmers, in a united front. That was it. The birth, the long awaited birth, the explosive generation of the United Labour Front.*

And Weekes' greatest secret joy. The oil workers had responded. He knew they would. He could have felt it building, that mood to fight. He was proud at how they had brought the contracting firms in the oil industry to heel. These firms had been viciously exploiting highly skilled workers, encouraged by the companies which also benefitted from the grossly under-priced labour. Talk and commissions since 1971 had not worked. But when he called for an offensive in September 1974 the oil workers responded. All through the industry they refused to work alongside contractors' workers. Some contractors tried to fight back through the courts. But writs or no writs the boycotts continued. Now they were panicking, the bosses themselves were coming for forms to sign up their workers in the union.[25]

Weekes was ecstatic, standing on a threshold. Leading where? To victory? To socialism? Defeat could not be possible. They prayed, prayer was the pattern now, for BREAD, PEACE AND JUSTICE.

If their prayers were heard in heaven, they were not answered in Whitehall. The government seemed to have no desire to de-fuse the situation. And neither justice nor legality were consider-ations, though enough cries of 'law and order' would be heard to justify their reactions. They made this clear when they refused to recognise the ruling of High Court judge, Justice John Braith-waithe, that sections of the Cane Farmers Cess Act (the infamous Act 1 of 1965) were unconstitutional. The Attorney General appealed this ruling which was handed down a few days before the mammoth rally at Skinner Park. By simply recognising this lawful decision of the court and so paving the way for the cane farmers to have representation of their choice, the government would have removed the major cause of strife in the sugar belt.

They did not want peace with Panday either. Information reaching the trade unionists was that the company, Caroni Limited, was prepared to discuss the question of profit sharing. It was the government, which owned 51% of the shares, that was instructing the company team not to entertain discussion on the issue.

---

* The 'United Labour Front' is the name the four union grouping gave itself.

THE ROAD TO BLOODY TUESDAY

The recalcitrance could have been mere vindictiveness and spite, especially where the question of recognition for the union led by "mutineer" Shah was concerned. This kind of vindictiveness had been part of the Williams' government.

Given the scale of confrontation the issues were provoking, there could have been other considerations at the later stages. No matter how just the causes were, no matter how much legal basis they had, an overriding concern of the government could have been the question of political stability. They were desperate to regain control of the country. Too many strikes and protests everywhere. To concede now, whether right or wrong, could have encouraged other causes, maybe with equal justice. Now was the time to stamp out causes in favour of political control, no matter what the cost in rights or freedoms, or even lives. Whatever the reasoning, government's actions were making confrontation inevitable and everybody could see they were going to get it.

The nervousness of vested interests in the society could be seen in the editorial of the *Express* the day after the Skinner Park rally. They called on the union leaders to "act responsibly". They did not want "an excuse for the government to declare a state of emergency". As one writer said, "the events of 1970 were still fresh in everybody's mind". Texaco cancelled its annual international sports meeting, Southern Games, for the first time in 37 years. The Employers Consultative Association hurriedly tried to get a meeting between themselves, the unions involved, the Council of Progressive Trade Unions (CPTU)* and the Labour Congress. The police commissioner immediately revoked Panday's firearm licence. On February 27th the state-owned radio station, Radio Guardian, banned the voice of Shah from the airwaves and then banned the voices of Weekes and Panday as well. Raoul Pantin, who was working at the station, criticised the policy and was fired. Leo De Leon was fired. Jimmy Bain, an old retired permanent secretary from the Gomes era, with archaic and fascist ideas, was brought in to take over direction of the country's only television station, state-owned Trinidad and Tobago Television, and Radio Guardian. The

---

* The CPTU was formed by the OWTU, TIWU, CWU (under the leadership of Lyle Townsend), Bank and General Workers Union (BGWU), led by Michael Als, and other unions opposed to Congress.

291

editor of the *Trinidad Guardian* also banned publication of photographs of Weekes in that daily newspaper.

Sugar workers stopped work all together. On March 12th Weekes called workers off their jobs, in the oil industry, from Fed Chem and from T&TEC to pray. On the same day he wrote Stibbs, the General Manager of Texaco, informing him that "our members employed at your company will from today continue their Prayers for the Peace that will flow from a speedy settlement and for Justice that will come forth from a speedy defacto recognition of the OWTU on behalf of monthly paid employees".

The tension mounted in the society. Expectancy grew as the day approached on which all minds were fixed, Tuesday March 18th. This was the day on which the workers in oil and sugar would begin their march from San Fernando to Port of Spain. No, not a "march". A "religious walk" for BREAD, PEACE AND JUSTICE. There were laws against marching, but there were no laws against a "religious walk". Weekes and the other leaders were going to try to squeeze tens of thousands of workers through a loophole in the law.

There was no questioning the widespread public support for the cause of the workers. Even the Trade Union Congress expressed public support. Articles in the newspaper brought home the tremendous level of sacrifice of the sugar workers and cane farmers. There was admiration for the courage and sacrifice of sugar workers especially, traditionally one of the lowest paid groups in the society. With an agreement for a 100% pay rise already secured, they were continuing to fight and deny themselves income on a principle, and, quite evidently, to give support to the struggle of the cane farmers for recognition by Caroni Limited.

Weekes had an unquestionable cause with the monthly-paid employees of Texaco as well. But if any issue was being questioned it was the demand of the OWTU for a 147% increase in pay for oil workers. Weekes raised a national debate here:

"147% for oil workers! Weekes mad or what?"

"Like you ent living in Trinidad. You ent see how prices rising. And is food going up the most. I working for the same salary as two years ago, and I can't buy half of what I used to buy.

The man right. Texaco could afford to pay, and they paying plenty more to workers in the States.*"

"Yeh. But this is Trinidad man. Them fellas in the oil making the most money already."

"All right, if Weekes don't get it for oil workers, who get it? Is not right back in the States the money going as profits? You rather it stay here in oil workers hands and they spend it here or it go outside and none ah we benefit?"

"I ent saying it should go outside. But if government get it, they could spread it around more, see that everybody benefit."

"Well that is just what Weekes saying all the time. If they take over the dam oil industry we wouldn't have that problem. Is the country will benefit. But if it in Texaco hands and the government don't want to take what the country deserve from it, then Weekes go fight for it for oil workers. And he tell them already, if they want to talk profit-sharing, he will settle for less pay. They don't want to talk that, they can't leave here with all the profits. Yuh know that gone up sky high since the baccahanal with oil. Yuh see what Weekes tell the Prime Minister in the letter he write him. Since 1972 to now Texaco profits gone up by over 400%. Yuh hear meh. They have to give up something, let them pay it in wages."

Even though the 147% demand remained an uneasy question in people's minds, at least two factors saved it from public rejection, despite the all-round attacks. One was psychological. There was a perception of a substantial increase in wealth in the society, though it had not yet started to filter down to the people. Everyone felt they had to fight for their share, especially with the crippling inflation. These factors brought about a new concept of a reasonable wage.

Another important factor in the 1975 context is the non-economic perception of what Weekes was doing. It would seem as though people understood that a major concern of Weekes at this time was for the oil workers to stand up side by side with their more unfortunate brothers and sisters in sugar. The P-Gee was admired for achieving this.

The cost of the achievement was a showdown.

As it drew near Weekes felt confident. He had no doubt where Police Commissioner Tony May would stand. This after all was

---

* short cut in conversation for 'United States'

a working class struggle, a reaction to working class pain and
. . . members of the privileged class, more so those that
are white, for reasons that are obvious do not have to
demonstrate in the streets for Peace, Bread and Justice
or for that matter anything. Why? Because the laws of
the country are specially made and brutally enforced
to protect their self-interest.

. . . the scales of what is called Justice by the system
in this society, are heavily on the side of the privileged
classes as can be clearly seen by the . . . law, which
permits you (Tony May) and others to deny the poor,
oppressed and exploited of their human and constitutional rights to demonstrate for Peace, Bread and
Justice . . .[26]

The countdown begins.

Police Commissioner Tony May decides "to deny the poor,
oppressed and exploited their human and constitutional rights".
The march by any name is forbidden . . .

All police leave has already been cancelled. They are confined
to barracks, waiting to be let loose . . .

The organisers are going ahead with what Weekes says is "a
peaceful religious walk to continue our prayers for justice, bread
and peace. If that is illegal, then where is justice in Trinidad?"

The country braces for the clash.

Texaco families begin an exodus from South, some an exodus
from the country. They head for Barbados.

The day has come — Tuesday March 18th 1975. The *Express*
says "laws as passed by parliament must be obeyed by everyone
regardless of the circumstances of the people involved".

Weekes leaves his home on the hill above the union
headquarters and walks down early in the morning. At 6.00 a.m.
many workers are already gathered. More are coming, growing
into thousands. Weekes feels an extra ounce of courage when he
sees Butler, clasping the hand of a little boy he has brought with
him. Jamadar is here. Millette is here. Today will not be a
repetition of 1969. A.N.R. Robinson is here. They all met with
the union leaders the night before to plan the day's strategy. The
demonstration would take a direction different to what the
police are expecting. Weekes addresses the throng that is waiting
to take to the streets. He lays down the rules of peace. His eyes
rest on Randolph Burroughs, parading through the workers

with an armed plain-clothes gang, toting machine guns. The people pray for peace . . .

Ten thousand leave from in front of Paramount Building. Religious leaders are at the front, Christian priests of various denominations, Muslim imams, Hindu pundits. Reports have come back to the leaders. The police are waiting outside the Mon Repos police station. Snipers with rifles are on the rooftops. To pick off leaders? Butler walks the first few yards to the first junction and bids luck to the demonstrators. Left is where the ambush is, as anticipated. The marchers turn right as the leaders decided the night before. The best protection for the demonstration is to pass through the areas where the crowds would be at their thickest.

They head along Coffee Street in San Fernando. Weekes is not worried. There is little fear this morning. His mind is on the horizon ahead, the horizon of tomorrow. This afternoon they would pause at Saith Park in Central Trinidad and overnight there after a meeting. Tomorrow they will descend on the capital city, Port of Spain. The government will have to answer to the demands of tens of thousands of workers, a virtual army of occupation, powerful enough to make its prayers heard . . .

The march stops. This is the moment of truth. The workers have been told what to do in case the march is forcefully broken up. They would re-assemble further along the way. The union leaders with their arms locked together go to the front. Assistant Commissioner Ramdwar commands on the megaphone. He calls on Weekes first to tell the crowd to disperse and then to each leader in turn in rapid succession. He does not give them time to debate or agree. He grabs Weekes, hands him over to burly Superintendent Wilson. Weekes is whisked down the road to a waiting police van, about 50ft away from the scene as the order is given to attack.

Weekes sits in the van where he is placed and only his ears tell the tale. He hears the explosions as the cannisters of tear gas are shot into the crowd. He hears screams. Where is Theresa? Where are the children? They were all on the march. So many other comrades had their wives and their children there too. There were so many women from the sugar belt, many of them quite advanced in age. Occasionally somebody runs past, terror on their faces.

Then he has the most horrifying experience. Some police men come in sight dragging an unresisting Jamadar, and another lawyer, Bridgenath. They are being really violently treated. Jamadar slips on the wet road. Weekes eyes open wide, his voice is frozen, he is welded with shock to the metal cage in which he is locked when he sees the savagery with which the police go at the fallen Jamadar with their long riot staffs. He is rolling helplessly on the ground. Oh God, they want to kill him. Then they lift him limp and dazed and throw him bodily into the van. As Jamadar recovers from the shock, he shakes his head. It is an experience that cannot be real. He stammers out the words:

> I cannot believe it. If anyone had told me that this could happen in our country, I would not have believed them. I have heard about police brutality from other people, from my clients, but I could not believe it ... like this ... I cannot believe it"

By the time 29 of them are packed in a small cell later, where they would have to overnight, Weekes gets a fuller appreciation of the horror. So many of his companions in the cell have been badly hurt. Some have bleeding heads. Teeth have been knocked out. He hears about the poor school children who were caught in the melee on their way to school and beaten mercilessly. He later learns of a pregnant woman going to the market who was beaten and ended up in the hospital. He learns too that escape routes were blocked. As the police charged, marchers and onlookers, reeling from the tear gas, tried to escape down side streets. They were followed by baton-wielding policemen and ran into cordons of others waiting to pelt blows on them. Winston Leonard was singled out for special attention by Burroughs' gang. Nobody knows if he is alive. Priests were not spared. The police ran into the Presbyterian Church to strike Reverend Idris Hamid. Press reporters and photographers were beaten, cameras seized and film exposed ...

The people were beaten but their wills were not. Weekes and the other leaders have to decide where to go from here. While Weekes is in prison on the afternoon of Bloody Tuesday, T&TEC workers indicate they are ready for battle. They throw the North of the country in darkness for three hours. 400 of them walk off the job.

The arrested men are given bail in court the next day. When Weekes comes out, he can feel it. If the country was tense before the march, it is hardly breathing now. The struggle is not over, it has now become more bitter, more dangerous. He sees violence in the eyes of those who were praying yesterday. This is a mood for a fight to the finish. Can they carry it? Is there another way, a peaceful way? Will the government and the companies compromise to clear the way for a ceasefire or will they push for all out war?

The leaders have to face the people gathered in Woodford Square in Port of Spain. When Weekes enters the square he can feel the powerful spiritual vibrations coming from the Indian women singing their bhajans. There is no pain in their voices, only defiance. It is not peace that is on their minds. The square is crowded and the mood today is different from what the leaders had created before the walk. You can just sense, people are prepared to leave here and do anything . . . anything . . .

The whole country is seething. The police action has released a force that might be uncontrollable. With this kind of mobilization and anger, Weekes could envisage multiplying acts of sabotage, guerilla strikes in revenge and in furtherance of the just cause for which hundreds have suffered physical injury. He decides with the other leaders to go the way of prayer and peace.

On April 24th in Woodford Square, Michael Als, the leader of the Bank and General Workers Union, is invited to speak at a ULF meeting. He attacks the leaders for compromising by holding talks with the Governor General as though he could do anything in the crisis and for pacifying the workers when they are poised to seize political power. Weekes is stung by the criticism from a union leader representing a younger generation. He was not so sure where a militant struggle would have gone, he probably did not feel the same certainty he would have felt (rightly or wrongly) in a similar situation before 1971. He knew the solution had to be a political solution. All the leaders were saying that. But a peaceful political solution.

Als' words sent his mind retracing the last hectic month. What should the ULF leadership have done? The country had gone through a nerve wracking period in the wake of Bloody Tuesday. Strong condemnation of police actions came from many quarters, including the Inter-Religious Organisation (IRO). The ECA called for repeal or amendment of the IRA, they wanted it replaced with "legislation which is workable". T&TEC workers kept up absences and warnings that the country could be paralysed. Problems cropped up at WASA. Bus workers went on a work-to-rule. The government postponed the common entrance examination which was due for March 21st. UWI students boycotted classes. Many organisations thought it better to postpone meetings and functions.

The government was hardly compromising. They amended the IRA to pave the way for OWTU to be able to represent Texaco monthly paid staff. A conciliator was eventually appointed to deal with the disputes in oil and sugar. But no quarter was really given on the fundamental issues. Instead they moved with increasing aggression, sending in army and police to transport gasoline supplies from March 21st and a few days later sending them to transport sugar to hospitals and other institutions.

Did the unions have the resources to opt for further confrontation?

By April 20th the path of prayer and peace could go no further. Government actions were relieving the strain on the public. The leaders avoided or defused actions which could be confrontational or lead to a possible emergency. The country was losing a fantastic amount of money, it would amount to some $200 million. But the government could afford the loss of revenue now. The workers, on the other hand, were suffering. Wages were being sacrificed by oil workers. Hunger was spreading in the sugar belt. With no signs of any movement towards victory, frustration was developing. The strikes had to be called off, before they broke down under the pressures. Panday tried to salvage what little pride he could in surrender. He told workers:

> If we do not go back to work now, Williams would have us crawling back in a week or two . . . We will go back with dignity.[27]

Oil workers resumed work on April 28th.

Later there would be the satisfaction of seeing Caroni have to recognise Shah. Texaco workers would get a 57% increase and OWTU would secure recognition for the monthly paid.

For these eventual achievements, the government extracted a hell of a price on Bloody Tuesday. But out of it would come a new political organisation, the United Labour Front. Weekes had survived another battle which involved grave physical danger and a lot of personal torment, which road to take at the critical time? But having chosen, he was going at it with all heart again. He was fighting again. Something had to give for African and Indian workers in Trinidad and Tobago.

CHAPTER 17

THE BATTLE NEVER ENDS

June 26th 1987

At 7.45 p.m. the capacity audience at the Farrell House Hotel stands. A young Surinamese musician, playing a march on a trumpet, leads the guest of honour into the hall. Among those standing on the stage to welcome George Weekes, accompanied by his wife, Theresa, are the Prime Minister of Trinidad and Tobago and his wife. The Prime Minister's presence at this farewell to George Weekes as President General of the OWTU is highly symbolic, symbolic of national political change and symbolic of change in the status of Weekes, a change that holds the aging fighter suspended somewhere between glory and a new agony.

After 25 years, labour's foremost hero and burden bearer in the era of Independence is retiring from the major office in the OWTU. With his voluntary retirement, an important chapter in the life of George Weekes closes. But even as this chapter is closing, another one is opening. In 1987 George Weekes is a Senator, a Government Senator. In the cabinet of the government there are other men who had linked arms with Weekes on Bloody Tuesday, 12 years before. John Humphrey is Minister of Works, Settlements and Infrastructure; Basdeo Panday is Minister of External Affairs, Marketing and Tourism. He is also Deputy Prime Minister. The Prime Minister is A.N.R. Robinson whom the police had decided against arresting on the infamous Tuesday, March 18th 1975.

After ruling Trinidad and Tobago for 30 years, the People's National Movement had finally been defeated in a national election in December of 1986 by the party led by Robinson, the National Alliance for Reconstruction. The new government appointed Senator Weekes, who was not a member of the NAR,

300

with an assurance that he would be allowed to function in the Senate as an independent voice for labour.*

By this time Eric Williams is only a memory. The decade of the 70's had to result in a major casualty. It turned out to be Williams. He had rallied under great psychological stress until March 1981. Then he departed with the angry sounds of mounting protest ringing in his ears. There were scandalous efforts to shade the truth about the demise of the man who led Trinidad and Tobago to Independence. It was too difficult to explain a Prime Minister dying in a diabetic coma (brought on by a prolonged period of deliberate avoidance of medication and abandonment of the rules of diet), and dying in the company of other senior members of the government who failed to call a doctor until it was too late.

Weekes had been an adversary to the end. Two months before Williams died George Weekes was demonstrating outside his Whitehall office with 3000 people: workers of Federation Chemicals Ltd, who were on strike from December 1980, their families, other workers who had been mobilised in their support, and aggrieved workers in other industries.[1] By then the welling tide against the PNM was getting stronger. On one occasion, before Parliament had ended its session for 1980, Williams had been forced to sneak out of the Red House like a fugitive, hiding in an ambulance. He did not want to face angry teachers protesting outside. As soon as parliament reconvened for 1981, the momentum built up again. When George Weekes was not protesting outside the Prime Minister's Whitehall office, he was leading Fed Chem workers around the Red House (the Parliament Building) calling for the nationalisation of Federation Chemicals. Teachers were marching for the repeal of a law that blocked them from representation by the union of their choice, the Trinidad and Tobago Unified Teachers Association. Squatters were there protesting against the destruction of their homes. Sugar workers were there . . .

The spirit of rebellion of the 70's had triumphed over repression. The decade had been a shameful one for the

---

* This is the second time in this period that Weekes has agreed, with the support of the OWTU General Council, to serve in the Senate under such conditions. The first was in 1986, when a number of groups in opposition formalized themselves into the National Alliance for Reconstruction. Weekes had also been a Senator for the United Labour Front in 1976.

government where human rights were concerned. From April 1970, when Williams and his cabinet hid trembling in the Hilton Hotel with a getaway jet on standby at Piarco airport, the government had embarked on a course of increasing use of repression as an instrument of survival and conflict resolution. In the first half of the 1970's, it was a sporadic kind of repression, reaching extremes at points. However repression was always sustained in relation to particular groups, such as NUFF, NJAC and OWTU, and in relation to particular individuals — for example, Weekes charged for fraud, Makandal Daaga* charged for possession of ammunition, Khafra Kambon** charged for armed robbery and shooting. After Bloody Tuesday in 1975 the assault on the people was directed with a new vehemence at industrial struggles, an area in which the government had been indecisive during the early 70's.

The repressive philosophy of the regime was expressed by Prime Minister Eric Williams at a public meeting in Point Fortin on April 11th 1975. He said openly that in Trinidad and Tobago there was "TOO MUCH FREEDOM".[2] Shortly afterwards, Senator Inskip Julien, in theory an independent senator, complemented these statements, which were especially facetious in the wake of Bloody Tuesday, by suggesting that what was needed was a dictatorship for five years to rid the country of its problems.[3] These preliminaries were followed by the presentation of a bill that came to be known as the Anti-Sabotage Bill. Lennox Pierre, the OWTU solicitor, considered it to be a more treacherous bill than the Public Order Bill which the people had rejected in 1970.

The stated purpose of the bill was to deal with incidents during periods of industrial conflict. Its penalties included life imprisonment for causing damage in an essential industry, clearly a bill aimed at Weekes and other OWTU militants. The bill also made provisions for compensation to be paid to companies in cases involving acts of sabotage. The most dangerous aspect of the bill however was that it shifted the burden of proof from the prosecution to the defendant. The defendant now had to prove innocence, rather than the accepted principle in British law where the prosecution had to prove guilt. An accused could be

---

* Formerly Geddes Granger
** Formerly Dave Darbeau

committed on a probability. In assessing the dangers of the bill, *Liberation*, the official organ of NJAC asked:

> ... if a molotov cocktail is thrown in the house of a strike breaker in the oil field, who is to say that it is not PROBABLE that George Weekes incited that.[4]

The bill never became law, but the mentality it reflected came to guide the enforcement agencies of the law. The deployment of the armed forces to transport oil and sugar in 1975 was only the beginning of a new role for the police and the army in industrial disputes. The dangerous new role went beyond the question of patrolling the picket lines and intimidating striking workers. In September of 1976, the response of the state to unrest at the Telephone Company and on the docks was to send in the police to invade and occupy those work places. Workers now had to work under the gun. A few months later a State of Emergency was declared in the postal services in response to a go-slow protest by postmen. The postmen were locked out. Ninety of them were suspended and charged with taking strike action under the IRA. The army was moved in to get mail delivered and young school leavers were recruited to act as postmen. The following year, just before carnival, BWIA pilots went on a go-slow; they called it "a withdrawal of enthusiasm". The government reacted by dismissing all 126 pilots and chartering US airlines to handle the heavy carnival traffic.

One report commented:

> ... it seems that the Government, as an Employer because of its favourable balance of payment position, has adopted a model of industrial relations that is based on conflict. This is a regressive attitude and is a throw-back to the era of the slave economy. This attitude can have serious implications for the industrial relations system and for the workers. Employers who, more often than not, are antagonistic to unions and have a direct-and-control attitude to workers could adopt the Government's attitude.

Government's brutal anti-strike actions of the late 70's did in fact set in train a pattern of aggression by employers that escalated in the 1980's. And they were fully backed by drastic police action. The report had expressed particular concern at the likely "adverse effect on workers who belong to a weak union (and) non-unionised workers" when employers adopted the same attitude as government. In fact even the most powerful union, the OWTU, found itself having increasingly serious problems with private employers and the state. In March 1980 for example, the police ransacked an unoccupied OWTU strike camp outside of the Bermudez biscuit company.[5] In another instance, workers at Fed Chem went on strike in December of 1980 and ended up outside for an unprecedented five months. During that strike the OWTU. leadership saw, "for the first time in our experience ... the use of vicious attack guard dogs to intimidate and harass peaceful picketers."[6] When the dispute reached the Ministry of Labour in 1981, the president of the company declared:

> We have not come here to negotiate, we have nothing
> more to offer, we are here only out of courtesy to the
> Minister.[7]

That was only a forerunner to prolonged strikes and lock-outs. When boom conditions in Trinidad and Tobago started to peter out around 1982, and the position of trade unions weakened with growing retrenchment, major employers became increasingly ruthless in their anti-labour, anti-union actions. They were willingly following the lead set by the government's drastic and repressive labour policies, feeling assured that a state which used terror tactics against its own employees would support similar tactics by private employers.

Outside of the industrial relations field, other forms of repression also continued into the second half of the 70's and new dimensions were added. In the aftermath of Bloody Tuesday, there was a period of intense police harassment of the people in the sugar belt, which included sacrilegious invasions of places of worship, Moslem mosques and Hindu mandirs, on the pretext of searching for arms and ammunition. New draconian measures were adopted to deal with squatters in the late 70's. Heavily armed battalions of soldiers and police would invade squatter settlements in pre-dawn hours, to forcefully evict families, break down and burn their dwellings. Propaganda campaigns were stepped up on political organisers, especially geared against NJAC. In May of 1979, the Commissioner of Police, Randolph Burroughs, in a radio broadcast deliberately linked armed robberies, murder and crime generally to a "militant group" and people who "have assumed African names".[8] The stage was set for another round of criminal frameups, with a new twist.

Emphasis was placed on seizing the cars owned by members of NJAC and holding them as "evidence" for court cases.

The government felt the need to resort to this kind of repression in the late 1970's because industrial strife, militant group protests, resistance to undesirable policies of employers and government just would not die. The number of man days lost through strikes reached a staggering 750,000 in 1975. Even though the strikes were so brutally suppressed, 1976 saw another 123,721 man days lost due to strikes, without counting those lost in the postal services. Protests of unemployed seeking jobs in Trinidad and Tobago, often involving defiance of the law, community level protests relating to specific community problems organised by various area action committees, a highly successful boycott campaign against merchants for Christmas 1975, the bombing and burning of several business places in 1977 and 1978, voices of protest in the arts, especially in calypso, all these were manifestations of the continuing volatility of the society.

The wave of protest that rocked the government in 1980 and 1981, therefore, was a spill over from the revolutionary 70's, even though qualitative differences from the earlier period had crept in. The change in ethos underlying the continuing militancy and the obviously political tone in the protests, could be seen in the inability of the OWTU to mobilise the kind of worker solidarity within the union which characterised the earlier post-70 period. In 1981 the union excused the relative inaction of its branches in relation to the prolonged Fed Chem strike on the grounds of the IRA's prohibition of sympathy strikes. But ten years before, more drastic clauses in the ISA had been ignored. Nevertheless, despite the decline of revolutionary consciousness and values throughout the society, the continuities from the decade of the 70's were significant enough to produce incessant political/industrial turbulence. Williams death really marked the end of that decade. It brought the truce that had eluded him in life.

Weekes' emotional response to the Prime Minister's death was a mixed one. In one way he felt that a weight had been lifted from the society. Williams had become tyrannical and increasingly remote and reclusive. He had betrayed the hopes and dreams which he himself had awakened in the society. At the end of his 25 years of unbroken rule the political atmosphere was almost suffocating. Weekes was particularly disturbed by the widespread corruption which was eating away at the soul of the nation. Williams, in his last years, had also violently assaulted the spirit of independence bred by the revolutionary 70's, with the introduction of an undisguisedly colonial policy termed "Government to Government arrangements". Under these arrangements, proclaimed in the 1979 budget, every area of the country's physical and infrastructural development was being handed over to foreign firms, with the governments of their respective countries having nominal responsibility for their performance. It was a shocking abandonment of responsibility by the Williams government, which was to have disastrous consequences for national morale and the financial viability of Trinidad and Tobago. The death of Williams the politician was therefore a welcome relief.

However Weekes could not help but feel another kind of emotion stirring in him. Williams was also the author of *Capitalism and Slavery*, he was the man who proclaimed "Massa Day Done", the man who stood up for the dignity of every Black man when he defied the white controllers of the Caribbean Commission. Weekes had been drawn to Williams in the early days. The critical part of him distinguished reasons for reservations. But emotionally he was absorbed in the new leader's charisma when he attended public meetings of the PNM. He felt a profound identification with the intense nationalism, Black pride and fighting spirit that emanated from Williams in the 50's. It made Weekes want to believe in Williams' promise, to give in to his emotional judgement. But in 1956 Weekes had matured enough ideologically to keep a political distance and assess with his head. He stood aloof from the euphoria and became an early critic of the Williams' regime. But he had been touched. He kept hoping in a peculiar kind of way that the author of *Capitalism and Slavery* would emerge from beneath the neo-colonial politician he saw developing. In his early days as leader of OWTU, he was even trying to call that Eric Williams forth. He felt that the mass movement of 1970 had reached that Williams, by then too sunk in failure, corruption and collusion with the forces he had condemned to ever come to light again, but with just enough lingering self consciousness to hold back his other self, the ruthless Prime Minister, from striking at the Black Power movement until the last moment. In Weekes' opinion, the

Black Power movement of 1970 represented what Williams knew he ought to have been, but didn't have the courage to be.

When Weekes walked past the draped and sealed casket, lying in state at the Red House, presumably containing the bloated body of the dead Prime Minister, he genuinely paid respect. He paid his respect not to the political foe who had capitulated by choosing death, but to that other self of Williams which Weekes imagined had a real existence. He had felt it.

Williams' death probably saved his party from defeat in the general elections of 1981. The emotion of the event drained the hostility to the regime just enough to prevent people from reaching in sufficient numbers for an alternative. Weekes played a stand-off role in that election, which the PNM won under a new leader, George Chambers. The OWTU President General and other members of his Executive had teamed up with Raffique Shah, Boodram Jattan and other trade union colleagues from the CPTU and other individuals such as Lennox Pierre, Allan Alexander and Ian Belgrave, to form the Committee for Labour Solidarity. Up to the 1986 election the CLS had not transformed itself into a political party, but it defined itself as a sort of preparatory political organisation to lay the basis for a party of the working class. CLS prepared a statement of direction for the workers in relation to the election of 1981 basically claiming that none of the parties contesting represented the working class. The statement caused some friction with the National Joint Action Committee, which was participating in elections for the first time, after years of eschewing conventional politics. A major concern of the CLS at the time was what they saw as a threat from the extreme right-wing in the country, represented by the newly-formed Organisation for National Reconstruction, led by former Attorney General, Karl Hudson-Phillips.

By that time Weekes himself had been burnt by his involvement in conventional politics. The trauma had come with the United Labour Front in its incarnation as a political party. It had come after a period of heady political promise that made the eventual fall all the harder.

The climb to initial political success began predictably in 1975. There had been little doubt in anybody's mind, after the mass rally of oil and sugar workers in Skinner Park on February 18th 1975, that the United Labour Front would declare itself a political party and contest the elections due for 1976. That rally and all the experiences leading up to the tragedy of Bloody Tuesday laid the basis for a far more serious political challenge to the Williams regime than the Workers and Farmers Party could possibly have mounted in 1966. The decision to transform the four union grouping into a political party was formally adopted on January 3rd 1976 and the founding Congress of the party was held on March 28th. Weekes was particularly elated because for the first time his union's General Council had decided to give official support to a political party.

Like the WFP had done before, the ULF fought the election with a working class projection. However the voting followed a painfully predictable pattern. The ULF won ten out of the 36 seats to form the opposition in the House of Parliament. The same ten the DLP, as the traditional Indian party would have won if it hadn't fallen into total discredit. Once the politics of the trade union radicals came off the streets, it became entangled in the web of racial perceptions.

Weekes had been through the wringer in 1966 with this subjective force that was a "monkey on the back" of the society, addicting it to self-destructiveness. He was impressed with the blows struck against African/Indian antagonism in 1970 and 1975. But he knew the demon was not dead. He knew the forces that would feed it and revive it in an election period. During general election campaigns every five years you could see them bait and nurture the historically bred fears, suspicions, insecurities and prejudices which gave the demon its virulent strength. The agents of discord, with vested interest in a helpless and plunderable society, or seeking some narrow selfish gain, would work in overt and covert ways, in house-to-house whispering campaigns, by snide remarks from public platforms, pointed suggestions in the media. One of the obvious examples of luring the racial demon out of its dormancy in 1976, Weekes felt, was the media's insistence on projecting Panday as leader of the ULF during the election campaign. The ULF hierarchy were trying to project the collective leadership of Weekes, Panday and Shah (which in fact opened the door to the media selection). Weekes was so irked by the deliberately subversive role of the media that he claimed, "manipulation of the press, which purposefully projected Mr Panday as the leader"[9] was responsible for the defeat of the ULF.

That was a statement of anger rather than analysis. It is true that at one stage the ULF campaign had built up such an astounding momentum that, on the surface, victory seemed attainable. But Weekes had not expected national victory. He expected the party to be defeated by the manipulable racial polarization. He had also anticipated negative effects on the anti-PNM campaign from the splintered image of the opposition forces. Conscious of the danger posed by opposition forces fighting against each other, the United Labour Front had sought unsuccessfully to form an alliance with the Democratic Action Congress, led by A.N.R. Robinson.[10] Eventually nine parties contested the election. Most of them were paper parties. Weekes knew it was hopeless for these unorganized fronts to pick up seats. The pseudo-parties could not dislodge the PNM in any of its strongholds and it was clear that no one could beat Panday and the ULF in the sugar belt. These groups however undermined the confidence of people opposed to the government by fostering an image of confusion and division in the opposing forces.

In making his early assessments too, Weekes was not underestimating the kind of propaganda that would be directed against a group identified as hostile to the system. Opposition to the system was more threatening than hostility aimed only at the government. He was not underestimating the venom that would be directed at a group which included him in its influential circle.

Weekes took it for granted therefore that the struggle would have to continue from fronts outside of parliament and the arena of electoral politics. He had taken a decision to play his major role outside of Parliament. Fundamentally he had to weigh the importance of concentrating effort on the rapidly expanding trade union base of the OWTU or plunging into the demanding exercise of organising a constituency and afterwards representing the constituency, if successful in the election. Weekes knew that he could have won at the polls this time. He had the option to select a "safe" seat. But he gave priority to the union, the membership of which had grown to 18,800. He however played his role on the public platforms of the ULF. After the 1976 election, he also accepted to serve the opposition ULF in the Senate since his work with the trade union could benefit from the prestige and exposure he would enjoy as a senator, without him incurring the burden of having to service a constituency.

Despite the narrow voting constituency of the ULF its entry into Parliament had a dramatic effect. Just the sight, captured by an *Express* photographer on the opening day of Parliament, of George Weekes, Basdeo Panday, Raffique Shah and Joe Young, entering those chambers, clad in shirt jac suits and raising their clenched fists, created a feeling that something different could be expected in the upcoming sessions. Conventional politics, parliament got a new focus. There was a potential for the future. The party could prove its dynamism. It could transcend the historically imposed base. It could build its image for the future, not just through its elected representatives, but by appointments in the Senate. The PNM could have its way in passing bills by force of numbers in the House, but the challenge of debate and whatever revolutionary strategies could be devised, would certainly bring the people back into the political arena. It was testing time for a new politics.

The promise did not materialise. Weekes had time to create some waves in 1977 when he raised questions about a report into corruption in the magistracy that had mysteriously disappeared in a distance of a few hundred yards between the President's house and the Prime Minister's office. The De Labastide Report (as it was called), with its damaging revelations, was baited out of the 'Bermuda triangle' into which it had dropped for five years. The political excitement had begun.

But soon, hopes collapsed in factionalism within the United Labour Front. The party Central Committee decided, by a very wide margin, to remove Panday as leader of the opposition and replace him with Shah. Weekes and the OWTU General Council supported the decision against Panday. Panday fought back and this resulted in the nation's President having to decide who was leader of the opposition. In April 1978, after months of the humiliating confusion, Weekes asked that his Senate appointment be revoked. Panday eventually got the nod of President Ellis Clarke to be opposition leader. But the damage done to the image of the opposition and the hopes of the people was incalculable. Worse, though racial conflict was nowhere at the source of the original problems, Panday's way of fighting back called up the demon the ULF was supposed to lay to rest.

The ULF victory had come against a background where left-wing parties have been spectacularly unsuccessful in electoral politics, not only in Trinidad and Tobago, but, with the exception of Guyana, throughout the English-speaking Caribbean. The shameful demise of the party therefore was a crushing blow to Weekes and others who had invested so much effort in raising the left to this triumphant political platform. Weekes had to be thankful that he had chosen the correct priority in 1976, especially as the struggles of the people demanded a lot of extra-parliamentary effort, and in particular efforts by the trade unions.

However, despite the political impact of trade union mobilisation in 1980-81, the trade union was no substitue for the political base that Weekes had lost through the ULF break-up. Up to 1976 Weekes had concretely experienced the oil workers distancing themselves from him politically, even though the OWTU General Council and COSSABO were totally involved in all the stages of the development of the ULF. In March 1976, the unions moving to form the embryonic ULF party, called a strike to protest against certain clauses considered dangerous in a proposed republican constitution for Trinidad and Tobago. The call succeeded in halting operations in the sugar belt, but the response in the oil industry was far more limited.

As the seventies progressed it became more difficult for Weekes to mesh the economic struggle in which he was involved as a trade unionist with the goals of revolutionary politics. This was a period in which the trade unions played an important role in spreading the effects of the economic boom precipitated by sharply rising oil prices. Thousands of workers benefitted directly from Weekes militant leadership of the OWTU during the period. Between 1978 and 1979 the union signed agreements to the value of $500 million.[11] In 1981 the OWTU secured further increases in wages and bonuses estimated at $110 million over the following three year period. The significance of the increases lay not just in their scale but in the fact that the union was able to boast:

> OWTU has been able to close the income gap
> between workers in the manufacturing industries of
> the North and oil workers in the South.[12]

Weekes was caught up in a contradiction. On the one hand he had to obey the demands inherent in trade union organisation, which made substantial wage claims inevitable in the psychological environment of economic prosperity and rampaging inflation - prices doubled between 1974 and 1978. On the other hand, he was committed to organising workers for revolutionary political change. He tried to resolve this contradiction by promoting the ideological development of the union membership through lectures, literature, the refurbishing and expansion of the union library, and the employment of young radical university graduates* to strengthen the education department of the union. He encouraged the participation of the union in the cultural life of the society. For example the union organised annual essay competitions and poster competitions in the schools in commemoration of Butler Day; the union sponsored a steelband, OWTU Free French, and promoted other cultural activities. He got the union to identify itself officially with international struggles for justice and freedom, struggles against imperialism and racism, in particular the struggle against apartheid in South Africa. He sought opportunities for members to travel to socialist countries and gain new political experiences.

But the tide was turning, against the revolution. Levels of social discontent remained demonstratively high because of specific irritations, in workplaces or communities, and because of the deplorable level of just about all social services. But the common language of complaint and political protest no longer reflected the concepts of revolutionary change. At the turn of the 80's, for all the rebelliousness that remained in the society, neither Weekes nor anyone else could halt the creeping corruption of values as money, drugs and repression took their toll on the spirit of the people.

By 1982 the industrial relations climate changed dramatically. As the Trinidad and Tobago economy went into a nose dive,[13] some employers welcomed strikes to relieve them of paying wages while inventories built up. When they could not provoke strikes, they resorted to lock outs. Given the growing levels of unemployment they could easily recruit scab labour to maintain minimal levels of production. Employers also received support action from the state. The police were unleashing

---

* The union's current treasurer (1987), David Abdulah, was brought into the union in this process as part of the Education and Research Department.

increasing brutality against strikers and locked out workers. The law courts were granting injunctions in favour of employers, restraining the workers from picketing within prescribed distances from the companies, thus undermining the effectiveness of protest. The OWTU developed a feeling that it was an organization under siege, similar to the way it was in 1971. There seemed to be a concerted effort on the part of employers to provoke the union into strikes, which the companies showed no inclination to settle, or to lock out OWTU workers. Seemingly interminable strikes and lock outs spread throughout many of the major companies where the union was the bargaining agent, in North and South Trinidad — Metal Box, Lever Brothers, Caribbean Packaging Industries, Dunlop, Fed Chem ... The list just kept growing.

Workers were showing tremendous courage. Weekes at times found that he had to be a restraining force. For example he had a difficult battle to persuade workers to leave the premises of Caribbean Packaging Industries, when the company secured a court injunction ordering them to leave. Workers argued vociferously against him. Some left with tears in their eyes.[14] But despite the courage, economic forces were against them, the revolutionary spirit of the 70's, which could have elicited support strikes, was no longer in evidence, and the state was acting ruthlessly against the interests of workers.

The economic forces, which strengthened the hands of the employers, had another grave effect on the OWTU. The membership was decimated by retrenchment in the 1980's. Overall some 10,000 members were lost between 1982 and 1986, most of them in the hard-hit oil industry. These were, in the main, inevitable losses, given the severe contraction of work in the industry. Both the inevitable losses and the deliberate machinations of employers were cause for alarm.

At the Annual Conference of Delegates in 1986 Weekes complained that the "big Employers" wanted

> to destroy the unions ...
>
> ... their major weapon, openly and remorselessly sanctioned by the ECA is the Lock out, followed by the unprincipled imposition of the retrograde individual contract on disturbed and bewildered workers.[15]

FOR BREAD JUSTICE AND FREEDOM

In September 1986, Weekes was speaking against a background of 14 lock outs by employers in the previous seven months. At the time of his resignation, a few months later, the menace of the lock outs and the individual contracts, had been contained by an amendment to the Industrial Relations Act passed by the new government. But the attitude of the employers to trade unions remained. After 50 years trade unions were a tolerated but not an accepted part of industrial relations. The mistaken notion still persisted in influential business quarters that the profitability of capital could best be served if the trade union movement was destroyed. An intense propaganda battle was on, waged by the Employers Consultative Association, the mass media and other allied forces, to undermine the confidence of workers in trade unions generally.

The new NAR government, too, even though it made an amendment to the IRA that was beneficial to the workers, demonstrated, by another action, a lack of confidence in trade unions. It suspended Cost of Living Allowances in the public service by an announcement of the drastic measure in the 1987 budget. There was no prior consultation with the trade unions. This example of unilateral action by the government further eroded the principle of collective bargaining. Even in this environment Weekes' many efforts to re-unite the trade union movement were meeting with no more than symbolic successes. Every hint of promise was followed by a paralysing inertia that seemed purposeful, leading Weekes to alternate between determined conciliatory efforts and harsh criticisms of Congress leaders. On June 19th 1987, six days before his retirement, there was one more hope of unity held out as Congress unions and unions of the Council of Progressive Trade Unions jointly observed the 50th Anniversary of the trade union movement in Fyzabad, a move strongly influenced by Weekes' initiatives.

But even as he sits on the stage of Farrell House on June 26th 1987, he can feel no assurance that the Butler Day demonstration of togetherness was any more than another of those gestures that pointed to recurring deadends in the quest for a united trade union movement.

However, on this special occasion such thoughts are out of place. The night of June 26th is a time when everyone can feel the strong emotion of the moment. You hear it in the short addresses. It envelops you as female members of the OWTU staff

314

render beautiful and relevant solos and when the staff choir sings. The emotion is a mixture of celebration of 25 years of struggle and achievement — those old faces from the union, looking at their retiring leader, are beaming that the achievement is his and it is theirs — and sadness, facing the inevitable end of an era. Weekes feels the embracing emotion. He feels tension too. The moment is approaching, the moment of the final handover of an office that is now a part of himself. He finds no comfort in the fact that he is placing a heavy weight on new shoulders.

The heaviness is not apparent at Farrell House on June 26th. There is no inkling of crisis in the glitter of the room. But George Weekes knows that the union is going through a critical phase. Tonight however that reality must be suspended from his imagination. That is what an appreciative audience is trying to communicate. In many minds there are questions about the future, but every face tries to make George Weekes enjoy the moment of glory. The force of the collective will is pushing the sense of crisis to the back of his mind, where it belongs on a special night like this.

On June 27th he would no longer have the responsibility but he would bear the burden in his thoughts. During his last years in office he had been troubled, not nearly as troubled by the external pressures affecting the trade union movement as a whole, as he was by the state of the union itself. The real danger to the OWTU was that it was not showing the internal cohesion and strength to deal with the combination of economic stringencies and the organised assault of anti-union forces. Several branches of the union were not functioning with the discipline, efficiency and motivation that existed in the past. Weekes, however, foresaw the union overcoming this handicap. As he told the Annual Conference of Delegates in 1986:

> I know that some of the older members in particular
> are worried that we have gone a bit soft over the past
> few years. That is a passing phase. We have to
> understand the process that is taking place. We must
> remember that many of the people who work in the
> oil industry today were not even born when the union
> was formed almost fifty (50) years ago. There are
> some who were not even born when I took up
> leadership nearly twenty five (25) years ago.

They came in when things were relatively easy and have taken the achievements of the union for granted. The new leadership will have to deal with this.[16]

Weekes recognised that the task of restoring the strength of the union was one for the "new leadership". His last three years in office had really been years of transition. Gradually he had been shifting responsibility for the affairs and direction of the union to the First Vice President, Errol McLeod, and other members of the Executive. He still made appearances in the war zones of industrial conflict He had to chair many crisis sessions of various bodies in the union, and generally his profile remained quite high in the activities of the OWTU. But his level of physical involvement was far reduced from what it was before. He concentrated more on guidance of the younger officers. But deep within him Weekes could not really conceive of himself as a trade union leader giving guidance and inspiration from the shelter of an office. He said at the 1986 Annual Conference of Delegates:

I am resigning because based on my standards and principles of trade union leadership, it is time for me to hand over to younger generals . . . .

As President General of the OWTU, . . . my Generalship has meant leadership out there on the frontline, where the protesting workers are, where the riot staffs and tear gas and the guns of the police are. It has meant nights in strike camps after days of combining office work, running around doing organising in the field, thrashing out issues in negotiations, more so during the battles of Beaumont Hill, Pointe-a-Pierre, against apartheid-loving Texaco, dealing with problems and struggling mainly with racist employers at the Ministry of Labour, attending and doing battles at international conferences, meeting individuals and delegations with problems etc.

Physically it is no longer possible for me to carry the strain. So the decision I have taken, sad as it may be, is a decision I had to take in my own interest and in the interest of you the workers.[17]

Weekes also made it clear that in his concept no one was "indispensable . . . to a properly functioning organisation" and he did not want members to see him in this light where the

OWTU was concerned. They had prevailed upon him not to hand over the leadership in 1984, when he first announced his intention to resign. But what had persuaded Weekes more than anything else, to remain in office until 1987, was the symbolism of resigning at the end of 25 unbroken years as President General and the symbolism of leading the union to mark the historic 50th Anniversary of the June 19th 1937 uprising. In 1987 he was also resigning in the year of the 50th Anniversary of the Oilfields Workers Trade Union.

It is probably no coincidence that Weekes first announced his decision to resign from the leadership of the OWTU in 1984, one year after the tragic extinction of the Grenada Revolution. Weekes was very close to Maurice Bishop, the leader of that revolution, who was brutally murdered by former colleagues, an act which recklessly paved the way for an invasion of the island by American troops. The revolution, which had triumphed with the armed overthrow of the Eric Gairy government in 1979, had brought new hope to Weekes. He saw an island in the English-speaking Caribbean boldly experimenting with socialist patterns of development, and for a time it looked as though the experiment would be successful. He was invigorated by the thought that this would open the eyes of the people in Trinidad and Tobago and other Caricom countries to other possibilities, give them the incentive to try new developmental strategies. Weekes strongly identified with the struggles and the progress of the revolution. The OWTU gave all the propaganda support it could. Weekes himself was treated like a hero in Grenada, always praised by the leadership, and given tremendous ovations by the people when he addressed rallies there. The self-destructive carnage in which the revolution ended was the most devastating blow that he had ever had to face. And it came at a time when the physical strain of his style of leadership was beginning to tell on his health.

Weekes, who was in his 63rd year at the time of Bishop's murder, had been like a father figure to a much younger generation of revolutionaries throughout the English-speaking Caribbean. But in the 1980's, it seemed that the sons and daughters were dying and leaving the father. Three years before the slaughter of Maurice Bishop, Unison Whiteman, Jacqueline Creft, Vincent Noel and the other martyrs of the Grenada Revolution, the victim was Walter Rodney in Guyana. Rodney was murdered while he sat in his car, by the blast of a bomb, disguised as a radio. That was on June 13th 1980. It was an outrageous political murder that shocked the sensibilities of Caribbean people. Walter Rodney was a young man who had returned to his homeland, Guyana, after years of lecturing at the University of Dar es Salaam in Tanzania. He had joined forces with Eusi Kwayana and other activists of the Working Peoples Alliance, seeking to make his dream of a liberated Guyana come true by organising and educating the people. In several islands people were mobilised to express condemnation and horror when he was killed. The OWTU was instrumental in forming the Committee Against Repression in Guyana (CARIG). June 19th 1980 was dedicated to the memory of Walter Rodney and to protest against his assassination.

But the nature of the events in Grenada in October of 1983 made any such response impossible. The American determination to invade the island paralysed a strong revolutionary response against the perpetrators of the massacre. At the same time, the fact that other leaders of the revolution had been the bloody executioners made the crime too numbing and shattering for anyone to be able to mobilise public outrage against the American invasion. The one meaningful gesture Weekes was able to organise for people to whom he had been so close and whose struggle and achievements had touched him so dearly was a Memorial Service at the Anglican Cathedral in Port of Spain, in December 1983. The service was attended by Bishop's mother and sister, two former ministers of the Bishop government, Kenneth Radix and George Louison, and several leaders of left-wing political organisations throughout the Caribbean.

The image of Weekes in the Caribbean had made the OWTU a fitting organisation to pull together this Caribbean tribute and memorial to martyred heroes of the struggle for liberation in the region. As leader of the Oilfields Workers Trade Union, Weekes had achieved Caribbean prominence, not only by his activities in Trinidad and Tobago, but by the concrete assistance he provided to other unions in other islands. To take one example; in 1977, the OWTU under Weekes leadership, provided material asistance to the Antigua Workers Union in its fight against repressive legislation in that island.[18] The prominence was also built on the close rapport he maintained with other unions and radical organisations in the region. They were often invited to send representatives to important functions of the OWTU. On the occasion of the union's 40th anniversary, which was addressed by Maurice Bishop, the leader of the New Jewel Movement in Grenada, trade unions and other organisations from throughout the Caribbean were represented.[19]

The reputation Weekes established as leader of the Oilfields Workers Trade Union, in fact extended beyond the Caribbean. In 1984, Dr Biodun Jeyifo, a lecturer at the University of Ife in Nigeria, and President of the Academic Staff Union of Universities (ASUU), told delegates at OWTU's Annual Conference:

> I met Comrade Weekes in Moscow and I introduced myself. Comrade Weekes wanted to know who I am, and I told him that he does not know me, but I know him well, and the Nigerian working class knows him.[20]

Tim Hector of the Antigua Caribbean Liberation Movement, speaking at the same Conference, related his own experience at the United Nations Security Council in 1978. He had been invited to give an account of violations of the UN arms embargo against South Africa, by a US/Canadian firm. The firm was using Antigua as a transhipment base to sell arms to the apartheid regime. Hector's organisation and a number of others in the Caribbean were struggling against this violation of UN sanctions and violation of the manhood and dignity of the Caribbean people. A US delegate questioned the information Tim Hector presented about the "great part played by George Weekes and the OWTU in that struggle".[21] Hector knew that he was on solid ground because Weekes had organised oil workers to stop handling shipments of oil to Antigua. In fact, as a result of Weekes' action, the OWTU even found itself battling against Texaco for dismissing workers who took part in the boycott. But Hector pointed out that he did not even need to reply to the US query. A woman delegate from Kuwait defended what he had said about George Weekes. He concluded:

> This showed me that the activities of George Weekes and the OWTU had not only spread throughout the Caribbean and Africa, but had reached as far as the Middle East.[22]

In October 1985, one year after Tim Hector made these observations, Weekes travelled to Britain to represent the

OWTU at an international conference against apartheid organised by maritime unions from Britain, Europe and Australia. Significantly, the OWTU was the only land-based union invited to the conference.

It is not surprising that a great deal of Weekes' international reputation was built on his fight against apartheid. George Weekes hardly ever spoke on any subject without including a condemnation of apartheid. He consistently attacked those companies in Trinidad and Tobago which maintained links with the racist South African regime. In 1978 he exposed the treachery of Texaco Trinidad Inc, local subsidiary of Texaco International, which was shipping oil from Trinidad and Tobago to South Africa, despite an official government ban on trade with the apartheid regime. The outcry that he made about this, once it had been brought to his attention by alert oil workers, forced the government to order a commission of enquiry into Texaco's operations in Trinidad. The commission was deliberately drawn out and aborted by government and company. But the issue of Texaco's links with South Africa formed part of the platform for an increasingly intense campaign Weekes led, for the nationalization of Texaco. The slogan was born: "Texaco Must Go".

Under Weekes' leadership, the OWTU also organised several seminars and public lectures, featuring speakers from the African National Congress and other revolutionary organisations in Africa, to sensitize the masses of people to the cruel realities of life in South Africa. Weekes and the OWTU often took part in the organisation of protests against events which violated Trinidad and Tobago's moral obligations to the oppressed black people of South Africa. One such protest in March 1986 led to the "grossly obscene spectacle of Black policemen brutalizing and bloodying Black people, unarmed and peaceful people, voicing their condemnation of apartheid".[23] The victims of the totally unprovoked brutality were citizens peacefully picketing outside the Queens Park Oval where English cricketers who had played in South Africa were engaged in a match against the West Indies cricket team. Several people were arrested and many more were injured by blows from the police, some of them seriously enough to be hospitalized. Weekes and the other organisers, led by the Committee in

Defence of West Indies Cricket, decided that the protests must continue and they did continue.

Weekes also gained recognition in some areas of the world as a political activist committed to the goals of socialism. As a result of this ideological identification, Weekes had several opportunities to travel to countries in Eastern Europe. However he only made use of those opportunities in the 1980's. He first visited Russia in 1983. The only Eastern European country he had visited before that was Poland. Later he travelled extensively in Eastern Europe.

On the whole the OWTU President General was not a frequent traveller for most of his years in office. After the trips which he made in the early years of his leadership on official trade union business and on government delegations, Weekes cut his foreign travel to a minimum. He always found it difficult to accept invitations to visit other countries because there were always pressing problems for him to deal with in his own country. Quite a great deal of his travel therefore was concentrated in his last few years as President General of the OWTU. Weekes' international reputation was really built by actions at home.

That international reputation helped to draw guests from many parts of the world to the observance of the 50th Anniversary of the June 19th 1937 uprising and the birth of important unions, including the OWTU. Guests came from the English, French, Dutch and Spanish speaking Caribbean, including Cuba. Some came from Africa, some from the United States, others from Western Europe and Eastern Europe.

Some of them have remained to be with Weekes at Farrell House on June 26th 1987. A number of speakers at the farewell function praise Weekes in turn. Jack Kelshall, Khafra Kambon, A.N.R. Robinson, Theresa Weekes, Errol McLeod, they all give brief impressions of the character and contribution of the man Robinson describes as a "Caribbean hero". Walter Annamunthodo, paying tribute as an old Rebel, ends his contribution in tears. A picture emerges of a man of courage, integrity and love, a man with the conviction to pursue his ideological beliefs, whatever the cost in sacrifice, who has spent his entire adult life fighting for justice, for workers power, for national ideals, for a more human world.

FOR BREAD JUSTICE AND FREEDOM

The whole image conveyed by the words spoken on June 26th 1987 may never be communicated. Historically, George Weekes may well be remembered in one dimension, a warring figure at the centre of social turmoil, to be praised or dammed for the conflicts he stirred. With time the balance in the perceived image would shift more and more away from "trouble maker" to "freedom fighter". But essentially what would be seen is the scowling, angry face of a man at war with the establishment, a man of harsh words, shouting his rage against injustice on platforms, a man defiant of authority, marching the streets against oppression and exploitation. Certainly Weekes demonstrated an appetite for controversy, confrontation and protest that can only be described as phenomenal. But the dominant image of this warlike exterior could hide something very fundamental about the man, a quality that was only barely touched by the credits given at his farewell function.

There had to be something to sustain Weekes spiritually through almost forty years of struggle, beginning with his entry into the Butler movement in the late 40's, to enable him to rise above crushing defeats, to shake off the most consistent and venomous criticism ever levelled at any individual in this society, to come to terms with betrayal and not allow it to deter his purpose, and, most of all, never to surrender to despair, never to abandon the will to fight. That invisible something was more than ideology. It was a deep love for fellow human beings that was reflected in positive acts of selfless struggle. It was also reflected in an absence of malice and a capacity for forgiveness which few leaders show.

The clearest demonstration of this aspect of Weekes' character was the redemption of John Rojas in the OWTU. When Rojas died in April 1985, he died at peace with the world and his union. He was given a hero's burial by the OWTU. The man responsible for that honour was George Weekes, the man whom Rojas had sought to destroy. Weekes put aside the anguish and rancour of the past and reached out to Rojas at a time when the former President General was ill in 1984. He got the union's General Council to pay the bills for Rojas to stay at a private hospital. Following his illness, Rojas was invited to attend and address the 45th Annual Conference of the union that year. When Rojas arrived at the hall, the past and present President Generals embraced each other for a prolonged period, with an emotional intensity that brought tears to the eyes of some observers. On that day, Weekes, talking from the heart, paid tribute to Rojas for his contribution to the union, quoting Rojas' own assessment of his record, which he had made at the time he resigned in 1962.

At that moment coherence and unity returned to the history of the union. A continuity that had been broken was re-established. That continuity had been symbolically demonstrated in 1962, when Adrian Cola Rienzi, John Rojas and George Weekes sat side by side on the platform at Palms Club at the first Annual Conference that George Weekes was attending as President General. But it had been consumed in the venom of succeeding years. It was a triumph for the union when, in 1984, the links that had been broken psychologically, by personal hostility, were mended by acts that came from a generosity of spirit. Yet it was more than generosity to an individual. It was a demonstration of a mature view of history and a desire, reflected before in the invitations to both former leaders to address the 1962 conference, to see a wholeness in the union's perception of itself. It was an implicit recognition that Rienzi and Rojas had to be assessed in terms of their time.

Neither of them had satisfied Weekes' personal ideal of leadership the way Butler* had done. But the fact is they had been able to build the union and pull it through difficult times. They had to convince workers, in the face of victimisation and discouragement by extremely hostile employers, that their interest lay in joining trade unions, maintaining their membership and making the unions strong. They had to operate in an environment dominated by the overwhelming power of colonialism. This created a dual problem. On one level there was the commonplace psychological problem, which Weekes was able to observe in later years in Rojas' dealings with the oil companies, the difficulty which so many colonials find in dealing with whites as equals in a face to face situation. On another level, that was as subversive as it appeared to be pragmatic, the unions found themselves relying on the colonial government and the British TUC for support in their battles against recalcitrant employers in the early years. The colonial government wanted

---

* Butler died in 1977. At the time he occupied a house built for him by the OWTU.

323

unions established and recognised, but to serve the government's interests as "the only guarantee against extremist tendencies . . .". The reliance of unions on this support, at a time when the alternative would have been battles against total hostility from state and companies, and armed repression, had its costs. The British government acquired inordinate weight in dictating the role and methods of the trade unions in Trinidad and Tobago.

A further disadvantage for the early trade unionists was that financially trade unions were weak. The financial crisis of the OWTU even worsened during the years of the Second World War. Many workers left the oilfields, attracted by higher salaries paid by the Americans on the military bases at Chaguaramas and Waller Field. At one point in this period all the union had in its bank account was $52.84.[24] Very likely, it was the financial strain more than anything else that had caused Rienzi to lay the burden down and take a job with the state in 1944. In 1947, the British trade unionist, F.W. Dalley, paid tribute to the achievements of the OWTU under the circumstances:

> The history of the OWTU, formed on the 25th of July
> 1937, yields an outstanding but by no means solitary
> example of difficulties encountered and overcome
> . . .[25]

But in dealing with the problems of the times, seeking to establish the trade union movement which they felt would ultimately be the salvation of the workers, men like Rienzi and Rojas, found themselves going against their own expressed radicalism, making compromises that a subsequent generation would find hard to tolerate. They adapted the form of trade unionism to secure and retain the perceived indispensable support of the British government. They adapted the form of trade unionism to the perceived need to emphasise to the companies and the government that colonial trade unions could be "responsible". The substantive objectives of the trade union movement thus became lost in the form, and the form itself, instead of serving the original objectives of the workers and founders of unions, increasingly moved away from, and eventually hindered and suppressed those objectives, a process which reached critical limits at the end of the 1950's.

This corruption of form and objective led to the corruption of the perspectives of the leaders too. Their own vision and goals, which had to be concealed in pretenses and adjustments, became entangled in the confusion. These early leaders survived by disguise. But the deception turned out to be self-deceiving. The plays became the reality, and the acted character became the actor's character. An essential difference between Butler and men like Rienzi and Rojas was that, whatever Butler's limitations, he had revolutionary instincts. Rienzi and Rojas lacked such instincts. Their radical ideology was more at the level of passive analysis. They were somewhat misplaced, therefore, in a context that also demanded revolutionary instincts and character. Personal failings and weaknesses only compounded the difficulty of the situation.

However, both the Butlerite and the Rienzi/Rojas tendencies played their part in getting the trade union movement off the ground and nurturing its strength, both tendencies are the heritage of the OWTU. While Weekes felt a greater spiritual kinship with Butler and his methods, he was able to appreciate and give credit to the first leaders who struggled hard against the odds to build the union.

Just as he inherited the mantle of leadership, the "crown of glory and crown of thorns", from them, another leader is about to inherit it from him at Farrell House on June 26th 1987. Here the formal ceremonies are coming to an end. Weekes has been talking for some time. But he is not really delivering a speech. He is saying "thank you" - to the Rebels, to the OWTU staff, to a number of individuals and organisations who have all played their part during the twenty five years he has led the OWTU. Then he lifts his voice above the low tone that has been dictated by emotion. He has a few parting messages. The most passionate one is about the economy — the next stage in ownership and control of the nation's productive resources. He is speaking against a background of change in the structure of ownership of economic resources, so radically different to what it was 25 years before, that the statistics convey the impression a revolution has taken place.

A substantial part of the oil industry is nationally owned. The once powerful Texaco has been nationalized. Weekes had tried hard for this transnational to be taken over in a manner consistent with national dignity. To this end, the OWTU had launched a strong "Texaco Must Go" campaign at the beginning of 1979. The union provided the government and the public with substantial information, gathered by the workers, indicating that Texaco was "running down" the refinery and its operations generally. The union publicised an analysis done by Trevor Farrell which concluded that Texaco's Trinidad and Tobago subsidiary had no future role in the plans of the transnational. Instead of taking the union's lead, the government allowed Texaco to "suck the orange dry and spit out the seed".[26] The final settlement in 1985 was a case of Texaco dumping a rundown refinery on the people of Trinidad and Tobago, at a high cost, rather than the well-timed takeover in the national interest for which Weekes and the OWTU had been struggling. The one laugh oil workers had on the company was the way its officials rushed to take down the Texaco sign in front of its main offices "like a thief in the night", when they learnt the workers were planning to take it down themselves.

Nevertheless, as Weekes is saying his last few words as President General of the OWTU, all the refining capacity and land-based oil resources are in national hands, with state companies Trintoc and Trintopec as the dominant owners. Though a foreign company, Amoco, still produces the most crude from its offshore operations, the advance in national ownership is indeed impressive. Much of the credit for this must go to the untiring struggles of George Weekes and the OWTU for national ownership and control of the commanding heights of the economy. At this time the government also has substantial participation in new industries based on natural gas which were introduced during the 1970's. It has fully nationalised the sugar industry and state ownership or participation in joint ventures extends to various industries and services throughout the economy.

In his parting remarks, George Weekes expresses two areas of concern. One is about the present thrust of the businessmen (a direction incorporated in the NAR manifesto) for privatisation of state companies and utilities. He has fought too hard, for too long, to accept the return of nationalized economic resources to the hands of a few profit seekers, local or foreign. His other area of concern is about the role of the workers. He himself has been appointed to the Board of Directors of Trintoc and generally the policy of the new government is to have worker representatives on the boards of national enterprises. Weekes welcomes this positive step but sees the need for workers to have a far deeper participatory role in the management of the enterprises, many of which have in their top management "people opposed to nationalization". He also wants workers to re-define their relationship to the nationalized industries and play a responsible role in ensuring their viability.

It is near to midnight when the symbolic handover of office takes place. George Weekes presents the keys to his office and a carved wooden gavel to the union's new President General, Errol McLeod, who first joined the Executive as 2nd Vice President in July 1980. McLeod strikes an appropriate note of continuity in his acceptance speech. He also announces the decision of the union Executive to appoint George Weekes as Honorary President of the union. He tells the Prime Minister and the audience that in the union's opinion, George Weekes deserves a Trinity Cross, the nation's highest honour. The Prime Minister responds, informing the audience that he has personally made such a recommendation to the committee which decides on such awards. The choir sings a rousing medley of calypsoes of struggle. A disturbance is caused by part of the platform breaking. George Weekes descends the stage, under the bright glare of recording cameras, making light the disturbance, and looking towards the future that looms in the shadows . . .

George Weekes left the stage of trade union leadership as engulfed in controversy as he had been in much of his time as leader of the OWTU. His acceptance of a NAR government senatorship was only mildly controversial at first. By and large it was generally accepted in the existing political environment. The government had been swept into power with an overwhelmingly popular mandate. But heated debate over Weekes' senatorship and hostile accusations against him were not long in coming. The government's suspension of COLA generated a widespread anger that enveloped those associated with them.

Weekes himself was aware of the precariousness of his position. A combination of strong rightwing elements within the NAR, the disastrous economic legacy of the PNM, and an unfavourable international economic climate, gave a nightmarish touch to the political situation for a man of his beliefs and ideological persuasion. There was no telling in what directions these forces could push the government at any time.

However Weekes was satisfied that he had made the right decision. The political paralysis of the left, the divisiveness and growing difficulties of the trade union movement, and the desperate need for action to save the country from economic and social ruin, are all factors that made him feel that he could not reject the opportunity to fight from another level. His belief that he could achieve anything at all from this level was rooted mainly in his confidence in the new Prime Minister, A.N.R. Robinson. He did not see Robinson as radical or socialist, but he credited him with honesty and a sincere concern for workers and the people, an image which he formed from his and the union's association with Robinson in the 1970's. Given all the circumstances, therefore, he thought it was important to strengthen Robinson's hand against the traditional "invisible government" of big business and the transnationals. Otherwise these interests would totally dominate the elected government and deny the masses of people any of the potential benefits of political change in a period that was extremely critical and dangerous.

It may seem unfortunate that, at the very last moment as it were, just as Weekes seemed on course for a smooth exit from his heavy responsibilities, he found himself once more at the centre of a storm. But given the pattern of Weekes' life, one gets the feeling that is how it had to be. His was the fate of a man with a dream of Freedom, a dream of a just and equal New World. He dared to struggle for that dream, a dream that was the hope of the dispossessed. But it was a dream which challenged the mighty and the powerful. The dream sowed the wind and the bearer, fortunately with the strength to endure and triumph, reaped the political hurricane.

CHAPTER REFERENCES

Chapter 1 – A Peephole on the Social Ferment

1. *Port of Spain Gazette*, January 21st 1920, p.8
Pierre, Lennox. *The Origins of our Trade Union Movement in Trinidad and Tobago.* (typewritten manuscript), 1962. p.5
2. Martin, Tony. *Race First*. Greenwood Press, Westport, Connecticut, 1976, p. 73
3. Pierre, Lennox. op.cit
4. Samaroo, Brinsley. *The Constitutional and Political Development of Trinidad, 1898-1925.* (Thesis). U.W.I. p.145
5. Basdeo, Sahadeo. *Indian Participation in Labour Politics in Trinidad 1919-1939.* UWI, St Augustine, Trinidad & Tobago., 1979. p.5
See also: Ryan, Selwyn. *Race and Nationalism in Trinidad and Tobago: a study of decolonization in a multiracial society.* University of Toronto Press, 1972. p.38
6. However it is to be noted that even where particular companies or industries thrived or were shielded from the depression by various mechanisms, they grossly underpaid their workers. The Forster Commission pointed out that very high dividends were paid by some of the larger oil companies — Apex and Trinidad Leaseholds Limited paid dividends of 35% and 25% respectively for the 1935-36 period. In the case of the Trinidad sugar industry, the impact of depressed international conditions was cushioned by preferences.
7. Basdeo. op. cit. p10
8. Martin, Tony. *Race First.* op.cit.
9. Lewis, W. Arthur. *Labour in the West Indies: The Birth of a Workers' Movement.* New Beacon Books, London. Port of Spain. 1977. pp.11-12
10. Butler, T.U.B. *WORKERS OF TRINIDAD, Attention Please.* Pamphlet distributed to workers on June 10th 1937.
11. Ryan op.cit. p.44 points out the strength of the mass reaction throughout the region. He indicates that the pleas of Selassie and lack of positive response from the "white democracies . . . left a searing imprint on the minds of the West Indian masses".

Chapter 2 – Love, War, and the Birth of Ideology

1. Weekes, George. *The President General's Address to the 47th Annual Conference of Delegates of the Oilfields Workers Trade Union.* Vanguard Publishing Co., San Fernando (1986), p. 7

329

2. Kambon, Khafra, "Interview with George Weekes" (unpublished), January 21st 1986
3. Kambon, Khafra, "Interview with Sybil Weekes" (unpublished), 1986
4. Kambon, Khafra, "Interview with George Weekes" (unpublished), May 12th 1986
5. Williams, Eric. *History of the People of Trinidad and Tobago.* Andre Deutsch, 1962. p. 237.
Solomon was very critical of the report of the commission led by O'Reilly because it was recommending the continued dominance of the Governor and nominated officials in the government of the country. His own emphasis was on the responsibility of people for their own development.

> The 'keynote' is responsibility which every people must shoulder sooner of later. (Quoted in Williams, p.241)

6. Kambon, Khafra, "Interview with George Weekes" (unpublished), 1986
7. Jacques-Garvey, Amy. *Philosophy and Opinions of Marcus Garvey, Volumes I & II.* Atheneum, New York, 1974. p.7

Chapter 3 – Turning Point for the OWTU

1. Kambon, Khafra, "Interview with George Weekes" (unpublished), July 9th 1986
2. Ibid.
3. Ibid
4. Ibid
5. Ibid
6. Ibid
7. Obika, Nyahuma. *An Introduction to the Life and Times of T.U.B. Butler The Father of the Nation.* Caribbean Historical Society, Point Fortin, Trinidad and Tobago. 1983
8. *Sunday Express.* Trinidad Express Newspapers Ltd., Port of Spain. 18th June 1967. Interview with A. Rienzi. Title: 'The Go-Between'.
9. Report of Forster Commission, 1937, p.67
10. Basdeo, Sahadeo. *Indian Participation in Labour Politics in Trinidad 1919-1939*
11. Ibid. p.21
12. Dalley, F.W. *Trade Union Organisation and Industrial Relations in Trinidad.* London, HMSO, 1947, p.35
13. Ibid
14. Annamunthodo Walter. *Tubal Uriah Buzz Butler, 1897-1977; The Father of the Nation; A tribute by Walter Annamunthodo.* Unique Services, San Fernando, 1986 (reprint), p.4
15. op. cit Dalley. Appendix 3. Letter from the OWTU to the commission.
16. op. cit Annamunthodo, p.4
17. *Trinidad Guardian.* Trinidad Publishing Co. Ltd., Port of Spain, 30/6/60 p.1
18. *Trinidad Guardian.* Trinidad Publishing Co. Ltd., Port of Spain, 5/7/60
19. Ibid
20. *Trinidad Guardian.* Trinidad Publishing Co. Ltd., Port of Spain, 13/7/60

CHAPTER REFERENCES

21. Kambon, Khafra, "Interview with Jack Kelshall" (unpublished), 1986
22. *The Nation.* PNM Publishing Co., Port of Spain. 29/7/60
23. Ibid
24. Ibid
25. Ibid
26. Ibid
27. *The Vanguard.* June 19th 1966. p. 7

Chapter 4 – OWTU gets a New Leader

1. John La Rose, in conversation with Khafra Kambon (Sept. 1987), quoted these statements of one of the WIIP members.
2. The History of the Union (1937-1977). In *Oilfields Workers Trade Union July 1937 — July 1977.* Oilfields Workers Trade Union, 1977. p.22
3. Kambon, Khafra, "Interview with Lennox Pierre (unpublished), 1986
4. Knowles, William H. *Trade Union Development and Industrial Relations in the British West Indies.* Berkeley and Los Angeles 1959. University of California Press. p.79
5. Leonard, Winston. "Interview with Walter Annamunthodo". (unpublished) 1986
6. Ibid
See also Selwyn Ryan, *Race and Nationalism.*
7. Williams, Eric. 'Aspects of Caribbean Economy'. Article in *PNM WEEKLY,* July 23rd 1956, p.6
8. op. cit Annamunthodo interview
9. op. cit *History of the Union.* p.25
10. *Trinidad Guardian.* Trinidad Publishing Co. Ltd., Port of Spain. April 14 1959
11. *Trinidad Chronicle.* June 27 1958
12. *Evening News.* Trinidad Publishing Co. Ltd., P.O.S., July 8 1960
13. *Trinidad Guardian.* Trinidad Publishing Co. Ltd., Port of Spain. May 6 1959

Chapter 5 – Confrontation Begins

1. *The Vanguard:* The Voice of Labour. Oilfield Workers Trade Union. Printed by The Vanguard Publishing Co., San Fernando. 30th April 1965, p.2
2. Ibid. p.2
3. *Trinidad Guardian.* Trinidad Publishing Co. Ltd., Port of Spain. Editorial, 17/2/63
4. Budget Speech 1961—. *Budget Speeches 1957-1981. Vol.I: 1957-1971.* Republic of Trinidad and Tobago, Trinidad and Tobago. p.155
5. Ibid. p.156
6. Kambon, Khafra, "Interview with George Weekes" (unpublished), July 2nd 1986

7. Lloyd Best, 'From Chaguaramas to Slavery', in *New World quarterly*; Vol.II No.1, Dead Season 1965. New World Group Ltd., Mona, Jamaica.

8. Budget Speech 1957—. *Budget Speeches 1957-1981. Vol.I: 1957-1971*. Republic of Trinidad and Tobago, Trinidad and Tobago . p.2

9. Carrington, Edwin, 'The Post-War Political Economy of Trinidad and Tobago'. In *New World quarterly*, Vol iv No.1. Dead Season 1967. p.60

10. Farrell, Trevor. *The Economics of Discontent*. Statistical tables indicate the following increases in G.D.P. :-
1954 — 3.6%; 1955 — 13.7%; 1956 — 15.4% p.46

11. James, C.L.R. *Party Politics in the West Indies*, Inprint Caribbean Ltd. Trinidad. 1984. p.154

12. op.cit. Carrington p.63

13. Ibid p.43

14. Budget Speech 1962—. *Budget Speeches 1957-1981. Vol.I: 1957-1971*. Republic of Trinidad and Tobago, Trinidad and Tobago. p.191

15. Budget Speech 1963. *Budget Speeches 1957- 1981. Vol.I: 1957-1971*. Republic of Trinidad and Tobago, Trinidad and Tobago. p.212

16. Farrell. op.cit. p.46

17. Budget Speech 1962. op.cit. p.185

18. Budget Speech 1963 op.cit. pp.240-241

19. Budget Speech 1962. op.cit. p.240

20. Budget Speech 1964. *Budget Speeches 1957-1981. Vol.I: 1957-1971*. Republic of Trinidad and Tobago, Trinidad and Tobago. p.252

21. Ibid.

22. Kambon, Khafra, "Interview with George Weekes" (unpublished)

23. *Sunday Guardian*. Trinidad Publishing Co. Ltd., Port of Spain, February 24th 1963.

24. *Trinidad Guardian*. Trinidad Publishing Co. Ltd., Port of Spain, March 7th 1963 p. 1

Chapter 6 – Rise to National Prominence

1. Rojas, John. *Rojas Summoned, Rojas Appeared, and Rojas Replied*. (pamphlet — a message from Rojas to oilworkers, following his answer to charges by a disciplinary committee of the OWTU executive in 1964) p.3

2. *Trinidad Guardian*. Trinidad Publishing Co. Ltd., Port of Spain, November 20th 1963

3. *The Vanguard*: The Voice of Labour. Vanguard Publishing Co., San Fernando, August 22nd 1970, p.1

4. *Trinidad Guardian*. Trinidad Publishing Co. Ltd., Port of Spain, 1st January 1963, p.3

5. Ibid.

6. *Trinidad Guardian*. Trinidad Publishing Co. Ltd., Port of Spain. 19th August 1963

7. *Trinidad Guardian*. Trinidad Publishing Co. Ltd., Port of Spain. 24th December 1963

CHAPTER REFERENCES

8. *Trinidad Guardian*. Trinidad Publishing Co. Ltd., Port of Spain, 11th July 1963
9. *Trinidad Guardian*. Trinidad Publishing Co. Ltd., Port of Spain. 1st January 1963
10. *Daily Mirror*. Port of Spain. 11th December 1963
11. *Trinidad Guardian*. Trinidad Publishing Co. Ltd., Port of Spain. 16th January 1964
12. *Sunday Guardian*. Trinidad Publishing Co. Ltd., Port of Spain. 24th Februrary 1963
13. *Trinidad Guardian*. Trinidad Publishing Co. Ltd., Port of Spain. 11th July 1963, p.13
14. *Evening News*. Trinidad Publishing Co. Ltd., Port of Spain. 19th September 1963

Chapter 7 – 1965: Democracy Threatened

1. *Daily Mirror*. Port of Spain. March 10th 1965, p.5
2. *Trinidad Guardian*. Trinidad Publishing Co. Ltd., Port of Spain, March 14th 1965
3. Kambon, Khafra, "Interview with George Weekes" (unpublished), March 19th 1986
4. Kambon, Khafra, "Telephone Interview with Cyril Weekes" (unpublished), 1987
5. Weekes, George. *Why I Resigned.* Dept. of Education and Research, Oilfields Workers Trade Union, 1965, p.13
6. Oilfields Workers Trade Union. 'Resolution No.3, 16th. Annual Conference of Delegates', November 20th 1955
7. Oilfields Workers Trade Union. General Council Resolution, March 16th 1965, in *The Vanguard*: The Voice of Labour. Vanguard Publishing Co., San Fernando, August 13th 1965, p.2
8. *The Vanguard*: The Voice of Labour. Vanguard Publishing Co., San Fernando, May 14th 1965, p.1
9. Ibid.
10. Ibid.
11. Opaluba, M.C. (article) 'Legal Restraints on Caribbean Trade Unions'. In *Caribbean Issues: A Journal of Caribbean Affairs.* Vol 1. No.2, August 1974. (Theme 'Industrial Relations'). UWI, St Augustine. p.23
12. OWTU General Council Resolution, March 1965. Op.cit.
13. *Daily Mirror*. Port of Spain. March 23rd 1965
14. Weekes, *Why I Resigned*. Op. cit. pp.10-11
15. Ibid. p.11
16. Ibid.
17. Ibid.
18. (Article) 'The "Rebel" Movement'. In *Twenty Years of Union Democracy under 'Rebel' Leadership. June 25th 1962 — June 25th 1982.* p.4. Article refers to CIA involvement in the union's elections in 1965 and 1968.

19. *Trinidad Guardian.* Trinidad Publishing Co. Ltd., Port of Spain. March 6th 1963, p.1

20. *Sunday Mirror.* Port of Spain. March 21st 1965

21. *Chronicle.* July 24th 1959. W.W. Sutton submitted his resignation as 3rd Vice President of the NTUC because he was not selected to represent Congress at a Conference on education in the West Indies at the University College of the West Indies in Jamaica.

22. *Trinidad Guardian.* Trinidad Publishing Co. Ltd., Port of Spain, July 13th 1965, p.9

23. *Trinidad Guardian.* Trinidad Publishing Co. Ltd., Port of Spain, March 22nd 1965

24. *Trinidad Guardian.* Trinidad Publishing Co. Ltd., Port of Spain, March 20th 1965, p.1

25. *Trinidad Guardian.* Trinidad Publishing Co. Ltd., Port of Spain, March 16th 1965, p.1

26. *Daily Mirror.* Port of Spain. April 12th 1965

27. *Trinidad Guardian.* Trinidad Publishing Co. Ltd., Port of Spain, November 12th 1961

28. *Trinidad Guardian.* Trinidad Publishing Co. Ltd., Port of Spain, March 17th 1965, p.1

29. *Trinidad Guardian.* Trinidad Publishing Co. Ltd., Port of Spain, March 18th 1965, p.1-2

30. *Trinidad Guardian.* Trinidad Publishing Co. Ltd., Port of Spain, March 19th 1965, p.1

31. Ibid.

32. Als, Michael. *Is Slavery Again : Some Factors leading up to the introduction of the Industrial Stabilization Act (I.S.A.) 1965, in Trinidad & Tobago.* Cacique Publishers (undated) p.15

33. Kambon, Khafra, "Interview with George Weekes" (unpublished), March 19th 1986

34. Weekes, *Why I Resigned.* Op. cit. p.14

35. Kambon, Khafra, "Interview with George Weekes" (unpublished), 1986

36. Ibid.

37. Ibid.

Chapter 8 – "Subversive elements. . .at work"

1. Weekes, George. President's Address to the 3rd Biennial Conference of Delegates of the National Trades Union Congress. January 30th 1965, (mimeo) p.4

2. Mahabir, Winston. Address delivered to the University of California, October 16th 1965. In *The Vanguard*: The voice of Labour. Vanguard Publishing Co., San Fernando, November 12 1965 p.3

3. James, C.L.R. *Party Politics in the West Indies.* Inprint Caribbean Ltd., Trinidad. 1984. p.157

CHAPTER REFERENCES

4. Weekes, George. 'Statement to Texaco Representatives at the opening of Wage Negotiations on April 6th 1965.' (mimeo). Oilfields Workers Trade Union, San Fernando, 1965. p.1

5. Farrell, Trevor. *The Economics of Discontent*, Oilfields Workers Trade Union, San Fernando, Trinidad and Tobago (1973), Table III, p.47

6. Budget Speech 1961. *Budget Speeches 1957-1981. Vol.I: 1957-1971.* Republic of Trinidad and Tobago, Trinidad and Tobago, p.153

7. Farrell op.cit. p.55

8. Budget Speech 1964. op.cit. p.255

9. Jacobs, Carl. (article) 'The Year in Print', in *Sunday Guardian*. Trinidad Publishing Co. Ltd., Port of Spain, January 6th 1963

10. *Trinidad Guardian*. Trinidad Publishing Co. Ltd., Port of Spain, February 20th 1965, p.1 (Evidence of Ossie Wilson, President of the Civil Service Association given before a High Court judge, during a challenge to the publication of the Mbanefo Commission report.)

11. Budget Speech 1965. op.cit. p.302

12. Ibid. p.286

13. Ibid.

14. *The Nation*. Peoples National Movement. April 23rd 1965

15. Williams, Eric. An Address to the Ninth Annual Convention of the People's National Movement.

16. Weekes, George. 'The Trade Union Struggle in Trinidad'. Article in Trevor Munroe and Rupert Lewis ed., *Readings in Government and Politics of the West Indies*, 1971 edition, Dept of Government, University of the West Indies, Mona, Jamaica. p.155

17. Williams, Eric. *Inward Hunger: The Education of a Prime Minister*, André Deutsch London, 1949

18. *The Nation*. People's National Movement. July 29th 1960.

19. Williams. *Inward Hunger*. op.cit.

20. Kambon, Khafra, "Interview with George Weekes" (unpublished) 1986

21. La Rose, John. Interviewed by Khafra Kambon.

Chapter 9 – David without the Sling Shot

1. *Trinidad Guardian*. Trinidad Publishing Co. Ltd., Port of Spain, March 16th 1965

2. *Trinidad Guardian*. Trinidad Publishing Co. Ltd., Port of Spain, March 20th 1965, p.1

3. *Trinidad Guardian*. Trinidad Publishing Co. Ltd., Port of Spain, April 13th 1965, p.1

4. *Trinidad Guardian*. Trinidad Publishing Co. Ltd., Port of Spain, March 20th 1965, p.2

5. Ibid.

6. *Trinidad Guardian*. Trinidad Publishing Co. Ltd., Port of Spain, March 20th 1965, p.2

7. *Trinidad Guardian*. Trinidad Publishing Co. Ltd., Port of Spain, March 31st 1965, p.1

8. *The People's Charter: A Statement of Fundamental Principles.* PNM Publishing Co., Port of Spain, 1956
9. Ibid. pp 11-12
10. Weekes, George. *High Treason : The Trade Union Congress and The Sugar Workers' Strike, Why I Resigned.* Oilfields Workers' Trade Union, San Fernando, Trinidad and Tobago. p.13
11. *The Daily Mirror.* Port of Spain. March 13th 1965, p.12
12. *The Vanguard:* The Voice of Labour. Vanguard Publishing Co., San Fernando, May 7th 1965 (?)
13. *Report of the Commission of Enquiry into Subversive Activities in Trinidad and Tobago.* House Paper No.2 of 1965. Government Printery, Trinidad, Trinidad and Tobago, 1965. p.33
14. Ibid. p.35
15. Ibid.
16. *Trinidad Guardian.* Trinidad Publishing Co. Ltd., Port of Spain, April 10th p.1
17. *Sunday Guardian.* Trinidad Publishing Co. Ltd., Port of Spain, March 28th 1965
18. Ibid.
19. *The Vanguard:* The Voice of Labour. Vanguard Publishing Co., San Fernando, May 7th 1965
20. Ibid.
21. Ibid.
22. *The Vanguard:* The Voice of Labour. Vanguard Publishing Co., San Fernando, April 30th 1965, p.8
23. *The Daily Mirror.* Port of Spain. December 17th 1965
24. Weekes, George. 'Statement to Texaco Representatives at opening of Wage Negotiations on April 6th 1965'. (mimeo) Oilfields Workers Trade Union, San Fernando, 1965. p.1
25. Ibid. p.2
26. Ibid. p.4
27. Ibid. p.5
28. *The Vanguard:* The Voice of Labour. Vanguard Publishing Co., San Fernando, December 10th 1965, p.3
29. *The Vanguard:* The Voice of Labour. Vanguard Publishing Co., San Fernando, December 23rd 1965, p.1
30. Ibid. p.5
31. *The Vanguard:* The Voice of Labour. Vanguard Publishing Co., San Fernando, August 20th 1965, p.7
32. Weekes, George. Lecture entitled "Trade Unions and Politics". In *The Vanguard:* The Voice of Labour. Vanguard Publishing Co., San Fernando, January 7th 1966, p.3

Chapter 10 – A Plunge into Conventional Politics

1. *The Vanguard:* The Voice of Labour. Vanguard Publishing Co., San Fernando, August 6th 1965. p.6

CHAPTER REFERENCES

2. Weekes, George. Lecture entitled, 'Trade Unions and Politics'. In *The Vanguard*: The Voice of Labour. Vanguard Publishing Co . . . San Fernando, January 7th 1966, p.3

3. Ibid.

4. Ibid.

5. Kambon, Khafra, "Interview with George Weekes" (unpublished) 1986

6. Ibid.

7. Kambon, Khafra, "Interview with George Weekes" (unpublished), June 26th 1986

8. Ibid.

9. Ibid.

10. Ibid.

11. James, C.L.R. *George Weekes.* (mimeo) (undated) p.7

12. Ibid. p.9

13. Ibid. p.3

14. Ibid. p.2

15. *The Vanguard*: The Voice of Labour. Vanguard Publishing Co., San Fernando, August 27th 1965, p.8
La Rose however was not as optimistic as James to project this phase as the "final defeat of the middle classes". He anticipated that there would still be "many see saws and zig zags to follow".

16. Dalley, F.W. *General Industrial Conditions and Labour Relations in Trinidad. A Report.* HMSO, London, 1954. p.38

17. *The Vanguard*: The Voice of Labour. Vanguard Publishing Co., San Fernando, February 18th 1966, p.1

18. *The Vanguard*: The Voice of Labour. Vanguard Publishing Co., San Fernando, August 6th 1965, p.6

19. Kambon, Khafra, "Interview with George Weekes" (unpublished), June 30th 1986

20. Ibid.

21. *Trinidad Guardian.* Trinidad Publishing Co. Ltd., Port of Spain, July 3rd 1965

22. *The Vanguard*: The Voice of Labour. Vanguard Publishing Co., San Fernando, February 18th 1966, p.1

23. Williams, Eric. *Inward Hunger: The Education of a Prime Minister.* Andre Deutsch Ltd., London, 1969. p.335

24. *The Vanguard*: The Voice of Labour. Vanguard Publishing Co., San Fernando, April 15th 1966. p.8

25. Kambon, Khafra, "Interview with George Weekes" (unpublished), June 30th 1986

Chapter 11 – The Eve of the Storm

1. *Trinidad Guardian.* Trinidad Publishing Co. Ltd., Port of Spain. May 4th 1969, p.12

2. *Trinidad Guardian.* Trinidad Publishing Co. Ltd., Port of Spain. (editorial) May 8th 1969, p.8

337

3. *Trinidad Guardian.* Trinidad Publishing Co. Ltd., Port of Spain. (editorial) May 3rd 1969, p.8

4. *Trinidad Guardian.* Trinidad Publishing Co. Ltd., Port of Spain. (editorial) May 5th 1969, p.6

5. *Daily Express.* Trinidad Express Newspapers Ltd., Port of Spain. April 22nd 1969

6. *Trinidad Guardian.* Trinidad Publishing Co. Ltd., Port of Spain. May 3rd 1969, p.2

7. Thomas, R.D. *The Adjustment of Displaced Workers in a Labour Surplus Economy: A Case Study of Trinidad and Tobago.* Institute of Social and Economic Research, University of the West Indies, Jamaica. 1972. p.46

8. *Trinidad Guardian.* Trinidad Publishing Co. Ltd., Port of Spain. May 6th 1969, p.9

9. Ibid.

10. Weekes, George. *"The Students of the World Today are my kind of People".* (pamphlet) (undated) Vanguard Publishing Co. Ltd, San Fernando.

11. Irvine, Keith. *The Rise of the Colored Races.* W. W.Norton & Company, Inc. New York, 1970. p.542

12. Kambon, Khafra, "Interview with George Weekes" (unpublished). July 2nd 1986

13. Weekes, George. President's Address to the 3rd Biennial Conference of Delegates of the National Trades Union Congress. January 30th 1965, (mimeo)

14. Kambon, Khafra, "Interview with George Weekes" (unpublished). 1986

15. Farrell, Trevor. *In Whose Interest? Nationalization and Bargaining with the Petroleum Multinationals: The Trinidad and Tobago Experience.* University of the West Indies, St Augustine, Trinidad and Tobago (mimeo). p.18

16. *Daily Express.* Trinidad Express Newspapers Ltd., Port of Spain. July 28th 1969.

17. *Daily Express.* Trinidad Express Newspapers Ltd., Port of Spain. July 22nd 1969

18. *Daily Express.* Trinidad Express Newspapers Ltd., Port of Spain. July 28th 1969.

19. *Daily Express.* Trinidad Express Newspapers Ltd., Port of Spain. July 1st 1969

20. *Daily Express.* Trinidad Express Newspapers Ltd., Port of Spain. September 24th 1967. p.1

21. *Daily Express.* Trinidad Express Newspapers Ltd., Port of Spain. June 22nd 1968

22. *The Vanguard:* The Voice of Labour. Vanguard Publishing Co., San Fernando, April 19th 1969. p.5

It is significant that an East Indian religious minister made the statements Baldeo did because there were many efforts to make Indians in Trinidad feel that Black Power was exclusively an African concern and even that it was anti-Indian. The Black Power movement in Trinidad and Tobago however consistently defined Indians as Black.

CHAPTER REFERENCES

Chapter 12 – Revolution!!

1. *The Vanguard*: The Voice of Labour. Vanguard Publishing Co., San Fernando, January 3rd 1971. p.1
2. *The Vanguard*: The Voice of Labour. Vanguard Publishing Co., San Fernando, January 3rd 1970. p.8
3. *Trinidad Guardian*. Trinidad Publishing Co. Ltd., Port of Spain. March 10th 1970
4. *The Vanguard*: The Voice of Labour. Vanguard Publishing Co., San Fernando, February 7th 1970. p.8
5. Thomas, R.D. *The Adjustment of Displaced Workers in a Labour Surplus Economy: A Case Study of Trinidad and Tobago*. Institute of Social and Economic Research, University of the West Indies, Jamaica. 1972. p.15
6. *Daily Express*. Trinidad Express Newspapers Ltd., Port of Spain. January 25th 1970
7. National Joint Action Committee. *From Slavery to Slavery*. National Joint Action Committee, Port of Spain. 1970
8. *The Vanguard*: The Voice of Labour. Vanguard Publishing Co., San Fernando, January 9th 1971, p.1
9. Kambon, Khafra, "Interview with George Weekes" (unpublished). July 17th 1986
10. *Daily Express*. Trinidad Express Newspapers Ltd., Port of Spain. March 5th 1970
11. Ibid.
12. *Daily Express*. Trinidad Express Newspapers Ltd., Port of Spain. June 2nd 1968
13. *Daily Express*. Trinidad Express Newspapers Ltd., Port of Spain. March 22nd 1970
14. Weekes, George. 'The Problem of Unemployment'. Lecture delivered to the Catholic Teachers Association on March 19th 1970. In *The Vanguard*: The Voice of Labour. Vanguard Publishing Co., San Fernando, April 4th 1970. p.4
15. Ibid.
16. Budget Speech 1971. *Budget Speeches 1957-1981. Vol.I: 1957-1971*. Republic of Trinidad and Tobago, Trinidad and Tobago. p.471
17. Weekes. Lecture on Unemployment. op.cit. p.5
18. *Daily Express*. Trinidad Express Newspapers Ltd., Port of Spain. March 15th 1970. p.1
19. 'OWTU Statement on the February Revolution'. OWTU General Council, April 4th 1970. In *The Vanguard*: The Voice of Labour. Vanguard Publishing Co., San Fernando, April 10th 1970. p.4
20. Ibid. p.5
21. *Trinidad Guardian*. Trinidad Publishing Co. Ltd., Port of Spain. April 11th 1970

Chapter 13 – "A Test of . . . My Manhood"

1. *Trinidad Guardian*. Trinidad Publishing Co. Ltd., Port of Spain. April 22nd 1970. p. 1

2. *The Vanguard*: The Voice of Labour. Vanguard Publishing Co., San Fernando, July 11th 1970, p.7
3. Oilfields Workers Trade Union. General Council Report to the 31st Annual Conference of Delegates. March 13th 1971. p.3
4. Ibid. p.2
5. Ibid. pp. 3-4
6. Weekes, George. *A Message by George Weekes, President General, Oilfield Workers Trade Union*; Moko Enterprises Ltd, 14 Riverside Road, Curepe, Trinidad W.I. (undated) pp.2-3
7. OWTU General Council Report. op.cit. p.70
8. Ibid. p.60
9. *The Vanguard*: The Voice of Labour. Vanguard Publishing Co., San Fernando, October 3rd 1970
10. Kambon, Khafra, "Interview with Jack Kelshall" (unpublished). 1986
11. An address to the nation, on June 30th 1970, by Eric Williams, Prime Minister of Trinidad and Tobago. The projections represented a substantial revision of the current Third Five Year Development Plan of the government and placed a new emphasis on economic nationalism and people's participation in the economy.
12. *Daily Express*. Trinidad Express Newspapers Ltd., Port of Spain. May 11th 1987. p. 8
13. *The Vanguard*: The Voice of Labour. Vanguard Publishing Co., San Fernando, October 24th 1970. p.7
14. Weekes, George. 'Message from Prison' In *The Vanguard*: The Voice of Labour. Vanguard Publishing Co., San Fernando, July 25th 1970
15. *Washington Post*. Washington, USA, April 23rd 1970.

Chapter 14 – From Crisis to Crisis

1. *The Vanguard*: The Voice of Labour. Vanguard Publishing Co., San Fernando, January 9th 1971, p.1
2. Ibid. p.4
3. Ibid. p.4
4. Ibid. p.2
5. Ibid. p.3
6. Ibid. p.1
7. OWTU General Council Report, May 19th 1971. pp. 81-82
8. General Council Report. op.cit.
9. Edwards, Hylton S. *Lengthening Shadows: Birth and Revolt of the Trinidad Army*. Inprint Caribbean Ltd., Trinidad and Tobago. 1982. p.125
10. Ryan, Selwyn; Greene, Eddie; Harewood, Jack. *The Confused Electorate — A Study of Political Attitudes and Opinions in Trinidad and Tobago*. St Augustine Research Associates, UWI. p.41
11. *The Vanguard*: The Voice of Labour. Vanguard Publishing Co., San Fernando, July 24th 1971, p.1
12. *The Vanguard*: The Voice of Labour. Vanguard Publishing Co., San Fernando, July 24th 1971, p.3

CHAPTER REFERENCES

13. OWTU General Council Report. May 27th 1972. p.20
14. Oilfields Workers Trade Union, Central Executive Election, 1979, MANIFESTO of The 'Rebel' Team. p.4
15. *Daily Express.* Trinidad Express Newspapers Ltd., Port of Spain. September 25th 1971
16. *Daily Express.* Trinidad Express Newspapers Ltd., Port of Spain. September 22nd 1971, p.1
17. Ibid. Eric Williams revealed this in his speech to the P.N.M. convention.
18. *Daily Express.* Trinidad Express Newspapers Ltd., Port of Spain. (Advertisment) October 9th 1971. p.2

Chapter 15 – The Intervention of Faith

1. Williams, Eric. In a radio and t.v. broadcast on the evening of October 19th 1971.
2. The History of the Union (1937-1977). In *Oilfields Workers Trade Union July 1937 — July 1977.* Oilfields Workers Trade Union, 1977. pp.38-39
3. Weekes, George. 'The Revolutionary 70's Continue'. New Year's Statement. In *The Vanguard.* January 9th 1971. p.7
4. Weekes, George. *A Message by George Weekes, President General, Oilfield Workers Trade Union*; Moko Enterprises Ltd, 14 Riverside Road, Curepe, Trinidad W.I. (undated) p.8
5. Baptiste, Owen ed. *Crisis.* Inprint Caribbean Ltd., Trinidad. 1976. p.274

Chapter 16 – The Road to Bloody Tuesday

1. Weekes, George. Letter to Minister of Labour, March 11th 1975. In *The Fight for Justice Peace and Bread.* (pamphlet). Oilfields Workers Trade Union, 1975. p13
2. Rennie, Bukka. *A History of the Working Class in the Twentieth Century: the Trinidad and Tobago experience. 1919-1956.* New Beginning Movement, Trinidad & Tobago, 1972. p.137
3. Weekes, George. *A Message by George Weekes, President General, Oilfield Workers Trade Union*; Moko Enterprises Ltd, 14 Riverside Road, Curepe, Trinidad W.I. (undated) p.8
4. Ibid. p.6
5. Ibid. p.8
6. Ibid. p.10
7. Ibid. p.11
8. Ibid. p.10
9. Ibid.
10. *Dialogue 1973: 33rd Annual Conference of Delegates.* May 1973. OWTU, San Fernando, 1973. pp.62,66.

11. Weekes, George. President General's Address to the Thirty Fourth Annual Conference of Delegates, 10th March 1974. In *Thirty-Fourth Annual Conference of Delegates; Addresses delivered by George Weekes & Allan Alexander. 10th March 1974.* Oilfields Workers Trade Union, Trinidad & Tobago. 1974. p.16
12. Baptiste, Owen ed. *Crisis.* Inprint Caribbean Ltd., Trinidad. 1976. p.17
13. *Liberation.* August 1973, p.7
14. Budget Speech 1974. In *Budget Speeches 1957 — 1981: Vol.II: 1972 — 1981.* Republic of Trinidad and Tobago (undated). p.604
15. *Liberation.* op.cit. p.4
16. Ibid. p.11
17. *Crisis.* op.cit. pp. 282-283
18. Budget Speech 1977. In *Budget Speeches.* op.cit. p.713
19. *Crisis.* op.cit. p.17
20. Ibid. p.285
21. Ibid. p.286 (adapted from reported to direct speech)
22. Weekes, George. Address to 34th Annual Conference. op.cit. p.16
23. Ibid. pp.9-10
24. Ibid. p.17
25. *OWTU General Council Report to the 35th Annual Conference of Delegates, 6th September 1975.* Oilfields Workers Trade Union. 1975. pp.9-10
26. Weekes, George. Letter to the Commissioner of Police, 27th November 1973. In *Dialogue.* Oilfields Workers Trade Union. 1974. p.10
27. *Crisis.* op.cit. p.167

Chapter 17 – The Battle Never Ends

1. *O.W.T.U. General Council Report to the 42nd Annual Conference of Delegates, 28th November 1981.* Oilfields Workers Trade Union. 1981. p.18
2. *Liberation.* May 1975. p.1
3. Ibid.
4. *Liberation,* National Joint Action Committee, Port of Spain, May 1975, p.1
5. *O.W.T.U. General Council Report to the 41st Annual Conference of Delegates, 15th October 1980.* Oilfields Workers Trade Union. 1980. p.35
6. *O.W.T.U. General Council Report 1981.* op.cit. p.17
7. Ibid.
8. *Liberation.* June 1979. p.1 (By this time many prominent members of NJAC had adopted African names.)
9. Ryan, Selwyn. *The Disunited Labour Front.* (mimeo) U.W.I. p.2
10. *U.L.F. — D.A.C. Alliance. The Truth about Why the Talks Failed.* (pamphlet) The United Labour Front, Trinidad & Tobago. August 24 1976
11. *O.W.T.U. General Council Report to the 40th Annual Conference of Delegates, 27th October 1979.* Oilfields Workers Trade Union. 1979. p.10
12. *O.W.T.U. General Council Report 1981.* op.cit. p.11
13. See *The Collapse of an Oil Economy: The Trinidad and Tobago Experience.* NJAC, 1983.
14. Ibid. pp.21-22

CHAPTER REFERENCES

15. Weekes, George. *The President General's Address to the 47th Annual Conference of Delegates of the Oilfields Workers Trade Union.* OWTU, 1986. p.12
16. Ibid. pp.8-9
17. Ibid. pp. 2-3
18. *O.W.T.U. General Council Report to the 37th Annual Conference of Delegates, 5th November 1977.* Oilfields Workers Trade Union. 1977. p.12
19. Ibid. p.37
20. *The Vanguard:* The Voice of Labour. Vanguard Publishing Co., San Fernando, November 2nd 1984. p.7
21. Ibid.
22. Ibid.
23. Weekes, George. Letter to Prime Minister, George Chambers. March 18th 1986. (mimeo) p.2
24. Rojas, John. Letter of resignation (from OWTU presidency) to OWTU General Secretary. 2nd April 1962.
25. Dalley, F.W. *Trade Union Organisation and Industrial Relations in Trinidad.* London HMSO, 1947. p.5
26. Paraphrased from *Our Fight for People's Ownership and Control of the Oil Industry: Memorandum submitted to the Government of Trinidad and Tobago by the Oilfields Workers Trade Union on the Nationalisation of the Oil Industry.* OWTU (booklet) Sept. 1982. p.45

INDEX

345

INDEX

INDEX

INDEX

INDEX

INDEX

351

INDEX

INDEX